the SEWING BOOK

the SEWING BOOK

ALISON SMITH

CONTENTS

346

354

104

INTRODUCTION

The Sewing Book provides a comprehensive guide to all sewing techniques, whether it be for dressmaking, tailoring, crafts, or soft furnishings. If you are new to sewing, you'll find many tips to help and guide you; if you have been sewing for many years, there will be lots of new ideas to try. I also hope the book will be a valuable reference for all students studying textiles and fashion.

Having sewn since my teenage years and taught dressmaking and fashion for all my adult life, I am truly passionate about sewing. It can be so therapeutic—relaxing and satisfying. The ability to produce a unique item of clothing or something for your home is truly rewarding.

The book is divided into three sections. The first, Tools, covers all the equipment required to sew, including sewing machines; gives an up-to-date guide to fabrics—their properties, care, and how to sew them; and explains how to alter patterns to make clothes that fit you perfectly.

The next section is Techniques, with over 300 different sewing techniques to try, all in a step-by-step photographic format, covering everything from basic stitches and seams to professional tailoring

techniques. Each chapter begins with a visual directory of what the techniques are used for, be it types of pleats or pockets, necklines or sleeves, or buttonhole shapes.

Dotted throughout the Techniques section are 10 gorgeous projects that range from quick and easy cushions to a shift dress and a Roman blind. Whatever your level of experience, there will be something to suit you. All the projects use techniques that appear in the second section of the book and will help you practise your sewing skills and develop new ones. The final section

contains patterns for the projects, as well as a useful glossary of sewing terms.

Enjoy, and happy sewing.

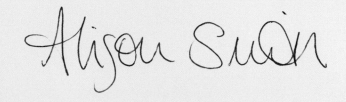

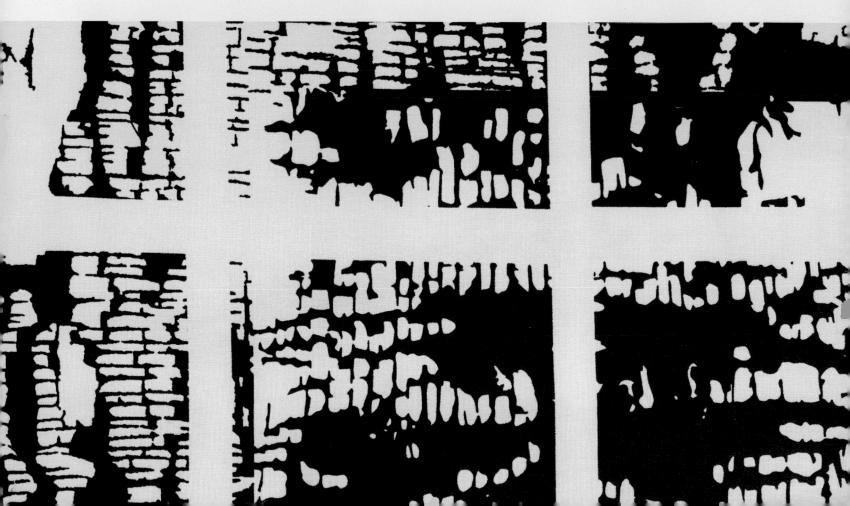

ABOUT **THIS BOOK**

For the photographs, we have used sewing threads of a contrast color to the fabric in order for the stitching to be visible. I recommend that you use a thread that matches your fabric as closely as possible.

All techniques and projects are graded by difficulty level, from * for the simple and straightforward to ***** for the more complex and challenging ones.

The visual directories at the start of each chapter show what the techniques within may be used for. They also show you the construction of the technique, with red dashed lines to indicate top-stitching and grey dotted lines to help you understand the structure beneath the fabric.

The fabric quantity given for each project is the minimum needed. If using fabric with a large-scale or directional pattern, you may need to buy extra to make sure the pattern works well on the finished item.

Always cut fabric on the straight grain unless instructed otherwise. The cutting layouts show fabric folded selvage to selvage for most projects, but this is not necessary for plain fabrics. Seam allowances are ⅝in (1.5cm) unless otherwise indicated.

Neatening of seams is not always shown in the photographs because this can distract from the technique (seam neatening is only shown when it forms part of the technique). I recommend that you neaten your seams using your preferred technique.

Many of the techniques shown may vary from those given on your pattern, but you might like to try an alternative technique. There are many to choose from.

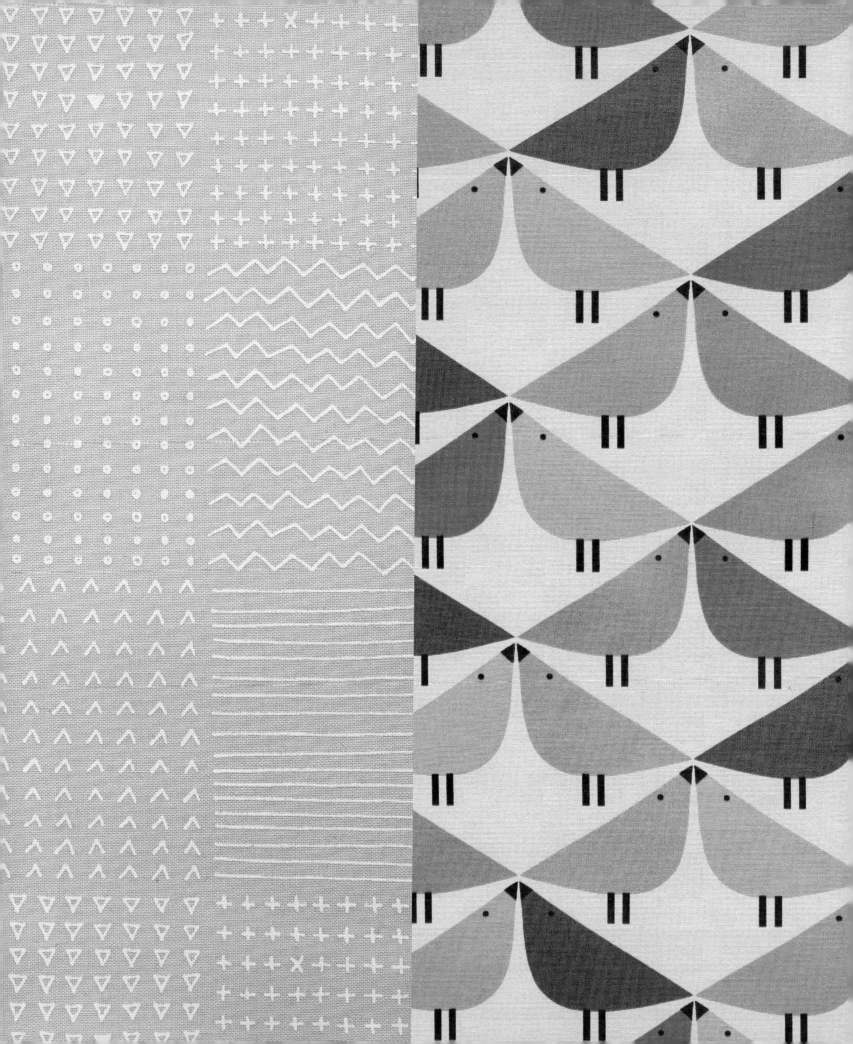

TOOLS

SEWING EQUIPMENT

As well as a few basic items—tape measure, scissors, pins, needles, thread, and seam ripper—you will need an iron for pressing. For eager sewers, a sewing machine—and possibly a serger—are essential, and there are also other handy gadgets available.

BASIC **SEWING KIT**

A well-equipped sewing kit will include all of the items shown below and many more, depending on the type of sewing that you do regularly. It is important that a suitable container is used to keep your tools together, so that they will be readily at hand, and to keep them organized.

◀ Seam ripper
To remove any stitches that have been sewn in the wrong place. Various sizes of seam rippers are available. Keep the cover on when not in use to protect the sharp point.
See p.16

Pins ▼
Needed by every sewer to hold the fabric together prior to sewing it permanently. There are different types of pins for different types of work.
See p.23

▲ Tape measure
Essential, not only to take body measurements, but also to help measure fabric, seams, etc. Choose one that shows both inches and centimeters. A tape made of plastic is best as it will not stretch.
See p.18

Cutting shears ▶
Required for cutting fabric. When buying, select a pair that feels comfortable in your hand and that is not too heavy.
See p.17

▼ Zippers
It is always a good idea to keep a couple of zippers in your sewing kit. Black, cream, and navy are the most useful colors.
See pp.284–293

▲ Safety pins
In a variety of sizes, these are useful for emergency repairs and threading elastics.
See p.23

Thimble ▲
This is useful to protect the end of your finger when hand sewing. Thimbles are available in various shapes and sizes.
See p.21

Sewing gauge ▲
A handy gadget for small measurements. The slide can be set to measure hem depths, buttonhole diameters, and much more.
See p.18

Threads ▲
A selection of threads for hand sewing and machine/serger sewing in a variety of colors. Some threads are made of polyester, while others are cotton or rayon.
See pp.24–25

Embroidery scissors ▼
Small pair of scissors with very sharp points, to clip threads close to the fabric.
See p.17

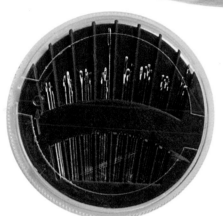

◀ Needles
A good selection of different types of needles for sewing by hand. This will enable you to tackle any hand sewing project.
See p.22

Pin cushion ▶
To keep your needles and pins safe and clean. Choose one that has a fabric cover and is firm.
See p.23

Notions ▼
All the odds and ends a sewer needs, including everything from buttons and snaps to trims and elastic. A selection of buttons and snaps in your basic kit is useful for a quick repair.
See pp.26–27

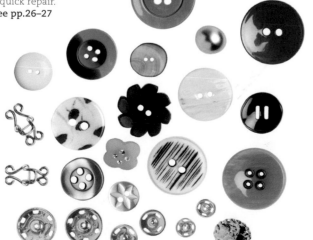

Buttonhole cutter ▲
An exceedingly sharp knife that gives a clean cut through machine buttonholes. Place a cutting mat underneath when using this tool, or you might damage the blade.
See p.16

BUILD UP FROM YOUR BASIC SEWING KIT

▶ **CUTTING TOOLS pp.16–17**
Appliqué scissors
Bent-handled shears
Cutting mat
Paper scissors
Pinking shears
Rotary cutter
Snips
Trimming scissors

▶ **MEASURING TOOLS p.18**
Flexible ruler
Gridded ruler
Other tape measures

▶ **MARKING AIDS p.19**
Chalk pencil
Chalk cartridge pencil
Heat-sensitive ink pen
Tailor's chalk
Tracing wheel
Carbon paper
Water/air-soluble pen

▶ **USEFUL EXTRAS pp.20–21**
14-in-1 measure
Awl
Beeswax
Collar point turner
Dress form
Emergency sewing kit
Glue stick
Liquid sealant
Loop turner
Pattern paper
Pliers
Bias tape maker
Tweezers

▶ **NEEDLE THREADERS p.22**

▶ **PRESSING AIDS pp.28–29**
Clapper
Iron
Ironing board
Mini iron
Pressing cloth
Pressing mat
Pressing mitten
Seam roll
Tailor's ham
Velvet mat

CUTTING TOOLS

There are many types of cutting tools, but one rule: buy good-quality products that can be re-sharpened. When choosing cutting shears, make sure you can comfortably open the whole blade with one action, which allows clean and accurate cutting lines. Everyone will at some point need a seam ripper to remove misplaced stitches or to unpick seams for mending. Rotary cutters that are used in conjunction with a special cutting mat and ruler are invaluable for cutting multiple straight edges.

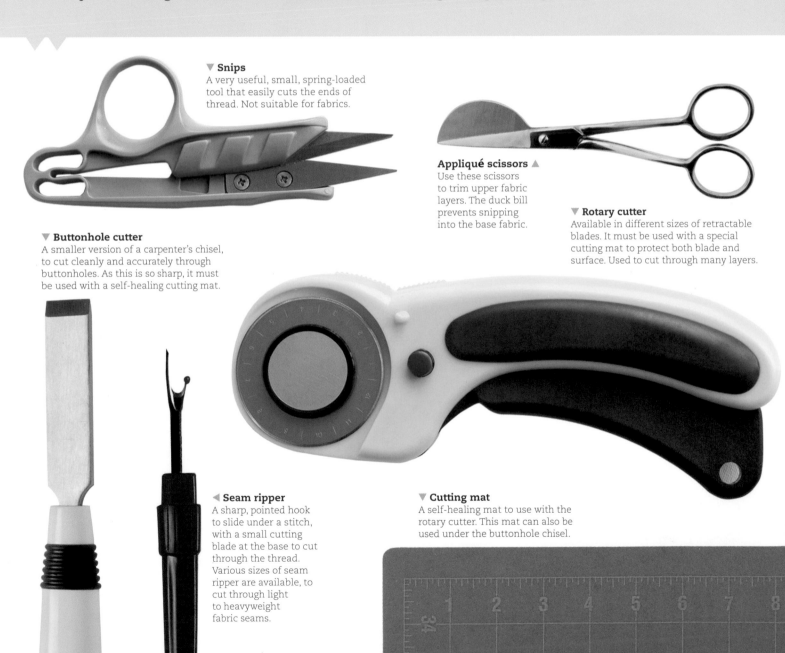

▼ Snips
A very useful, small, spring-loaded tool that easily cuts the ends of thread. Not suitable for fabrics.

Appliqué scissors ▲
Use these scissors to trim upper fabric layers. The duck bill prevents snipping into the base fabric.

▼ Buttonhole cutter
A smaller version of a carpenter's chisel, to cut cleanly and accurately through buttonholes. As this is so sharp, it must be used with a self-healing cutting mat.

▼ Rotary cutter
Available in different sizes of retractable blades. It must be used with a special cutting mat to protect both blade and surface. Used to cut through many layers.

◄ Seam ripper
A sharp, pointed hook to slide under a stitch, with a small cutting blade at the base to cut through the thread. Various sizes of seam ripper are available, to cut through light to heavyweight fabric seams.

▼ Cutting mat
A self-healing mat to use with the rotary cutter. This mat can also be used under the buttonhole chisel.

◀ Bent-handled shears
This type of shear has a blade that can sit flat against the table when cutting out, due to the angle between the blade and handle. Popular for cutting long, straight edges.

Pinking shears ▶
Similar in size to cutting shears, but with a blade that cuts with a zigzag pattern. Used for neatening seams and decorative edges.

▼ Cutting shears
The most popular type of shear, used for cutting large pieces of fabric. The length of the blade can vary from 8–12in (20–30cm).

▲ Trimming Scissors
These scissors have a 4in (10cm) blade and are used to trim away surplus fabric and neaten ends of machining.

▼ Embroidery scissors
A small and very sharp scissor used to get into corners and clip threads close to the fabric.

◀ Paper scissors
Use these to cut around pattern pieces—cutting paper will dull blades of fabric scissors and shears.

MEASURING TOOLS AND MARKING AIDS

A huge range of tools enables a sewer to measure accurately. Choosing the correct tool for the task at hand is important, so that your measurements are precise. The next step is to mark your work using the appropriate marking technique or tool. Some tools are very specific to one job, while others are specific to types of sewing.

MEASURING TOOLS

There are many tools available to help you measure everything from the width of a seam or hem, to body dimensions, to the area of a window. One of the most basic yet invaluable measuring tools is the tape measure. Be sure to keep yours in good condition—once it stretches or gets snipped on the edges it will no longer be accurate and should be replaced.

▼ **Extra-long tape**
This is usually twice the length of a normal tape measure, at 10ft (300cm) long. Use it when making home goods. It's also useful to help measure the length of bridal trains.

▲ **Metal tape for windows**
A metal tape that can be secured when extended is used to measure windows and soft furnishings.

Sewing gauge ▲
A handy small tool about 6in (15cm) long, marked in inches and centimeters, with a sliding tab. Use as an accurate measure for small measurements such as hems.

Retractable tape ▶
Very useful to have in your purse when shopping as you never know when you may need to measure something!

Tape measure ▲
Available in various colors and widths. Try to choose one that is the same width as standard seam allowance (⅝in/1.5cm), because it will prove very useful.

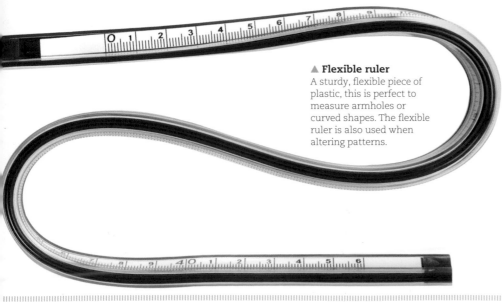

▲ **Flexible ruler**
A sturdy, flexible piece of plastic, this is perfect to measure armholes or curved shapes. The flexible ruler is also used when altering patterns.

Gridded ruler ▼
This type of ruler is larger than a normal ruler and is marked with an inch or centimeter grid. Used together with the rotary cutter and mat, and also for marking bias strips.

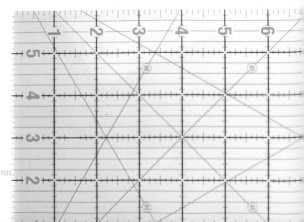

MARKING AIDS

Marking certain parts of your work is essential, to make sure that things such as pockets and darts are placed correctly and seamlines are straight as drawn on the pattern. With some marking tools, such as pens and a tracing wheel and carbon paper, it is always a good idea to test on a scrap of fabric first to make sure that the mark made will not be permanent.

▼ Chalk cartridge pencil
Chalk leads of different colors can be inserted into this pencil, making it a very versatile marking tool. The leads can be sharpened.

Combined set square and curve ▲
A plastic curved tool, used primarily when drafting or altering patterns.

◀ Tailor's chalk
Also known as French chalk, this solid piece of chalk in either a square or triangular shape is available in a large variety of colors. The chalk easily brushes off fabric.

◀ Water/air-soluble pen
This resembles a felt marker. Marks made can be removed from the fabric with either a spray of water or by leaving to air-dry. Be careful—if you press over the marks, they may become permanent.

Tracing wheel and carbon paper ▼
These two items are used together to transfer markings from a paper pattern or a design on to fabric. Not suitable for all types of fabric though, as marks may not be easily removable.

◀ Chalk pencil
Available in blue, pink, and white. As it can be sharpened like a normal pencil, it will draw accurate lines on fabric.

Heat-sensitive ink pen ▶
This pen draws clear fine lines on fabric and will vanish once ironed. However, test it first as the ink can reappear in cold conditions.

USEFUL **EXTRAS**

There are many more accessories that can be purchased to help with your sewing, and knowing which products to choose and for which job can be daunting. The tools shown here can be useful aids, although it depends on the type of sewing that you do—dressmaking, craft work, making soft furnishings, or running repairs—as to whether you would need all of them in your sewing kit.

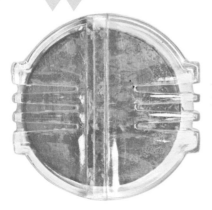

◀ **Beeswax**
When hand sewing, this will prevent the thread from tangling, and will strengthen it. First draw the thread through the wax, then press the wax into the thread by running your fingers along it.

▲ **Awl**
This sharp tool is used to make holes in fabric for eyelet insertion or for the rounded end of a keyhole buttonhole.

◀ **Bias tape maker**
Available in ½, ¾, and 1in (12, 18, and 25mm) widths, this tool evenly folds the edges of a fabric strip, which can then be pressed to make binding.

▼ **Tweezers**
These can be used for removing stubborn basting stitches that have become caught in the machine stitching. An essential aid to threading the serger.

Loop turner ▶
A thin metal rod with a latch at the end. Use to turn narrow fabric tubes or to thread ribbons through a slotted lace.

Liquid sealant ▶
Used to seal the cut edge of ribbons and trims to prevent fraying. Also useful to seal the ends of serger stitching.

▼ **Emergency sewing kit**
All the absolute essentials to fix loose buttons or dropped hems while away from your sewing machine. Take it with you when traveling.

Glue stick ▶
Similar to a glue stick for paper, this will hold fabric or trims temporarily in place until they can be secured with stitches. It will not damage the fabric or make the sewing needle sticky.

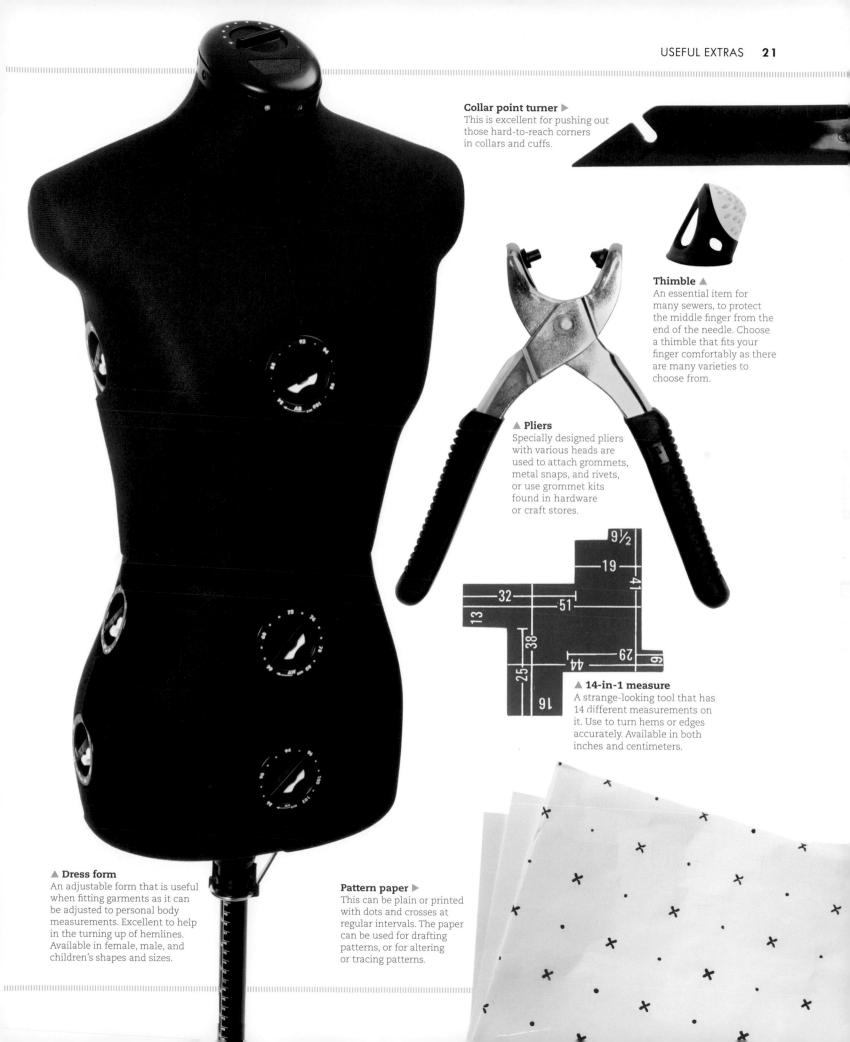

Collar point turner ▶
This is excellent for pushing out those hard-to-reach corners in collars and cuffs.

Thimble ▲
An essential item for many sewers, to protect the middle finger from the end of the needle. Choose a thimble that fits your finger comfortably as there are many varieties to choose from.

▲ **Pliers**
Specially designed pliers with various heads are used to attach grommets, metal snaps, and rivets, or use grommet kits found in hardware or craft stores.

▲ **14-in-1 measure**
A strange-looking tool that has 14 different measurements on it. Use to turn hems or edges accurately. Available in both inches and centimeters.

▲ **Dress form**
An adjustable form that is useful when fitting garments as it can be adjusted to personal body measurements. Excellent to help in the turning up of hemlines. Available in female, male, and children's shapes and sizes.

Pattern paper ▶
This can be plain or printed with dots and crosses at regular intervals. The paper can be used for drafting patterns, or for altering or tracing patterns.

TOOLS

NEEDLES AND PINS

Using the correct pin or needle for your work is so important, as the wrong choice can damage fabric or leave small holes. Needles are made from steel and pins from steel or occasionally brass. Take care of them by keeping pins in a pin cushion and needles in a needle case—if kept together in a small container, they could become scratched and blunt.

NEEDLES AND THREADERS

Needles are available for all types of fabrics and projects. A good selection of needles should be on hand at all times, whether it be for emergency mending of tears, sewing on buttons, or adding trims to special-occasion wear. With a special needle threader, inserting the thread through the eye of the needle is simplicity itself.

Sharps
A general-purpose hand-sewing needle, with a small, round eye. Available in sizes 1 to 12. For most hand sewing use a size 6 to 9.

Crewel
Also known as an embroidery needle, a long needle with a long, oval eye that is designed to take multiple strands of embroidery thread.

Milliners or straw
A very long, thin needle with a small, round eye. Good for hand sewing and basting as it doesn't damage fabric. A size 8 or 9 is most popular.

Quilting or betweens
Similar to a milliner's needle but very short, with a small, round eye. Perfect for fine hand stitches and favored by quilters.

Beading
Long and extremely fine, to sew beads and sequins to fabric. As it is prone to bending, keep it wrapped in tissue when not in use.

Darning
A long, thick needle that is designed to be used with wool or thick yarns and to sew through multiple layers.

Tapestry
A medium-length, thick needle with a blunt end and a long eye. For use with wool yarn in tapestry. Also for darning in serger threads.

Chenille
This looks like a tapestry needle but it has a sharp point. Use with thick or wool yarns for darning or heavy embroidery.

Bodkin
A strange-looking needle with a blunt end and a large, fat eye. Use to thread elastic or cord. There are larger eyes for thicker yarns.

Self-threading needle
A needle that has a double eye. The thread is placed in the upper eye through the gap, then pulled into the eye below for sewing.

Wire needle threader
A handy gadget, especially useful for needles with small eyes. Also helpful in threading sewing-machine needles.

Automatic needle threader
This threader is operated with a small lever. The needle, eye down, is inserted and the thread is wrapped around.

PINS

There is a wide variety of pins available, in differing lengths and thicknesses, and ranging from plain straight pins to those with colored balls or flower shapes on their ends.

Straight
General-purpose pins of a medium length and thickness. Can be used for all types of sewing.

Quilting
A long pin of medium thickness, designed to hold multiple layers of fabric together.

Pearl-headed
Longer than straight pins, with a colored pearl head. They are easy to pick up and use.

Lace or bridal
A fine, short pin designed to be used with fine fabrics, such as those for bridal gowns, because the pin will not damage the fabric.

Flowerhead
A long pin of medium thickness with a flat, flower-shaped head. It is designed to be pressed over, as the head lays flat on the fabric.

Extra fine
Extra long and extra fine, this pin is favored by many professional dressmakers, because it is easy to use and doesn't damage finer fabrics.

Glass-headed
Similar to pearl-headed pins but shorter. They have the advantage that they can be pressed over without melting.

Dressmaker's
Similar to a straight pin in shape and thickness, but slightly longer. These are the pins for beginners to choose.

Safety pins
Available in a huge variety of sizes and made either of brass or stainless steel. Used for holding two or more layers together.

Staple
A strong pin that looks like a very large staple, used for pinning loose covers to furniture. Take care as staple pins are very sharp.

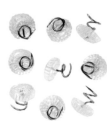

Spiral
Shaped like a spiral with a very sharp point at one end to enable it to be twisted in and out easily. Used to secure loose covers to furniture.

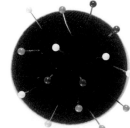

Pin cushion
To keep pins clean and sharp. Choose a fabric-cover: a foam cushion may blunt pins.

THREADS

There are so many threads available that knowing which ones to choose can be confusing. There are specialist threads designed for special tasks, such as machine embroidery or quilting. Threads also vary in fiber content, from pure cotton to rayon to polyester. Some threads are very fine, while others are thick and coarse. Failure to choose the correct thread can spoil your project and lead to problems with the stitch quality of the sewing machine or serger.

Cotton thread
A 100% cotton thread. Smooth and firm, this is designed to be used with cotton fabrics and is much favored by quilters.

Polyester all-purpose thread
A cotton-coated polyester thread that has a very slight "give," making it suitable to sew all types of fabrics and garments, as well as home goods. The most popular type of thread.

Silk thread
A sewing thread made from 100% silk. Used for machining delicate silk garments. It is also used for basting or temporary stitching in areas that are to be pressed, such as jacket collars, because it can be removed without leaving an imprint.

Elastic thread
A thin, round elastic thread normally used on the bobbin of the sewing machine for stretch effects such as shirring.

Embroidery thread

Often made from a rayon yarn for shine. This is a finer thread designed for machine embroidery. Available on much larger reels for economy.

Serger thread

A dull yarn on a larger reel designed to be used on the serger. This type of yarn is normally not strong enough to use on the sewing machine.

Button thread

A thicker polyester thread used for decorative top-stitching and buttonholes. Also for hand sewing buttons on thicker fabrics and some soft furnishings.

Metallic thread

A rayon and metal thread for decorative machining and machine embroidery. This thread usually requires a specialist sewing-machine needle.

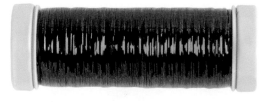

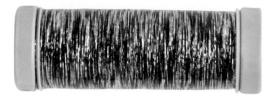

TOOLS

NOTIONS

The term notions covers all the bits and pieces that sewers tend to need, for example fasteners such as buttons, snaps, hooks and eyes, and Velcro™. But notions also includes elastics, ribbons, trims of all types, and boning.

BUTTONS

Buttons can be made from almost anything—shell, bone, coconut, nylon, plastic, brass, silver. They can be any shape, from geometric to abstract to animal shapes. A button may have a shank or have holes on the surface to enable it to be attached to fabric.

OTHER FASTENERS

Hooks and eyes (below left), snaps (below center), and Velcro™ (below right) all come in a wide variety of forms, differing in size, shape, and color. Some hooks and eyes are designed to be seen, while snaps and Velcro™ are intended to be hidden fasteners.

TRIMS, DECORATIONS, FRINGES, AND BRAIDS

Decorative finishing touches—fringes, strips of sequins, braids, feathers, pearls, bows, flowers, and beads—can dress up a garment, embellish a bag, or personalize soft furnishings. Some are designed to be inserted into seams, while others are surface-mounted.

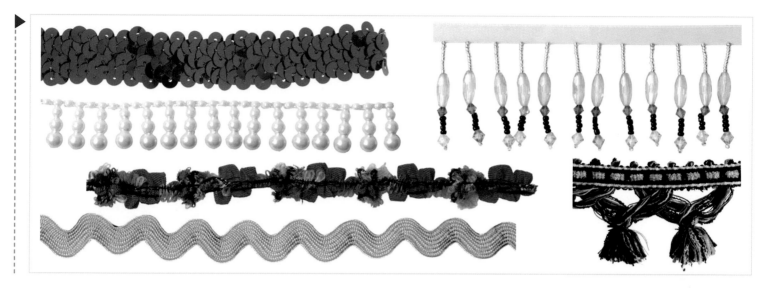

RIBBONS

From the narrowest strips to wide widths, ribbons are made from a variety of yarns, such as nylon, polyester, and cotton. They can be printed or plain and may feature metallic threads or wired edges.

ELASTIC

Elastic is available in many forms, from very narrow, round cord to wide strips (below left). It may have buttonhole slots in it (below right) or even have a decorative edge.

BONING

You can buy various types of boning in varying widths. Polyester boning (bottom left), used in boned bodices, can be sewn through, while nylon boning (bottom right), also used on boned bodices, has to be inserted into a casing. Specialist metal boning (below left and right), which may be either straight or spiral, is for corsets and bridal wear.

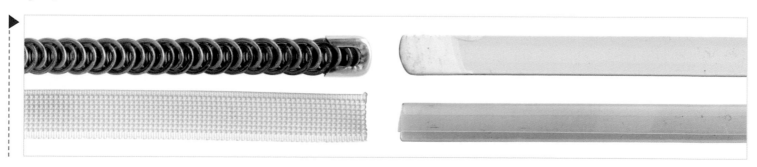

PRESSING **AIDS**

Successful sewing relies on successful pressing. Without the correct pressing equipment, sewing can look too "homemade" whereas if correctly pressed, any sewn item will have a neat, professional finish.

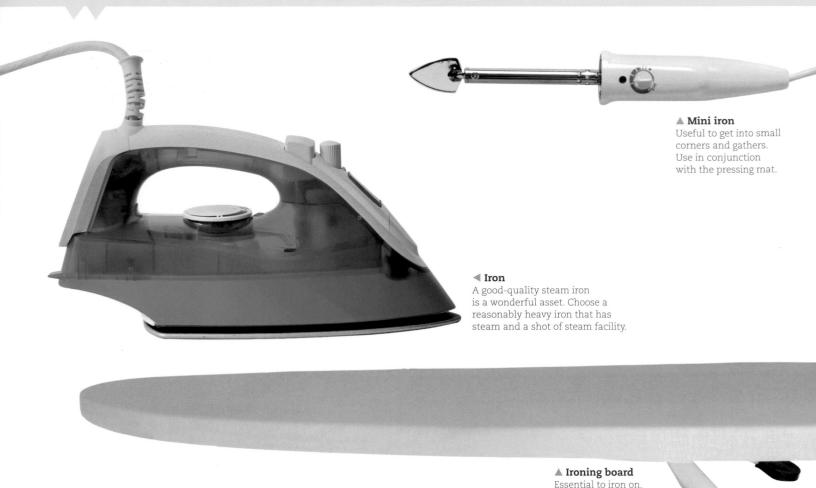

▲ **Mini iron**
Useful to get into small corners and gathers. Use in conjunction with the pressing mat.

◀ **Iron**
A good-quality steam iron is a wonderful asset. Choose a reasonably heavy iron that has steam and a shot of steam facility.

▲ **Ironing board**
Essential to iron on. Make sure the board is height-adjustable.

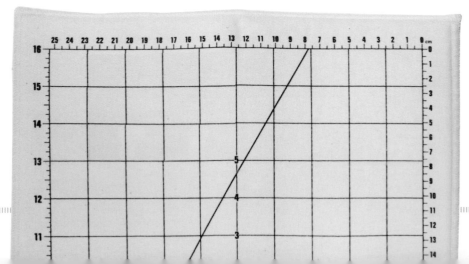

◀ **Pressing mat**
A heat-resistant mat for pressing small items.

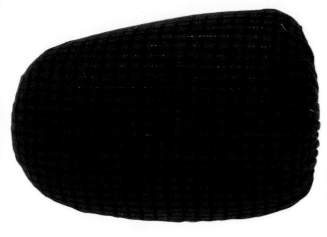

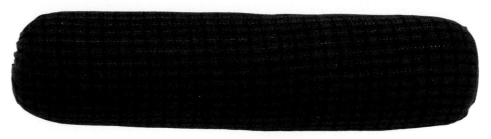

◄ Tailor's ham
A ham-shaped pressing cushion that is used to press darts and the shape into curves of collars and shoulders, and in making tailored garments.

▲ Seam roll
This tubular pressing aid is used to press seams open on fabrics that mark, as the iron only touches the seam on top of the roll. Also used for sleeve and pant seams.

▲ Clapper
A wooden aid that pounds creases into a heavy fabric after steaming. The top section is used to help press collar seams and points.

Pressing cloth ▶
Choose a cloth made from silk organza or muslin as you can see through it. The cloth will stop the iron from marking fabric and prevent burning delicate fabrics.

▼ Velvet mat
A pressing mat with a tufted side to aid the pressing of pile fabrics, such as velvet.

Pressing mitten ▶
Slips on to your hand to enable more control over where you are pressing.

SEWING **MACHINE**

A sewing machine will quickly speed up any job, whether it be a quick repair or a huge home-sewing project. Most sewing machines today are aided by computer technology, which enhances stitch quality and ease of use. Always spend time trying out a sewing machine before you buy, to really get a feel for it.

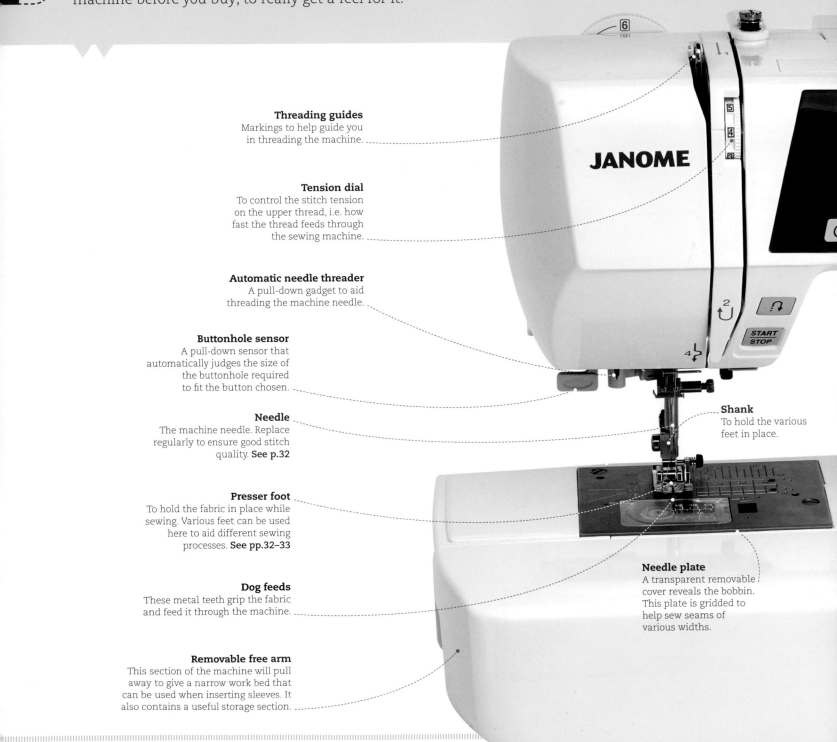

Threading guides
Markings to help guide you in threading the machine.

Tension dial
To control the stitch tension on the upper thread, i.e. how fast the thread feeds through the sewing machine.

Automatic needle threader
A pull-down gadget to aid threading the machine needle.

Buttonhole sensor
A pull-down sensor that automatically judges the size of the buttonhole required to fit the button chosen.

Needle
The machine needle. Replace regularly to ensure good stitch quality. **See p.32**

Presser foot
To hold the fabric in place while sewing. Various feet can be used here to aid different sewing processes. **See pp.32–33**

Dog feeds
These metal teeth grip the fabric and feed it through the machine.

Removable free arm
This section of the machine will pull away to give a narrow work bed that can be used when inserting sleeves. It also contains a useful storage section.

Shank
To hold the various feet in place.

Needle plate
A transparent removable cover reveals the bobbin. This plate is gridded to help sew seams of various widths.

JANOME

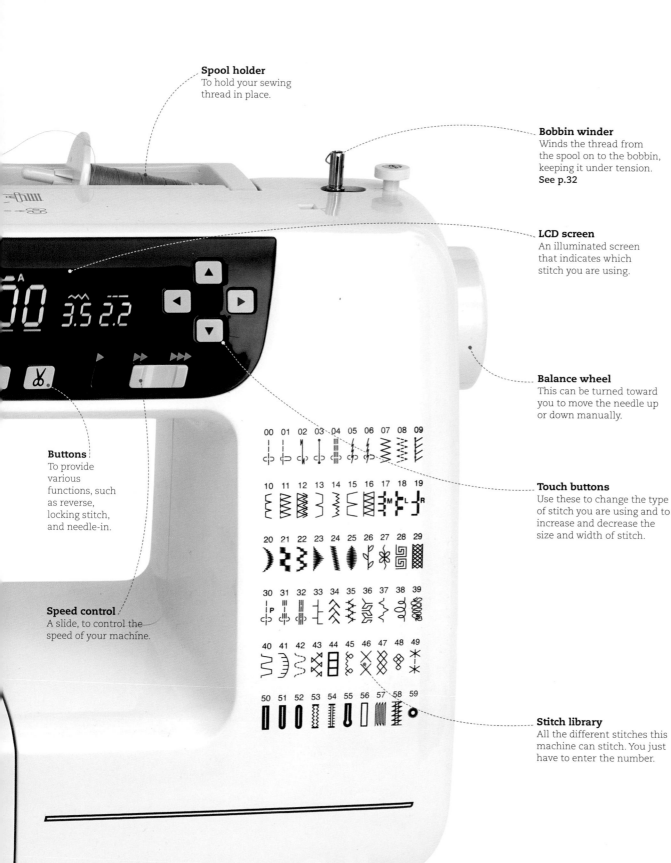

Spool holder
To hold your sewing thread in place.

Bobbin winder
Winds the thread from the spool on to the bobbin, keeping it under tension.
See p.32

LCD screen
An illuminated screen that indicates which stitch you are using.

Balance wheel
This can be turned toward you to move the needle up or down manually.

Buttons
To provide various functions, such as reverse, locking stitch, and needle-in.

Touch buttons
Use these to change the type of stitch you are using and to increase and decrease the size and width of stitch.

Speed control
A slide, to control the speed of your machine.

Stitch library
All the different stitches this machine can stitch. You just have to enter the number.

SEWING-MACHINE ACCESSORIES

Many accessories can be purchased for your sewing machine to make certain sewing processes so much easier. There are different machine needles not only for different fabrics, but also for different types of threads. There is also a huge number of sewing-machine feet, and new feet are constantly coming on to the market. Those shown here are some of the most popular.

Plastic bobbin
The bobbin is for the lower thread. Some machines take plastic bobbins, others metal. Always check which kind of bobbin your machine uses as the incorrect choice can cause stitch problems.

Metal bobbin
Also known as a universal bobbin, this is used on many types of sewing machines. Be sure to check that your machine needs a metal bobbin before you buy.

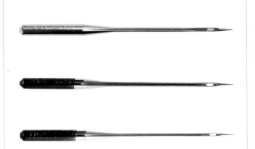

Machine needles
There are different types of sewing machine needles to cope with different fabrics. Machine needles are sized from 60 to 100, a 60 being a very fine needle. There are special needles for machine embroidery and also for metallic threads.

Overedge foot
A foot that runs along the raw edge of the fabric and holds it stable while an overedge stitch is worked.

Embroidery foot
A clear plastic foot with a groove underneath that allows linear machine embroidery stitches to pass under.

Free embroidery or darning foot
A foot designed to be used when the dog feeds on the machine are lowered. This enables a free motion stitch to be worked.

Buttonhole foot
This extends and the button is placed in the back of the foot. The machine will sew a buttonhole to fit due to the buttonhole sensor.

Blind hem foot
Use this foot in conjunction with the blind hem stitch to create a neat hemming stitch.

Rolled hem foot
This foot rolls the fabric while sewing with a straight stitch or a zigzag stitch.

Walking foot
This odd-looking foot "walks" across the fabric, so that the upper layer of fabric does not push forward. Great for matching checkers and stripes and also for difficult fabrics, like quilts.

Zipper foot
This foot fits to either the right- or left-hand side of the needle to enable you to sew close to a zipper.

Invisible zipper foot
A foot that is used to insert a concealed zipper—the foot holds open the coils of the zipper, enabling you to sew behind them.

Pin tuck foot
A foot with grooves underneath to allow multiple pin tucks to be sewn.

Piping foot
A deep groove in this foot allows a piping cord to fit underneath, enabling sewing close to the cord.

Ribbon foot
A foot that will feed either one or two ribbons evenly under the machine needle to ensure accurate sewing.

Beading foot, narrow
This foot has a narrow groove and is used to attach small beads or decorative cords.

Beading foot, wide
Beads on a string will fit under the foot, which has a wide groove, and they can then be zigzag stitched over.

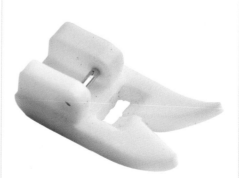

Ultra-glide foot
A foot made from Teflon™ that glides over the fabric. Useful for synthetic leathers.

SERGER

This machine is often used in conjunction with the sewing machine as it gives a very professional finish to your work. The serger has two upper threads and two lower threads (the loopers), with a knife that removes the edge of the fabric. Used extensively for neatening the edges of fabric, it can also be used for construction of stretch knits.

SERGER STITCHES

As the serger works, the threads wrap around the edge to give a professional finish. The 3-thread stitch is used primarily for neatening. A 4-thread stitch can also be used for neatening, as well as for construction due to its having the extra thread.

▶ **3-THREAD SERGER STITCH**

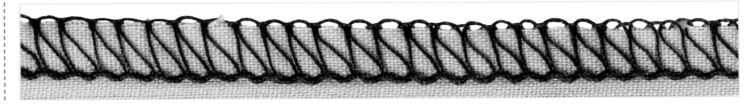

▶ **4-THREAD SERGER STITCH**

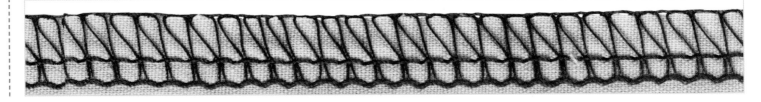

SERGER ACCESSORIES

You can purchase additional feet for the serger. Some will speed up your sewing by performing tasks such as gathering.

▶

Serger needles
The serger uses a ballpoint needle, which creates a large loop in the thread for the loopers to catch and produce a stitch. If a normal sewing machine needle is used, it could damage the serger.

Serger foot
The standard foot used for most processes.

Cording foot
A foot with a coil on one side through which a thin cord or fishing line is fed. Use in conjunction with a rolled hem setting for decorative effects.

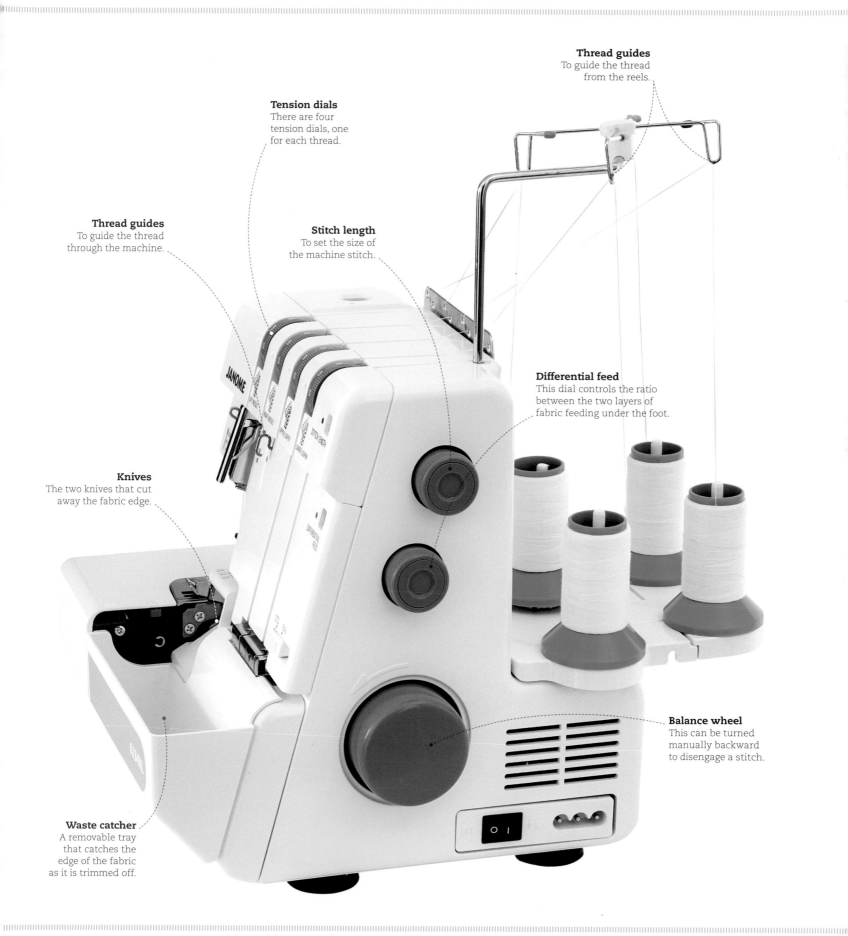

Thread guides
To guide the thread
from the reels.

Tension dials
There are four
tension dials, one
for each thread.

Thread guides
To guide the thread
through the machine.

Stitch length
To set the size of
the machine stitch.

Differential feed
This dial controls the ratio
between the two layers of
fabric feeding under the foot.

Knives
The two knives that cut
away the fabric edge.

Balance wheel
This can be turned
manually backward
to disengage a stitch.

Waste catcher
A removable tray
that catches the
edge of the fabric
as it is trimmed off.

EMBROIDERY **MACHINE**

A machine that does not sew but embroiders, this enables you to produce embellished clothing or home wares. Computer-controlled, the machine has plenty of built-in embroidery designs and there are many more designs that can be purchased to use with it. The machine works best with special embroidery threads and bobbin threads.

EMBROIDERY DESIGNS

Here are some examples of the many types of design that can be embroidered, to personalize and embellish clothing and accessories as well as place mats, tablecloths, napkins, pillows, baby blankets, and many other items.

EMBROIDERY MACHINE ACCESSORIES

Hoops of varying shapes and sizes fit on to the machine carriage to enable the embroidery to be stitched.

A gridded template on the bottom of the embroidery hoop aids placement of the design.

Once the fabric is stretched in the hoop, the ring is pressed down and secured. The fabric must be held taut.

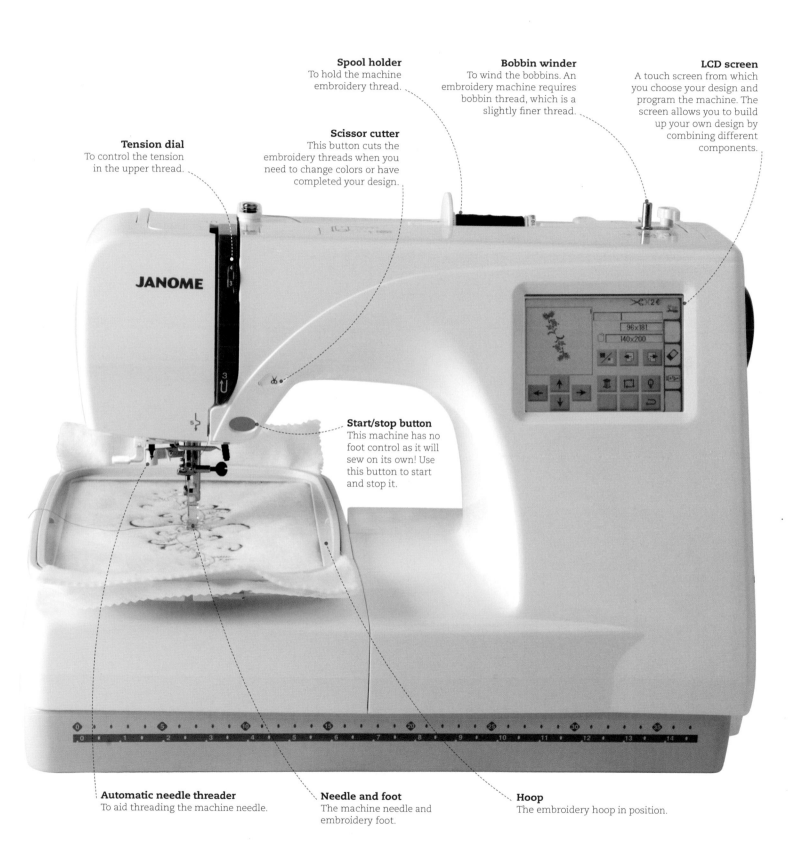

Spool holder
To hold the machine embroidery thread.

Bobbin winder
To wind the bobbins. An embroidery machine requires bobbin thread, which is a slightly finer thread.

LCD screen
A touch screen from which you choose your design and program the machine. The screen allows you to build up your own design by combining different components.

Scissor cutter
This button cuts the embroidery threads when you need to change colors or have completed your design.

Tension dial
To control the tension in the upper thread.

Start/stop button
This machine has no foot control as it will sew on its own! Use this button to start and stop it.

Automatic needle threader
To aid threading the machine needle.

Needle and foot
The machine needle and embroidery foot.

Hoop
The embroidery hoop in position.

FABRICS

Whether making clothes, soft furnishings, or crafts, it's important to choose the right fabric for your project. You need to consider weight and drape of the fabric, the width, the cost, and the care—some have to be dry-cleaned.

TOOLS

WOOL FABRICS

A natural fiber, wool comes primarily from sheep—Australian merino sheep's wool is considered to be the best. However, we also get wool fibers from goats (mohair and cashmere), rabbits (angora), camels (camel hair), and llamas (alpaca). A wool fiber is either short and fluffy, when it is known as a woollen yarn, or it is long, strong, and smooth, when it is called worsted. The term virgin (or new) wool denotes wool fibers that are being used for the first time. Wool may be reprocessed or reused and is then often mixed with other fibers.

PROPERTIES OF WOOL

▶ **Comfortable to wear** in all climates as it is available in many weights and weaves

▶ **Warm in the winter** and cool in the summer, because it will breathe with your body

▶ **Absorbs moisture** better than other natural fibers—will absorb up to 30 percent of its weight before it feels wet

▶ **Flame-resistant**

▶ **Relatively** crease-resistant

▶ **Ideal to tailor** as it can be easily shaped with steam

▶ **Often blended** with other fibers to reduce the cost of fabric

▶ **Felts if exposed** to excessive heat, moisture, and pressure

▶ **Will be bleached** by sunlight with prolonged exposure

▶ **Can be damaged** by moths

CASHMERE

Wool from the Kashmir goat, and the most luxurious of all the wools. A soft yet hard-wearing fabric available in different weights.

Cutting out: as cashmere often has a slight pile, use a nap layout

Seams: plain, neatened with serger stitch or pinking shears (a zigzag stitch would curl the edge of the seam)

Thread: a silk thread is ideal, or a polyester all-purpose thread

Needle: machine size 12/14, depending on the thickness of the fabric; sharps for hand sewing

Pressing: steam iron on a steam setting, with a pressing cloth and seam roll

Use for: jackets, coats, men's wear; knitted cashmere yarn for sweaters, cardigans

CHALLIS

A fine wool fabric, made from a worsted yarn that has an uneven surface texture. Challis is often printed as well as plain.

Cutting out: a nap layout is not required unless the fabric is printed

Seams: plain, neatened with serger or zigzag stitch; a run and fell seam can also be used

Thread: polyester all-purpose thread

Needle: machine size 11/12; sharps for hand sewing

Pressing: steam iron on a steam setting, with a pressing cloth; fabric will stretch while warm so handle with care

Use for: dresses, jackets, garments with pleating or draping detail

CREPE

A soft fabric made from a twisted yarn, which is what produces the uneven surface. It is important to preshrink this fabric prior to use by giving it a good steaming, because it will have stretched on the bolt and it is prone to shrinkage.

Cutting out: use a regular layout

Seams: plain, neatened with serger (a zigzag stitch may curl the edge of the seam)

Thread: polyester all-purpose thread

Needle: machine size 12; sharps or milliner's for hand sewing

Pressing: steam iron on a wool setting; a pressing cloth is not always required

Use for: all types of clothing

FLANNEL

A wool with a lightly brushed surface, featuring either a plain or twill weave. Used in the past for underwear.

Cutting out: use a nap layout

Seams: plain, neatened with serger or zigzag stitch or Hong Kong finish

Thread: polyester all-purpose thread

Needle: machine size 14; sharps for hand sewing

Pressing: steam iron on a wool setting with a pressing cloth; use a seam roll as the fabric is prone to marking

Use for: bedding, sleepwear, men's wear

GABARDINE

A hard-wearing suiting fabric with a distinctive weave. Gabardine often has a sheen and is prone to shine. It can be difficult to handle as it is springy and frays badly.

Cutting out: a nap layout is advisable as the fabric has a sheen

Seams: plain, neatened with serger or zigzag stitch

Thread: polyester all-purpose thread or 100 percent cotton thread

Needle: machine size 14; sharps for hand sewing

Pressing: steam iron on a wool setting; use just the toe of the iron and a silk organza pressing cloth as the fabric will mark and may shine

Use for: men's wear, jackets, pants

MOHAIR

From the wool of the Angora goat. A long, straight, and very strong fiber that produces a hairy cloth.

Cutting out: use a nap layout, with the fibers brushing down the pattern pieces in the same direction, from neck to hem

Seams: plain, neatened with serger or pinking shears

Thread: polyester all-purpose thread

Needle: machine size 14; sharps for hand sewing

Pressing: steam iron on a wool setting; "stroke" the iron over the wool, moving in the direction of the nap

Use for: jackets, coats, men's wear, soft furnishings; knitted mohair yarns for sweaters

TARTAN

An authentic tartan belongs to a Scottish clan, and each has its own unique design that can only be used by that clan. The fabric is made using a twill weave from worsted yarns.

Cutting out: check the design for even/uneven check as it may need a nap layout or even a single layer layout

Seams: plain, matching the pattern and neatened with serger or zigzag stitch

Thread: polyester all-purpose thread

Needle: machine size 14; sharps for hand sewing

Pressing: steam iron on a wool setting; may require a pressing cloth, so test first

Use for: traditionally kilts, but these days also skirts, pants, jackets, home goods

CUTTING OUT pp.76—83 • MACHINE STITCHES AND SEAMS pp.92—109

TOOLS

TWEED, MODERN

A mix of chunky and nubby wool yarns. Modern tweed is often found in contemporary color palettes as well as plain, and with interesting fibers in the weft such as metallics and paper. It is much favored by fashion designers.

Cutting out: use a nap layout

Seams: plain, neatened with serger or zigzag stitch; the fabric is prone to fraying

Thread: polyester all-purpose thread

Needle: machine size 14; sharps for hand sewing

Pressing: steam iron on a wool setting; a pressing cloth may not be required

Use for: jackets, coats; also skirts, dresses, home goods

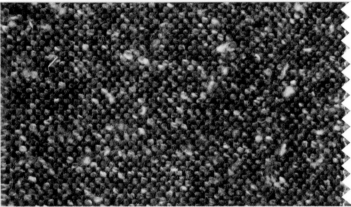

TWEED, TRADITIONAL

A rough fabric with a distinctive warp and weft, usually in different colors, and often forming a small check pattern. Traditional tweed is associated with the English countryside.

Cutting out: a nap layout is not required unless the fabric features a check

Seams: plain, neatened with serger or zigzag stitch; can also be neatened with pinking shears

Thread: polyester all-purpose thread or 100 percent cotton thread

Needle: machine size 14; sharps for hand sewing

Pressing: steam iron on a steam setting; a pressing cloth may not be required

Use for: jackets, coats, skirts, men's wear, home goods

VENETIAN

A wool with a satin weave, making a luxurious, expensive fabric.

Cutting out: use a nap layout

Seams: plain, neatened with serger or zigzag stitch

Thread: polyester all-purpose thread or 100 percent cotton thread

Needle: machine size 14; sharps for hand sewing

Pressing: steam iron on a steam setting with a silk organza cloth to avoid shine; use a seam roll under the seams to prevent them from showing through

Use for: jackets, coats, men's wear

WOOL WORSTED

A light and strong cloth, made from good-quality thin, firm filament fibers. Always steam prior to cutting out as the fabric may shrink slightly after having been stretched around a bolt.

Cutting out: use a nap layout

Seams: plain, neatened with serger or zigzag stitch or Hong Kong finish

Thread: polyester all-purpose thread

Needle: machine size 12/14, depending on fabric; milliner's or sharps for hand sewing

Pressing: steam iron on a wool setting, with a pressing cloth; use a seam roll to prevent the seam from showing through

Use for: skirts, jackets, coats, pants

NEEDLES AND PINS **pp.22–23** • THREADS **pp.24–25** • PRESSING AIDS **pp.28–29**

COTTON FABRICS

One of the most versatile and popular of all fabrics, cotton is a natural fiber that comes from the seed pods, or bolls, of the cotton plant. It is thought that cotton fibers have been in use since ancient times. Today, the world's biggest producers of cotton include the United States, India, and countries in the Middle East. Cotton fibers can be filament or staple, with the longest and finest used for top-quality bed linen. Cotton clothing is widely worn in warmer climates as the fabric will keep you cool.

PROPERTIES OF COTTON

▶ **Absorbs moisture** well and carries heat away from the body

▶ **Stronger wet than dry**

▶ **Does not build up** static electricity

▶ **Dyes well**

▶ **Prone to shrinkage** unless it has been treated

▶ **Will deteriorate** from mildew and prolonged exposure to sunlight

▶ **Creases easily**

▶ **Soils easily,** but launders well

EYELET

A fine, plain-weave cotton that has been embroidered to make small holes. Usually white or a pastel color.

Cutting out: may need layout to place embroidery at hem edge

Seams: plain, neatened with serger or zigzag stitch; a French seam can also be used

Thread: polyester all-purpose thread

Needle: machine size 12/14; sharps for hand sewing

Pressing: steam iron on a cotton setting; a pressing cloth is not required

Use for: baby clothes, summer skirts, blouses

CALICO

A plain weave fabric that is usually unbleached and quite stiff. Available in many different weights, from very fine to extremely heavy.

Cutting out: use a regular layout

Seams: plain, neatened with serger or zigzag stitch

Thread: polyester all-purpose thread

Needle: machine size 11/14, depending on thickness of thread; sharps for hand sewing

Pressing: steam iron on a steam setting; a pressing cloth is not required

Use for: muslins (test garments), home goods

CHAMBRAY

A light cotton that has a colored warp thread and white weft thread. Chambray can also be found as a check or a striped fabric.

Cutting out: use a regular layout

Seams: plain, neatened with serger or zigzag stitch

Thread: polyester all-purpose thread

Needle: machine size 11; sharps for hand sewing

Pressing: steam iron on a cotton setting; a pressing cloth is not required

Use for: blouses, men's shirts, children's wear

CHINTZ

A floral print or plain cotton fabric with a glazed finish that gives it a sheen. It has a close weave and is often treated to resist dirt.

Cutting out: use a nap layout

Seams: plain, neatened with serger or zigzag stitch; a run and fell seam can also be used

Thread: polyester all-purpose thread or 100 percent cotton thread

Needle: machine size 14; milliner's for hand sewing

Pressing: steam iron on a cotton setting; a pressing cloth may be required due to sheen on fabric

Use for: home goods

CUTTING OUT **pp.76–83** ● MACHINE STITCHES AND SEAMS **pp.92–109**

TOOLS

CORDUROY

A soft pile fabric with distinctive stripes (known as wales or ribs) woven into it. The name depends on the size of the ribs: baby or pin cord has extremely fine ribs; needle cord has slightly thicker ribs; corduroy has 10–12 ribs per 1in (2.5cm); and elephant or jumbo cord has thick, heavy ribs.

Cutting out: use a nap layout with the pile on the corduroy, brushing the pattern pieces from neck to hem, to give depth

Seams: plain, stitched using a walking foot and neatened with serger or zigzag stitch

Thread: polyester all-purpose thread

Needle: machine size 12/16; sharps or milliner's for hand sewing

Pressing: steam iron on a cotton setting; use a seam roll under the seams with a pressing cloth

Use for: pants, skirts, men's wear

CRINKLE COTTON

Looks like an exaggerated version of seersucker (see p.46), with creases added by a heat process. Crinkle cotton may require careful laundering as it often has to be twisted into shape when wet to put the creases back in.

Cutting out: a nap layout is not required unless the fabric is printed

Seams: plain, neatened with serger or zigzag stitch

Thread: polyester all-purpose thread

Needle: machine size 12; milliner's for hand sewing

Pressing: steam iron on a cotton setting; take care not to press out the crinkles

Use for: blouses, dresses, children's wear

DAMASK

A cotton that has been woven on a jacquard loom to produce a fabric usually with a floral pattern in a self color. May have a sheen to the surface. May also be made of silk or linen.

Cutting out: use a nap layout

Seams: plain, neatened with serger or zigzag stitch

Thread: polyester all-purpose thread or 100 percent cotton thread

Needle: machine size 14; sharps for hand sewing

Pressing: steam iron on a cotton setting; a pressing cloth may be required if the fabric has a sheen

Use for: home furnishings; colored jacquards for jackets, skirts

DENIM

Named after Nîmes in France. A hard-wearing twill-weave fabric (see p.53) with a colored warp and white weft, usually made into jeans. Available in various weights and often mixed with an elastic thread for stretch. Denim is usually blue, but is also available in a variety of other colors.

Cutting out: use a regular layout

Seams: run and fell or top-stitched plain

Thread: polyester all-purpose thread with top-stitching thread for detail top-stitching

Needle: machine size 14/16; sharps for hand sewing

Pressing: steam iron on a cotton setting; a pressing cloth should not be required

Use for: jeans, jackets, children's wear

NEEDLES AND PINS **pp.22–23** ● THREADS **pp.24–25** ● PRESSING AIDS **pp.28–29**

DRILL

A hard-wearing twill or plain-weave fabric with the same color warp and weft. Drill frays badly on the cut edges.

Cutting out: use a regular layout

Seams: run and fell; or plain, neatened with serger or zigzag stitch

Thread: polyester all-purpose thread with top-stitching thread for detail top-stitching

Needle: machine size 14; sharps for hand sewing

Pressing: steam iron on a cotton setting; a pressing cloth is not required

Use for: men's wear, casual jackets, pants

GINGHAM

A fresh, two-color cotton fabric that features checkers of various sizes. A plain weave made by having groups of white and colored warp and weft threads.

Cutting out: usually an even check, so nap layout is not required but recommended; pattern will need matching

Seams: plain, neatened with serger or zigzag stitch

Thread: polyester all-purpose thread

Needle: machine size 11/12; sharps for hand sewing

Pressing: steam iron on a cotton setting; a pressing cloth should not be required

Use for: children's wear, dresses, shirts, home furnishings

JERSEY

A fine cotton yarn knitted to give stretch, making the fabric very comfortable to wear. Drapes well.

Cutting out: a nap layout is recommended

Seams: 4-thread serger stitch; or plain seam stitched with a small zigzag stitch; seam allowances stitched together with a zigzag

Thread: polyester all-purpose thread

Needle: machine size 12/14; a ballpoint needle may be required for serger and for hand sewing

Pressing: steam iron on a wool setting as jersey may shrink on a cotton setting

Use for: underwear, drapey dresses, leisurewear, bedding

COTTON LAWN

A plain weave fabric woven from fine, high-count yarns, which results in a silky, smooth feel.

Cutting out: a nap layout is not required unless the fabric has a one-way print

Seams: plain, neatened with serger or zigzag stitch; French

Thread: pure cotton thread; or a polyester all-purpose thread

Needle: machine size 11; or a milliner's size 9 for hand sewing

Pressing: steam iron on a cotton setting; a pressing cloth should not be required

Use for: blouses, shirts, dresses, children's wear, interlining

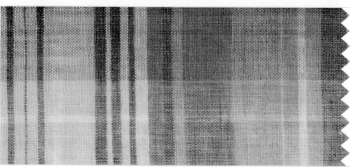

MADRAS

A plaid fabric made from a fine cotton yarn, usually from India. Often found in bright colors. An inexpensive cotton fabric.

Cutting out: use a nap layout and match the pattern

Seams: plain, neatened with serger or zigzag stitch

Thread: polyester all-purpose thread

Needle: machine size 12/14; sharps for hand sewing

Pressing: steam iron on a cotton setting; a pressing cloth is not required

Use for: shirts, skirts, home furnishings

CUTTING OUT **pp.76–83** ● MACHINE SEWING AND SEAMS **pp.92–109**

MUSLIN

A fine, plain, open-weave cotton. Can be found in colors but usually sold a natural/unbleached or white. Makes great pressing cloths and interlinings. It is a good idea to wash prior to use.

Cutting out: use a regular layout

Seams: 4-thread serger stitch; or plain seam, neatened with serger or zigzag stitch; or a French seam

Thread: polyester all-purpose thread

Needle: machine size 11; milliner's for hand sewing

Pressing: steam iron on a cotton setting; a cloth is not required

Use for: curtaining and other household uses, as well as test patterns or muslins

SEERSUCKER

A woven cotton that has a bubbly appearance woven into it, due to stripes of puckers. Do not over-press, or the surface effect will be damaged.

Cutting out: use a nap layout, due to puckered surface effect

Seams: plain, neatened with serger or zigzag stitch

Thread: polyester all-purpose thread

Needle: machine size 11/12; milliner's for hand sewing

Pressing: steam iron on a cotton setting (be careful not to press out the wrinkles)

Use for: summer clothing, skirts, shirts, children's wear

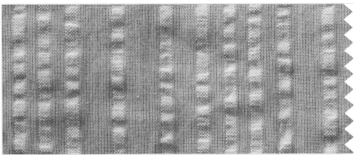

SHIRTING

A closely woven, fine cotton, with colored warp and weft yarns making stripes or checks.

Cutting out: use a nap layout if fabric has uneven stripes

Seams: plain, neatened with serger or zigzag stitch; a run and fell seam can also be used

Thread: polyester all-purpose thread

Needle: machine size 12; milliner's for hand sewing

Pressing: steam iron on a cotton setting; a pressing cloth is not required

Use for: ladies' and men's shirts

TERRY CLOTH

A cotton fabric with loops on the surface; top-quality terry cloth has loops on both sides. It is highly absorbent. Wash before use to preshrink and make it fluffy.

Cutting out: use a nap layout

Seams: 4-thread serger stitch; or plain seam, neatened with serger or zigzag stitch

Thread: polyester all-purpose thread

Needle: machine size 14; sharps for hand sewing

Pressing: steam iron on a cotton setting; a pressing cloth is not required

Use for: bathrobes, beachwear, towels

VELVET

A pile-weave fabric, made by using an additional yarn that is then cut to produce the pile. Difficult to handle and can be easily damaged if seams have to be unpicked.

Cutting out: use a nap layout with the pile brushing up from hem to neck, to give depth of color

Seams: plain, stitched using a walking foot (stitch all seams from hem to neck) and neatened with serger or zigzag stitch

Thread: polyester all-purpose thread

Needle: machine size 14; milliner's for hand sewing

Pressing: only if you have to; use a velvet board, a bit of steam, toe of iron, and silk organza cloth

Use for: jackets, coats

◀ **NEEDLES AND PINS pp.22–23** ● **THREADS pp.24–25** ● **PRESSING AIDS pp.28–29**

LINEN FABRICS

Linen is a natural fiber that is derived from the stem of the flax plant. It is available in a variety of qualities and weights, from very fine linen to heavy suiting weights. Coarser than cotton, it is sometimes woven with cotton as well as being mixed with silk.

PROPERTIES OF LINEN

- ▶ Cool and comfortable to wear
- ▶ Absorbs moisture well
- ▶ Shrinks when washed
- ▶ Does not ease well
- ▶ Has a tendency to wrinkle
- ▶ Prone to fraying
- ▶ Resists moths but is damaged by mildew

COTTON AND LINEN BLEND

Two fibers may have been mixed together in the yarn or may have mixed warp and weft yarns. It has lots of texture in the weave. Silk and linen mix is treated in the same way.

Cutting out: use a regular layout

Seams: plain, neatened with serger or zigzag stitch

Thread: polyester all-purpose thread

Needle: machine size 14; sharps for hand sewing

Pressing: a steam iron on a steam setting, with a silk organza pressing cloth

Use for: summer-weight jackets, tailored dresses

DRESS-WEIGHT LINEN

A medium-weight linen with a plain weave. The yarn is often uneven, which causes slubs in the weave.

Cutting out: use a regular layout

Seams: plain, neatened with serger or zigzag stitch or a Hong Kong finish

Thread: polyester all-purpose thread with a top-stitching thread for top-stitching

Needle: machine size 14; sharps for hand sewing

Pressing: steam iron on a cotton setting

Use for: dresses, pants, skirts

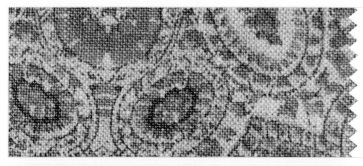

PRINTED LINENS

Many linens today feature prints or even embroidery. The fabric may be light- to medium weight, with a smooth yarn that has few slubs.

Cutting out: use a nap layout

Seams: plain, neatened with serger or zigzag stitch

Thread: polyester all-purpose thread

Needle: machine size 14; sharps for hand sewing

Pressing: steam iron on a cotton setting (steam is required to remove creases)

Use for: dresses, skirts

SUITING LINEN

A heavier yarn is used to produce a linen suitable for suits for men and women. Can be a firm, tight weave or a looser weave.

Cutting out: use a regular layout

Seams: plain, neatened with serger or a zigzag stitch and sharps hand-sewing needle

Thread: polyester all-purpose thread with a top-stitch thread for top-stitching

Needle: machine size 14; sharps for hand sewing

Pressing: steam iron on a cotton setting (steam is required to remove creases)

Use for: men's and women's suits, pants, coats

CUTTING OUT **pp.76–83** ● MACHINE STITCHES AND SEAMS **pp.92–109**

TOOLS

SILK FABRICS

Often referred to as the queen of all fabrics, silk is made from the fibers of the silkworm's cocoon. This strong and luxurious fabric dates back thousands of years to its first development in China, and the secret of silk production was well protected by the Chinese until 300 CE. Silk fabrics can be very fine or thick and chunky. They need careful handling as some silk fabrics can be easily damaged.

PROPERTIES OF SILK

▸ **Keeps you warm** in winter and cool in summer
▸ **Absorbs moisture** and dries quickly
▸ **Dyes well,** producing deep, rich colors
▸ **Static electricity** can build up and fabric may cling
▸ **Will fade in prolonged** strong sunlight

▸ **Prone to shrinkage**
▸ **Best dry-cleaned**
▸ **Weaker when** wet than dry
▸ **May water-mark**

CHIFFON

A very strong and very fine, transparent silk with a plain weave. Will gather and ruffle well. Difficult to handle.

Cutting out: place tissue paper under the fabric and pin the fabric to the tissue, cutting through all layers if necessary; use extra-fine pins

Seams: French

Thread: polyester all-purpose thread

Needle: machine size 9/11; fine milliner's for hand sewing

Pressing: dry iron on a wool setting

Use for: special-occasion wear, over-blouses

CREPE DE CHINE

Medium weight, with an uneven surface due to the twisted silk yarn used. Drapes well and often used on bias-cut garments.

Cutting out: if to be bias-cut, use a single layer layout; otherwise use a nap layout

Seams: a seam for a difficult fabric or French

Thread: polyester all-purpose thread

Needle: machine size 11; milliner's or betweens for hand sewing

Pressing: dry iron on a wool setting

Use for: blouses, dresses, special-occasion wear

DUCHESS SATIN

A heavy, expensive satin fabric used almost exclusively for special-occasion wear.

Cutting out: use a nap layout

Seams: plain, with pinked edges

Thread: polyester all-purpose thread

Needle: machine size 12/14; milliner's for hand sewing

Pressing: steam iron on a wool setting with a pressing cloth; use a seam roll under the seams to prevent shadowing

Use for: special-occasion wear

DUPIONI

Similar to shantung (see p.49) but woven using a much smoother yarn to reduce the amount of nubbly bits in the weft.

Cutting out: use a nap layout to prevent shadowing

Seams: plain, neatened with serger or zigzag stitch

Thread: polyester all-purpose thread

Needle: machine size 12; milliner's for hand sewing

Pressing: steam iron on a wool setting, with a pressing cloth as fabric may water-mark

Use for: dresses, skirts, jackets, special-occasion wear, soft furnishings

NEEDLES AND PINS **pp.22—23** ● THREADS **pp.24—25** ● PRESSING AIDS **pp.28—29**

SHANTUNG

The most popular of all the silks. A distinctive weft yarn with many nubbly bits. Available in hundreds of colors. Easy to handle, but it does fray badly.

Cutting out: use a nap layout as the fabric shadows

Seams: plain, neatened with serger or zigzag stitch

Thread: polyester all-purpose thread

Needle: machine size 12; milliner's for hand sewing

Pressing: steam iron on a wool setting, with a pressing cloth to avoid water-marking

Use for: dresses, special-occasion wear, jackets, soft furnishings

GEORGETTE

A soft, filmy silk fabric that has a slight transparency. Does not crease easily.

Cutting out: place tissue paper under the fabric and pin fabric to tissue, cutting through all layers if necessary; use extra-fine pins

Seams: French

Thread: polyester all-purpose thread

Needle: machine size 11; milliner's for hand sewing

Pressing: dry iron on a wool setting to avoid damage by steam

Use for: special-occasion wear, loose-fitting overshirts

HABUTAI

Originally from Japan, a smooth, fine silk that can have a plain or a twill weave. Fabric is often used for silk painting.

Cutting out: use a regular layout

Seams: French

Thread: polyester all-purpose thread

Needle: machine size 9/11; very fine milliner's or betweens for hand sewing

Pressing: steam iron on a wool setting

Use for: lining, shirts, blouses

MATKA

A silk suiting fabric with an uneven-looking yarn. Matka can be mistaken for linen.

Cutting out: use a nap layout as silk may shadow

Seams: plain, neatened with serger or zigzag stitch or Hong Kong finish

Thread: polyester all-purpose thread

Needle: machine size 12/14; milliner's for hand sewing

Pressing: steam iron on a wool setting with a pressing cloth; a seam roll is recommended to prevent the seams from showing through

Use for: dresses, jackets, pants

ORGANZA

A sheer fabric with a crisp appearance that will crease easily.

Cutting out: use a regular layout

Seams: French or a seam for a difficult fabric

Thread: polyester all-purpose thread

Needle: machine size 11; milliner's or betweens for hand sewing

Pressing: steam iron on a wool setting; a pressing cloth should not be required

Use for: sheer blouses, shrugs, interlining, interfacing

CUTTING OUT pp.76–83 ● **MACHINE SEWING AND SEAMS pp.92–109**

TOOLS

SATIN

A silk with a satin weave that can be very light to quite heavy in weight.

Cutting out: use a nap layout in a single layer as fabric is slippery

Seams: French; on thicker satins, a seam for a difficult fabric

Thread: polyester all-purpose thread (not silk thread as it becomes weak with wear)

Needle: machine size 11/12; milliner's or betweens for hand sewing

Pressing: steam iron on a wool setting, with a pressing cloth as fabric may water-mark

Use for: blouses, dresses, special-occasion wear

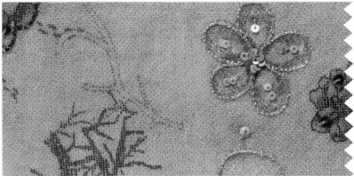

SILK AND WOOL BLEND

A fabric made by mixing wool and silk fibers or wool and silk yarns. The fabric made may be fine in quality or thick, like a coating.

Cutting out: use a nap layout

Seams: plain, neatened with serger or zigzag stitch

Thread: polyester all-purpose thread

Needle: machine size 11/14, depending on fabric; sharps for hand sewing

Pressing: steam iron on a wool setting; seams will require some steam to make them lie flat

Use for: suits, skirts, pants, coats

TAFFETA

A smooth, plain-weave fabric with a crisp appearance. It makes a rustling sound when worn. Can require special handling and does not wear well.

Cutting out: use a nap layout, with extra-fine pins in seams as they will mark the fabric

Seams: plain; fabric may pucker, so sew from the hem upward, keeping the fabric taut under the machine; neaten with serger or pinking shears

Thread: polyester all-purpose thread

Needle: machine size 11; milliner's or betweens for hand sewing

Pressing: cool iron, with a seam roll under the seams

Use for: special-occasion wear

LEATHER AND SUEDE

Leather and suede are natural fabrics derived from either pigskin or cowhide. Depending on the curing process that has been used, the skin will be either a suede or a leather. The fabrics require special handling.

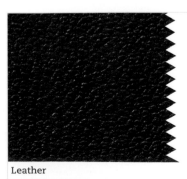

Leather

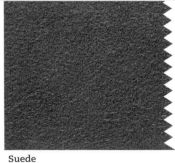

Suede

LEATHER AND SUEDE

Pattern pieces cannot be pinned on—you must draw around them using tailor's chalk. After cutting out, chalk will rub off and not damage the skin.

Cutting out: a complete pattern is required, left- and right-hand halves; use a nap layout for suede, as it will brush one way

Seams: lapped or plain, using a walking foot or an ultra glide foot; neatening is not required

Thread: polyester all-purpose thread

Needle: machine size 14 (a special leather needle may actually damage the skin); hand sewing is not recommended

Pressing: Avoid steam when ironing; set the iron on the rayon setting and use a 100% cotton cloth between the iron and leather

Use for: skirts, pants, jackets, home goods

 NEEDLES AND PINS **pp.22–23** ● THREADS **pp.24–25** ● PRESSING AIDS **pp.28–29**

MAN-MADE FABRICS

The term "man-made" applies to any fabric that is not 100 percent natural. Many of these fabrics have been developed over the last hundred years, which means they are new compared to natural fibers. Some man-made fabrics are made from natural elements mixed with chemicals while others are made entirely from non-natural substances. The properties of man-made fabrics vary from fabric to fabric.

ACETATE

Introduced in 1924, acetate is made from cellulose and chemicals. The fabric has a slight shine and is widely used for linings. Acetate can also be woven into fabrics such as acetate taffeta, acetate satin, and acetate jersey.

Properties of acetate:
• dyes well
• can be heat-set into pleats
• washes well

Cutting out: use a nap layout due to sheen on fabric

Seams: plain, neatened with serger or zigzag stitch, or 4-thread serger stitch

Thread: polyester all-purpose thread

Needle: machine size 11; sharps for hand sewing

Pressing: steam iron on a cool setting (fabric can melt)

Use for: special-occasion wear, linings

ACRYLIC

Introduced in 1950, acrylic fibers are made from ethylene and acrylonitrile. The fabric resembles wool and makes a good substitute for machine-washable wool. Often seen as a knitted fabric, the fibers can be mixed with wool.

Properties of acrylic:
• little absorbency
• tends to retain odors
• not very strong

Cutting out: use a regular layout

Seams: 4-thread serger stitch on knitted fabrics; plain seam on woven fabrics

Thread: polyester all-purpose thread

Needle: machine size 12/14, but a ballpoint needle may be required on knitted fabrics; sharps for hand sewing

Pressing: steam iron on a wool setting (fabric can be damaged by heat)

Use for: knitted yarns for sweaters; wovens for skirts, blouses

NYLON

Developed by DuPont in 1938, the fabric takes its name from a collaboration between New York (NY) and London (LON). Nylon is made from polymer chips that are melted and extruded into fibers. The fabric can be knitted or woven.

Properties of nylon:
• very hard-wearing
• does not absorb moisture

• washes easily, although white nylon can discolor easily
• very strong

Cutting out: a nap layout is not required unless the fabric is printed

Seams: plain, neatened with serger or zigzag stitch

Thread: polyester all-purpose thread

Needle: machine size 14, but a ballpoint needle may be required for knitted nylons; sharps for hand sewing

Pressing: steam iron on a silk setting (fabric can melt)

Use for: sportswear, underwear

SCUBA/NEOPRENE

A relatively new fabric, scuba is a lofty double-knit fabric of finely spun polyester fibers that create a super smooth handle, low sheen, and a full-bodied drape. It is often digitally printed to great effect.

Properties of scuba:
• takes dye well, especially digital prints

• holds its shape after construction
• does not absorb moisture well

Cutting out: a nap layout is not required unless the fabric is printed

Seams: plain seam; no need to neaten but you can pink the edge or serger stitch

Thread: polyester all-purpose thread

Needle: machine size 14; some scubas may require a ballpoint needle

Pressing: steam iron, with a pressing cloth (fabric can melt)

Use for: skirts and dresses

CUTTING OUT **pp.76–83** • MACHINE STITCHES AND SEAMS **pp.92–109**

POLYESTER

One of the most popular of the man-made fibers, polyester was introduced in 1951 as a washable man's suit. Polyester fibers are made from petroleum by-products and can take on any form, from a very fine sheer fabric to a thick, heavy suiting.

Properties of polyester:
• non-absorbent
• does not crease
• can build up static
• may "pill"

Cutting out: a nap layout is only required if the fabric is printed

Seams: French, plain, or 4-thread serger, depending on the weight of the fabric

Thread: polyester all-purpose thread

Needle: machine size 11/14; sharps for hand sewing

Pressing: steam iron on a polyester setting

Use for: workwear, school uniforms

RAYON

Also known as viscose and often referred to as artificial silk, this fiber was developed in 1889. It is made from wood pulp or cotton linters mixed with chemicals. Rayon can be knitted or woven and made into a wide range of fabrics. It is often blended with other fibers.

Properties of rayon:
• is absorbent
• is not static
• dyes well
• frays badly

Cutting out: a nap layout is only required if the fabric is printed

Seams: plain, neatened with serger or zigzag stitch

Thread: polyester all-purpose thread

Needle: machine size 12/14; sharps for hand sewing

Pressing: steam iron on a silk setting

Use for: dresses, blouses, jackets

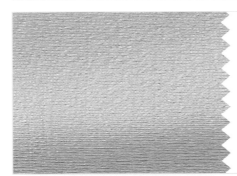

SPANDEX

Introduced in 1958, this is a lightweight, soft fiber than can be stretched 500 percent without breaking. A small amount of spandex is often mixed with other fibers to produce wovens with a slight stretch.

Properties of spandex:
• resistant to body oils, detergents, sun, sea, and sand
• can be difficult to sew
• can be damaged by heat
• not suitable for hand sewing

Cutting out: use a nap layout

Seams: 4-thread serger stitch or a seam stitched with a small zigzag

Thread: polyester all-purpose thread

Needle: machine ballpoint size 14 or a machine stretch needle

Pressing: steam iron on a wool setting (spandex can be damaged by a hot iron)

Use for: swimwear, foundation wear, sportswear

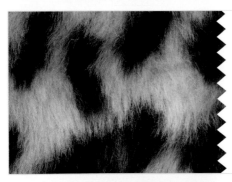

SYNTHETIC FURS

Created using a looped yarn that is then cut on a knitted or a woven base, synthetic fur can be made from nylon or acrylic fibers. The furs vary tremendously in quality and some are very difficult to tell from the real thing.

Properties of synthetic furs:
• require careful sewing
• not as warm as real fur

• can be heat-damaged by pressing

Cutting out: use a nap layout, with the fur pile brushed from the neck to the hem; cut just the backing carefully and not through the fur pile

Seams: plain, with a longer stitch and a walking foot; no neatening is required

Thread: polyester all-purpose thread

Needle: machine size 14; sharps for hand sewing

Pressing: if required, use a cool iron (synthetic fur can melt under a hot iron)

Use for: outerwear

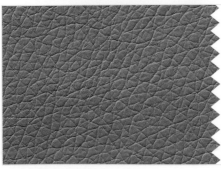

SYNTHETIC LEATHER AND SUEDE

Made from polymers, these are non-woven fabrics. Some synthetic leathers and suedes can closely resemble the real thing.

Properties of synthetic leather and suede:
• do not fray
• do not ease well

• can be difficult to sew by hand, so this is not recommended

Cutting out: use a nap layout

Seams: plain, stitched using a walking foot and neatened with pinking shears; can also use top-stitched seams and lapped seams

Thread: polyester all-purpose thread

Needle: machine size 11/14

Pressing: steam iron on a wool setting, with a pressing cloth

Use for: jackets, skirts, pants, home goods

 NEEDLES AND PINS **pp.22—23** ● THREADS **pp.24—25** ● PRESSING AIDS **pp.28—29**

FABRIC CONSTRUCTION

Most fabric is made by either knitting or weaving. A knitted fabric is constructed by interlocking looped yarns. For a woven fabric, horizontal and vertical yarns go under and over each other. The warp yarn, which is the strongest, runs vertically and the weft crosses it at right angles. There are also non-woven fabrics created by a felting process where tiny fibers are mixed and squeezed together, then rolled out.

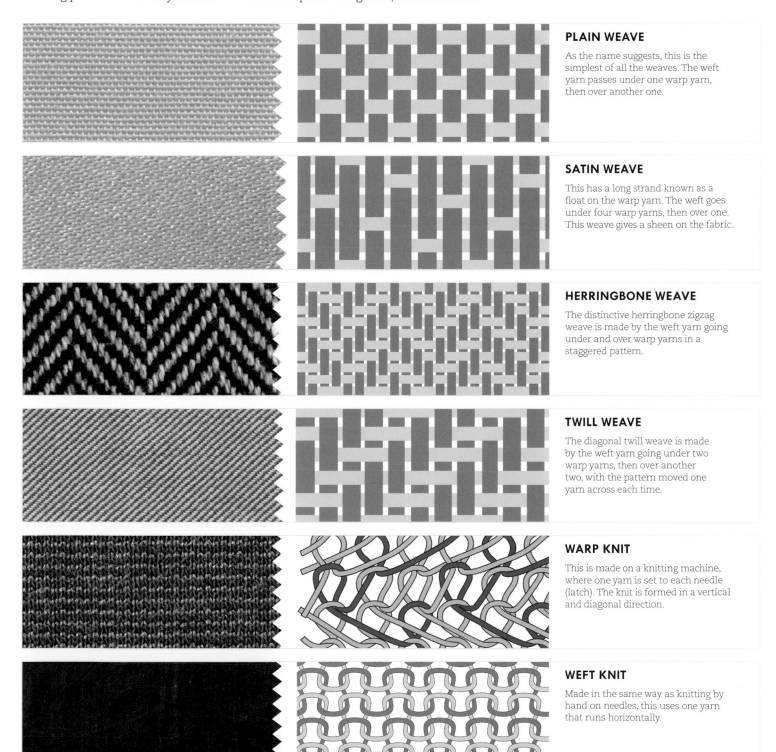

PLAIN WEAVE

As the name suggests, this is the simplest of all the weaves. The weft yarn passes under one warp yarn, then over another one.

SATIN WEAVE

This has a long strand known as a float on the warp yarn. The weft goes under four warp yarns, then over one. This weave gives a sheen on the fabric.

HERRINGBONE WEAVE

The distinctive herringbone zigzag weave is made by the weft yarn going under and over warp yarns in a staggered pattern.

TWILL WEAVE

The diagonal twill weave is made by the weft yarn going under two warp yarns, then over another two, with the pattern moved one yarn across each time.

WARP KNIT

This is made on a knitting machine, where one yarn is set to each needle (latch). The knit is formed in a vertical and diagonal direction.

WEFT KNIT

Made in the same way as knitting by hand on needles, this uses one yarn that runs horizontally.

CUTTING OUT **pp.76–83** ● MACHINE SEWING AND SEAMS **pp.92–109**

INTERFACINGS

An interfacing is a piece of fabric that is attached to the main fabric to give it support or structure. An interfacing fabric may be woven, knitted, or non-woven. It may also be fusible or non-fusible. A fusible interfacing (also called iron-on) can be bonded to the fabric by applying heat, whereas a non-fusible interfacing needs to be sewn to the fabric with a basting stitch. Always cut interfacings on the same grain as the fabric, regardless of its construction.

FUSIBLE INTERFACINGS

Be sure to buy fusibles designed for the home sewer, because the adhesive on the back of fusible interfacings for commercial use cannot be released with a normal steam iron. Do all pattern markings after the interfacing has been applied to the fabric.

WOVEN

A woven fusible is always a good choice for a woven fabric as the two weaves will work together. Always cut on the same grain as the fabric. This type of interfacing is suitable for crafts and for more structured garments.

LIGHTWEIGHT WOVEN

A very light, woven fusible that is almost sheer, this can be difficult to cut out as it tends to stick to the scissors. It is suitable for all light to medium-weight fabrics.

KNITTED

A knitted fusible is ideally suited to a knit fabric as the two will be able to stretch together. Some knitted fusibles only stretch one way, while others will stretch in all directions. A knitted fusible is also a good choice on fabrics that have a percentage of stretch.

NON-WOVEN

Non-woven fusibles are available in a wide variety of weights—choose one that feels lighter than your fabric. You can always add a second layer if one interfacing proves to be too light. This interfacing is suitable for supporting collars and cuffs, and facings on garments.

▶ HOW TO APPLY A FUSIBLE INTERFACING

1 Place fabric on pressing surface, wrong side up, making sure it is straight and not wrinkled.

2 Place the chosen interfacing sticky side down on the fabric (the sticky side feels gritty).

3 Cover with a dry pressing cloth and spray the cloth with a fine mist of water.

4 Place a steam iron, on a steam setting, on top of the pressing cloth.

5 Leave the iron in place for at least 10 seconds before moving it to the next area of fabric.

6 Check to see if the interfacing is fused to the fabric by rolling the fabric—if the interfacing is still loose in places, repeat the pressing process.

7 When the fabric has cooled down, the fusing process will be complete. Then pin the pattern back on to the fabric and transfer the pattern markings as required.

NON-FUSIBLE INTERFACINGS

These sew-in interfacings require basting to the wrong side of facings or the main garment fabric around the seam allowances. They are useful for sheer or fine fabrics where the adhesive from a fusible interfacing might show through.

ALPACA

A tailorings canvas made from wool and alpaca, this interfacing is excellent to use in difficult fabrics such as velvet, because the alpaca can be steamed into shape.

VOILE AND BATISTE

Voile (shown) is a lightweight, semi-sheer, 100 percent cotton fabric. It is perfect as an underlining or for interfacing silks and cotton lawns. It can also be used in heirloom sewing and smocking. Batiste is very similar but slightly firmer, and can be used in the same ways.

MUSLIN

A cotton muslin interfacing is a good choice on summer dresses as well as for special-occasion wear. Muslin can also be used to line fine cotton dresses.

ORGANZA

A pure silk organza makes an excellent interfacing for sheer fabric to give support and structure. It can also be used for structure in much larger areas such as bridal skirts.

NON-WOVEN SEW-IN INTERFACING

A non-woven material is ideal for crafts and small areas of garments, such as cuffs and collars. Use it in garments when a woven or fusible alternative is not available.

▶ HOW TO APPLY A NON-FUSIBLE INTERFACING

1 Place the interfacing on to the wrong side of the fabric, aligning the cut edges.

2 Pin in place.

3 Using a basting stitch, baste the interfacing to the fabric at ⅜in (1cm) within the seam allowance.

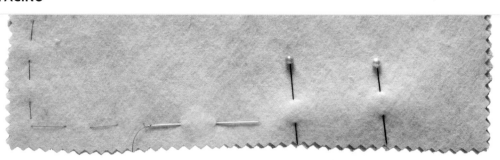

STITCHES FOR HAND SEWING **pp.88–91** ● APPLYING INTERFACING TO A FACING **p.153** ● LININGS AND INTERFACINGS **pp.322–333**

PATTERNS

Patterns are available not only for clothes but for a whole range of crafts and soft furnishing projects. It is always a good idea to test out a pattern in muslin before using the real fabric—this is known as making a muslin.

TOOLS

READING PATTERNS

Paper patterns are available for clothing, crafts, and home furnishings. A pattern has three main components: the envelope gives an illustration of the item, together with fabric suggestions and requirements. The pattern sheets inside the envelope are normally printed on tissue paper and contain a wealth of information, while the instructions tell you how to construct the item.

READING A PATTERN ENVELOPE

The envelope front illustrates the finished garment or item. This may be a line drawing or a photograph. The different versions are known as views. On the reverse of the envelope, there is usually an illustration of the back view and the standard body measurement chart that has been used for this pattern, plus a chart that will help you purchase the correct amount of fabric for each view. Suitable fabrics are also suggested alongside notions, which are all the bits and pieces you need to complete the project.

Number of pattern pieces

Code number for ordering

Description of garment or item, giving details of style and different views included in pattern

Suggested fabrics suitable for garment or item as well as unsuitable fabrics

Notions required for each view

5678
15 PIECES

MISSES' UNLINED JACKET, SKIRT, SHORTS, AND PANTS. Unlined, semifitted, V-neck jacket has short sleeves, front buttons, optional waistline darts, and optional breast pocket. Straight skirt, above mid-knee, and pants or shorts with straight legs, have waistband, front pleats, side seam pockets, and back zipper.

FABRICS: Jacket, skirt, shorts, and pants: wool crepe, soft cottons, sheeting, linen, silk, silk types, and lightweight woollens. Skirt, shorts, and pants also challis, jacquards, and crepe. Unsuitable for fabrics printed with obvious diagonals. Allow extra fabric in order to match plaids, stripes, or one-way design fabrics.

Use nap yardages/layouts for shaded, pile, or one-way design fabrics. *with nap. ** without nap
NOTIONS: Thread. Jacket: three ⅞ in (1.2 cm) buttons; ¼ in (6 mm) shoulder pads. Skirt, pants: pkg of 1¼ in (3.2 cm) waistband interfacing; 7 in (18 cm) zipper; and one hook and eye closure.

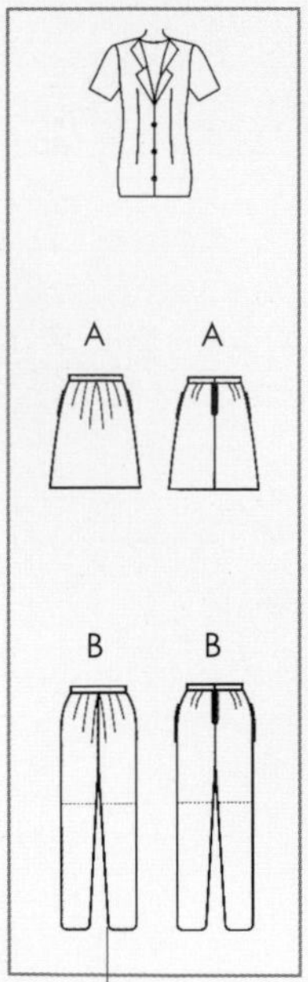

IMPERIAL

Body measurements	(6	8	10)	(12	14	16)	(18	20	22)	
Bust	30½	31½	32½	34	36	38	40	42	44	in
Waist	23	24	25	26½	28	30	32	34	37	in
Hip	32½	33½	34½	36	38	40	42	44	46	in

Fabric needed		(6	8	10)	(12	14	16)	(18	20	22)	
Jacket	45 in*/**	1⅞	1⅞	1⅞	1⅞	2	2⅜	2⅜	2⅜	2⅜	yd
	60 in*/**	1⅜	1⅜	1⅜	1½	1⅞	1⅞	1⅞	1⅞	2	yd
Interfacing		1⅛ yd of 22–36 in lightweight fusible or non-fusible									
Skirt A	45 in*/**	1¾	1⅞	1⅞	1⅞	2	2	2	2	2⅛	yd
	60 in*/**	1¼	1¼	1⅜	1⅜	1⅜	1⅜	1½	1½	1⅝	yd
Shorts B	45 in*/**	1¾	1¾	1¾	1¾	2	2	2	2	2⅛	yd
	60 in*/**	1¼	1¼	1⅜	1⅜	1⅜	1⅜	1½	1½	1⅝	yd
Pants B	45 in*/**	2⅝	2⅝	2⅝	2⅝	2⅝	2⅝	2⅝	2⅞	2⅞	yd
	60 in*	2⅛	2⅛	2⅛	2⅛	2¼	2¼	2⅜	2½	2½	yd
	60 in **	1¾	1¾	1⅞	2⅛	2⅛	2¼	2⅜	2½	2½	yd

Garment measurements	(6	8	10)	(12	14	16)	(18	20	22)	
Jacket bust	36¼	37¼	38¼	39¾	41¾	43¾	45¼	47¾	49¾	in
Jacket waist	31¾	32¾	33¾	35¼	37¼	39¼	41¼	43¼	45¼	in
Jacket back length	28¾	29	29¼	29½	29¾	30	30¼	30½	30¾	in
Skirt A lower edge	39	40	41	42	44	46	48	50	52	in
Skirt A length	24	24	24	24¾	24¾	24¾	25½	25½	25½	in
Shorts B leg width	28	29	30	32	34	37	39	41	43	in
Shorts B side length	19½	19¾	20	20¼	20½	20¾	21	21¼	21½	in
Pants B leg width	21	21	22	22	23	23	24	24	25	in
Pants B side length	40½	40½	40½	40½	40½	40½	40½	40½	40½	in

METRIC

Body measurements	(6	8	10)	(12	14	16)	(18	20	22)	
Bust	78	80	83	87	92	97	102	107	112	cm
Waist	58	61	63.5	66	71	76	81	86	94	cm
Hip	81	84	86	91	96.5	102	107	112	117	cm

Fabric needed		(6	8	10)	(12	14	16)	(18	20	22)	
Jacket	115 cm*/**	1.70	1.70	1.70	1.80	1.80	2.10	2.20	2.20	2.20	m
	150 cm*/**	1.30	1.30	1.30	1.40	1.70	1.70	1.70	1.80	1.80	m
Interfacing		1 m of 55–90 cm lightweight fusible or non-fusible									
Skirt A	115 cm*/**	1.6	1.6	1.6	1.6	1.9	1.9	1.9	1.9	2	m
	150 cm*/**	1.2	1.2	1.3	1.3	1.3	1.3	1.4	1.4	1.5	m
Shorts B	115 cm*/**	1.6	1.6	1.6	1.6	1.9	1.9	1.9	1.9	2	m
	150 cm*/**	1.2	1.2	1.3	1.3	1.3	1.3	1.4	1.4	1.5	m
Pants B	115 cm*/**	2.4	2.4	2.4	2.4	2.4	2.4	2.4	2.7	2.7	m
	150 cm*	2	2	2	2	2.1	2.1	2.2	2.3	2.3	m
	150 cm**	1.6	1.6	1.8	2	2	2.1	2.2	2.3	2.3	m

Garment measurements	(6	8	10)	(12	14	16)	(18	20	22)	
Jacket bust	92	94.5	97	101	106	111	116	121	126	cm
Jacket waist	81	83	86	89.5	94.5	100	105	110	116	cm
Jacket back length	73	73.5	74	75	75.5	76	77	77.5	78	cm
Skirt A lower edge	99	101	104	106	112	117	122	127	132	cm
Skirt A length	61	61	61	63	63	63	65	65	65	cm
Shorts B leg width	71	73.5	76	81	86.5	94	99	104	109	cm
Shorts B side length	49.5	50	51	51.5	52	52.5	53.5	54	54.5	cm
Pants B leg width	53.5	53.5	56	56	58.5	58.5	61	61	63.5	cm
Pants B side length	103	103	103	103	103	103	103	103	103	cm

Outline drawing of garment or item, including back views, with darts and zipper positions

Garment measurements box gives actual size of finished garment

Chart to follow for required fabric quantity, indicating size across top, and chosen view and correct width down the side

FIGURE SHAPES

Most people fall into one of these four basic figure shapes. Pattern books and envelopes may feature these symbols and they can be used to help you choose suitable patterns for your figure.

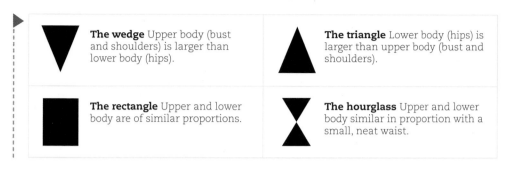

The wedge Upper body (bust and shoulders) is larger than lower body (hips).

The triangle Lower body (hips) is larger than upper body (bust and shoulders).

The rectangle Upper and lower body are of similar proportions.

The hourglass Upper and lower body similar in proportion with a small, neat waist.

SINGLE-SIZE PATTERNS

Some patterns contain a garment or craft project of one size only. If you are using a single-size pattern, cut around the tissue on the thick black cutting line before making any alterations.

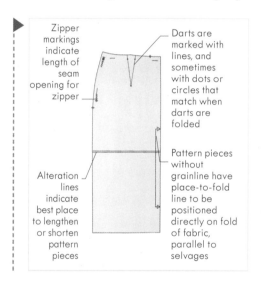

Zipper markings indicate length of seam opening for zipper

Darts are marked with lines, and sometimes with dots or circles that match when darts are folded

Alteration lines indicate best place to lengthen or shorten pattern pieces

Pattern pieces without grainline have place-to-fold line to be positioned directly on fold of fabric, parallel to selvages

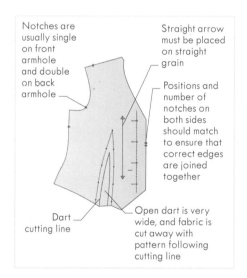

Notches are usually single on front armhole and double on back armhole

Straight arrow must be placed on straight grain

Positions and number of notches on both sides should match to ensure that correct edges are joined together

Dart cutting line

Open dart is very wide, and fabric is cut away with pattern following cutting line

MULTI-SIZE PATTERNS

Many patterns today have more than one size printed on the tissue. Each size is clearly labeled and the cutting lines are marked with a different type of line for each size.

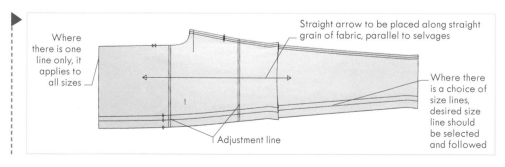

Where there is one line only, it applies to all sizes

Straight arrow to be placed along straight grain of fabric, parallel to selvages

Where there is a choice of size lines, desired size line should be selected and followed

Adjustment line

PATTERN MARKINGS

Each pattern piece will have a series of lines, dots, and other symbols printed on it. These symbols are to help you alter the pattern and join the pattern pieces together. The symbols are universal across all major paper patterns.

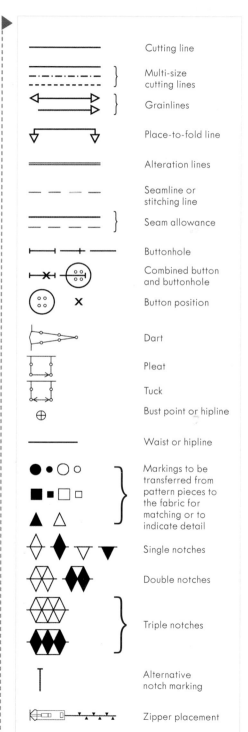

Cutting line

Multi-size cutting lines

Grainlines

Place-to-fold line

Alteration lines

Seamline or stitching line

Seam allowance

Buttonhole

Combined button and buttonhole

Button position

Dart

Pleat

Tuck

Bust point or hipline

Waist or hipline

Markings to be transferred from pattern pieces to the fabric for matching or to indicate detail

Single notches

Double notches

Triple notches

Alternative notch marking

Zipper placement

TOOLS

BODY **MEASURING**

Accurate body measurements are needed to determine the correct pattern size to use and if any alterations are required. Pattern sizes are usually chosen by the hip or bust measurement; for tops follow the bust measurement, but for skirts or pants use the hip measurement. If you are choosing a dress pattern, go by whichever measurement is the largest.

TAKING BODY MEASUREMENTS

1 You'll need a tape measure and ruler as well as a helper for some of the measuring, and a hard chair or stool.

2 Wear close-fitting clothes such as a leotard and leggings.

3 Tie a piece of elastic or ribbon snugly around your waist prior to taking any measurements. The elastic will find your natural waist, which may not be where you think it is.

4 Do not wear any shoes.

HOW TO MEASURE YOUR HEIGHT

Most paper patterns are designed for a woman 5ft 5in to 5ft 6in (165-168cm). If you are shorter or taller than this you may need to adjust the pattern prior to cutting out your fabric.

1 Remove your shoes.

2 Stand straight, with your back against the wall.

3 Place a ruler flat on your head, touching the wall, and mark the wall at this point.

4 Step away and measure the distance from the floor to the marked point.

▶ CHEST

Measure above the bust, high under the arms, keeping the tape measure flat and straight across the back.

▶ FULL BUST

Make sure you are wearing a good-fitting bra and measure over the fullest part of the bust. If your cup size is in excess of a B, you will probably need to do a bust alteration, although some patterns are now cut to accommodate larger cup sizes.

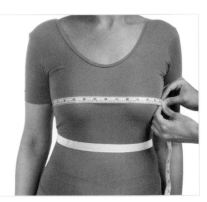

▶ WAIST

This is the measurement around the smallest part of your waist. Wrap the tape around first to find your natural waist, then measure.

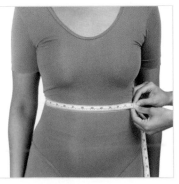

◀ MEASURING TOOLS AND MARKING AIDS **pp.18–19**

HIPS

This measurement must be taken around the fullest part of the hips, between the waist and legs.

HIGH HIP

Take this just below the waist and just above the hip bones to give a measurement across the tummy.

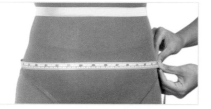

SHOULDER

Hold the end of the tape measure at the base of your neck (where a necklace would lie) and measure to the dent at the end of your shoulder. To find this dent raise your arm slightly.

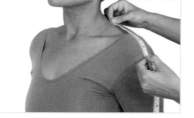

NECK

Measure around the neck—snugly but not too tight—to determine collar size.

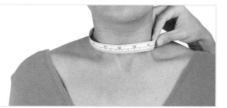

BACK WAIST

Take this measurement down the center of the back, from the lumpy bit at the top of the spine, in line with the shoulders, to the waist.

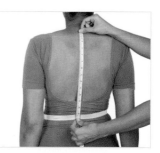

OUTSIDE LEG

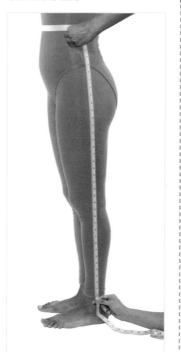

Measure the side of the leg from the waist, over the hip, and straight down the leg to the ankle bone.

INSIDE LEG

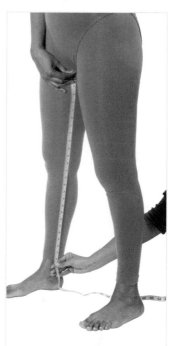

Stand with your legs apart and measure the inside of one leg from the crotch to the ankle bone.

ARM

Bend your elbow and place your hand on your hip, then measure from the end of the shoulder over the elbow to the wrist bone.

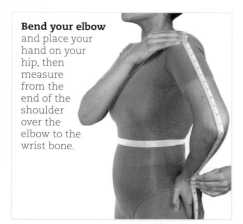

CROTCH DEPTH

Sit upright on a hard chair or stool and measure from the waist vertically down to the chair.

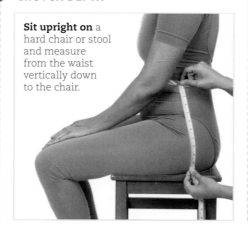

CROTCH LENGTH

Stand with your legs slightly apart. Measure from your center front waist, between your legs, to the center back waist.

ALTERING PATTERNS **pp.62–73** ● MAKING A MUSLIN **pp.74–75** ● MARKING A HEMLINE **p.263**

ALTERING **PATTERNS**

It is unlikely that your body measurements will be exactly the same as those of your chosen pattern, so you will need to alter the pattern to accommodate your figure. Here is how to lengthen and shorten pattern pieces, and how to make specific alterations at the bust, waist and hips, shoulders and back, and to sleeves and pants.

EQUIPMENT

▶ **In addition to scissors and pins or tape**, you will need a pencil, an eraser, a ruler that is clearly marked, and possibly a set square. For many alterations, you will also need pattern paper.

▶ **After pinning or taping the piece of pattern tissue to the paper**, you can redraw the pattern lines. Trim away the excess tissue or paper before pinning the pattern pieces to the fabric for cutting out.

EASY MULTI-SIZE PATTERN ALTERATIONS

Using a multi-size pattern has many advantages, as you can cut it to suit your unique individual shape—for example, to accommodate a hip measurement that may be two sizes different to a waist measurement, or your not being precisely one size or another.

▶ **INDIVIDUAL PATTERN ADJUSTMENT**

To adjust for a wider hip measurement, when cutting from one size to another, make the lines a gentle curve to follow the contours of the body.

▶ **BETWEEN SIZES**

If your body measurements fall between two pattern sizes, cut carefully between the two cutting lines for the different sizes.

LENGTHENING AND SHORTENING PATTERNS

If you are shorter or taller, or your arms or legs are shorter or longer, than the pattern pieces, you will need to adjust the paper pattern prior to cutting out. There are lines printed on the pattern pieces that will guide you as to the best places to adjust. However, you will need to compare your body shape against the pattern. Alter the front and back by the same amount at the same points, and always check finished lengths.

▶ **FOR A FITTED SLEEVE**

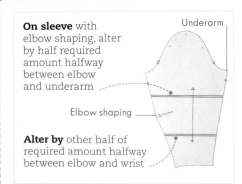

On sleeve with elbow shaping, alter by half required amount halfway between elbow and underarm

Underarm

Elbow shaping

Alter by other half of required amount halfway between elbow and wrist

▶ **FOR A STRAIGHT SLEEVE**

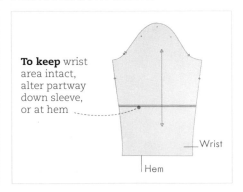

To keep wrist area intact, alter partway down sleeve, or at hem

Wrist

Hem

▶ **FOR A BODICE**

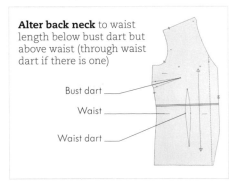

Alter back neck to waist length below bust dart but above waist (through waist dart if there is one)

Bust dart

Waist

Waist dart

▶ FOR A FITTED DRESS

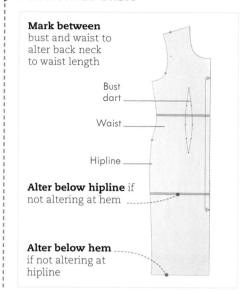

Mark between bust and waist to alter back neck to waist length

Bust dart

Waist

Hipline

Alter below hipline if not altering at hem

Alter below hem if not altering at hipline

▶ FOR A PRINCESS DRESS

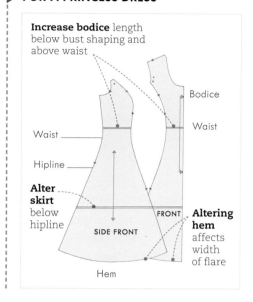

Increase bodice length below bust shaping and above waist

Bodice

Waist

Waist

Hipline

Alter skirt below hipline

Altering hem affects width of flare

FRONT

SIDE FRONT

Hem

▶ FOR SHORTS

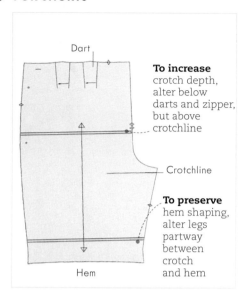

Dart

To increase crotch depth, alter below darts and zipper, but above crotchline

Crotchline

To preserve hem shaping, alter legs partway between crotch and hem

Hem

▶ FOR A SKIRT

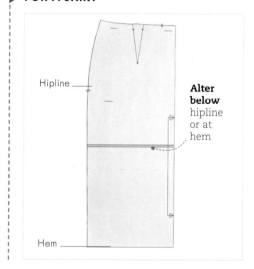

Hipline

Alter below hipline or at hem

Hem

▶ FOR SHAPED-LEG PANTS

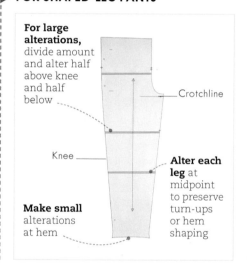

For large alterations, divide amount and alter half above knee and half below

Crotchline

Knee

Make small alterations at hem

Alter each leg at midpoint to preserve turn-ups or hem shaping

▶ FOR STRAIGHT TROUSERS

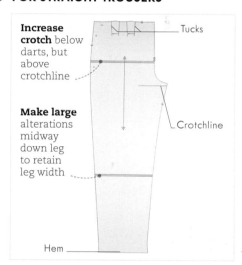

Increase crotch below darts, but above crotchline

Tucks

Crotchline

Make large alterations midway down leg to retain leg width

Hem

▶ HOW TO LENGTHEN A PATTERN PIECE

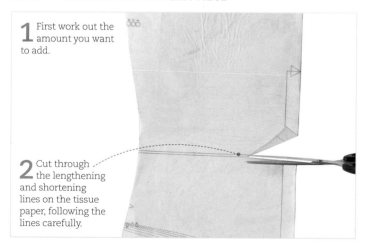

1 First work out the amount you want to add.

2 Cut through the lengthening and shortening lines on the tissue paper, following the lines carefully.

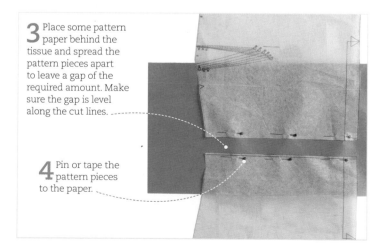

3 Place some pattern paper behind the tissue and spread the pattern pieces apart to leave a gap of the required amount. Make sure the gap is level along the cut lines.

4 Pin or tape the pattern pieces to the paper.

MAKING A MUSLIN **pp.74–75** ● MARKING A HEMLINE **p.263**

▶ HOW TO SHORTEN A PATTERN PIECE

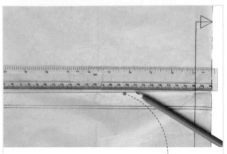

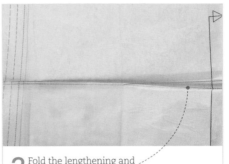

1 Work out the amount you want to lose. Mark this amount above the lengthening and shortening lines, then draw a line through the marks using the ruler as a guide.

2 Fold the lengthening and shortening line on to the drawn line so the two lines meet neatly.

3 Press with your fingers to crease the fold sharply, then secure the fold in the pattern piece with tape.

▶ HOW TO LENGTHEN ACROSS DARTS

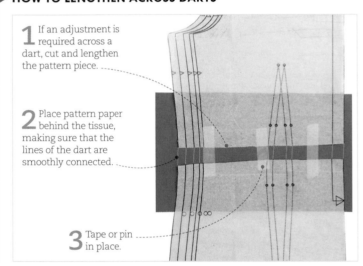

1 If an adjustment is required across a dart, cut and lengthen the pattern piece.

2 Place pattern paper behind the tissue, making sure that the lines of the dart are smoothly connected.

3 Tape or pin in place.

▶ HOW TO SHORTEN ACROSS DARTS

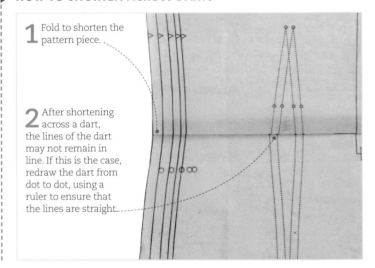

1 Fold to shorten the pattern piece.

2 After shortening across a dart, the lines of the dart may not remain in line. If this is the case, redraw the dart from dot to dot, using a ruler to ensure that the lines are straight.

▶ HOW TO LENGTHEN A HEM EDGE

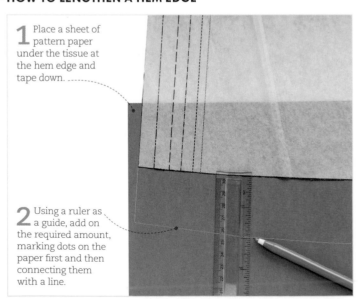

1 Place a sheet of pattern paper under the tissue at the hem edge and tape down.

2 Using a ruler as a guide, add on the required amount, marking dots on the paper first and then connecting them with a line.

▶ HOW TO SHORTEN A HEM EDGE

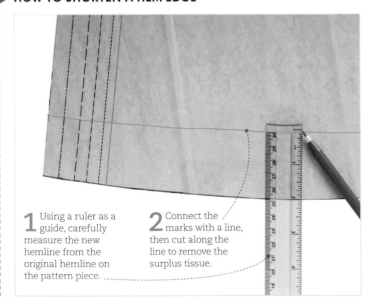

1 Using a ruler as a guide, carefully measure the new hemline from the original hemline on the pattern piece.

2 Connect the marks with a line, then cut along the line to remove the surplus tissue.

BUST

Some paper patterns today feature various cup sizes, but the majority of patterns are cut to accommodate a B cup. If you are larger than this, you will probably need to adjust your pattern before cutting out. As a general rule, when spreading the pattern pieces apart, try adjusting by ¼ in (6mm) per cup size over a B cup. Other pattern alterations can be made for bust position, raising it higher or lowering it. If the bust dart is altered, the waist dart may also need to be adjusted.

▶ RAISING A BUST DART

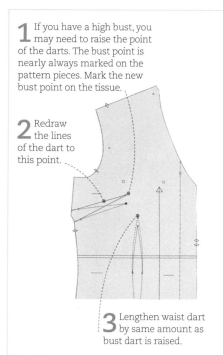

1 If you have a high bust, you may need to raise the point of the darts. The bust point is nearly always marked on the pattern pieces. Mark the new bust point on the tissue.

2 Redraw the lines of the dart to this point.

3 Lengthen waist dart by same amount as bust dart is raised.

▶ RAISING A BUST DART SUBSTANTIALLY

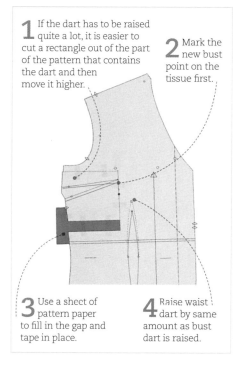

1 If the dart has to be raised quite a lot, it is easier to cut a rectangle out of the part of the pattern that contains the dart and then move it higher.

2 Mark the new bust point on the tissue first.

3 Use a sheet of pattern paper to fill in the gap and tape in place.

4 Raise waist dart by same amount as bust dart is raised.

▶ INCREASING A BUST DART

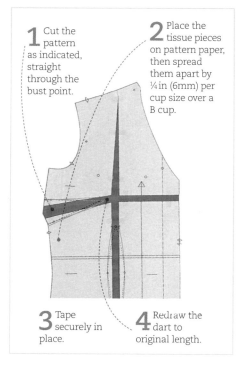

1 Cut the pattern as indicated, straight through the bust point.

2 Place the tissue pieces on pattern paper, then spread them apart by ¼ in (6mm) per cup size over a B cup.

3 Tape securely in place.

4 Redraw the dart to original length.

▶ LOWERING A BUST DART

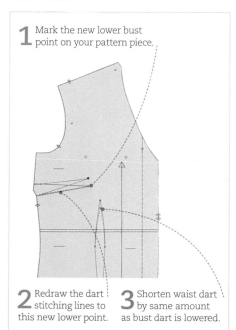

1 Mark the new lower bust point on your pattern piece.

2 Redraw the dart stitching lines to this new lower point.

3 Shorten waist dart by same amount as bust dart is lowered.

▶ LOWERING A BUST DART SUBSTANTIALLY

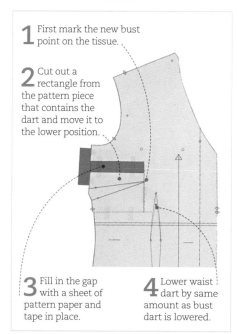

1 First mark the new bust point on the tissue.

2 Cut out a rectangle from the pattern piece that contains the dart and move it to the lower position.

3 Fill in the gap with a sheet of pattern paper and tape in place.

4 Lower waist dart by same amount as bust dart is lowered.

▶ INCREASING A FRENCH DART

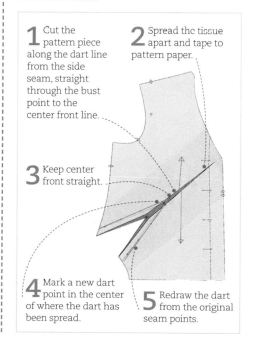

1 Cut the pattern piece along the dart line from the side seam, straight through the bust point to the center front line.

2 Spread the tissue apart and tape to pattern paper.

3 Keep center front straight.

4 Mark a new dart point in the center of where the dart has been spread.

5 Redraw the dart from the original seam points.

MAKING A MUSLIN pp.74–75 ● **SHAPING DARTS TO FIT p.114** ● **MARKING A HEMLINE p.263**

▶ RAISING A CURVED BUST SEAM

1 Fold a pleat in the shoulder pattern to bring the bust point up by the required amount.

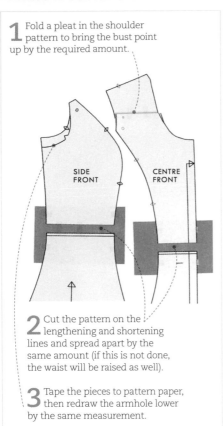

2 Cut the pattern on the lengthening and shortening lines and spread apart by the same amount (if this is not done, the waist will be raised as well).

3 Tape the pieces to pattern paper, then redraw the armhole lower by the same measurement.

▶ LOWERING A CURVED BUST SEAM

1 Cut the shoulder pattern piece and spread apart by the required amount, then tape to a sheet of pattern paper.

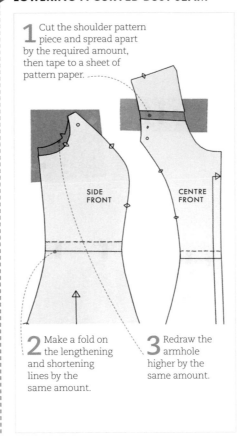

2 Make a fold on the lengthening and shortening lines by the same amount.

3 Redraw the armhole higher by the same amount.

▶ ADJUSTING A CURVED SEAM

1 For a larger bust, place a sheet of pattern paper under the tissue pieces in the bust area.

2 Add the required amount to each piece, split equally—if you need to increase by ½ in (1.2cm), add ¼ in (6 mm) on to each piece.

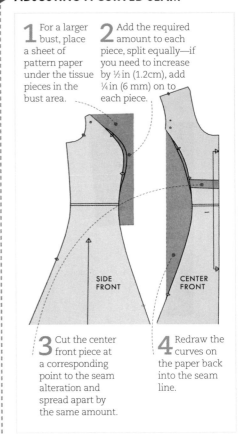

3 Cut the center front piece at a corresponding point to the seam alteration and spread apart by the same amount.

4 Redraw the curves on the paper back into the seam line.

WAIST AND HIPS

Most people's waists and hips are out of proportion when compared to the measurements of a paper pattern. To alter the pattern to suit your body shape, adjust the pieces for the waist first and then do the hip pieces.

▶ INCREASING THE WAIST AT A SEAM

1 On a fitted skirt, increase the waist at the side seams. Divide the amount to be increased by four as there are four seamlines.

2 Tape pattern paper behind the tissue pieces and add the increase on at the waist edge.

3 Draw a new seamline from this point, tapering it back into the skirt side seam.

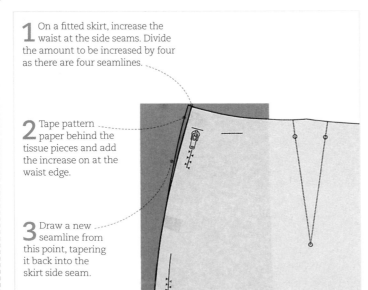

▶ INCREASING THE WAIST ON A GORED SKIRT

1 As there are many seams on a gored skirt, divide the increase amount by the number of seamlines.

2 Tape the tissue pieces on to pattern paper and add one of these small amounts to each seamline at the waist.

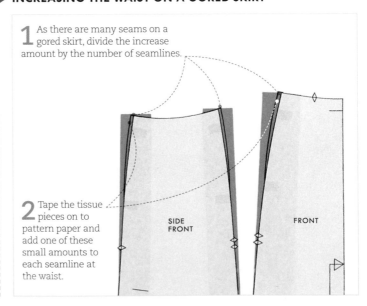

▶ INCREASING THE WAIST ON A FULL-CIRCLE SKIRT

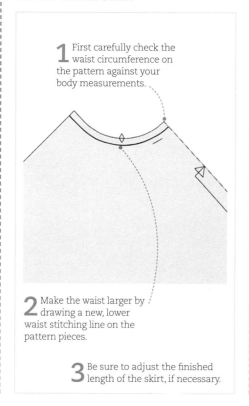

1 First carefully check the waist circumference on the pattern against your body measurements.

2 Make the waist larger by drawing a new, lower waist stitching line on the pattern pieces.

3 Be sure to adjust the finished length of the skirt, if necessary.

▶ INCREASING THE WAIST ON A FITTED DRESS

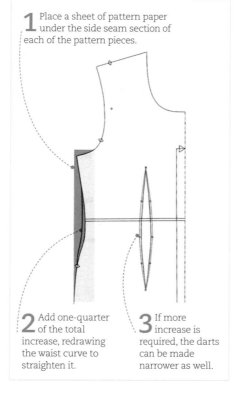

1 Place a sheet of pattern paper under the side seam section of each of the pattern pieces.

2 Add one-quarter of the total increase, redrawing the waist curve to straighten it.

3 If more increase is required, the darts can be made narrower as well.

▶ INCREASING THE WAIST ON A PRINCESS-LINE DRESS

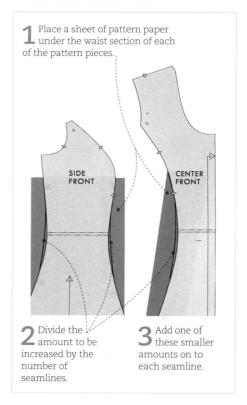

SIDE FRONT

CENTER FRONT

1 Place a sheet of pattern paper under the waist section of each of the pattern pieces.

2 Divide the amount to be increased by the number of seamlines.

3 Add one of these smaller amounts on to each seamline.

▶ DECREASING THE WAIST AT A SEAM

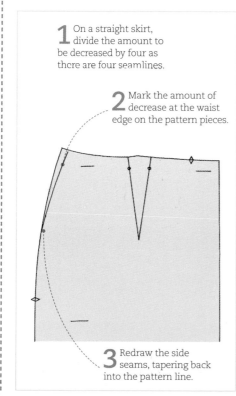

1 On a straight skirt, divide the amount to be decreased by four as there are four seamlines.

2 Mark the amount of decrease at the waist edge on the pattern pieces.

3 Redraw the side seams, tapering back into the pattern line.

▶ DECREASING THE WAIST ON A GORED SKIRT

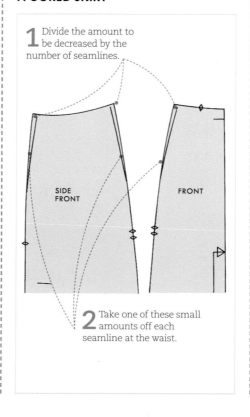

SIDE FRONT

FRONT

1 Divide the amount to be decreased by the number of seamlines.

2 Take one of these small amounts off each seamline at the waist.

▶ DECREASING THE WAIST ON A FULL-CIRCLE SKIRT

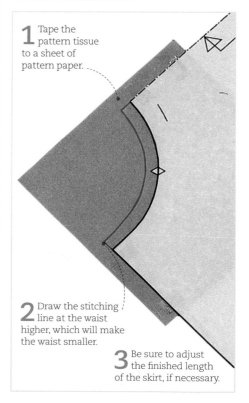

1 Tape the pattern tissue to a sheet of pattern paper.

2 Draw the stitching line at the waist higher, which will make the waist smaller.

3 Be sure to adjust the finished length of the skirt, if necessary.

MAKING A MUSLIN **pp.74–75** ● SHAPING DARTS TO FIT **p.114** ● WAISTLINES **pp.184–193**

▶ DECREASING THE WAIST ON A FITTED DRESS

1 To reduce the waist seam, you need to redraw the side seamline on each pattern piece. Divide the total decrease by four.

2 Measure one-quarter of the total amount to be decreased at the waist.

3 Draw a curved line from above and below to this point.

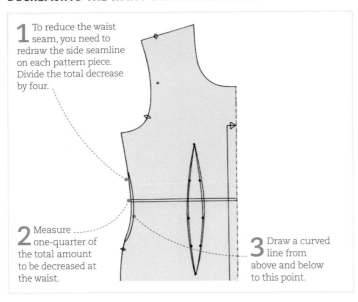

▶ DECREASING THE WAIST ON A PRINCESS-LINE DRESS

1 Divide the total amount of reduction by the number of seamlines, then mark the required amount of decrease at the waist on each pattern piece.

2 Redraw the seams, curving each one in to the marked point.

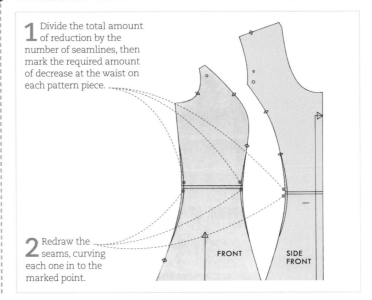

FRONT   SIDE FRONT

▶ WIDENING A FITTED SKIRT AT THE HIPLINE

1 To increase the hip dimension on a fitted skirt, divide the amount of the increase by four. Place the tissue pieces on pattern paper and increase each side seam at the hip point by the required amount.

2 Redraw the seamline from the hip increase, gradually tapering into the waistline.

3 It is more flattering to take the adjustment all the way down the skirt, so redraw the seamline straight down from the hip to the hem.

▶ ADJUSTING A FITTED SKIRT FOR EXTRA-LARGE HIPS

1 For an increase over 2in (5cm), cut each pattern piece vertically between the dart and the side seam.

2 Place on pattern paper and spread apart by one-quarter of the total amount of increase.

3 If the waist is to remain the same, draw in a second dart to remove the increase at the waist.

▶ ADJUSTING A FITTED SKIRT FOR PROMINENT HIPS

1 Place the tissue on pattern paper and add the required amount from the waist to the hip point as for a fitted skirt (see left), tapering the line back into the seam.

2 Increase the width of the dart by the same amount, redrawing the dart lines to the new center point.

▶ ADJUSTING A FITTED SKIRT FOR A LARGE BOTTOM

1 Cut through the skirt back pattern piece, vertically through the dart to the hem.

2 Cut across the hipline, but not through the side seam.

3 Spread apart the tissue on pattern paper as much as needed and tape in place.

4 Redraw the dart.

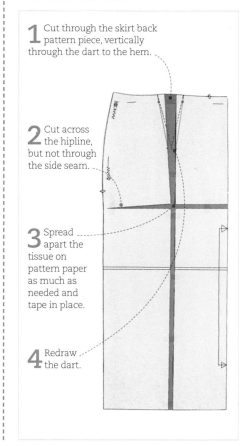

▶ DECREASING THE HIPLINE ON A FITTED SKIRT

1 Divide the amount to be reduced by four and mark the reduction amount on each pattern piece at the hipline.

2 Redraw the side seam, tapering the line into the waist and from the hipline, drawing straight down to the hem.

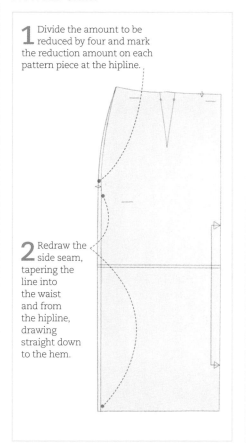

▶ ADJUSTING THE HIPLINE ON A GORED SKIRT OR PRINCESS DRESS

1 Divide the amount to be reduced or added by the number of seamlines.

2 If widening, tape the pieces of tissue to pattern paper.

3 Mark the reduction or addition at the hipline on each piece.

4 Redraw the seamlines, tapering them into the waist and drawing straight down to the hem.

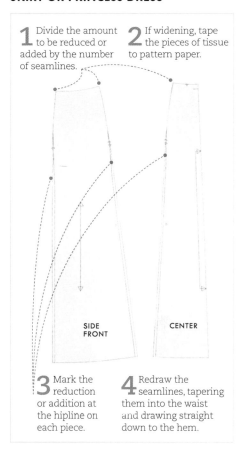

SIDE FRONT   CENTER

▶ MAKING A LARGE INCREASE AT THE HIPLINE ON A FITTED DRESS

1 Make a cut into each pattern piece horizontally just below the waist by one-quarter of the total amount to be increased.

2 Cut vertically to the hem.

3 Spread the tissue apart and tape to a sheet of pattern paper.

4 Redraw the side seam.

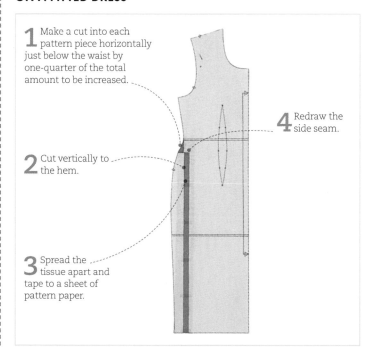

▶ ADJUSTING AT THE HIPLINE TO ALLOW FOR A SWAY BACK

1 A sway back requires a shorter center back seam. Draw a line on the pattern piece across the hipline, from the center back.

2 Fold along the line to make a pleat of the required reduction, tapering it to nothing at the side seam. Tape in place.

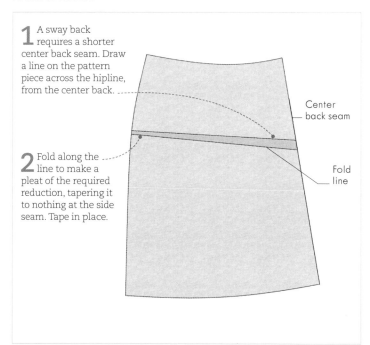

Center back seam

Fold line

MAKING A MUSLIN **pp.74–75** ● WAISTLINES **pp.184–193**

SHOULDERS, BACK, AND SLEEVES

Alterations can be made to accommodate sloping shoulders, square shoulders, and backs that may be wider or narrower than the pattern allowances. It's important to ensure that these alterations have a minimum effect on the armhole. Sleeves need to allow for movement, so should not be too tight, and pattern pieces can be enlarged as necessary. Alterations can also be made for thin arms.

▶ ADJUSTING TO FIT SQUARE SHOULDERS

1 Starting at the armhole, slash the pattern piece about 1¼ in (3cm) below and parallel with the shoulder line, not cutting through the neck seamline.

2 Spread the tissue apart to make the shoulder line straighter. Tape to pattern paper.

3 Redraw the line across the gap created.

4 Raise the armhole by the amount added at the shoulder.

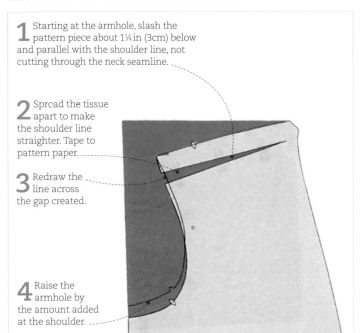

▶ ADJUSTING TO FIT SLOPING SHOULDERS

1 Slash from the armhole across the pattern piece 1¼ in (3cm) below the shoulder line and parallel with it.

2 Overlap the tissue by the required amount and tape in place.

3 Lower the armhole by the same amount, drawing a new seamline on the tissue.

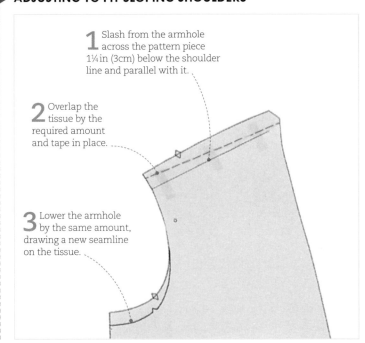

▶ PREPARING THE PATTERN FOR BROAD OR NARROW SHOULDER ALTERATIONS

1 Draw a vertical line 8in (20cm) long from the middle of the shoulder line.

2 Next, draw a second line horizontally from the end of this line to the armhole.

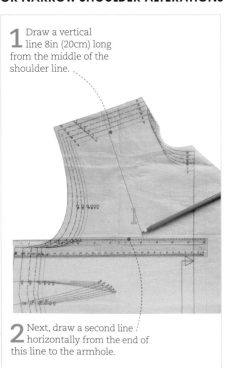

▶ ADJUSTING TO FIT BROAD SHOULDERS

1 Cut along the lines that have been drawn and spread the pieces of tissue apart on pattern paper, to accommodate the increase in shoulder length.

2 Tape in place and redraw the shoulder line.

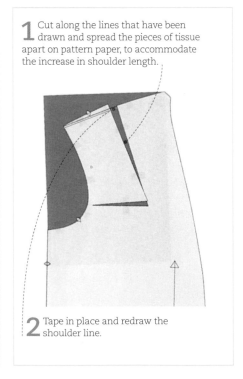

▶ ADJUSTING TO FIT NARROW SHOULDERS

1 Cut along the drawn lines.

2 Slide the cut-out piece of tissue in to overlap the cut edges and reduce the shoulder length.

3 Tape on to pattern paper and redraw the shoulder line.

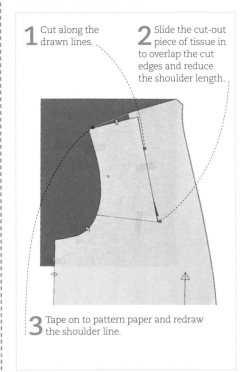

MEASURING TOOLS AND MARKING AIDS pp.18–19 ● **BODY MEASURING pp.60–61**

▶ ENLARGING A FITTED SLEEVE

1 Cut the sleeve pattern piece vertically down the center.

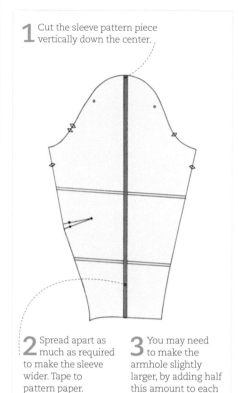

2 Spread apart as much as required to make the sleeve wider. Tape to pattern paper.

3 You may need to make the armhole slightly larger, by adding half this amount to each bodice side seam.

▶ ENLARGING THE HEAD ON A FITTED SLEEVE

1 Cut the pattern piece vertically down the center, not cutting through the wrist seamline.

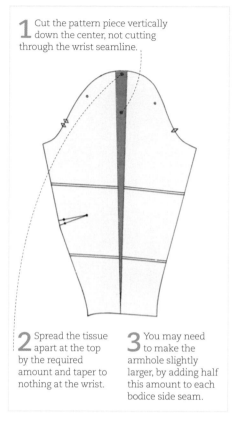

2 Spread the tissue apart at the top by the required amount and taper to nothing at the wrist.

3 You may need to make the armhole slightly larger, by adding half this amount to each bodice side seam.

▶ ENLARGING A FITTED SLEEVE AT THE ELBOW

1 Cut horizontally at an angle from just above the elbow dart to the center, then cut vertically almost to the top.

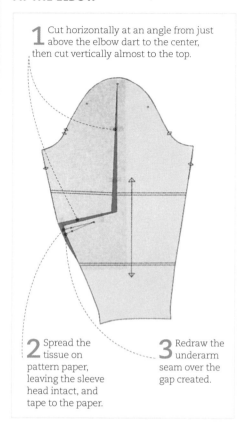

2 Spread the tissue on pattern paper, leaving the sleeve head intact, and tape to the paper.

3 Redraw the underarm seam over the gap created.

▶ INCREASING AT THE UNDERARM ON A FITTED SLEEVE

1 If the underarm is tight, cut the pattern horizontally from armhole to armhole, then cut the top piece of tissue vertically almost to the sleeve head.

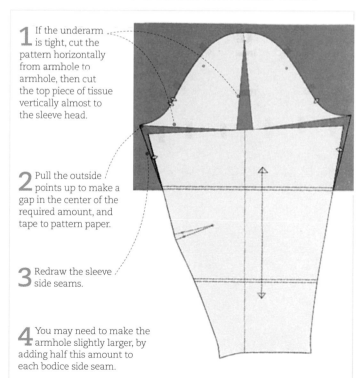

2 Pull the outside points up to make a gap in the center of the required amount, and tape to pattern paper.

3 Redraw the sleeve side seams.

4 You may need to make the armhole slightly larger, by adding half this amount to each bodice side seam.

▶ DECREASING A FITTED SLEEVE FOR THIN ARMS

1 To decrease the width of a sleeve, make a vertical pleat in the center of the sleeve pattern piece, from wrist to sleeve head.

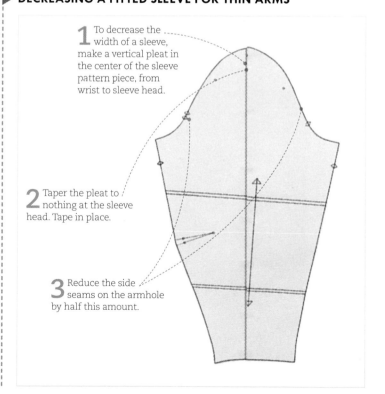

2 Taper the pleat to nothing at the sleeve head. Tape in place.

3 Reduce the side seams on the armhole by half this amount.

MAKING A MUSLIN **pp.74—75** ● SLEEVES **pp.210—215**

TOOLS

PANTS

Pant alterations, to accommodate a large stomach, wide hips, or a prominent or flat bottom, can be more complicated than those on other pattern pieces, and need to be done in the correct order. Crotch depth alterations are done first, followed by width alterations, then crotch length alterations, and finally pant leg length. The crotch depth line is only marked on the back pattern pieces.

▶ INCREASING DEPTH AT CROTCH SEAM

1 Adjust both back and front pattern pieces by the same amount. Cut along the upper lengthening and shortening lines.

2 Spread the pattern tissue apart by the required amount at the center back and center front seams, tapering to nothing at the side seam. Tape the tissue to pattern paper.

3 Redraw the crotch edge.

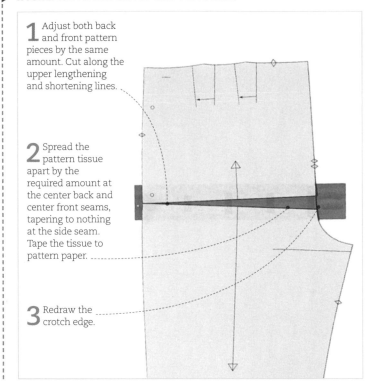

▶ DECREASING DEPTH AT CROTCH SEAM

1 Adjust both back and front pattern pieces by the same amount. Cut each of the pattern pieces along the lengthening and shortening lines.

2 Overlap by the amount to be reduced, working from the center and tapering to nothing at the side seam.

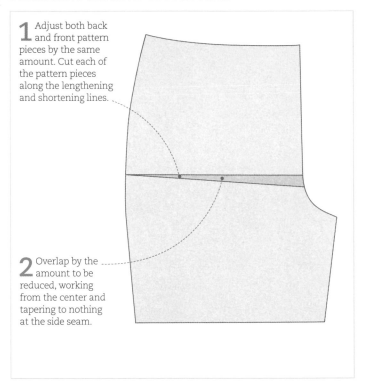

▶ INCREASING THE WAISTLINE

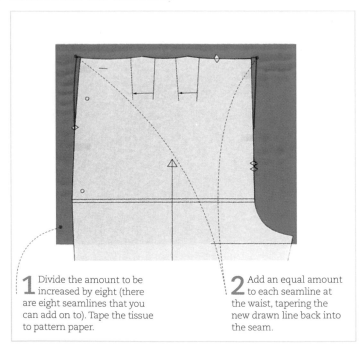

1 Divide the amount to be increased by eight (there are eight seamlines that you can add on to). Tape the tissue to pattern paper.

2 Add an equal amount to each seamline at the waist, tapering the new drawn line back into the seam.

▶ DECREASING THE WAISTLINE

1 Take the amount to be decreased and divide it by eight.

2 Reduce each of the waist seamlines by this amount.

3 Draw a new line from the decrease point back into the seamline on the pattern.

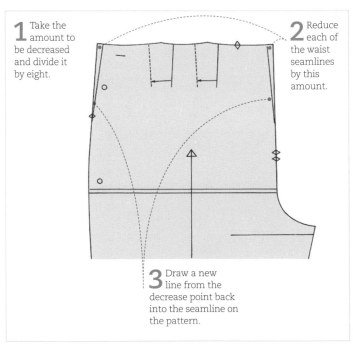

▶ INCREASING AT THE HIPLINE

1 Take the amount to be increased and divide it by four.

2 Place a sheet of pattern paper under the hip area on the side seam of each pattern piece.

3 Add the required amount to each of the seamlines at the hip, tapering the new seamline into the waist and thigh.

4 For straight pants, draw the new seamline straight down from the hip to the hem.

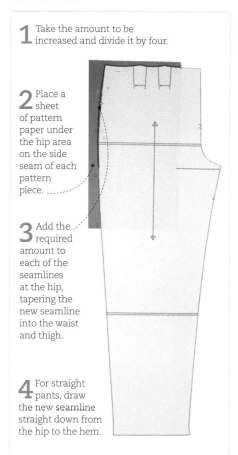

▶ ADJUSTING FOR A LARGE BOTTOM

1 Cut through the pant back pattern pieces at the hipline.

2 Place the tissue on pattern paper and spread apart by the required amount, then tape the tissue to the paper.

3 Redraw the crotch edge. This adjustment may be in addition to a crotch depth adjustment.

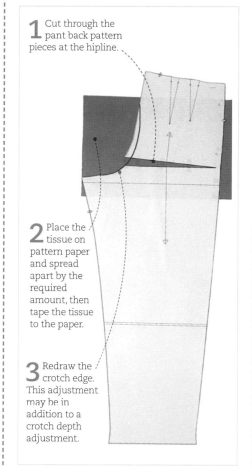

▶ DECREASING AT THE HIPLINE

1 For fitted pants, divide the amount to be decreased by four.

2 Reduce the side seam at the hipline on each pattern piece by one-quarter of the total reduction.

3 Taper the new drawn seamline to waist and thigh.

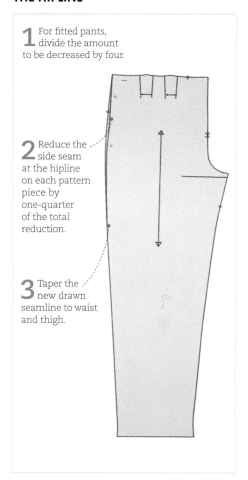

▶ INCREASING LENGTH AT CROTCH POINT

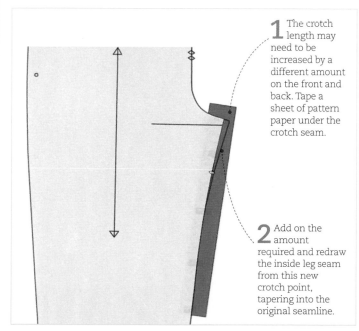

1 The crotch length may need to be increased by a different amount on the front and back. Tape a sheet of pattern paper under the crotch seam.

2 Add on the amount required and redraw the inside leg seam from this new crotch point, tapering into the original seamline.

▶ DECREASING LENGTH AT CROTCH POINT

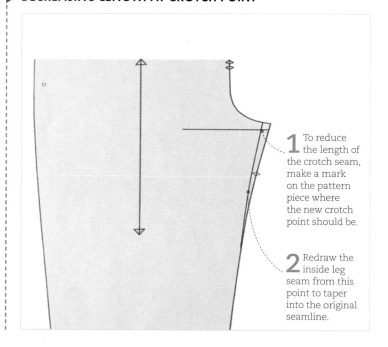

1 To reduce the length of the crotch seam, make a mark on the pattern piece where the new crotch point should be.

2 Redraw the inside leg seam from this point to taper into the original seamline.

MAKING A MUSLIN **pp.74–75** ● WAISTLINES **pp.184–193**

TOOLS

MAKING A MUSLIN

When using a new pattern for the first time, or if you have made pattern alterations, it is always a good idea to try out the pattern in muslin, to make a test garment called a muslin. This will tell you if the garment is going to fit you, or whether more alterations are required. It is also a good opportunity to confirm that the style suits your figure type. You will need a helper, or failing that, a dress form.

MUSLIN TOO BIG

When you try the muslin on, if it is too big there will be surplus fabric. Pleat and pin out the surplus fabric, making the pleating equal on both the left and right-hand sides of the garment. Take off the muslin and measure the surplus amount. Alter the pattern pieces to match, by pinning out the surplus tissue.

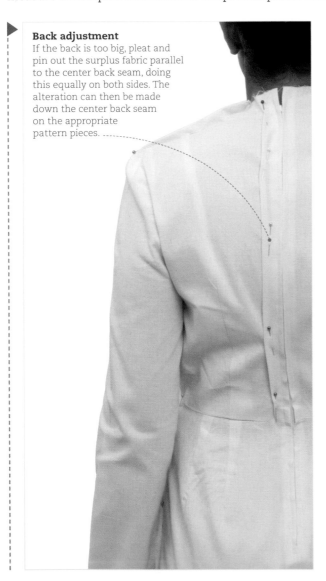

Back adjustment
If the back is too big, pleat and pin out the surplus fabric parallel to the center back seam, doing this equally on both sides. The alteration can then be made down the center back seam on the appropriate pattern pieces.

Shoulder adjustment
If the shoulder is too wide it will need a sloping shoulder adjustment (see page 70).

The waist on the bodice and skirt
If the waist is too big, this can easily be adjusted by taking more fabric into the bust dart, thus making the waist smaller. If you adjust the bust dart on the bodice, you will need to alter the skirt dart too, so they join up.

The hip on the skirt
If the hip is too loose, pleat and pin out the surplus fabric, doing this equally on both side seams. Measure the surplus amount and take in the hipline on the pattern pieces accordingly (see Decreasing the hipline on a fitted skirt, page 69).

MUSLIN TOO SMALL

If the muslin is too small, the fabric will "pull" where it is too tight. The garment shown below is too tight over the bust and also over the high hip area. The pattern will need adjusting to allow more fabric in these areas. It is also snug at the top of the sleeve, which will need adjusting.

The bust on the bodice
If a small increase is required in the bust, rip out the side seams and measure the increase required. Then make the required alteration to the pattern pieces. If a larger increase is required, the whole pattern piece will need to be altered and a new front cut out (see Increasing a bust dart, page 65). To be sure the alteration is successful, make up a new muslin bodice to try.

Shoulder adjustment
If the sleeve is tight at the top, or at the underarm, it is best to alter the pattern pieces (see page 71) and then to make up a new sleeve for the muslin.

HOW TO ADJUST A MUSLIN THAT IS TOO SMALL

If the muslin is too tight, it will require more fabric and you will need to make further alterations to the pattern pieces. For small increases (up to 1½ in/4cm), you can adjust the muslin as described below and then alter the pattern pieces accordingly, redrawing the seamlines. For larger increases, after altering the pattern pieces you will need to make up a new muslin.

1 Where the muslin is too tight, rip out the side seam on either side, until the garment will hang without pulling.

2 Measure the gap between the sewn lines where the seam has been opened at the fullest point. It should be the same on both sides of the body.

3 Divide this measurement by four (four seams)— for example, if the gap is 1½ in (4cm) at the fullest point, then ⅜ in (1cm) needs to be added to each seamline.

4 Using a marker, mark directly on the muslin the top and bottom of the alteration. Also mark the fullest point of the alteration.

5 When the muslin has been removed, add muslin to the seam in the given area at the fullest point, tapering back to the original seam at either end.

6 Try the muslin on again to be sure your alterations have made it fit you properly, then measure them and make adjustments to the relevant pattern pieces.

The hip on the skirt
Rip out the side seams and measure the increase required. When you have adjusted the muslin with extra fabric to be sure the fit is right, you can alter the pattern pieces accordingly (see p.68).

DARTS **pp.112–117**

TOOLS

CUTTING OUT

Cutting out correctly can make or break your project. But first you need to examine the fabric in the store, looking for any flaws, such as a crooked pattern, and checking to see if the fabric has been cut properly from the roll—that is at a right angle to the selvage. If not you will need to straighten the edge. If the fabric is creased, press it; if washable, wash it to avoid shrinkage later. After this preparation, you will be ready to lay the pattern pieces on the fabric, pin in place, and cut out.

FABRIC GRAIN AND NAP

It is important that the pattern pieces are cut on the correct grain, as this will make the fabric hang correctly and produce a longer-lasting item. The grain of the fabric is the direction in which the yarns or threads that make up the fabric lie. The majority of pattern pieces need to be placed with the straight of grain symbol running parallel to the warp yarn. Some fabrics have a nap due to the pile, which means the fabric shadows when it is smoothed in one direction. A fabric with a one-way design or uneven stripes is also described as being with nap. Fabrics with nap are generally cut out with the nap running down, whereas those without nap can be cut out at any angle.

▶ GRAIN ON WOVEN FABRICS

The selvage is the woven, non-frayable edge that runs parallel to the warp grain.

Yarns that run the length of the fabric are called warp yarns. They are stronger than weft yarns and less likely to stretch.

Weft

Selvage

Selvage

Weft yarns run crosswise, over and under the warp yarns.

Bias

Warp

The bias grain is diagonal—running at 45 degrees to the warp and weft. A garment cut on the bias will follow the contours of the body.

▶ GRAIN ON KNITTED FABRICS

Warp

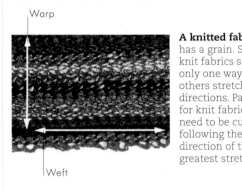

Weft

A knitted fabric also has a grain. Some knit fabrics stretch only one way while others stretch in both directions. Patterns for knit fabrics often need to be cut following the direction of the greatest stretch.

▶ NAP DUE TO PILE

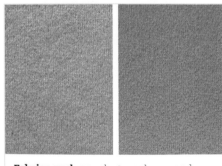

Fabrics such as velvet, corduroy, and velour will show a difference in color, depending on whether the nap is running up or down.

▶ NAP IF ONE-WAY DESIGN

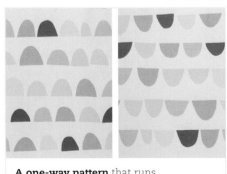

A one-way pattern that runs lengthwise in the fabric will be upside-down on one side when the fabric is folded back on itself.

▶ NAP IF STRIPED

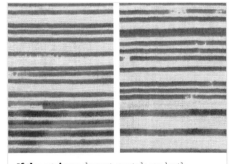

If the stripes do not match on both sides when the fabric is folded back, they are uneven and the fabric will need a nap layout.

CUTTING TOOLS pp.16–17 ● **MARKING AIDS p.19** ● **FABRICS pp.40–52**

FABRIC PREPARATION

To check if the fabric has been cut properly from the roll, smooth it out flat, with the selvages lying together. If the cut ends are uneven and do not match, use one of the following methods to make the edge straight. Then press the fabric.

▶ PULLING A THREAD TO OBTAIN A STRAIGHT EDGE

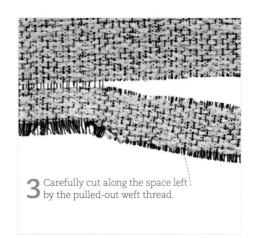

1 On a loose-woven fabric you can pull a weft thread to get a straight edge. First snip the selvage, then find a single thread and tug it gently to pull it out.

2 The fabric will gather along the single weft thread until the thread can be removed completely.

3 Carefully cut along the space left by the pulled-out weft thread.

▶ CUTTING ON A STRIPE LINE

On plaid and stripes, cut along the edge of one of the boldest stripes to achieve a straight edge.

▶ CUTTING ON A STITCH LINE ON KNIT FABRICS

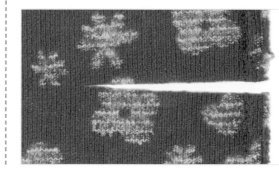

On jersey and other knit fabrics, if you look carefully, you can cut along a row of stitches.

PATTERN PREPARATION

Before cutting out, sort out all the pattern pieces that are required for the item you are making. Check them to see if any have special cutting instructions. Make pattern alterations, if necessary. If there are no alterations, just trim patterns to your size.

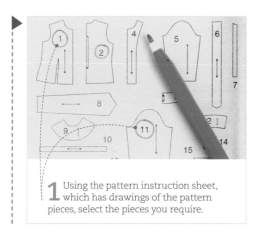
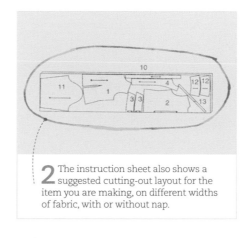
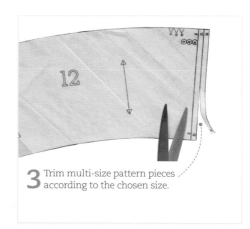

1 Using the pattern instruction sheet, which has drawings of the pattern pieces, select the pieces you require.

2 The instruction sheet also shows a suggested cutting-out layout for the item you are making, on different widths of fabric, with or without nap.

3 Trim multi-size pattern pieces according to the chosen size.

TOOLS

PATTERN LAYOUT

Fabric is usually folded selvage to selvage. With the fabric folded, the pattern is pinned on top, and both the right and left side pieces are cut at the same time. If pattern pieces have to be cut from single layer fabric, remember to cut matching pairs. For a fabric with a design, it is a good idea to have this on the outside so that you can arrange the pattern pieces to show off the design. If you have left and right side pattern pieces, they are cut on single fabric with the fabric right side up and the pattern pieces right side up.

▶ PINNING THE PATTERN TO THE FABRIC

1 The "to fold" symbol indicates the pattern piece is to be pinned carefully to the folded edge of the fabric.

2 To check the straight of grain on the other pattern pieces, place the grain arrow so that it looks parallel to the selvedge, then pin to secure at one end of the arrow.

3 Measure from the pinned end to the selvage.

4 Measure from the other end of the arrow to the selvage.

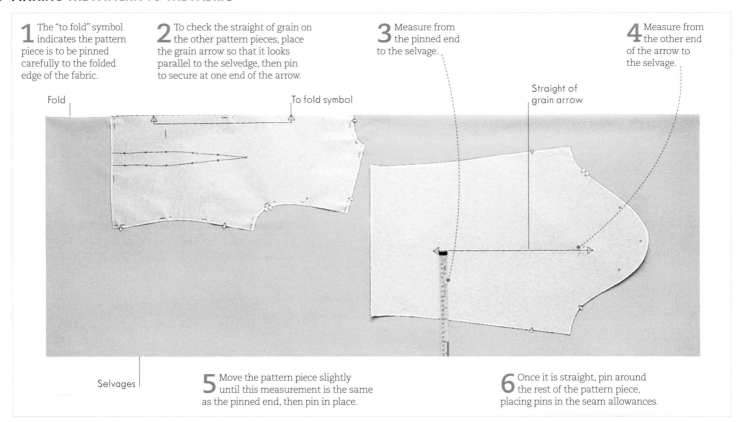

Fold

To fold symbol

Straight of grain arrow

Selvages

5 Move the pattern piece slightly until this measurement is the same as the pinned end, then pin in place.

6 Once it is straight, pin around the rest of the pattern piece, placing pins in the seam allowances.

▶ GENERAL GUIDE TO LAYOUT

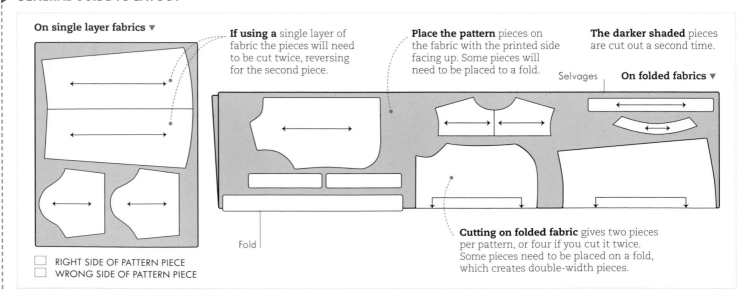

On single layer fabrics ▼

If using a single layer of fabric the pieces will need to be cut twice, reversing for the second piece.

Place the pattern pieces on the fabric with the printed side facing up. Some pieces will need to be placed to a fold.

The darker shaded pieces are cut out a second time.

Selvages

On folded fabrics ▼

Fold

☐ RIGHT SIDE OF PATTERN PIECE
☐ WRONG SIDE OF PATTERN PIECE

Cutting on folded fabric gives two pieces per pattern, or four if you cut it twice. Some pieces need to be placed on a fold, which creates double-width pieces.

▶ LAYOUT FOR FABRICS WITH A NAP OR A ONE-WAY DESIGN

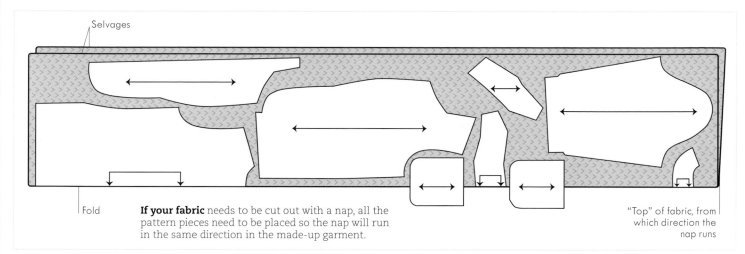

Selvages

Fold

If your fabric needs to be cut out with a nap, all the pattern pieces need to be placed so the nap will run in the same direction in the made-up garment.

"Top" of fabric, from which direction the nap runs

▶ LAYOUT ON A CROSSWISE FOLD

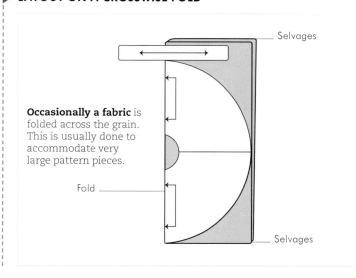

Selvages

Fold

Selvages

Occasionally a fabric is folded across the grain. This is usually done to accommodate very large pattern pieces.

▶ LAYOUT ON A CROSSWISE FOLD WITH A NAP

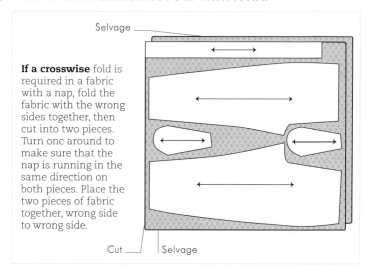

Selvage

If a crosswise fold is required in a fabric with a nap, fold the fabric with the wrong sides together, then cut into two pieces. Turn one around to make sure that the nap is running in the same direction on both pieces. Place the two pieces of fabric together, wrong side to wrong side.

Cut

Selvage

▶ LAYOUT ON A PARTIAL FOLD

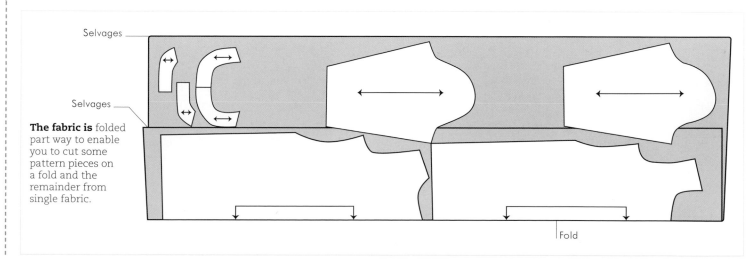

Selvages

Selvages

The fabric is folded part way to enable you to cut some pattern pieces on a fold and the remainder from single fabric.

Fold

READING PATTERNS **pp.58–59** ● FABRIC GRAIN AND NAP **p.76**

STRIPES AND PLAID

For fabrics with a stripe or plaid pattern, a little more care is needed when laying out the pattern pieces. If the stripes and plaid are running across or down the length of the fabric when cutting out, they will run the same direction in the finished garment. So it is important to place the pattern pieces to ensure that the plaid and stripes match and that they run together at the seams. If possible, try to place the pattern pieces so each has a stripe down the center. With plaid, be aware of the hemline placement on the pattern.

▶ **EVEN STRIPES**

When a corner of the fabric is folded back diagonally, the stripes will meet up at the fold.

▶ **UNEVEN STRIPES**

When a corner of the fabric is folded back diagonally, the stripes will not match at the fold.

▶ **EVEN PLAID**

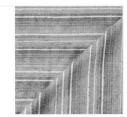

When a corner is folded back diagonally, the plaid will be symmetrical on both of the fabric areas.

▶ **UNEVEN PLAID**

When a corner of the fabric is folded back diagonally, the plaid will be uneven lengthwise, widthwise, or both.

▶ **MATCHING STRIPES OR PLAID ON A SKIRT**

1 Place one of the skirt pattern pieces on the fabric and pin in place.

2 Mark on the tissue the position of the boldest lines of the plaid or stripes.

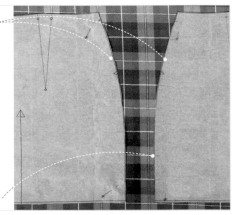

3 Place the adjoining skirt pattern piece alongside, with notches matching and side seams even. Transfer the marks across.

4 Move the second pattern piece away, matching up the bold lines, and pin it in place.

▶ **MATCHING STRIPES OR PLAID AT THE SHOULDER**

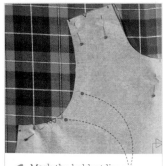

1 Mark the boldest lines of the stripes or plaid around the armhole on the front bodice pattern.

2 Place the sleeve pattern on to the armhole, matching the notches, and copy the marks on to the sleeve pattern.

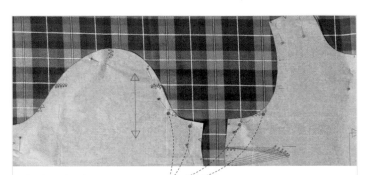

3 Place the sleeve pattern on to the fabric, matching the marks to the corresponding bold lines, and pin in place.

CUTTING TOOLS pp.16–17 ● **FABRICS pp.40–52** ● **FABRIC GRAIN AND NAP pp.76**

▶ LAYOUT FOR EVEN PLAID ON FOLDED FABRIC

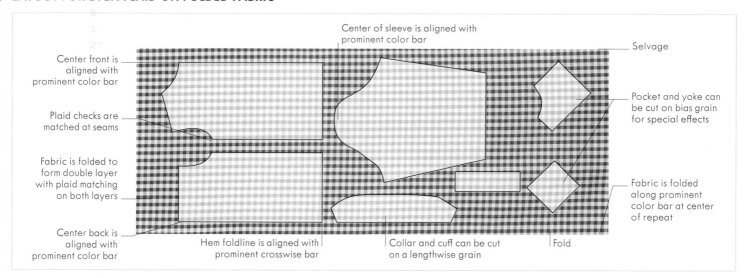

Center of sleeve is aligned with prominent color bar

Selvage

Center front is aligned with prominent color bar

Plaid checks are matched at seams

Fabric is folded to form double layer with plaid matching on both layers

Center back is aligned with prominent color bar

Pocket and yoke can be cut on bias grain for special effects

Fabric is folded along prominent color bar at center of repeat

Hem foldline is aligned with prominent crosswise bar

Collar and cuff can be cut on a lengthwise grain

Fold

▶ LAYOUT FOR EVEN STRIPES ON FOLDED FABRIC

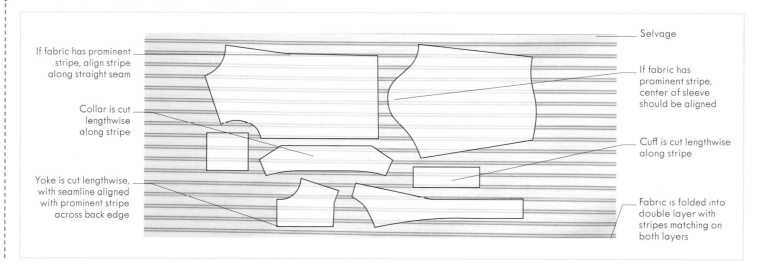

Selvage

If fabric has prominent stripe, align stripe along straight seam

Collar is cut lengthwise along stripe

Yoke is cut lengthwise, with seamline aligned with prominent stripe across back edge

If fabric has prominent stripe, center of sleeve should be aligned

Cuff is cut lengthwise along stripe

Fabric is folded into double layer with stripes matching on both layers

▶ LAYOUT FOR UNEVEN PLAID OR STRIPES ON UNFOLDED FABRIC

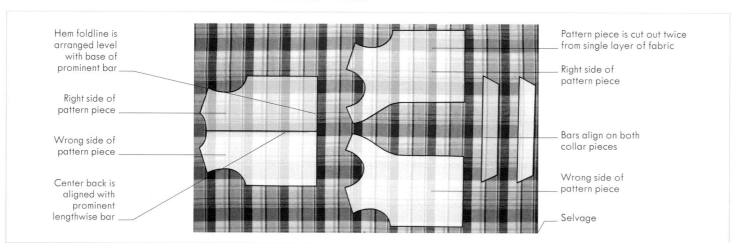

Hem foldline is arranged level with base of prominent bar

Right side of pattern piece

Wrong side of pattern piece

Center back is aligned with prominent lengthwise bar

Pattern piece is cut out twice from single layer of fabric

Right side of pattern piece

Bars align on both collar pieces

Wrong side of pattern piece

Selvage

PATTERN LAYOUT pp.78–79

CUTTING OUT ACCURATELY

Careful, smooth cutting around the pattern pieces will ensure that they join together accurately. Always cut out on a smooth, flat surface such as a table—the floor is not ideal—and be sure your scissors are sharp. Use the full blade of the scissors on long, straight edges, sliding the blades along the fabric; use smaller cuts around curves. Do not nibble or snip at the fabric.

▶ HOW TO CUT

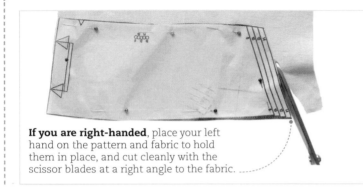

If you are right-handed, place your left hand on the pattern and fabric to hold them in place, and cut cleanly with the scissor blades at a right angle to the fabric.

▶ MARKING NOTCHES

These symbols need to be marked on to the fabric as they are matching points. One of the easiest ways to do this is to cut the mirror image of the notches out into the fabric. Rather than cutting out each notch separately, cut straight across from point to point.

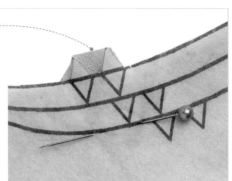

▶ MARKING DOTS

You can cut a small clip into the fabric to mark the dots that indicate the top of the shoulder on a sleeve. Alternatively, these can be marked with tailor's tacks (see opposite page).

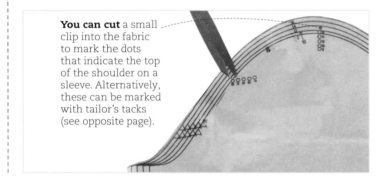

▶ CLIPPING LINES

A small clip or snip into the fabric is a useful way to mark some of the lines that appear on a pattern, such as the center front line and foldlines.

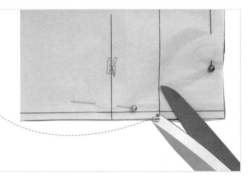

PATTERN MARKING

Once the pattern pieces have been cut out, you will need to mark the symbols shown on the tissue through to the fabric. There are various methods to do this. Tailor's tacks are good for circles and dots, or mark these with a water- or air-soluble pen (when using a pen, it's a good idea to test it on a piece of scrap fabric first). For lines, you can use trace basting or a tracing wheel with dressmaker's carbon paper.

▶ TRACE BASTING

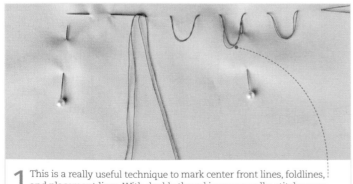

1 This is a really useful technique to mark center front lines, foldlines, and placement lines. With double thread in your needle, stitch a row of loopy stitches, sewing along the line marked on the pattern.

2 Carefully pull away the tissue. Cut through the loops, then gently separate the layers of fabric to show the threads. Snip apart to leave thread tails in both of the fabric layers.

▶ TAILOR'S TACKS

1 As there are often dots of different sizes, it is a good idea to choose a different color thread for each dot size. It is then easy to match the colors as well as the dots. Have double thread in your needle, unknotted. Insert the needle through the dot from right to left, leaving a tail of thread. Be sure to go through the tissue and both layers of fabric.

2 Now stitch through the dot again, this time from top to bottom to make a loop. Cut through the loop, then snip off excess thread to leave a tail.

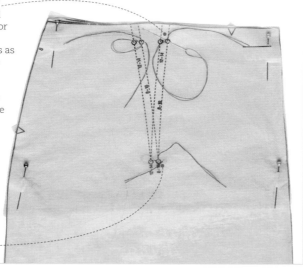

3 Carefully pull the pattern tissue away. On the top side, you will have four threads marking each dot. When you turn the fabric over, the dot positions will be marked with an X.

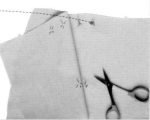

4 Gently turn back the two layers of fabric to separate them, then cut through the threads so that thread tails are left in both pieces of fabric.

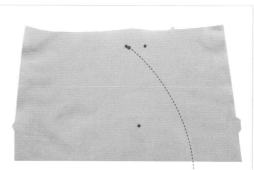

▶ TRACING PAPER AND WHEEL

1 This method is not suitable for all fabrics as the marks may not be able to be removed easily. Slide dressmaker's carbon paper against the wrong side of the fabric.

2 Run a tracing wheel along the pattern lines (a ruler will help you make straight lines).

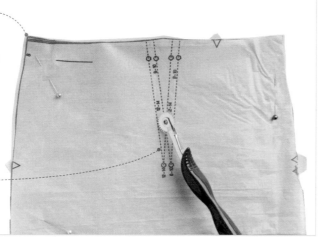

3 Remove the carbon paper and carefully pull off the pattern tissue. You will have dotted lines marked on your fabric.

▶ MARKERS

1 This method can only be used with a single layer of fabric. Press the point of the pen into the center of the dot marked on the pattern piece.

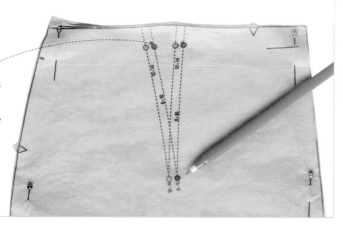

2 Carefully remove the pattern. The pen marks will have gone through the tissue on to the fabric. Be sure not to press the fabric before the pen marks are removed or they may become permanent.

FABRICS **pp.40–52** ● PATTERN LAYOUT **pp.78–79**

TECHNIQUES

SEWING ESSENTIALS

Seams and stitches are the essential construction elements of your work. Some stitches are created by hand, while others are made on the sewing machine or serger.

STITCHES FOR HAND SEWING

Although modern sewing machines have eliminated the need for a lot of hand sewing, it is still necessary to use hand sewing to prepare the fabric prior to permanent stitching—these temporary pattern marking and basting stitches will eventually be removed. Permanent hand sewing is used to finish a garment and to attach fasteners, as well as to help out with a quick repair.

THREADING THE NEEDLE

When sewing by hand, cut your piece of thread to be no longer than the distance from your fingertips to your elbow. If the thread is much longer than this, it will knot as you sew.

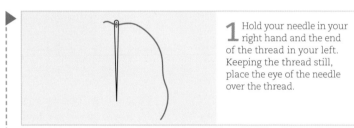

1 Hold your needle in your right hand and the end of the thread in your left. Keeping the thread still, place the eye of the needle over the thread.

2 If the needle will not slip over the thread, dampen your fingers and run the moisture across the eye of the needle.

3 At the other end of the thread, tie a knot as shown (left) or secure the thread (shown right).

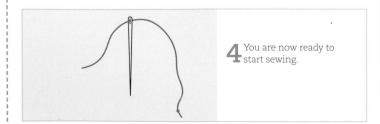

4 You are now ready to start sewing.

SECURING THE THREAD

The ends of the thread must be secured firmly, especially if the hand sewing is to be permanent. A knot (see left) is frequently used and is the preferred choice for temporary stitches. For permanent sewing, a double stitch is a better option.

▶ DOUBLE STITCH

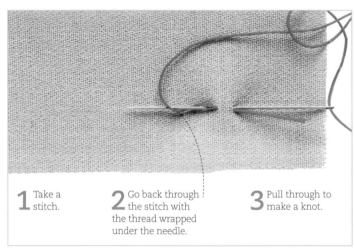

1 Take a stitch.

2 Go back through the stitch with the thread wrapped under the needle.

3 Pull through to make a knot.

▶ BACK STITCH

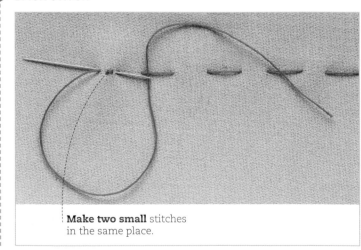

Make two small stitches in the same place.

NEEDLES AND THREADERS p.22 ● **THREADS pp.24—25**

BASTING STITCHES

Each of the many types of basting stitches has its own individual use. Trace bastes are used to transfer pattern markings to fabric. Basic bastes and bar bastes hold two or more pieces of fabric together. Long and short bastes are an alternative version of the basic basting stitch, often used when the basting will stay in the work for some time. Thread chain bastes work in a similar way to bar bastes but are much finer as they are made by looping a single thread through itself. Diagonal bastes hold folds or overlaid fabrics together, while slip bastes are used to hold a fold in fabric to another piece of fabric.

▶ BASIC BASTES

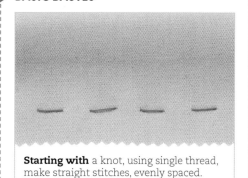

Starting with a knot, using single thread, make straight stitches, evenly spaced.

▶ DIAGONAL BASTES

Work vertically, taking horizontal stitches.

▶ SLIP BASTES

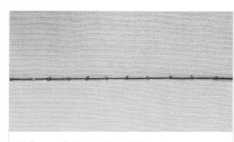

Take a stitch into the fold and then a stitch into the base fabric.

▶ LONG AND SHORT BASTES

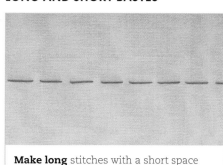

Make long stitches with a short space between each one.

▶ BAR BASTES

1 Using double thread, make two or three loops between the two layers of fabric.

2 Work a buttonhole stitch (see p.91) across the loops.

▶ THREAD CHAIN BASTES

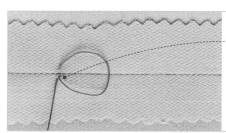

1 Start with a stitch in the fabric and make a loop.

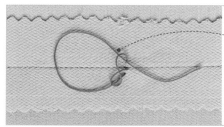

2 Make another loop from the thread and push through the first loop, then pull to tighten the first loop.

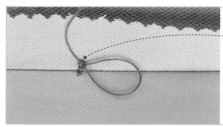

3 Repeat the process. Eventually you will have made a thread chain.

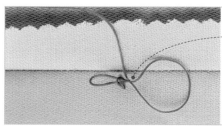

4 To finish, take a single thread through the last loop and pull to tighten. Use the thread end to stitch the loop as required.

PATTERN MARKING **pp.82—83**

TECHNIQUES

HAND SEWING

There are a number of hand stitches that can be used during construction of a garment or other item. Some are for decorative purposes while others are more functional.

▶ BACK STITCH

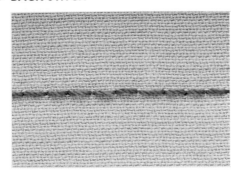

A strong stitch that could be used to construct a piece of work. Work from right to left. Bring the needle up, leaving a space, and then take the thread back to the end of the last stitch.

▶ RUNNING STITCH

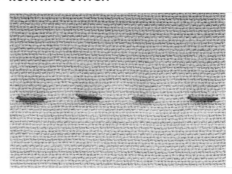

Very similar to basting (see p.89), but used more for decorative purposes. Work from right to left. Run the needle in and out of the fabric to create even stitches and spaces.

▶ PRICK STITCH

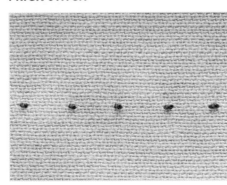

Often used to highlight the edge of a completed garment, such as a collar. Work from right to left. Make small stitches about ¹⁄₁₆in (2mm) long, with spaces between of at least three times that length.

▶ WHIP STITCH

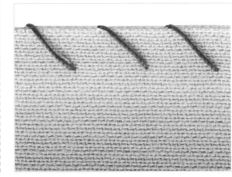

A diagonal stitch sewn with a single thread along a raw edge to prevent fraying. Work right to left. Take a stitch through the edge of the fabric. For a thin fabric, take a shallow stitch. As a rule, stitch depth should be 0.2mm minimum, 0.5mm maximum.

▶ HERRINGBONE STITCH

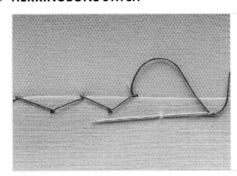

A useful stitch that is secure yet has some movement. It is used to secure hems and interlinings. Work left to right. Take a small (not more than 0.5mm) horizontal stitch into one layer and then the other, so the thread crosses itself.

▶ FLAT FELL STITCH

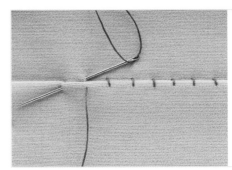

A strong, secure stitch to hold two layers permanently together. This stitch is often used to secure bias bindings and linings. Work from right to left. Make a short, straight stitch at the edge of the fabric.

▶ SLIP HEM STITCH

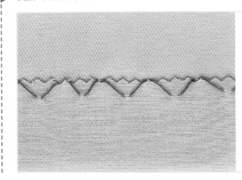

Also called a catch stitch, this is used primarily for securing hems. It looks similar to herringbone (above). Work from right to left. Take a short horizontal stitch into one layer and then the other.

▶ BLIND HEM STITCH

As the name suggests this is for hemming a garment. As the stitch is under the edge of the fabric it should be discreet. Work from right to left and use a slip hem stitch (left).

NEEDLES AND THREADERS p.22 ● **THREADS pp.24—25**

▶ BUTTONHOLE STITCH

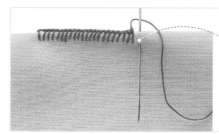

1 Used to make hand-worked buttonholes and also to secure fastenings. It is always stitched on an edge with no spaces between the stitches. Work from right to left. Push the needle from the top edge into the fabric.

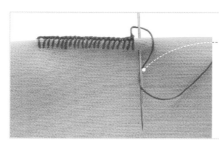

2 Wrap the thread behind the needle as the needle goes in and again as the needle leaves the fabric. Pull through and a knot will appear at the edge. This is an essential stitch for all sewers and is not difficult to master.

▶ BLANKET STITCH

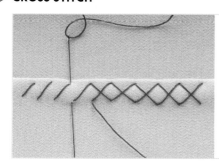

Similar to buttonhole stitch (above) but without the knot. Blanket stitch is useful to neaten edges and for decorative purposes. Always leave a space between the stitches. Push the needle into the fabric and, as it appears at the edge, wrap the thread under the needle.

▶ CROSS STITCH

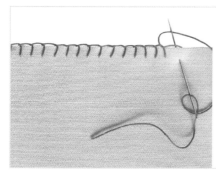

A temporary securing stitch used to hold pleats in place after construction. It can also be used to secure linings. Work a row of even diagonal stitches in one direction and then a row back over them to make crosses.

▶ SLIP STITCH/LADDER STITCH

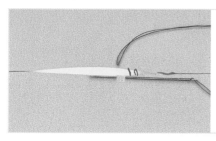

A stitch worked in double thread from right to left to secure a gap in a seam. Take a small horizontal stitch on one side and then a small horizontal stitch on the opposite side. When tightened, the gap is seamlessly closed.

HAND-STITCHED ARROWHEADS

Difficulty level

An arrowhead is a triangular shape made by working straight stitches in a set order. This is a permanent stitch placed at an area of strain or stress, such as the top of a split.

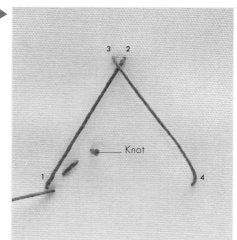

1 Mark a triangle on the fabric, with sides about 0.8 mm each. Start with a knot. Bring the needle up through **1** and down through **2**.

2 Then bring the needle up through **3** and down through **4**. Repeat the stitch.

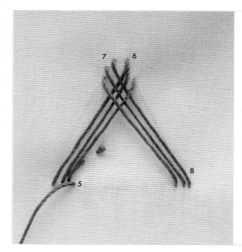

3 Continue the stitches, up through **5** and down through **6**, up through **7** and down through **8**.

4 Make about 10 alternating stitches to complete the arrowhead.

MACHINE ARROWHEADS **p.93** ● MACHINE-MADE BUTTONHOLES **p.306**

TECHNIQUES

MACHINE STITCHES AND SEAMS

Fabric is joined together using seams—whether it be for an item of clothing, craft work, or home goods. The most common seam is a plain seam, which is suitable for a wide variety of fabrics and items. However, there are many other seams to be used as appropriate, depending on the fabric and item being constructed. Some seams are decorative and can add detail to structured garments.

SECURING THE THREAD

Machine stitches need to be secured at the end of a seam to prevent them from coming undone. This can be done by hand, tying the ends of the thread, or using the machine with a reverse stitch or a locking stitch, which stitches three or four stitches in the same place.

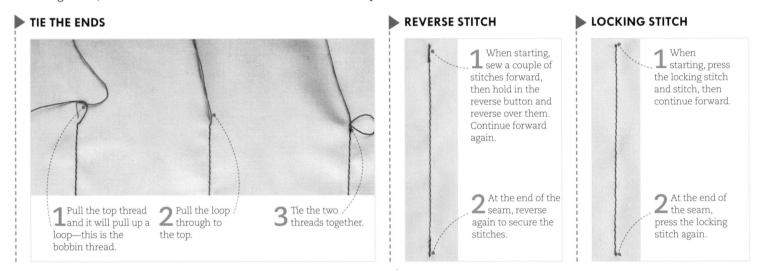

▶ **TIE THE ENDS**

1 Pull the top thread and it will pull up a loop—this is the bobbin thread.

2 Pull the loop through to the top.

3 Tie the two threads together.

▶ **REVERSE STITCH**

1 When starting, sew a couple of stitches forward, then hold in the reverse button and reverse over them. Continue forward again.

2 At the end of the seam, reverse again to secure the stitches.

▶ **LOCKING STITCH**

1 When starting, press the locking stitch and stitch, then continue forward.

2 At the end of the seam, press the locking stitch again.

STITCHES MADE WITH A MACHINE

The sewing machine will sew plain seams and decorative seams as well as buttonholes of various styles. The length and width of all buttonholes can be altered to suit the garment or craft item.

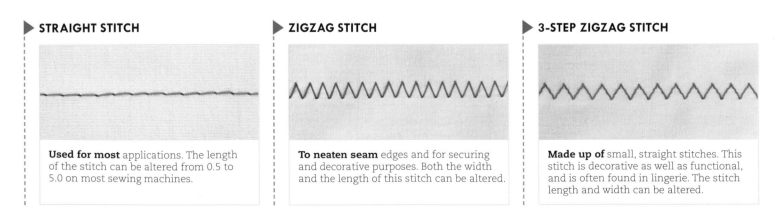

▶ **STRAIGHT STITCH**

Used for most applications. The length of the stitch can be altered from 0.5 to 5.0 on most sewing machines.

▶ **ZIGZAG STITCH**

To neaten seam edges and for securing and decorative purposes. Both the width and the length of this stitch can be altered.

▶ **3-STEP ZIGZAG STITCH**

Made up of small, straight stitches. This stitch is decorative as well as functional, and is often found in lingerie. The stitch length and width can be altered.

SEWING MACHINE **pp.30–31** ● SEWING MACHINE ACCESSORIES **pp.32–33** ● SERGER **pp.34–35**

▶ BLIND HEM STITCH

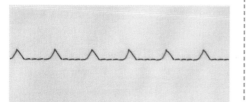

Made in conjunction with the blind hem foot. A combination of straight stitches and a zigzag stitch (see opposite page). Used to secure hems.

▶ OVEREDGE STITCH

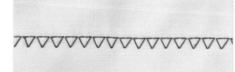

Made in conjunction with the overedge foot. The stitch is used for neatening the edge of fabric. The width and length of the stitch can be altered.

▶ STRETCH STITCH

Also known as a lightning stitch. This stitch is recommended for stretch knits, but is better used to help control difficult fabrics.

▶ BASIC BUTTONHOLE STITCH

Square on both ends. Used on all styles of garment.

▶ ROUND-END BUTTONHOLE STITCH

One square end and one round end. Used on jackets.

▶ KEYHOLE BUTTONHOLE STITCH

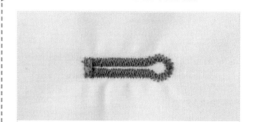

One square end and one end shaped like a loop. Used on jackets.

▶ DECORATIVE STITCHES

CORN STITCH

FLOWER STITCH

STAR STITCH

Sewing machines are capable of producing decorative linear stitches. These can be used to enhance the surface of work or a seam as they add interest to edges. Or, when worked as many rows together, they can be used to create a piece of embroidered fabric.

▶ 3-THREAD SERGER STITCH

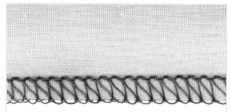

Stitched using three threads on the serger. Used to neaten the edge of fabric to prevent fraying.

▶ 4-THREAD SERGER STITCH

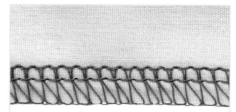

Made using four threads on the serger. Used to neaten edges and to construct stretch knits.

▶ MACHINE ARROWHEADS

This is a built-in stitch on many sewing machines. Used to secure weak points.

SEAM NEATENING **p.95** ● MACHINED HEMS **p.266** ● BUTTONHOLES **pp.304–311**

TECHNIQUES

HOW TO MAKE A PLAIN SEAM

Difficulty level ✱✱✱✱✱

A plain seam is ⅝in (1.5cm) wide. It is important that the seam is sewn accurately at this measurement, otherwise the item being made will come out the wrong size and shape. There are guides on the plate of the sewing machine that can be used to help align the fabric.

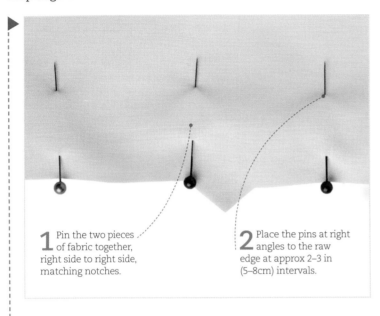

1 Pin the two pieces of fabric together, right side to right side, matching notches.

2 Place the pins at right angles to the raw edge at approx 2–3 in (5–8cm) intervals.

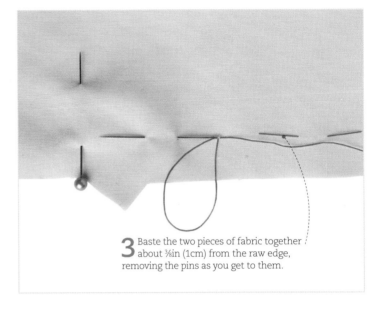

3 Baste the two pieces of fabric together about ⅜in (1cm) from the raw edge, removing the pins as you get to them.

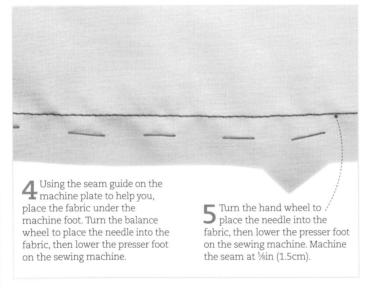

4 Using the seam guide on the machine plate to help you, place the fabric under the machine foot. Turn the balance wheel to place the needle into the fabric, then lower the presser foot on the sewing machine.

5 Turn the hand wheel to place the needle into the fabric, then lower the presser foot on the sewing machine. Machine the seam at ⅝in (1.5cm).

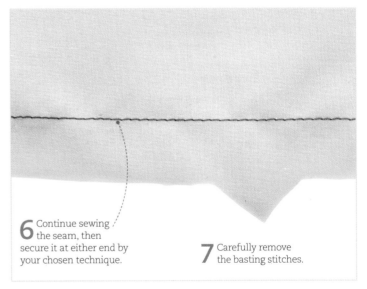

6 Continue sewing the seam, then secure it at either end by your chosen technique.

7 Carefully remove the basting stitches.

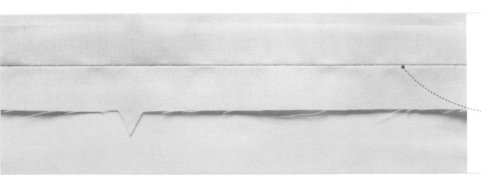

8 Press the seam flat as it was sewn, then press the seam open.

SEAM NEATENING

It is important that the raw edges of the seam are neatened or finished—this will make the seam hard-wearing and prevent fraying. The method of neatening will depend on the style of item that is being made and the fabric you are using.

▶ **PINKED**

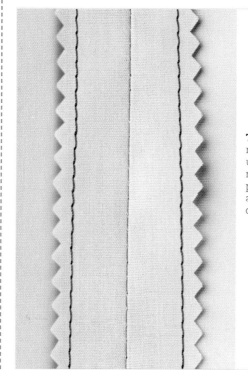

This method of neatening is ideal to use on fabrics that do not fray badly. Using pinking shears, trim as little as possible off the raw edge.

▶ **ZIGZAGGED**

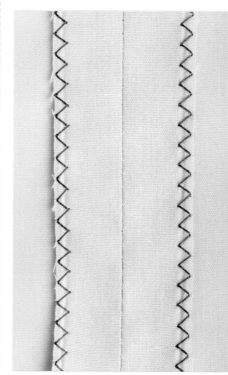

All sewing machines will make a zigzag stitch. It is an ideal stitch to use to stop the edges fraying and is suitable for all types of fabric. Sew in from the raw edge, then trim back to the zigzag stitch. On most fabrics, use a stitch width of 2.0 and a stitch length of 1.5.

▶ **OVEREDGE SEWING**

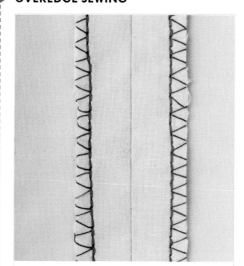

This is found on most sewing machines. Select the overedge stitch on your machine. Using the overedge machine foot and the pre-set stitch length and width, machine along the raw edge of the seam.

▶ **CLEAN FINISHED**

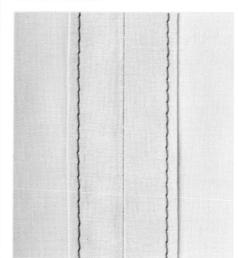

This is a very hard-wearing finish and is ideal for cottons and fine fabrics. Using a straight stitch, turn under the raw edge of the seam allowance by ⅛in (3mm) and sew straight along the fold.

▶ **3-THREAD SERGED**

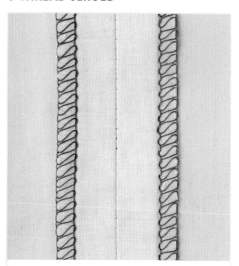

If you have a serger, you can neaten seams with a 3-thread serger stitch. It is one of the most professional ways to finish seams and is suitable for all types of fabric and items.

BASTING STITCHES **p.89** • STITCHES MADE WITH A MACHINE **pp.92–93**

TECHNIQUES

HONG KONG FINISH

Difficulty level ✳✳✳✳✳

This is a great finish to use on wools and linens, to neaten the seams on unlined jackets. It is made by wrapping the raw edge with bias-cut strips.

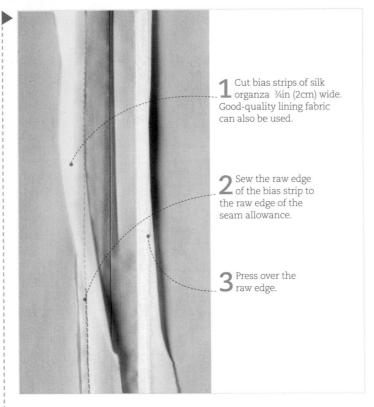

1 Cut bias strips of silk organza ¾in (2cm) wide. Good-quality lining fabric can also be used.

2 Sew the raw edge of the bias strip to the raw edge of the seam allowance.

3 Press over the raw edge.

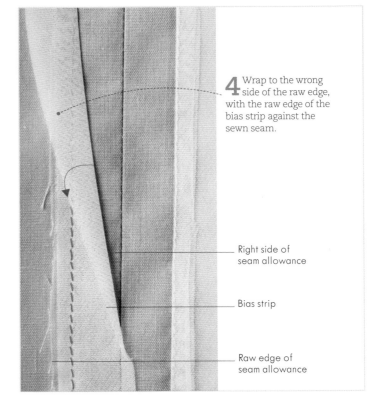

4 Wrap to the wrong side of the raw edge, with the raw edge of the bias strip against the sewn seam.

Right side of seam allowance

Bias strip

Raw edge of seam allowance

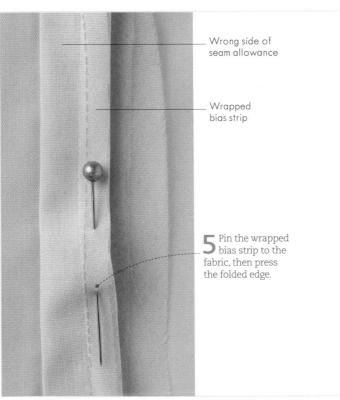

Wrong side of seam allowance

Wrapped bias strip

5 Pin the wrapped bias strip to the fabric, then press the folded edge.

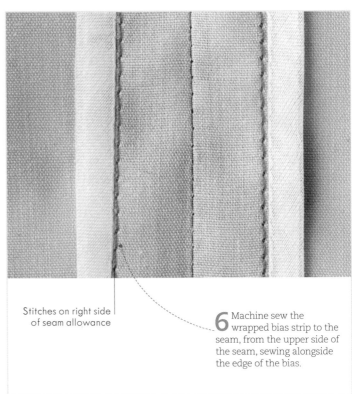

Stitches on right side of seam allowance

6 Machine sew the wrapped bias strip to the seam, from the upper side of the seam, sewing alongside the edge of the bias.

FRENCH SEAM

A French seam is a seam that is sewn twice, first on the right side of the work and then on the wrong side, enclosing the first seam. The French seam has traditionally been used on delicate garments such as lingerie and on sheer and silk fabrics.

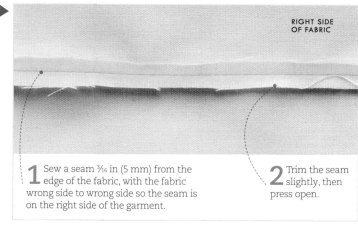

RIGHT SIDE OF FABRIC

1 Sew a seam ³⁄₁₆ in (5 mm) from the edge of the fabric, with the fabric wrong side to wrong side so the seam is on the right side of the garment.

2 Trim the seam slightly, then press open.

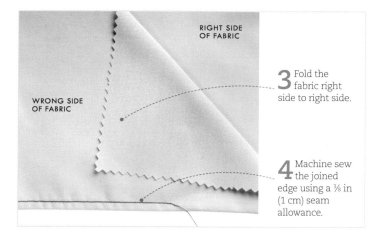

WRONG SIDE OF FABRIC

RIGHT SIDE OF FABRIC

3 Fold the fabric right side to right side.

4 Machine sew the joined edge using a ⅜ in (1 cm) seam allowance.

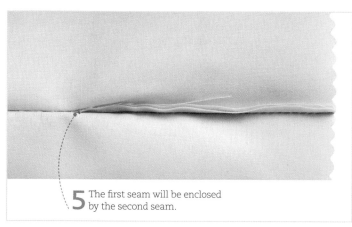

5 The first seam will be enclosed by the second seam.

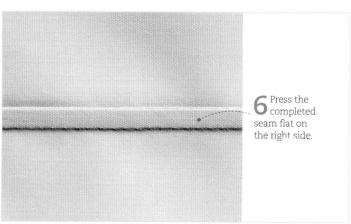

6 Press the completed seam flat on the right side.

MOCK FRENCH SEAM

When this seam is completed, it looks very similar to the French seam. A mock French seam is best used on cotton or firmer fine fabrics. It is constructed on the wrong side of the work.

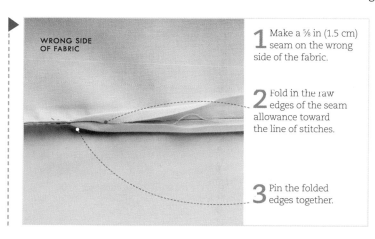

WRONG SIDE OF FABRIC

1 Make a ⅝ in (1.5 cm) seam on the wrong side of the fabric.

2 Fold in the raw edges of the seam allowance toward the line of stitches.

3 Pin the folded edges together.

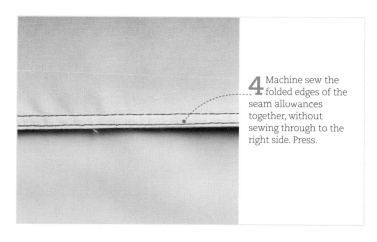

4 Machine sew the folded edges of the seam allowances together, without sewing through to the right side. Press.

HOW TO CUT BIAS STRIPS **p.154**

FLAT FELL SEAM

Difficulty level ✱✱✱✱✱

Some garments require a strong seam that will withstand frequent washing and wear and tear. A flat fell seam is very strong. It is made on the right side of a garment and is used on the inside leg seam of jeans, and on men's tailored shirts.

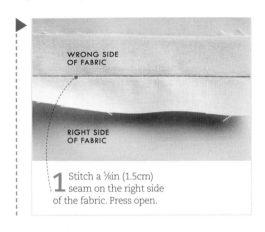

WRONG SIDE OF FABRIC

RIGHT SIDE OF FABRIC

1 Stitch a ⅝in (1.5cm) seam on the right side of the fabric. Press open.

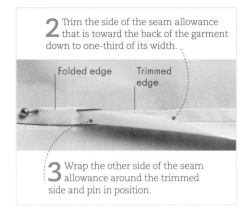

2 Trim the side of the seam allowance that is toward the back of the garment down to one-third of its width.

Folded edge   Trimmed edge

3 Wrap the other side of the seam allowance around the trimmed side and pin in position.

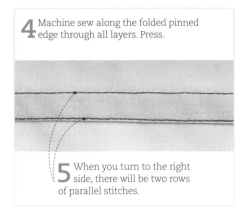

4 Machine sew along the folded pinned edge through all layers. Press.

5 When you turn to the right side, there will be two rows of parallel stitches.

SELF-BOUND SEAM

Difficulty level ✱✱✱✱✱

Another strong seam, this is constructed in a similar way to the flat fell seam (see above), but on the wrong side of the work. It is used in children's wear.

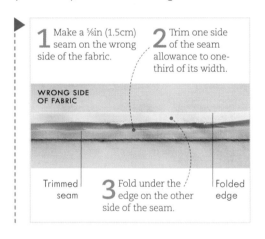

1 Make a ⅝in (1.5cm) seam on the wrong side of the fabric.

2 Trim one side of the seam allowance to one-third of its width.

WRONG SIDE OF FABRIC

Trimmed seam

3 Fold under the edge on the other side of the seam.

Folded edge

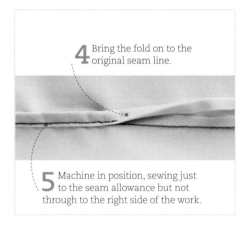

4 Bring the fold on to the original seam line.

5 Machine in position, sewing just to the seam allowance but not through to the right side of the work.

6 The finished seam can only be seen on the wrong side. On the right side there is just a seamline.

TOP-STITCH SEAM

Difficulty level ✱✱✱✱✱

A top-stitch seam is very useful as it is both decorative and practical. This seam is often used on crafts and home goods as well as garments.

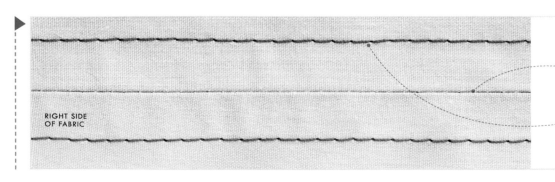

RIGHT SIDE OF FABRIC

1 Make a ⅝in (1.5cm) seam on the wrong side of the fabric. Press the seam open.

2 Working from the right side of the work, sew down either side of the seam. Press.

CUTTING TOOLS **p.16** ● HOW TO MAKE A PLAIN SEAM **p.94**

LAPPED SEAM

Also called an overlaid seam, a lapped seam is constructed on the right side of the garment. It is a very flat seam when it is finished.

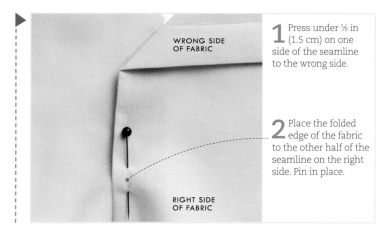

1 Press under ⅝ in (1.5 cm) on one side of the seamline to the wrong side.

2 Place the folded edge of the fabric to the other half of the seamline on the right side. Pin in place.

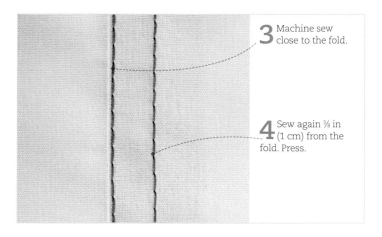

3 Machine sew close to the fold.

4 Sew again ⅜ in (1 cm) from the fold. Press.

SLOTTED SEAM

A slotted seam is a decorative seam, shown on the right side. The edges of the seam open to reveal an under layer, which could be a contrasting fabric.

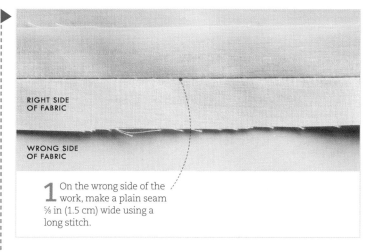

1 On the wrong side of the work, make a plain seam ⅝ in (1.5 cm) wide using a long stitch.

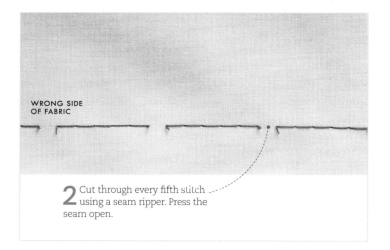

2 Cut through every fifth stitch using a seam ripper. Press the seam open.

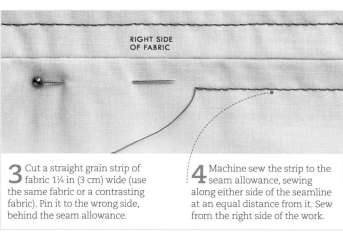

3 Cut a straight grain strip of fabric 1¼ in (3 cm) wide (use the same fabric or a contrasting fabric). Pin it to the wrong side, behind the seam allowance.

4 Machine sew the strip to the seam allowance, sewing along either side of the seamline at an equal distance from it. Sew from the right side of the work.

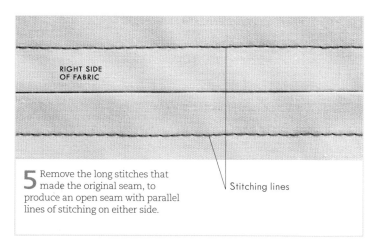

5 Remove the long stitches that made the original seam, to produce an open seam with parallel lines of stitching on either side.

Stitching lines

STITCHES MADE WITH A MACHINE pp.92–93

TECHNIQUES

CORDED SEAM

Difficulty level ✱✱✱✱✱

A seam with piping in it can add interest to an otherwise plain garment. This is also a useful technique if you are joining two fabrics that are different. The piping is made first, prior to its being inserted in the seam.

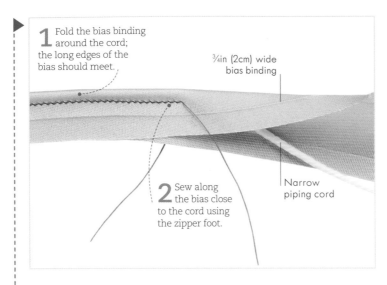

1 Fold the bias binding around the cord; the long edges of the bias should meet.

¾in (2cm) wide bias binding

2 Sew along the bias close to the cord using the zipper foot.

Narrow piping cord

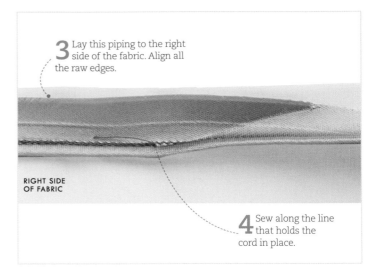

3 Lay this piping to the right side of the fabric. Align all the raw edges.

RIGHT SIDE OF FABRIC

4 Sew along the line that holds the cord in place.

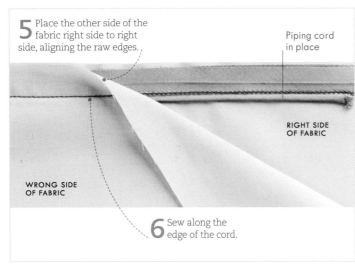

5 Place the other side of the fabric right side to right side, aligning the raw edges.

Piping cord in place

RIGHT SIDE OF FABRIC

WRONG SIDE OF FABRIC

6 Sew along the edge of the cord.

7 On the right side, the finished corded seam is neat and decorative.

MAKING A SEAM WITH THE SERGER

Difficulty level ✱✱✱✱✱

Use this when constructing stretch knits.

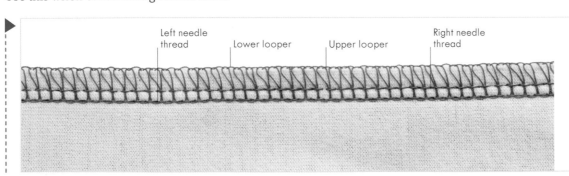

Left needle thread

Lower looper

Upper looper

Right needle thread

1 Put the fabric together, right side to right side.

2 Remove all the pins as they could damage the serger.

3 Stitch the seam with a 4-thread serger stitch.

SEAMS ON DIFFICULT FABRICS

Difficulty level ★★☆☆

Some fabrics require special care for seam construction because they are very bulky, as you find with a fur fabric, or so soft and delicate that they appear too soft to sew. On a sheer fabric, the seam used is an alternative to a French seam; it is very narrow when finished and presses very flat. Making a seam on suede is done by means of a lapped seam. As some suede-effect fabric has a fake fur on the other side, the seam is reversible.

▶ **A SEAM ON SHEER FABRIC**

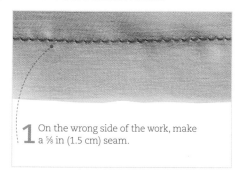

1 On the wrong side of the work, make a ⅝ in (1.5 cm) seam.

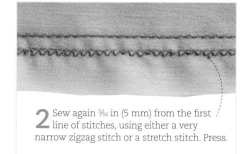

2 Sew again ³⁄₁₆ in (5 mm) from the first line of stitches, using either a very narrow zigzag stitch or a stretch stitch. Press.

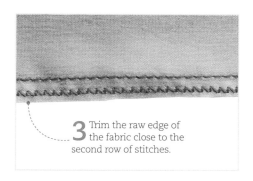

3 Trim the raw edge of the fabric close to the second row of stitches.

▶ **A SEAM ON SUEDE OR SUEDE-EFFECT FABRIC**

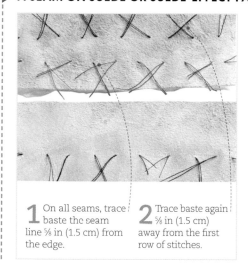

1 On all seams, trace baste the seam line ⅝ in (1.5 cm) from the edge.

2 Trace baste again ⅝ in (1.5 cm) away from the first row of stitches.

3 Overlap one side of the seam over the other, matching the ⅝ in (1.5 cm) baste lines. The raw edge should touch the second row of bastes.

4 Using a walking foot and a longer than normal stitch length of 3.5, sew the two layers together along the bastes marking the ⅝ in (1.5 cm) seam allowance.

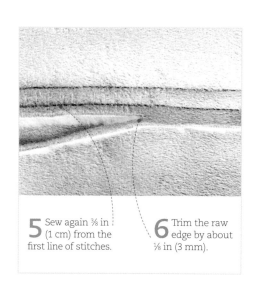

5 Sew again ⅜ in (1 cm) from the first line of stitches.

6 Trim the raw edge by about ⅛ in (3 mm).

▶ **A SEAM ON FUR FABRIC**

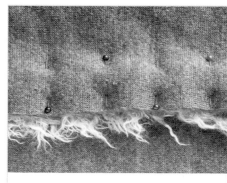

1 Pin the fabric together right side to right side, placing the pins in alternate directions to stop the fur moving.

2 Using a walking foot and a longer than normal stitch length, sew the seam.

3 Finger press the seam open.

4 Trim the surplus fur fabric off the seam allowances.

STITCHES MADE WITH A MACHINE **pp.92–93**

TECHNIQUES

SEWING CORNERS AND CURVES

Not all sewing is straight lines. The work will have curves and corners that require negotiation, to produce sharp clean angles and curves on the right side. The technique for sewing a corner shown below applies to corners of all angles. On a thick fabric, the technique is slightly different, with a stitch taken across the corner, and on a fabric that frays badly the corner is reinforced with a second line of stitches.

Difficulty level ✱✱✱✱✱

▶ SEWING A CORNER

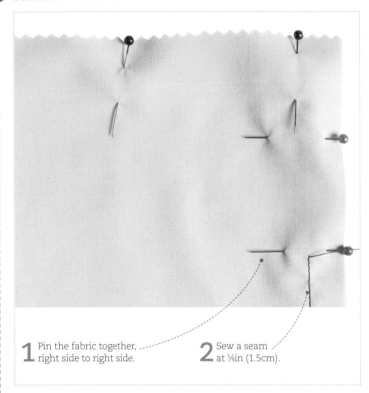

1 Pin the fabric together, right side to right side.

2 Sew a seam at ⅝in (1.5cm).

3 On reaching the corner, insert the machine needle into the fabric.

4 Raise the presser foot and turn the fabric through 90 degrees (this is pivoting at the corner).

5 Lower the presser foot and continue sewing in the other direction.

6 The sewn lines are at right angles to each other, which means the finished corner will have a sharp point when turned through to the right side.

▶ SEWING A CORNER ON HEAVY FABRIC

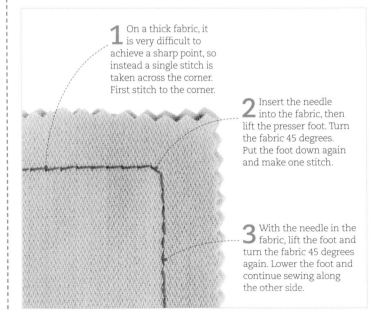

1 On a thick fabric, it is very difficult to achieve a sharp point, so instead a single stitch is taken across the corner. First stitch to the corner.

2 Insert the needle into the fabric, then lift the presser foot. Turn the fabric 45 degrees. Put the foot down again and make one stitch.

3 With the needle in the fabric, lift the foot and turn the fabric 45 degrees again. Lower the foot and continue sewing along the other side.

▶ **SEWING A REINFORCED CORNER**

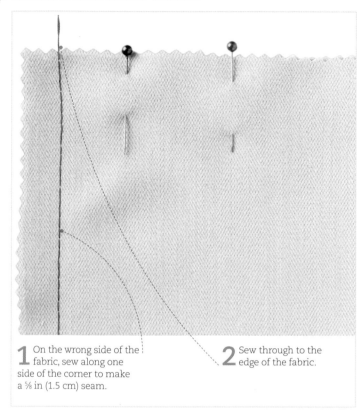

1 On the wrong side of the fabric, sew along one side of the corner to make a ⅝ in (1.5 cm) seam.

2 Sew through to the edge of the fabric.

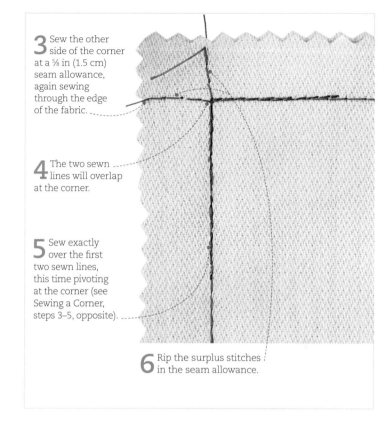

3 Sew the other side of the corner at a ⅝ in (1.5 cm) seam allowance, again sewing through the edge of the fabric.

4 The two sewn lines will overlap at the corner.

5 Sew exactly over the first two sewn lines, this time pivoting at the corner (see Sewing a Corner, steps 3–5, opposite).

6 Rip the surplus stitches in the seam allowance.

▶ **SEWING AN INNER CORNER**

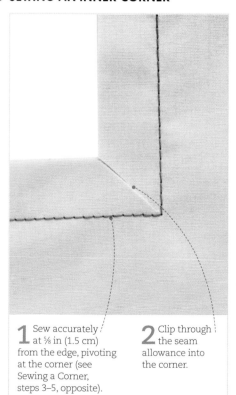

1 Sew accurately at ⅝ in (1.5 cm) from the edge, pivoting at the corner (see Sewing a Corner, steps 3–5, opposite).

2 Clip through the seam allowance into the corner.

▶ **SEWING AN INNER CURVE**

1 Place the right sides of the fabric together.

2 Sew a seam at ⅝ in (1.5 cm) from the edge. Be sure the sewn line follows the curve (use the stitch guides on the plate of the machine to help).

▶ **SEWING AN OUTER CURVE**

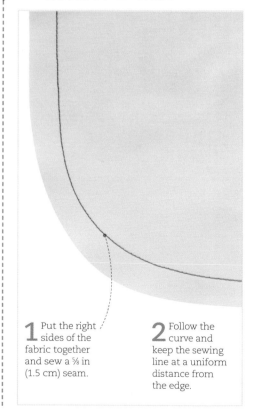

1 Put the right sides of the fabric together and sew a ⅝ in (1.5 cm) seam.

2 Follow the curve and keep the sewing line at a uniform distance from the edge.

REDUCING SEAM BULK pp.108–109

TWO-TONE **TOTE BAG**

At the beginning of your sewing career, the best projects are those that are easy to make and look anything but! This tote bag certainly meets the challenge of an ideal beginner project because it's made up of simple rectangles, brought together with straightforward seam and top-stitching techniques.

TECHNIQUES USED How to apply a fusible interfacing **p.54**, Sewing a corner **p.100**, Top-stitching **p.109**

PROJECT

YOU WILL NEED

- 36 x 43in (50 x 110cm) medium-weight cotton for outer fabric A
- 36 x 43in (25 x 110cm) medium-weight cotton for outer fabric B
- 36 x 43in (50 x 110cm) quilting-weight cotton for the lining
- 2 pieces 17 x 17in (43 x 43cm) light- to medium-weight fusible woven interfacing for outer pieces
- 2 pieces 26 x 3½in (66 x 9cm) light- to medium-weight fusible woven interfacing for handles
- 2 pieces 16 x 15½in (40 x 39cm) medium-loft fusible fleece batting for outer pieces
- Matching thread

PIECES TO CUT

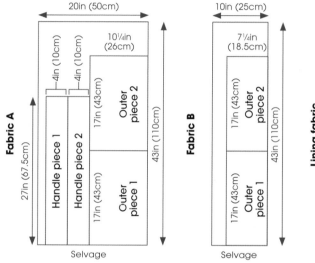

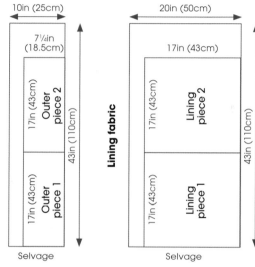

▶ MAKE THE HANDLES

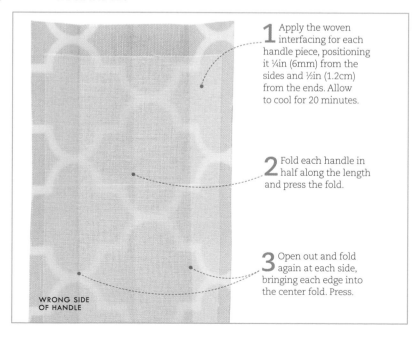

1 Apply the woven interfacing for each handle piece, positioning it ¼in (6mm) from the sides and ½in (1.2cm) from the ends. Allow to cool for 20 minutes.

2 Fold each handle in half along the length and press the fold.

3 Open out and fold again at each side, bringing each edge into the center fold. Press.

WRONG SIDE OF HANDLE

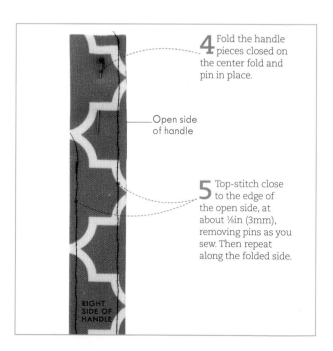

4 Fold the handle pieces closed on the center fold and pin in place.

Open side of handle

5 Top-stitch close to the edge of the open side, at about ⅛in (3mm), removing pins as you sew. Then repeat along the folded side.

RIGHT SIDE OF HANDLE

PRESSING AIDS **pp.28—29**

▶ **MAKE THE LINING**

WRONG SIDE
OF FABRIC

1 Pin the lining pieces together right side to right side and mark a 5in (12cm) turning gap on one side.

2 Sew along the two sides and the bottom except for the marked gap using a ⅜in (1cm) seam allowance.

3 On both corners, pinch the fabric to bring the bottom and side seams together.

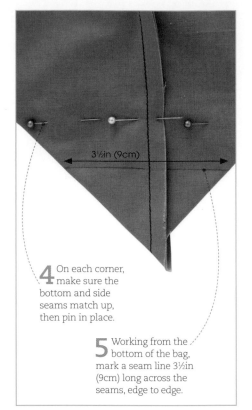

3½in (9cm)

4 On each corner, make sure the bottom and side seams match up, then pin in place.

5 Working from the bottom of the bag, mark a seam line 3½in (9cm) long across the seams, edge to edge.

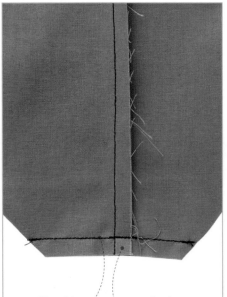

6 Still working from the bottom of the bag, create boxed corners by sewing across the marked lines. Reverse stitch across the central bag seam to reinforce.

7 Trim the corner seams to ⅜in (1cm).

▶ **MAKE THE OUTER LAYER**

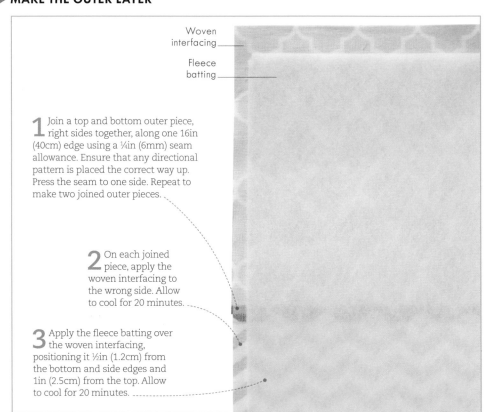

Woven interfacing

Fleece batting

1 Join a top and bottom outer piece, right sides together, along one 16in (40cm) edge using a ¼in (6mm) seam allowance. Ensure that any directional pattern is placed the correct way up. Press the seam to one side. Repeat to make two joined outer pieces.

2 On each joined piece, apply the woven interfacing to the wrong side. Allow to cool for 20 minutes.

3 Apply the fleece batting over the woven interfacing, positioning it ½in (1.2cm) from the bottom and side edges and 1in (2.5cm) from the top. Allow to cool for 20 minutes.

4 Position the handle ends 4in (10cm) from each side with the folded edges facing outward and make sure the handle is not twisted. Sew in place at ⅛in (3mm) from the top edge.

5 On the right side, top-stitch along the bottom piece, ⅛in (3mm) from the seam. You may wish to use a decorative stitch.

6 Pin the outer pieces right sides together, ensuring the seams line up, and sew along the side and bottom edges using a ¼in (6mm) seam allowance.

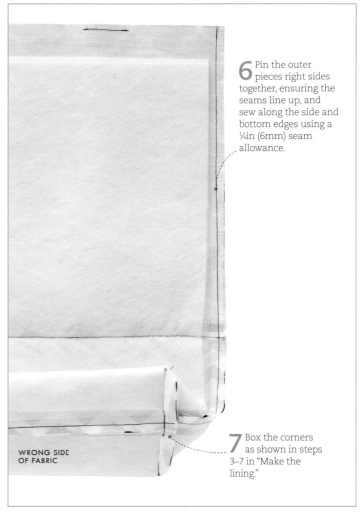

WRONG SIDE OF FABRIC

7 Box the corners as shown in steps 3–7 in "Make the lining."

▶ SEW LAYERS TOGETHER

1 Turn the outer layer right side out and place inside the lining, which is wrong side out, so the right sides face each other with the handles tucked inside. Line up the side seams on the two layers and pin in place. Baste together along the top edge.

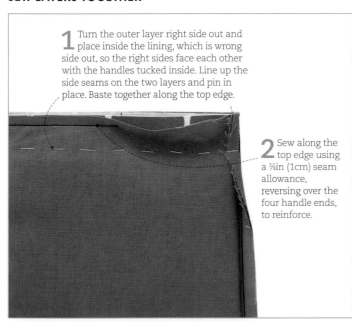

2 Sew along the top edge using a ⅜in (1cm) seam allowance, reversing over the four handle ends, to reinforce.

3 Turn the bag right side out through the turning gap in the lining. Press the top edge well. Top-stitch around the top at ⅛in (3mm).

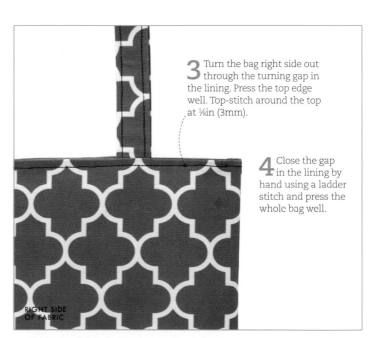

4 Close the gap in the lining by hand using a ladder stitch and press the whole bag well.

RIGHT SIDE OF FABRIC

TECHNIQUES

REDUCING **SEam BULK**

It is important that the seams used for construction do not cause bulk on the right side. To make sure this does not happen, the seam allowances need to be reduced in size by a technique known as layering a seam. They may also require V shapes to be removed, which is known as notching, or the seam allowance may be clipped.

LAYERING A SEAM

Difficulty level ✱✱✱✱✱

On the majority of fabrics, if the seam is on the edge of the work, the fabric in the seam needs reducing. The seam allowance closest to the outside of the garment or item stays full width, while the seam allowance closest to the body or inside is reduced.

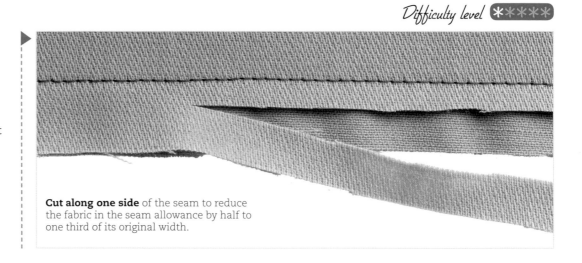

Cut along one side of the seam to reduce the fabric in the seam allowance by half to one third of its original width.

REDUCING SEAM BULK ON AN INNER CURVE

Difficulty level ✱✱✱✱✱

For an inner curve to lie flat, the seam will need to be layered and notched, then understitched to hold it in place (see opposite page).

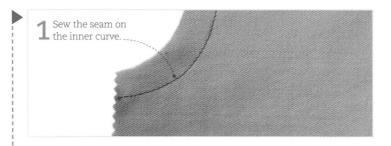

1 Sew the seam on the inner curve.

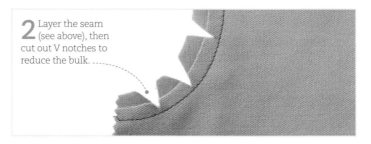

2 Layer the seam (see above), then cut out V notches to reduce the bulk.

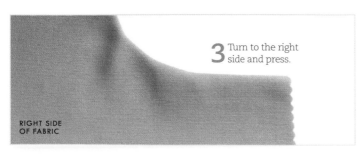

3 Turn to the right side and press.

RIGHT SIDE OF FABRIC

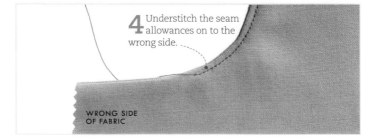

4 Understitch the seam allowances on to the wrong side.

WRONG SIDE OF FABRIC

HOW TO MAKE A PLAIN SEAM p.94 ● **SEWING CORNERS AND CURVES pp.102–103**

REDUCING SEAM BULK ON AN OUTER CURVE

Difficulty level ✶✶✶✶✶

An outer curve also needs layering and notching or clipping to allow the fabric to turn to the right side, after which it is understitched.

▶ **1** Make the seam, sewing along the outer curve.

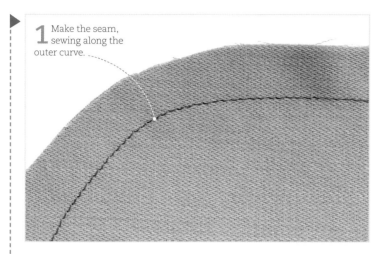

2 Layer the seam (see opposite page).

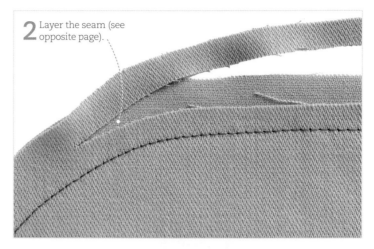

3 Clip through the seam allowances to reduce bulk.

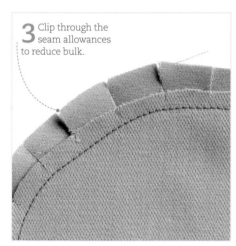

RIGHT SIDE OF FABRIC

4 Turn through to the right side and press.

WRONG SIDE OF FABRIC

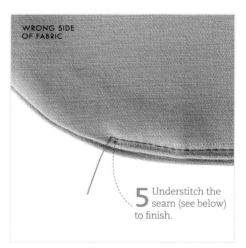

5 Understitch the seam (see below) to finish.

SEWN FINISHES

Difficulty level ✶✶✶✶✶

Top-stitching and understitching are two methods to finish edges. Top-stitching is meant to be seen on the right side of the work, whereas understitching is not visible from the right side.

▶ **TOP-STITCHING**

A top-stitch is a decorative, sharp finish to an edge. Use a longer stitch length, of 3.0 or 3.5, and machine on the right side of the work, using the edge of the machine foot as a guide.

▶ **UNDERSTITCHING**

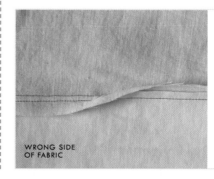

WRONG SIDE OF FABRIC

Understitching is used to secure a seam that is on the edge of a piece of fabric. It helps to stop the seam from rolling to the right side. First make the seam, then layer, turn, and press on to the right side. Open the seam again and push the seam allowance over the layered seam allowance. Sew the seam allowance down.

COMBINATION NECK AND ARMHOLE FACING **p.159** • INSERTING A SET-IN SLEEVE **p.211**

DARTS, TUCKS, PLEATS, AND GATHERS

Shape is put into a piece of flat fabric by means of a dart, a tuck, a pleat, or a gather. It may be to shape the fabric around the body or shape for crafts and home goods.

DARTS

A dart is used to give shape to a piece of fabric so that it can fit around the contours of the body. Some darts are sewn using straight sewn lines and other darts are sewn using a slightly curved line. Always sew a dart from the point to the wide end because you are able to sink the machine needle into the point accurately and securely.

DIRECTORY OF DARTS

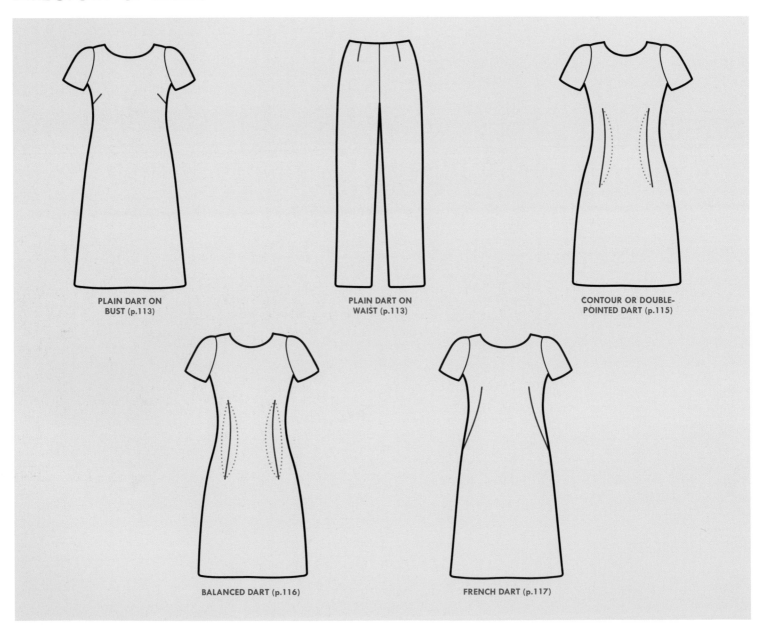

PLAIN DART ON
BUST (p.113)

PLAIN DART ON
WAIST (p.113)

CONTOUR OR DOUBLE-
POINTED DART (p.115)

BALANCED DART (p.116)

FRENCH DART (p.117)

BODY MEASURING pp.60–61 • ALTERING PATTERNS **pp.64–65**

PLAIN DART

Difficulty level ✳✳✳✳✳

This is the most common type of dart and is used to give shaping to the bust in the bodice. It is also found at the waist in skirts and pants to give shape from the waist to the hip.

1 Tailor tack the points of the dart as marked on the pattern, making one tack at the point and two to mark the wide ends.

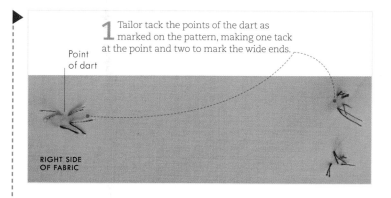

Point of dart

RIGHT SIDE OF FABRIC

2 Fold the fabric right side to right side, matching the tailor's tacks.

3 Pin through the tailor's tacks to match them.

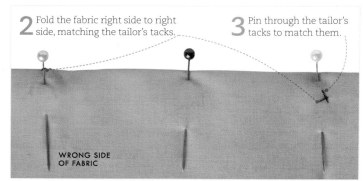

WRONG SIDE OF FABRIC

4 Baste along the dart line, joining the tailor's tacks. Remove the pins.

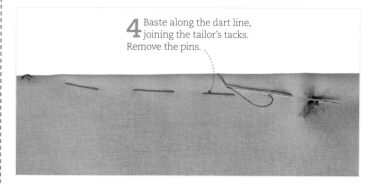

5 Machine sew alongside the basting line. Remove the bastes.

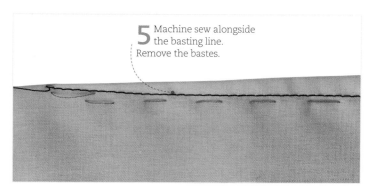

6 Sew the machine threads back into the line of the dart to secure them.

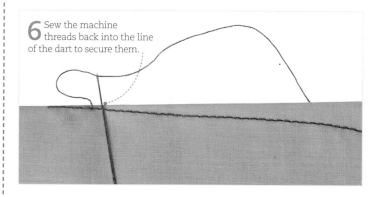

7 Press the dart to one side (see p.114).

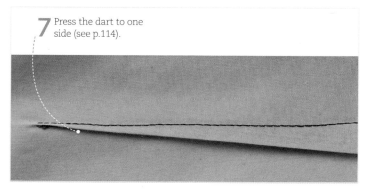

8 The finished dart on the right side.

RIGHT SIDE OF FABRIC

MAKING A MUSLIN **pp.74–75** ● PATTERN MARKING **pp.82–83**

SHAPING DARTS TO FIT

Difficulty level ❋❋❋❋❋

Our bodies often curve, and the straight line of the dart may not sit closely enough to our own personal shape. The dart can be sewn slightly concave or convex so it follows our contours. Do not move the curve out by more than ⅛in (3mm).

▶ **CONVEX DART**

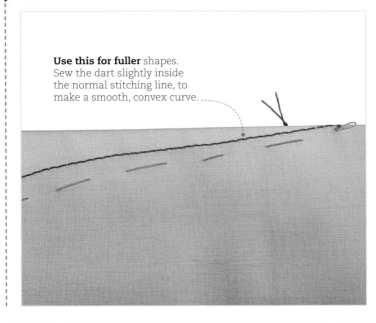

Use this for fuller shapes. Sew the dart slightly inside the normal stitching line, to make a smooth, convex curve.

▶ **CONCAVE CURVE**

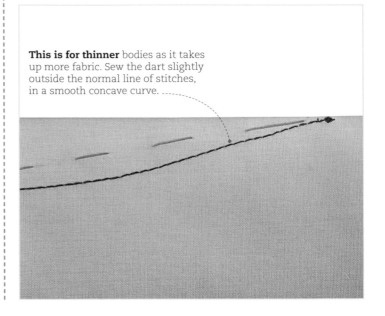

This is for thinner bodies as it takes up more fabric. Sew the dart slightly outside the normal line of stitches, in a smooth concave curve.

PRESSING A DART

If a dart is pressed incorrectly, this can spoil the look of a garment. For successful pressing, you will need a tailor's ham and a steam iron on a steam setting. A pressing cloth may be required for delicate fabrics such as silk, satin, and chiffon, and for lining fabrics.

1 Place the fabric piece, right side down, on the tailor's ham. The point of the dart should be over the end of the ham.

2 Press the fabric around the point of the dart.

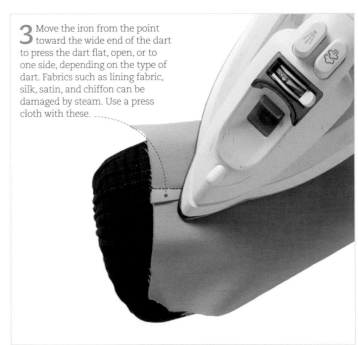

3 Move the iron from the point toward the wide end of the dart to press the dart flat, open, or to one side, depending on the type of dart. Fabrics such as lining fabric, silk, satin, and chiffon can be damaged by steam. Use a press cloth with these.

 PRESSING AIDS **pp.28–29** ● ALTERING PATTERNS **pp.64–65** ● PATTERN MARKING **pp.82–83**

CONTOUR OR DOUBLE-POINTED DART

Difficulty level ✶✶✶✶✶

This type of dart is like two darts joined together at the fat end. It is used to give shape at the waist of a garment. It will contour the fabric from the bust into the waist and then out again for the hip.

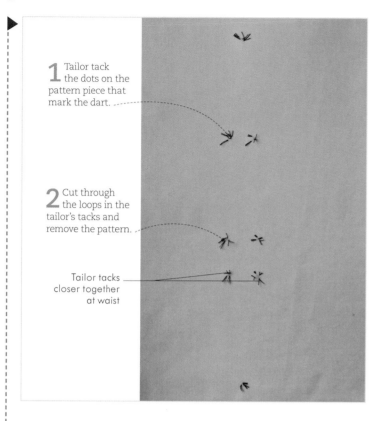

1 Tailor tack the dots on the pattern piece that mark the dart.

2 Cut through the loops in the tailor's tacks and remove the pattern.

Tailor tacks closer together at waist

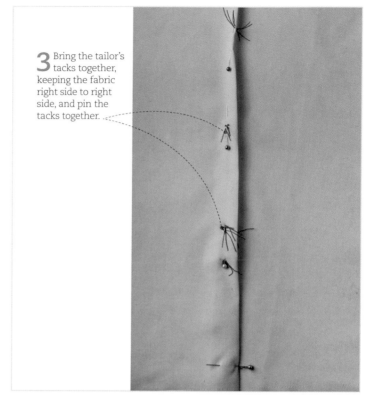

3 Bring the tailor's tacks together, keeping the fabric right side to right side, and pin the tacks together.

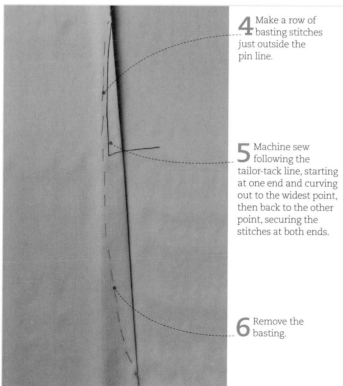

4 Make a row of basting stitches just outside the pin line.

5 Machine sew following the tailor-tack line, starting at one end and curving out to the widest point, then back to the other point, securing the stitches at both ends.

6 Remove the basting.

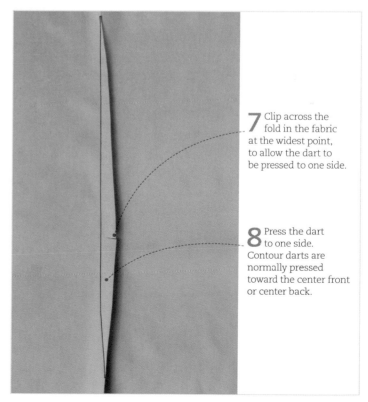

7 Clip across the fold in the fabric at the widest point, to allow the dart to be pressed to one side.

8 Press the dart to one side. Contour darts are normally pressed toward the center front or center back.

BASTING STITCHES p.89 ● **STITCHES MADE WITH A MACHINE pp.92—93**

BALANCED DART

Difficulty level ❋❋❋❋❋

This dart is used on thicker fabrics such as wool crepe or tweed, as well as on fabrics that mark when pressed. The addition of a balancing strip helps distribute the fabric on either side of the dart on the wrong side, making it less conspicuous on the worn garment.

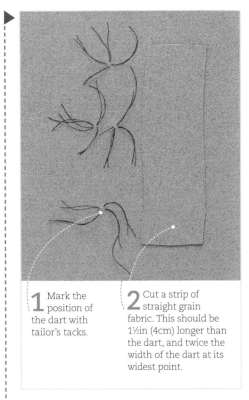

1 Mark the position of the dart with tailor's tacks.

2 Cut a strip of straight grain fabric. This should be 1½in (4cm) longer than the dart, and twice the width of the dart at its widest point.

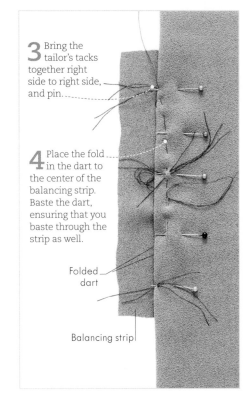

3 Bring the tailor's tacks together right side to right side, and pin.

4 Place the fold in the dart to the center of the balancing strip. Baste the dart, ensuring that you baste through the strip as well.

Folded dart

Balancing strip

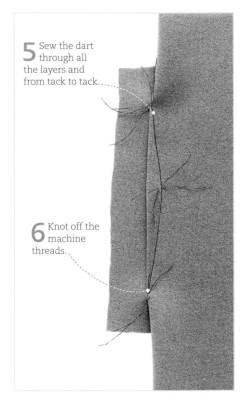

5 Sew the dart through all the layers and from tack to tack.

6 Knot off the machine threads.

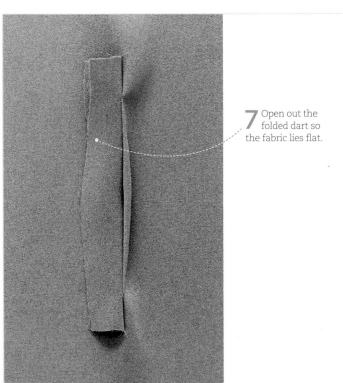

7 Open out the folded dart so the fabric lies flat.

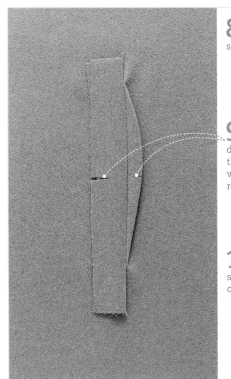

8 Press the dart to one side and the balancing strip to the other.

9 If the fabric is tight, clip the center of the dart and the center of the balancing strip at their widest points. This will release tension.

10 Trim back the strip to a neat rectangle shape to reflect the shape of the dart.

PRESSING AIDS **pp.28–29** • ALTERING PATTERNS **pp.64–65** • PATTERN MARKING **pp.82–83**

FRENCH DART

A French dart is used on the front of a garment only. It is a curved dart that extends from the side seam at the waist to the bust point. As this is a long dart that is shaped, it will need to be slashed prior to construction, in order for it to fit together and then lie flat when pressed.

Difficulty level ★★★★★

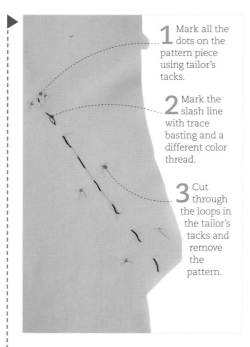

1 Mark all the dots on the pattern piece using tailor's tacks.

2 Mark the slash line with trace basting and a different color thread.

3 Cut through the loops in the tailor's tacks and remove the pattern.

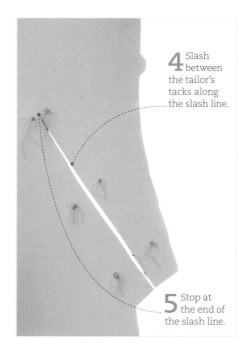

4 Slash between the tailor's tacks along the slash line.

5 Stop at the end of the slash line.

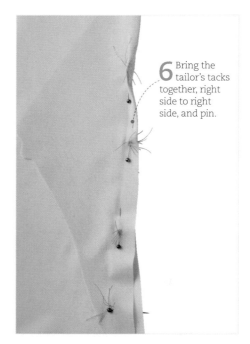

6 Bring the tailor's tacks together, right side to right side, and pin.

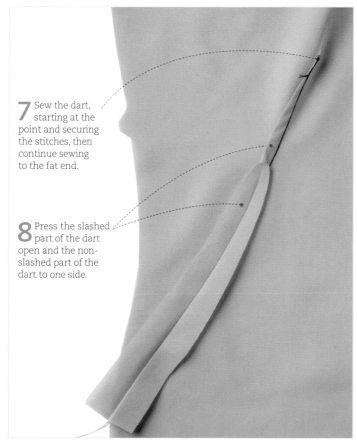

7 Sew the dart, starting at the point and securing the stitches, then continue sewing to the fat end.

8 Press the slashed part of the dart open and the non-slashed part of the dart to one side.

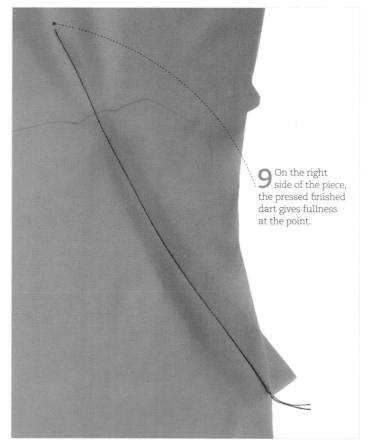

9 On the right side of the piece, the pressed finished dart gives fullness at the point.

TUCKS

A tuck is a decorative addition to any piece of fabric, and can be big and bold or very delicate. Tucks are made by sewing evenly spaced folds into the fabric on the right side, normally on the straight grain of the fabric. As the tucks take up additional fabric, it is best to make them prior to cutting out.

DIRECTORY OF TUCKS

PLAIN TUCKS (p.119)

SPACED TUCKS (p.119)

PIN TUCKS (p.119)

TWIN NEEDLE TUCKS (p.119)

BLIND TUCKS (p.119)

SHELL TUCKS (p.120)

CORDED OR PIPED TUCKS (p.121)

DARTED TUCKS (p.121)

CROSS TUCKS (p.121)

MARKING AIDS p.19 ● PRESSING AIDS pp.28–29 ● SEWING-MACHINE ACCESSORIES pp.32–33

PLAIN TUCKS

A plain tuck is made by marking and creasing the fabric at regular intervals. A row of machine stitches are then worked adjacent to the fold.

Difficulty level ★★☆☆☆

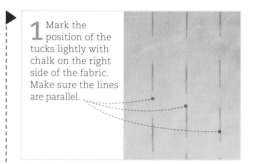

1 Mark the position of the tucks lightly with chalk on the right side of the fabric. Make sure the lines are parallel.

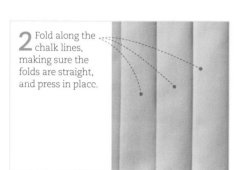

2 Fold along the chalk lines, making sure the folds are straight, and press in place.

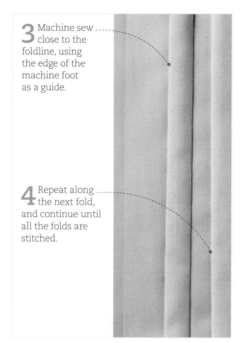

3 Machine sew close to the foldline, using the edge of the machine foot as a guide.

4 Repeat along the next fold, and continue until all the folds are stitched.

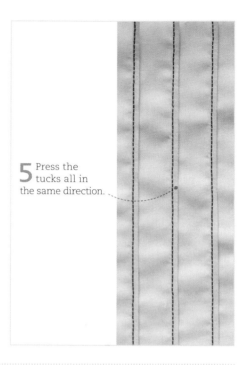

5 Press the tucks all in the same direction.

OTHER SIMPLE TUCKS

Difficulty level ★★☆☆☆

These tucks are also made by marking and creasing the fabric. The positioning of the sewn line determines the type of tuck.

▶ SPACED TUCKS

These are similar to a plain tuck, but with wider regular spacing. Press the tucks in place along the foldlines and pin. Sew ⅜in (1cm) from the foldline. Press all the tucks in one direction.

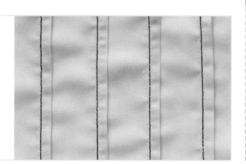

▶ PIN TUCKS

These narrow, regularly spaced tucks are stitched very close to the foldline, which may require moving the machine needle closer to the fold. Use the pintuck foot on the sewing machine.

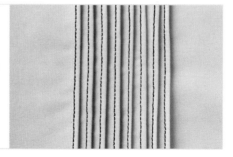

▶ TWIN NEEDLE TUCKS

For these regularly spaced tucks, use the twin needle on the sewing machine. The twin needle produces a shallow tuck that looks very effective when multiple rows are stitched.

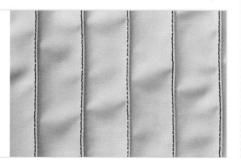

▶ BLIND TUCKS

These are wide tucks that are sewn so no stitching shows—the fold of each tuck covers the machine stitching of the previous tuck.

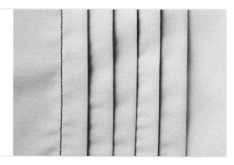

STITCHES MADE WITH A MACHINE pp.92—93

TECHNIQUES

SHELL TUCKS

Difficulty level ✳✳✳✳✳

A shell tuck is very decorative as it has a scalloped edge. Shell tucks can be easily sewn using the sewing machine. On heavy fabric and delicate fabrics, it may be preferable to make the tucks by hand.

▶ MACHINE SHELL TUCKS

1 Mark the foldlines on the fabric, then fold and press.

2 Baste the folds in place.

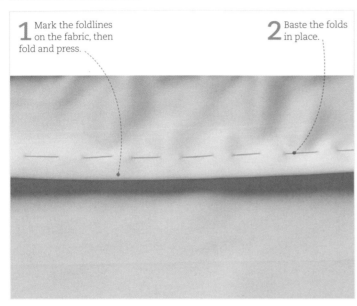

3 Use the embroidery foot on the sewing machine and set the sewing machine to a shell hem stitch.

4 Sew along the fold, keeping the fold close to the inside opening of the machine foot.

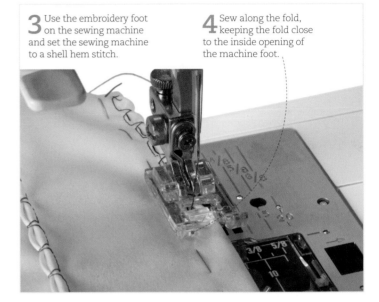

5 The finished tucks should be stitched at regular intervals.

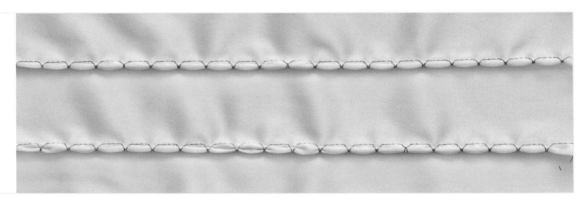

SHELL TUCKS BY HAND

1 Baste the foldlines for the tucks in place.

2 Using a double thread in the needle, make two or three running stitches.

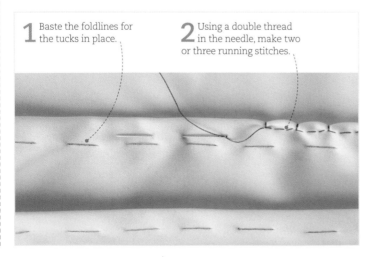

3 Every ½in (1.25cm), make an over-stitch through the fold to produce a scallop.

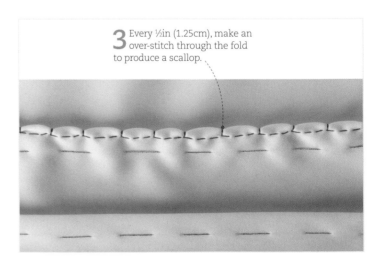

PIPED TUCKS

These are very substantial tucks that stand proud on the fabric. This type of tuck is best used in home goods.

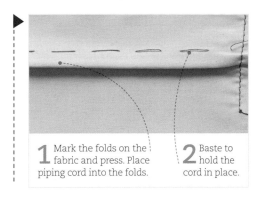

1 Mark the folds on the fabric and press. Place piping cord into the folds.

2 Baste to hold the cord in place.

3 Using the zip foot on the sewing machine, sew close to the cord.

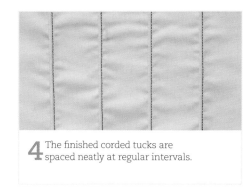

4 The finished corded tucks are spaced neatly at regular intervals.

DARTED TUCKS

A tuck that stops to release the fullness is known as a darted tuck. It can be used to give fullness at the bust or hip. The shaped darted tuck is sewn at an angle to release less fabric, while the plain darted tuck is sewn straight on the grainline.

▶ **SHAPED DARTED TUCKS**

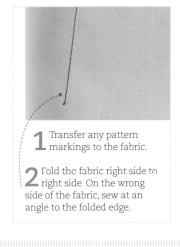

1 Transfer any pattern markings to the fabric.

2 Fold the fabric right side to right side. On the wrong side of the fabric, sew at an angle to the folded edge.

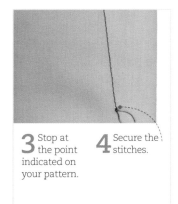

3 Stop at the point indicated on your pattern.

4 Secure the stitches.

▶ **PLAIN DARTED TUCKS**

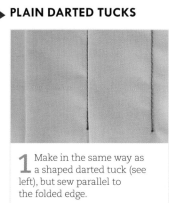

1 Make in the same way as a shaped darted tuck (see left), but sew parallel to the folded edge.

2 Stop as indicated on the pattern.

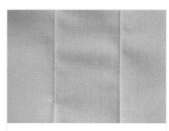

3 The tuck as seen from the right side.

CROSS TUCKS

These are tucks that cross over each other by being sewn in opposite directions.

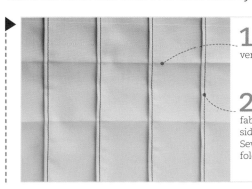

1 Press the crease lines into the fabric, both vertically and horizontally.

2 Sew all the vertical tucks first: fold the fabric wrong side to wrong side along the crease lines. Sew ³⁄₁₆in (5mm) from the folded edge.

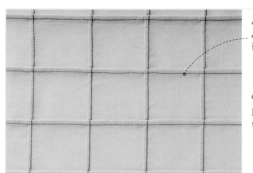

3 Sew all the horizontal tucks in the same way.

4 Press all the vertical or horizontal tucks in the same direction.

PLEATS

A pleat is a fold or series of folds in fabric. Pleats are most commonly found in skirts where the pleats are made to fit around the waist and hip and then left to fall in crisply pressed folds, giving fullness at the hemline. It is important that pleats are made accurately, otherwise they will not fit the body and will look uneven. Foldlines and placement lines, or foldlines and crease lines, are marked on the fabric from the pattern. It is by using a combination of these lines and the spaces between them that the pleats are made.

DIRECTORY OF PLEATS

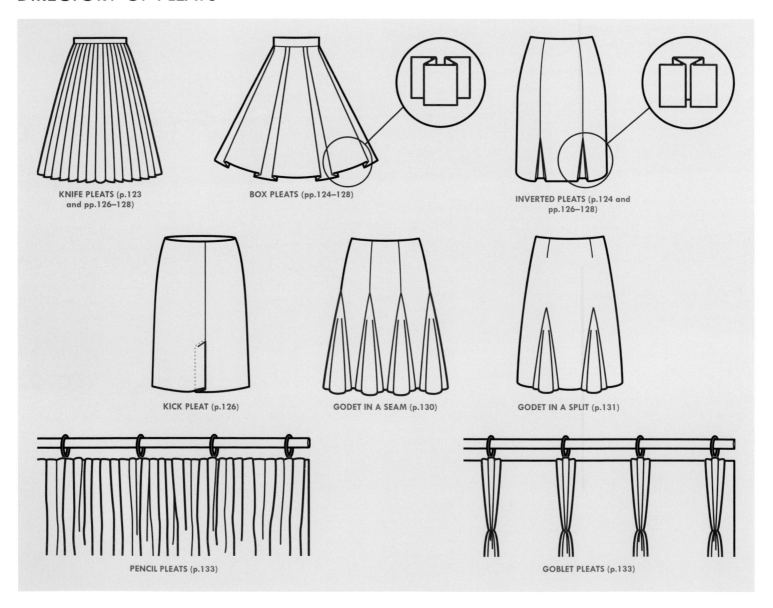

KNIFE PLEATS (p.123 and pp.126–128)

BOX PLEATS (pp.124–128)

INVERTED PLEATS (p.124 and pp.126–128)

KICK PLEAT (p.126)

GODET IN A SEAM (p.130)

GODET IN A SPLIT (p.131)

PENCIL PLEATS (p.133)

GOBLET PLEATS (p.133)

PLEATS ON THE RIGHT SIDE

Difficulty level ✱✱✱✱

Knife pleats are normally formed on the right side of fabric. They can all face the same direction or may face opposite directions from opposite sides of the garment. Knife pleats have foldlines and placement lines.

1 Mark the placement lines and foldlines with trace tacks. Use one color thread, such as red, for placement lines.

2 Use a contrasting color thread, such as blue, to mark foldlines.

3 Cut through the thread loops and remove the pattern pieces carefully.

Placement line

Fold line

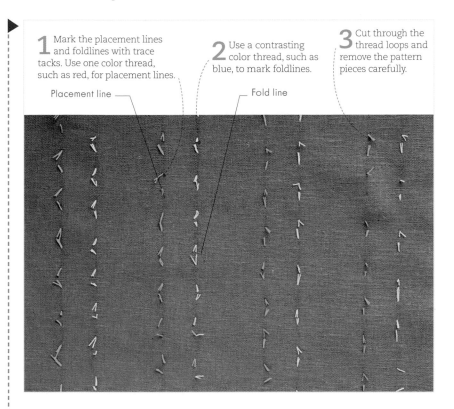

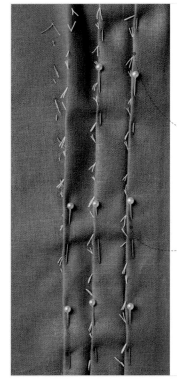

4 Fold the fabric along the foldline, creasing accurately along the trace tacks.

5 Bring the creased line on to the placement line. Pin to secure.

6 Baste along the foldlines about ⅟₁₆in (2mm) from the folded edge, through all the layers.

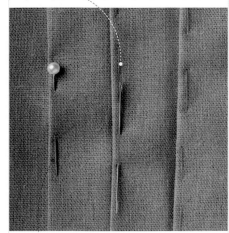

7 Remove the pins and the trace basting on this part of the pleat.

8 With the right side of the fabric uppermost, cover with a silk organza pressing cloth.

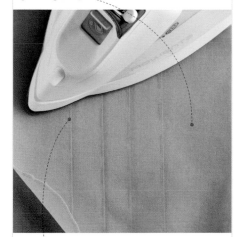

9 Using a steam iron on a steam setting, press the pleats in place. Keep the iron still as opposed to moving it around, and eject a shot of steam each time you lift it to a new position. Repeat this action across all of the pleats.

10 Turn the fabric to the wrong side and insert thin strips of construction paper under the pleat fabric.

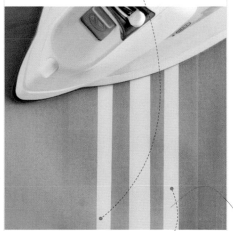

11 Press again with the steam iron and a silk organza cloth. The paper will prevent the fabric from leaving an imprint on the right side.

PATTERN MARKING **pp.82–83** ● BASTING STITCHES **p.89**

TECHNIQUES

PLEATS ON THE WRONG SIDE

Difficulty level ★★☆☆☆

Some pleats, including box (shown below) and inverted pleats, are formed on the wrong side of the fabric. As the pleats are made on the wrong side, you can mark the crease lines and foldlines with a tracing wheel and dressmaker's carbon paper. Use a ruler to guide the tracing wheel, because these pleats need to be straight lines.

1 Mark the crease lines and foldlines on the wrong side of the fabric, using different colors for the different lines. The lines must be marked down the full length of the fabric.

2 Also mark the stop line that shows where to stop stitching. Remove the pattern pieces.

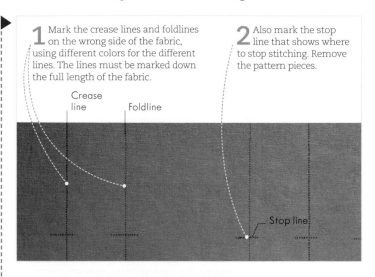

Crease line

Foldline

Stop line

3 Bring the two crease lines that are either side of the foldline together and pin in place.

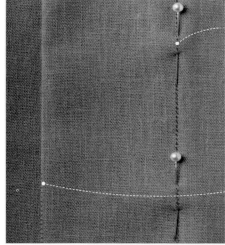

4 Be sure the foldline is along the fold in the fabric.

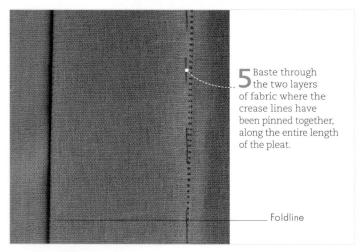

5 Baste through the two layers of fabric where the crease lines have been pinned together, along the entire length of the pleat.

Foldline

6 Sew along the crease lines.

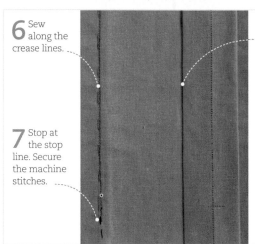

7 Stop at the stop line. Secure the machine stitches.

8 Flatten the pleat on the wrong side so that the foldline is lying on top of the machine stitches. Make sure that the fabric on either side of this foldline to the crease line is equal on both sides.

9 Cover the pleats on the wrong side with a silk organza pressing cloth and press, using a steam iron with a shot of steam.

10 Press each section of the pleat in turn, lifting the iron rather than moving it on the fabric.

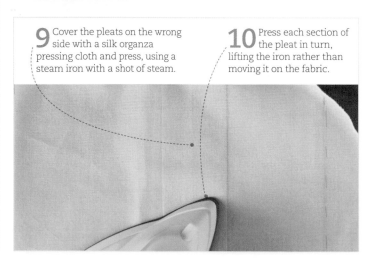

11 If the fabric is in danger of being marked on the right side with the pleats, place some strips of construction paper under the pleats on the wrong side, then press again on the wrong side.

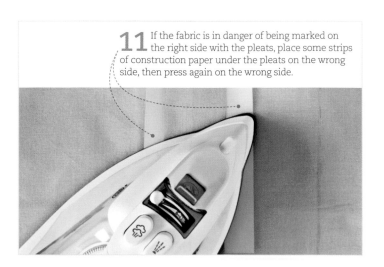

PLEATS WITH A SEPARATE UNDERLAY

Difficulty level ★★★★★

Sometimes a box pleat is constructed with a separate piece of fabric or underlay. This technique is usually done on large, single box pleats or on a pleat made using thicker fabric, because it reduces the bulk. The seam to make this pleat is much wider than normal, as it is the width of the pleat.

1 Mark the sewing line with trace bastes. Cut through the thread loops and carefully pull away the pattern piece.

2 Place the two pieces of fabric together, right side to right side. Match the notches and trace basting.

3 Baste along the trace bastes that mark the sewn line, removing the trace basting as you do so.

4 Sew the seam to the stop point.

5 Press the seam open along its full length.

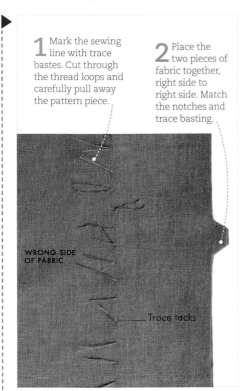

WRONG SIDE OF FABRIC

Trace tacks

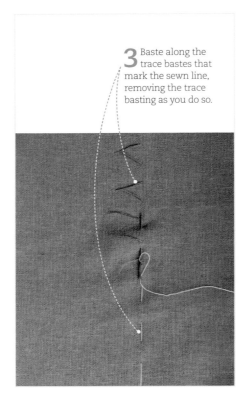

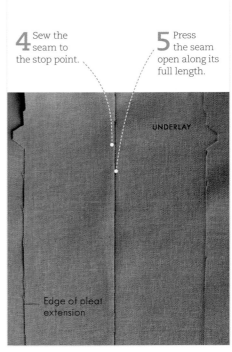

UNDERLAY

Edge of pleat extension

6 Take the underlay and place carefully on to the pressed seam, matching the notches. The wrong side of the underlay should be uppermost.

7 Pin the underlay in place, being careful to pin it just to the edge of the seam and not through to the main fabric.

8 On this type of pleat, the hem has to be constructed before all the pleats can be made. Sew either side of the underlay to the edge of the pleat, stopping at least 4in (10cm) above the raw hem edge.

9 Remove the basting stitches that are holding the pleat together.

10 Turn up the hem including the pleat. Separately turn up the underlay to match.

11 Pin the underlay and the pleat back together from where the machine sewing stopped, down through the hem. Make sure that on the right side the hem is even through this area.

WRONG SIDE OF UNDERLAY

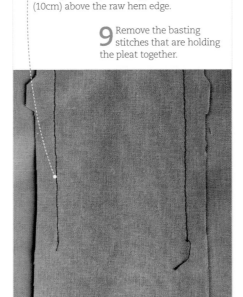

12 Neaten the seams using your preferred method.

13 Remove the lower edge of the underlay/pleat seam, then blanket stitch or whip stitch. Finish by pressing.

TOP-STITCHING AND EDGE-STITCHING PLEATS

Difficulty level ★★★★★

If a pleat is top-stitched or edge-stitched, it will hang correctly and always look crisp. It will also help the pleats on the skirt to stay in shape when you are sitting. Try to sew both the top-stitching and the edge-stitching the entire length of the skirt, from the hem to the waist.

▶ TOP-STITCHING KNIFE PLEATS

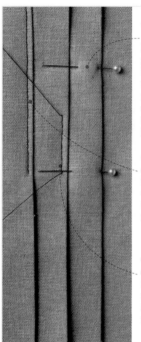

1 Once the knife pleats have been pressed and all bastes and markings removed, place some pins across the pleat to stop it from moving.

2 Machine sew from the right side approx ⅟₁₆in (2mm) from the fold.

3 Start sewing at the lower end of the pleat and sew to the waist.

▶ TOP-STITCHING BOX PLEATS THAT HAVE A SQUARE END

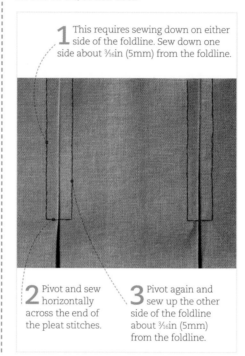

1 This requires sewing down on either side of the foldline. Sew down one side about ³⁄₁₆in (5mm) from the foldline.

2 Pivot and sew horizontally across the end of the pleat stitches.

3 Pivot again and sew up the other side of the foldline about ³⁄₁₆in (5mm) from the foldline.

▶ TOP-STITCHING BOX PLEATS THAT HAVE A POINTED END

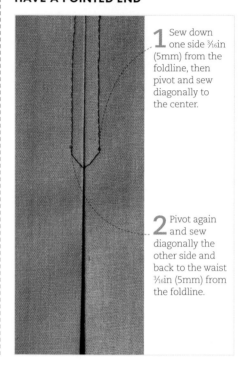

1 Sew down one side ³⁄₁₆in (5mm) from the foldline, then pivot and sew diagonally to the center.

2 Pivot again and sew diagonally the other side and back to the waist ³⁄₁₆in (5mm) from the foldline.

▶ EDGE-STITCHING KNIFE PLEATS

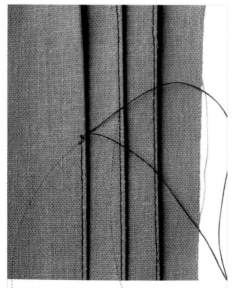

1 After pressing the pleats into shape, stitch ⅟₁₆in (2mm) from the fold.

2 Sew along the entire length of the fold.

▶ EDGE-STITCHING AND TOP-STITCHING PLEATS

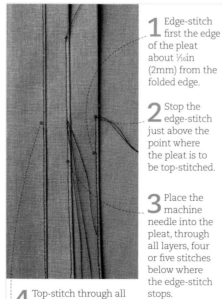

1 Edge-stitch first the edge of the pleat about ⅟₁₆in (2mm) from the folded edge.

2 Stop the edge-stitch just above the point where the pleat is to be top-stitched.

3 Place the machine needle into the pleat, through all layers, four or five stitches below where the edge-stitch stops.

4 Top-stitch through all the layers, continuing at ⅟₁₆in (2mm) from the fold, to the waist.

▶ TOP-STITCHING KICK PLEATS OR INVERTED PLEATS

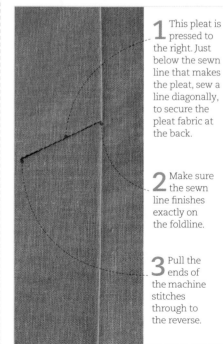

1 This pleat is pressed to the right. Just below the sewn line that makes the pleat, sew a line diagonally, to secure the pleat fabric at the back.

2 Make sure the sewn line finishes exactly on the foldline.

3 Pull the ends of the machine stitches through to the reverse.

HAND SEWING **pp.90–91** ● SEWING CORNERS AND CURVES **pp.102–103** ● REDUCING SEAM BULK **pp.108–109** ● SEWN FINISHES **p.109**

STAYING PLEATS

Staying a pleat is a technique used to reduce the bulk of the pleat, especially in the hip area. There are various ways of doing this and the method chosen will depend on the type of pleat, the fabric used, and your personal preference.

▶ SELF-STAYING BOX PLEATS OR INVERTED PLEATS

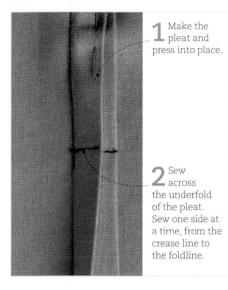

1 Make the pleat and press into place.

2 Sew across the underfold of the pleat. Sew one side at a time, from the crease line to the foldline.

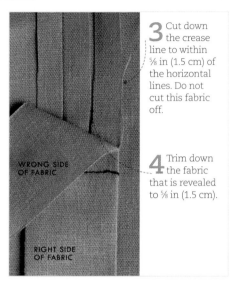

WRONG SIDE OF FABRIC

RIGHT SIDE OF FABRIC

3 Cut down the crease line to within ⅝ in (1.5 cm) of the horizontal lines. Do not cut this fabric off.

4 Trim down the fabric that is revealed to ⅝ in (1.5 cm).

5 Flip the underfold back into place and secure at the waist edge.

▶ STAYING KNIFE PLEATS ON THICKER FABRIC

1 On the wrong side, sew across the underfold.

Fold of pleat

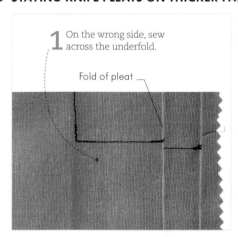

2 Remove the bulk of the underfold fabric with a curve.

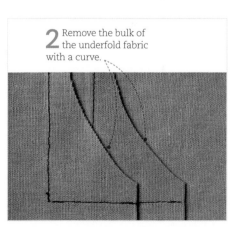

3 Cut a piece of lining large enough to cover the pleated section.

4 Clean finish the lower edge.

5 Baste to secure along the waist edge (to make this fabric fit at the waist, tuck the lining at the waist).

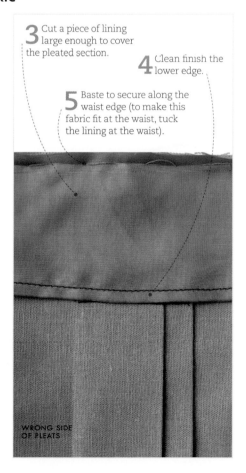

WRONG SIDE OF PLEATS

6 Hand sew, using a flat fell stitch, the edge of the lining to the seam on the underfold.

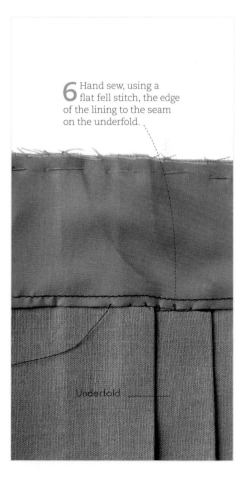

Underfold

HAND-SEWN HEMS: CLEAN FINISH **p.264**

HEMMING PLEATS

Most pleated garments or home goods are hemmed after the pleats have been constructed; however, in some cases pleats can be hemmed first. This technique is only used for garments with all-around pleats or that have to follow a checker or stripe.

Difficulty level ★★★★☆

▶ HEMMING KNIFE PLEATS OR INVERTED PLEATS

1 Make sure the pleat has been well pressed. Press the hem up into place, then open the pleat out to reveal the crease lines.

2 Reduce the bulk in the seam in the area of the hem, from the raw edge to the top edge of the hem when folded into place.

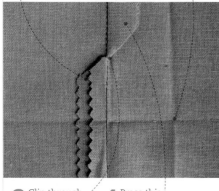

3 Clip through the seam allowance.

4 Press this part of the seam allowance in the opposite direction to the seam.

5 Turn up the hem.

6 Press the pleat back into position.

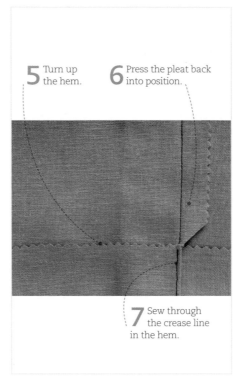

7 Sew through the crease line in the hem.

▶ HEMMING BOX PLEATS BEFORE THE GARMENT IS FINISHED

1 Turn up the hem.

2 Make the seam and press open.

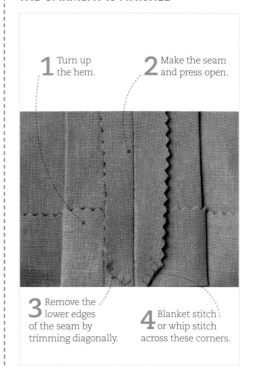

3 Remove the lower edges of the seam by trimming diagonally.

4 Blanket stitch or whip stitch across these corners.

▶ HEMMING BOX PLEATS AFTER THE GARMENT IS FINISHED

1 Press the pleat into position and press the hem into position.

2 Reduce the seam allowance below the crease line of the hem.

3 Turn up the hem.

4 Match the sewn lines and press the pleat for the final time.

▶ SECURING PLEATS AT THE HEM

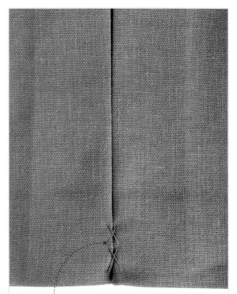

The bottom of every pleat on a garment can be secured temporarily with two or three cross stitches.

ALTERING PATTERNS **pp.62–63** ● PATTERN MARKING **pp.82–83** ● HAND SEWING **pp.90–91** ● REDUCING SEAM BULK **pp.108–109**

ADJUSTING PLEATS TO FIT

Difficulty level ✦✦✦✶✶

If a pleated skirt is either too big or too tight at the waist or hip, a small adjustment on each pleat can make a huge difference. Simply take the amount to be added or removed and divide it by the number of pleats. If the adjustment is not the same on all the pleats, they will look unbalanced.

▶ LETTING OUT PLEATS FORMED ON THE RIGHT SIDE

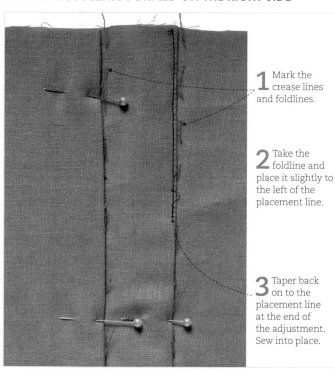

1 Mark the crease lines and foldlines.

2 Take the foldline and place it slightly to the left of the placement line.

3 Taper back on to the placement line at the end of the adjustment. Sew into place.

▶ TAKING IN PLEATS FORMED ON THE RIGHT SIDE

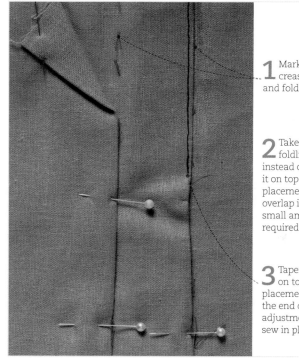

1 Mark the crease lines and foldlines.

2 Take the foldline and, instead of placing it on top of the placement line, overlap it by the small amount required.

3 Taper back on to the placement line at the end of the adjustment, then sew in place.

▶ LETTING OUT PLEATS FORMED ON THE WRONG SIDE

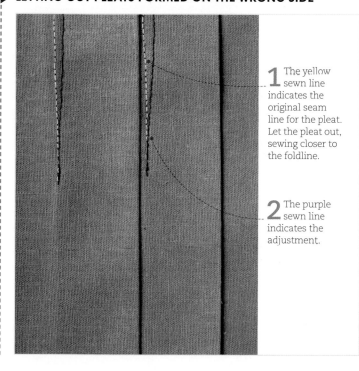

1 The yellow sewn line indicates the original seam line for the pleat. Let the pleat out, sewing closer to the foldline.

2 The purple sewn line indicates the adjustment.

▶ TAKING IN PLEATS FORMED ON THE WRONG SIDE

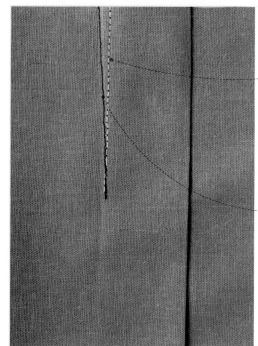

1 The yellow sewn line indicates the original seam line for the pleat. Take the pleat in, sewing further from the foldline.

2 The purple sewn line indicates this adjustment.

HEMS **pp.262–267**

TECHNIQUES

GODET IN A SEAM

A godet is a type of pleat that is inserted into a garment to give fullness at the hem edge. It is a segment of a circle, usually triangular in shape, but also sometimes a half circle—the size of the godet depends on the fullness required. The godet may go from hem to knee or even hem to thigh, according to the style of the skirt. The easiest way to insert a godet is in a seam.

Difficulty level ★★★★✱

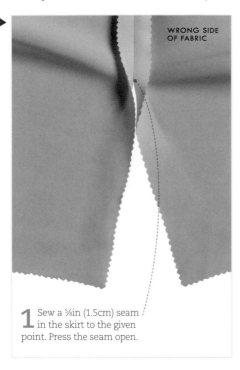

1 Sew a ⅝in (1.5cm) seam in the skirt to the given point. Press the seam open.

WRONG SIDE OF FABRIC

2 Cut out the godet. Tailor tack to mark where the stitching in the skirt stops.

WRONG SIDE OF GODET

3 Place the godet to the split in the skirt seam, right side to right side.

4 Join one side of the godet to the skirt, sewing along the edge, from the hem to the tailor's tack.

5 Sew the other side of the godet to the skirt, from hem to tailor's tack.

All three seam lines meet at tailor's tack

6 Snip through the skirt seam to release tension and allow the godet-to-skirt to be pressed open.

RIGHT SIDE OF FABRIC

7 Finish the godet by pressing carefully on the right side.

GODET IN A SPLIT

Sometimes there are not enough seams in a garment for the number of godets that you would like to insert. If that is the case, a split must be made in the fabric at the hemline to accommodate each godet. A piece of silk organza is sewn on to the point of the split to strengthen it.

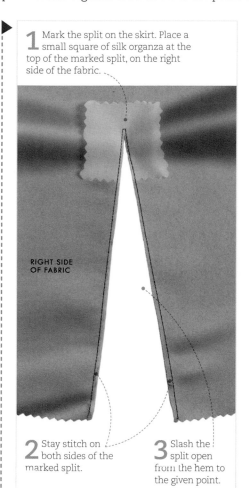

1 Mark the split on the skirt. Place a small square of silk organza at the top of the marked split, on the right side of the fabric.

RIGHT SIDE OF FABRIC

2 Stay stitch on both sides of the marked split.

3 Slash the split open from the hem to the given point.

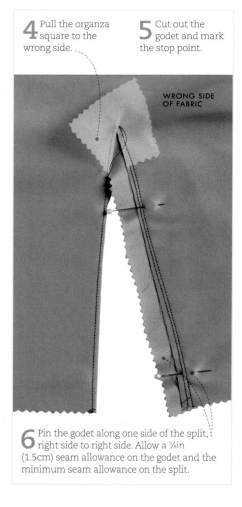

4 Pull the organza square to the wrong side.

5 Cut out the godet and mark the stop point.

WRONG SIDE OF FABRIC

6 Pin the godet along one side of the split, right side to right side. Allow a ⅝in (1.5cm) seam allowance on the godet and the minimum seam allowance on the split.

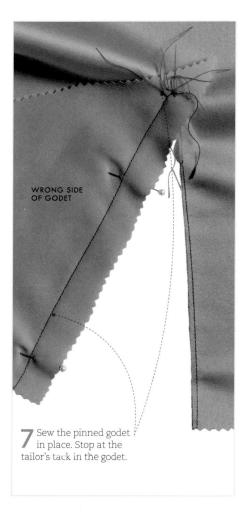

WRONG SIDE OF GODET

7 Sew the pinned godet in place. Stop at the tailor's tack in the godet.

8 Sew the other side of the godet to the split. Make sure the seam lines meet exactly at the point of the split.

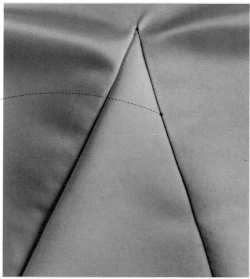

9 On the right side, there should be no creases at the top of the godet. Press gently to finish, using just the toe of the iron.

STITCHES MADE WITH A MACHINE **pp.92–93** ● HOW TO MAKE A PLAIN SEAM **p.94**

PLEATS ON CURTAINS

Difficulty level ✷✷✷✷✷

Pleats are used in home goods, particularly at the top of curtains, to reduce the fabric so that the curtain will fit on to its track and fit the window. The easiest way to pleat the upper edge of a curtain is to apply a curtain tape. Tapes are available in various depths and will pull the curtain into pencil pleats or goblet pleats. The most common tape used for pencil pleating is 3¼in (8cm) deep. A curtain is normally cut two-and-a-half to three times the width of the window. The curtain tape will reduce the fabric by this much as it pleats up.

▶ PREPARING THE CURTAIN TO TAKE THE TAPE

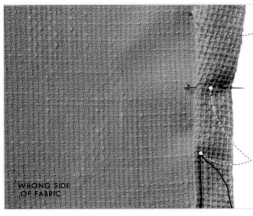

1 Turn under the two side edges of the curtain by using a double hem of 1in (2.5cm), i.e. turn the fabric 1in (2.5cm) once and then the same again.

2 Pin the hem edges on the sides of the curtains, then sew.

WRONG SIDE OF FABRIC

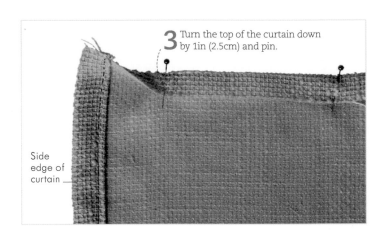

3 Turn the top of the curtain down by 1in (2.5cm) and pin.

Side edge of curtain

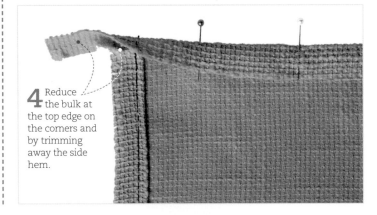

4 Reduce the bulk at the top edge on the corners and by trimming away the side hem.

5 Baste the upper edge of the curtain down into place. To ensure the corners are square, after pivoting realign the edge of the fabric with the stitch guide on the faceplate of the machine.

▶ MAKING A POCKET FOR THE STRINGS

1 Before the tape is applied, a small pocket needs to be made to take the strings that are used to pull up the tape. Cut a rectangle of spare fabric 6 x 3¼in (15 x 8cm).

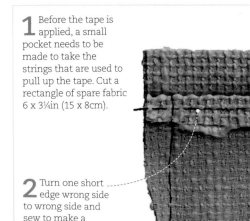

2 Turn one short edge wrong side to wrong side and sew to make a single hem.

3 Fold the rectangle right side to right side with a ¾in (2cm) seam at the upper edge free.

4 Sew down the sides and clip the corners.

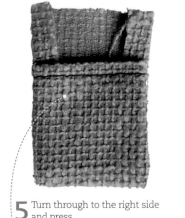

5 Turn through to the right side and press.

▶ PENCIL PLEATS

1 Take the curtain tape and release the strings at the one end, making sure they are all visible on the same side.

2 Place the top of the tape ³⁄₁₆in (5mm) down from the folded edge of the curtain. Pin in place, stretching the tape as you do so. Turn under the short end, avoiding the strings and pin.

3 Sew the upper edge of the tape to the curtain fabric. Make sure the strings stay free.

4 Before sewing the lower edge of the tape, place the pocket you made under the end of the tape.

5 Pin the tape and the pocket in place. Sew the tape and pocket into the curtain fabric.

6 At the opposite end of the tape, sew across each string individually to prevent it from being pulled out.

7 Pull up the strings in the tape from the end with the pocket to make the pleats.

8 Tie the strings together and place in the pocket.

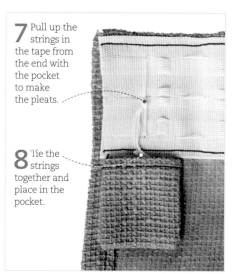

9 Turn the curtain over to check that the pencil pleats are evenly spaced and will fit the window. Adjust if necessary.

▶ GOBLET PLEATS

1 Goblet pleats are three pleats together at regular intervals. When the tape is pulled up, the pleats are close together at the base and fan out at the top. Prepare the curtain to take the tape and make the pocket (see opposite page).

2 Attach the tape in the same way as for pencil pleats (above).

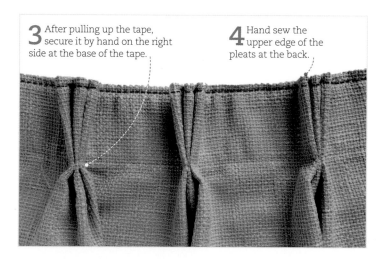

3 After pulling up the tape, secure it by hand on the right side at the base of the tape.

4 Hand sew the upper edge of the pleats at the back.

TECHNIQUES

GATHERS

Gathers are an easy way to draw up a piece of larger fabric so that it will fit on to a smaller piece of fabric. They often appear at waistlines or yoke lines. The gather stitch is inserted after the major seams have been constructed, and it is best worked on the sewing machine using the longest stitch length that is available. On the majority of fabrics two rows of gather stitches are required, but for very heavy fabrics it is advisable to make three rows. Try to stitch the rows so that the stitches line up under one another.

DIRECTORY OF GATHERS

GATHERS (p.135)

CORDED GATHERS (p.136)

SHIRRING (p.138)

WAFFLE SHIRRING (p.138)

CORDED SHIRRING (p.139)

SMOCKING (p.140)

HOW TO MAKE AND FIT GATHERS

Difficulty level ✱✱✱✱✱

Once all the main seams have been sewn, stitch the two rows of gathers so that the stitches are inside the seam allowance. This should avoid the need to remove them, because removing gathers after they have been pulled up can damage the fabric.

1 Sew one row of gathers at ⅜in (1cm) and the second row at ½in (1.2cm). Leave long tails of thread for gathering. Break the sewn lines at the seams.

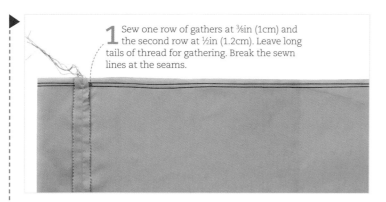

2 Place the piece to be gathered to the other garment section, right side to right side.

Other garment section

3 Match the notches and seams, and pin these first.

Section to be gathered

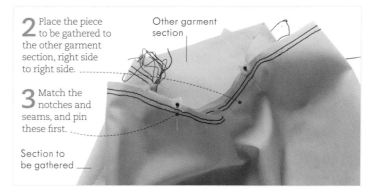

4 Gently pull on the two ends of the thread on the wrong side—the fabric will gather along the thread.

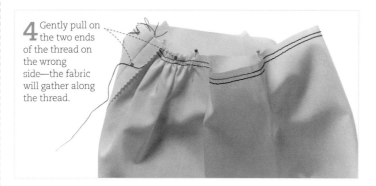

5 Secure the threads at the one end to prevent the stitches from pulling out.

6 Even out the gathers and pin.

7 When all the gathers are in place, use a standard machine stitch to sew a ⅝in (1.5cm) wide seam.

8 Sew with the gathers uppermost and keep pulling them to the side to stop them creasing up.

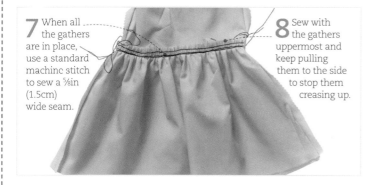

9 Turn the other garment section inside. Using a mini iron, press the seam very carefully to avoid creasing the gathers.

10 Neaten the seam by sewing both edges together. Use either a zigzag stitch or a 3-thread serger stitch.

11 Press the seam up.

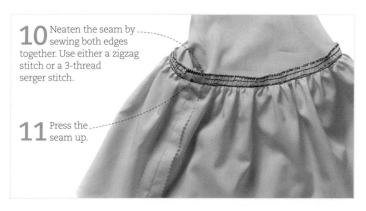

12 Press the gathers using the mini iron.

Seam pressed up

STITCHES MADE WITH A MACHINE pp.92–93 ● **HOW TO MAKE A PLAIN SEAM p.94**

CORDED GATHERS

Corded gathers are gathers that are pulled up over a narrow piping cord or thick thread. This technique is used for furnishing fabrics, where machine gathers may not be strong enough.

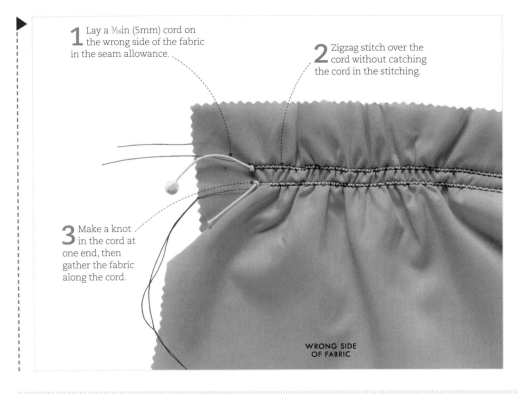

1 Lay a ³⁄₁₆in (5mm) cord on the wrong side of the fabric in the seam allowance.

2 Zigzag stitch over the cord without catching the cord in the stitching.

3 Make a knot in the cord at one end, then gather the fabric along the cord.

WRONG SIDE OF FABRIC

4 Turn to the right side to check that the gathers are even. Knot the other end of the cord.

RIGHT SIDE OF FABRIC

KEEP A GATHERED SEAM

A gathered seam is often kept gathered by sewing on cotton stay tape, to ensure the gathers remain in place and also to help strengthen the seam.

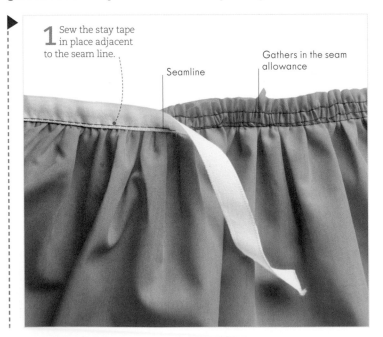

1 Sew the stay tape in place adjacent to the seam line.

Seamline

Gathers in the seam allowance

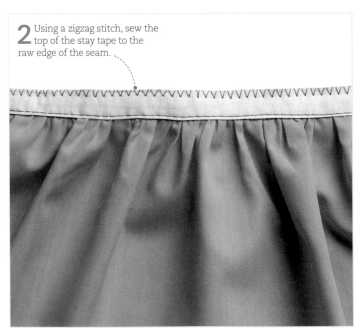

2 Using a zigzag stitch, sew the top of the stay tape to the raw edge of the seam.

JOINING TWO GATHERED EDGES TOGETHER

Difficulty level ✱✱✱✱✱

On some garments it may be necessary to join together two gathered edges. This usually happens when gathering a skirt on to a gathered bodice. The one side, usually the skirt, is gathered first on to a stay tape and the second side is gathered to fit, then sewn in place.

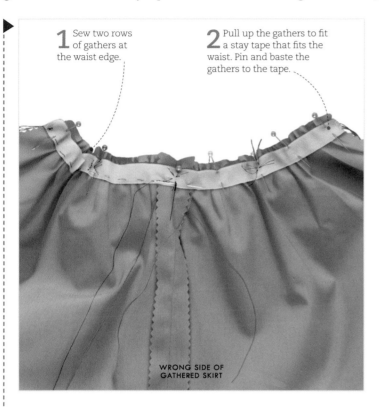

1 Sew two rows of gathers at the waist edge.

2 Pull up the gathers to fit a stay tape that fits the waist. Pin and baste the gathers to the tape.

WRONG SIDE OF GATHERED SKIRT

3 Sew two rows of gathers at the waist edge of the bodice.

4 Place the bodice waist, right side to right side, to the skirt waist, matching seams and notches.

5 Pull up the bodice gathers to fit the skirt.

6 Pin the two layers together.

Ungathered bodice

WRONG SIDE OF GATHERED SKIRT

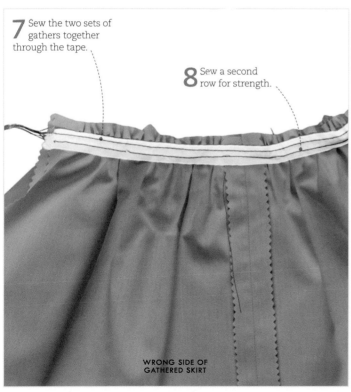

7 Sew the two sets of gathers together through the tape.

8 Sew a second row for strength.

WRONG SIDE OF GATHERED SKIRT

9 The waist of the bodice is now gathered to fit the skirt waist.

WRONG SIDE OF BODICE

INTERLININGS **p.324**

SHIRRING

Difficulty level ✷✷✴✴✴

Shirring is the name given to multiple rows of gathers. It is an excellent way to give fullness in a garment. If made using shirring elastic in the bobbin, shirring gathers can stretch. On heavier fabrics, such as for home goods, static shirring is more suitable.

▶ MACHINE SHIRRING

1 Hand wind shirring elastic on to the bobbin.

2 Insert the bobbin into the sewing machine and pull the elastic through the tension on the bobbin case. Use all-purpose thread on the top.

3 Set the machine to a stitch length of 5.0. Sew a row of stitches across the fabric.

4 Sew a second row of stitches, ⅝in (1.5cm) from seam. Make sure the sewing rows are parallel.

5 Continue sewing as many rows of shirring as required.

6 Knot the ends of the elastic together.

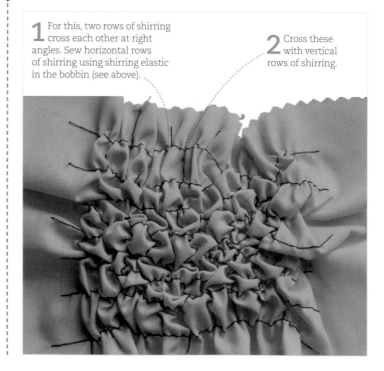

▶ WAFFLE SHIRRING

1 For this, two rows of shirring cross each other at right angles. Sew horizontal rows of shirring using shirring elastic in the bobbin (see above).

2 Cross these with vertical rows of shirring.

▶ **CORDED SHIRRING**

WRONG SIDE OF FABRIC

1 This is a way of shirring that is static. Fold the fabric right side to right side and sew a piece of piping cord into the fold made. Use the zipper foot, and sew ¹⁄₁₆in (2mm) from the cord.

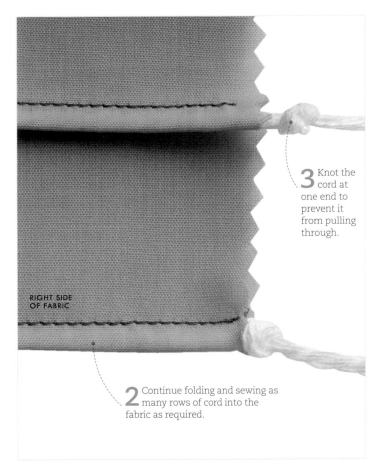

RIGHT SIDE OF FABRIC

3 Knot the cord at one end to prevent it from pulling through.

2 Continue folding and sewing as many rows of cord into the fabric as required.

4 Push the fabric along the cord to create the shirred gathers.

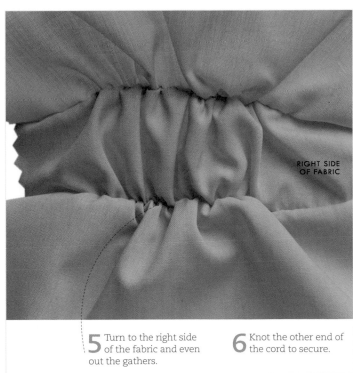

RIGHT SIDE OF FABRIC

5 Turn to the right side of the fabric and even out the gathers.

6 Knot the other end of the cord to secure.

SMOCKING

Difficulty level ★★★★★

Smocking is one of the oldest ways of gathering fabric. It is very decorative and can add interest to a garment. Smocking involves pulling up multiple rows of gathers that have been sewn in by hand, in line with each other, to produce fine tubes in the fabric. These tubes are then sewn over. Smocking dots that can be heat-transferred to the fabric are used as a guide for the hand gathers. Dots can be purchased with different spaces between them.

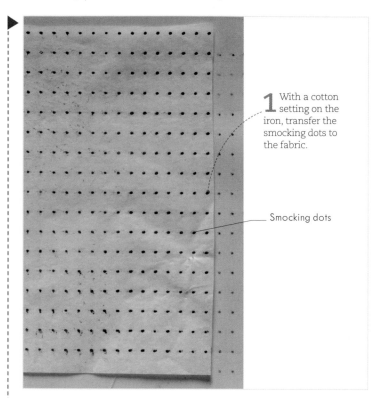

1 With a cotton setting on the iron, transfer the smocking dots to the fabric.

Smocking dots

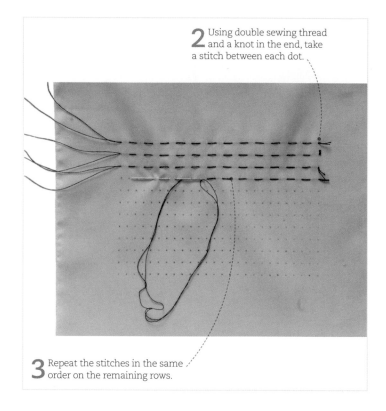

2 Using double sewing thread and a knot in the end, take a stitch between each dot.

3 Repeat the stitches in the same order on the remaining rows.

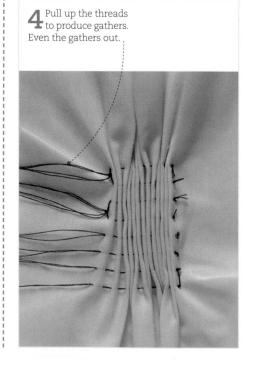

4 Pull up the threads to produce gathers. Even the gathers out.

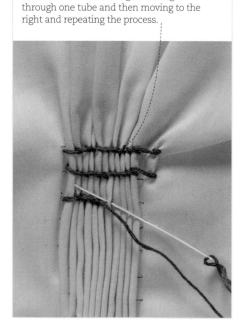

5 Sew across each tube using a back stitch. Work left to right, sewing through one tube and then moving to the right and repeating the process.

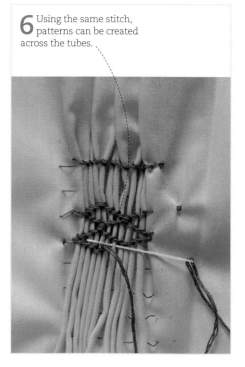

6 Using the same stitch, patterns can be created across the tubes.

SMOCKING FOR CUSHIONS

Smocking can be used in a much larger format to produce a decorative effect on cushions.
Patterns and templates can be purchased for this effect.

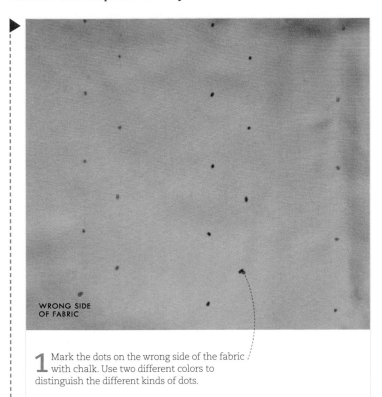

WRONG SIDE
OF FABRIC

1 Mark the dots on the wrong side of the fabric
with chalk. Use two different colors to
distinguish the different kinds of dots.

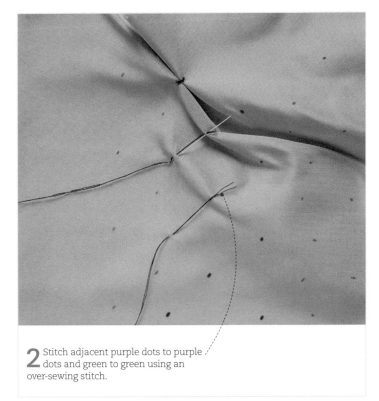

2 Stitch adjacent purple dots to purple
dots and green to green using an
over-sewing stitch.

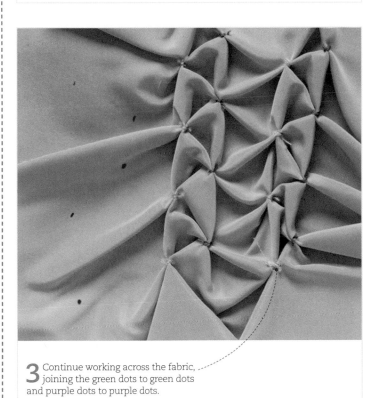

3 Continue working across the fabric,
joining the green dots to green dots
and purple dots to purple dots.

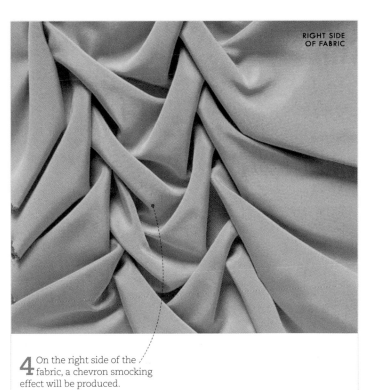

RIGHT SIDE
OF FABRIC

4 On the right side of the
fabric, a chevron smocking
effect will be produced.

HAND SEWING **pp.90–91**

RUFFLES

Ruffles can be single layer or double layer and are used to give a decorative gathered effect to a garment. The amount of fullness in a ruffle depends on the fabric used—to achieve a similar result, a fine, thin fabric will need twice the fullness of a thicker fabric.

DIRECTORY OF RUFFLES

PLAIN RUFFLE
(p.143)

RUFFLE WITH A HEADING
(p.143)

DOUBLE RUFFLE 1
(p.144)

DOUBLE RUFFLE 2
(p.144)

DOUBLE RUFFLE 3
(p.144)

CIRCULAR RUFFLE
(pp.148–149)

PLAIN RUFFLE

Difficulty level ✱✱✱✱

A plain ruffle is normally made from a single layer of fabric cut on the straight of the grain. The length of the fabric needs to be at least two and a half times the length of the seam into which it is to be inserted or of the edge to which it is to be attached. The width of the ruffle depends on where it is to be used.

▶

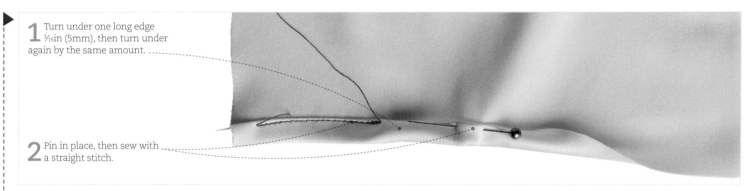

1 Turn under one long edge ³⁄₁₆in (5mm), then turn under again by the same amount.

2 Pin in place, then sew with a straight stitch.

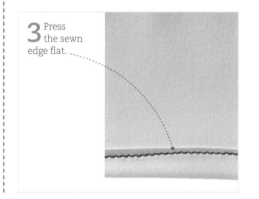

3 Press the sewn edge flat.

4 Place two rows of gather stitches along the raw edge—one row at ³⁄₈in (1cm) and the second row at ½in (1.2cm). Pull the threads to gather the fabric. The ruffle is now ready to be attached.

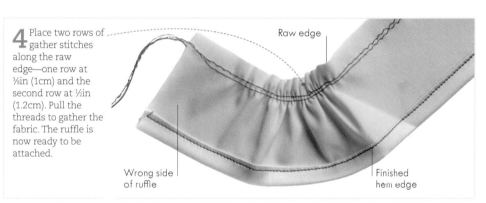

Raw edge

Wrong side of ruffle

Finished hem edge

GATHERED RUFFLE

Difficulty level ✱✱✱✱✱

This type of ruffle can give a decorative effect on clothing and home goods.

▶

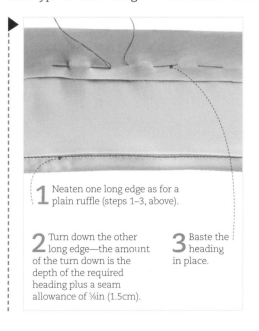

1 Neaten one long edge as for a plain ruffle (steps 1–3, above).

2 Turn down the other long edge—the amount of the turn down is the depth of the required heading plus a seam allowance of ⅝in (1.5cm).

3 Baste the heading in place.

Threads to pull up gathers

Basting stitches

4 Insert the two rows of gather stitches.

5 Pull up the stitches to make the gathers.

6 After gathering, there will be gathers with a ruffle on one side of the stitch line and a short gathered heading on the other. Pull out the basting stitches.

HOW TO MAKE AND FIT GATHERS p.135

DOUBLE RUFFLE VERSION 1

This is a great ruffle on fine fabrics as it can be highly decorative. Attach the ruffle to the garment by stitching through the center of the gather lines.

Difficulty level ✱✱✱✱✱

1 Neaten both long edges by turning the fabric once and then again, and sewing (see Plain ruffle, steps 1–3, page 135).

WRONG SIDE OF FABRIC

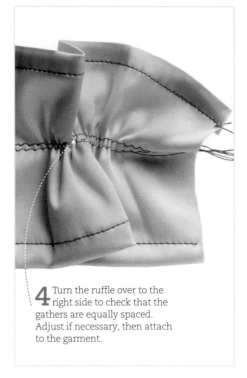

2 Work two rows of gather stitches lengthwise down the center of the fabric.

3 Pull up the gather stitches to create a ruffle to fit.

4 Turn the ruffle over to the right side to check that the gathers are equally spaced. Adjust if necessary, then attach to the garment.

DOUBLE RUFFLE VERSION 2

Difficulty level ✱✱✱✱✱

This ruffle has one side longer than the other and is fashioned from two plain ruffles.

1 Cut two pieces of fabric for the ruffle, one wider than the other. Neaten one long edge of each piece (see Plain ruffle, steps 1–3, page 135).

2 Pin the pieces of fabric together along the raw edges, right sides up, making sure the shorter piece is on the top.

3 Insert two rows of gather stitches through the two layers.

4 Pull the threads to gather the double ruffle to fit.

DOUBLE RUFFLE VERSION 3

Difficulty level ✱✱✱✱✱

This is a useful ruffle on a fabric that is prone to fraying.

1 Cut the fabric for the ruffle twice the required depth.

2 Fold the fabric lengthwise, wrong side to wrong side.

3 Pin the raw edges together.

4 Insert gathers along the raw edge.

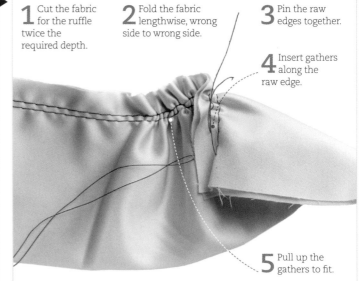

5 Pull up the gathers to fit.

SEWING INTO A SEAM

Once the ruffle has been constructed it can either be inserted into a seam or attached to the edge of the fabric (see page 138). The two techniques below apply to both single and double ruffles.

Difficulty level ★★☆☆☆

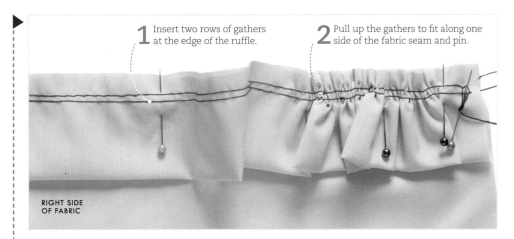

1 Insert two rows of gathers at the edge of the ruffle.

2 Pull up the gathers to fit along one side of the fabric seam and pin.

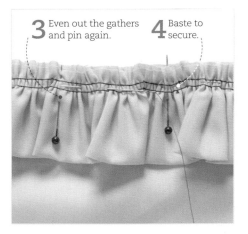

3 Even out the gathers and pin again.

4 Baste to secure.

RIGHT SIDE OF FABRIC

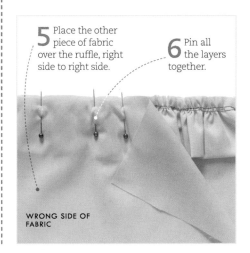

5 Place the other piece of fabric over the ruffle, right side to right side.

6 Pin all the layers together.

7 Sew through all the layers using a ⅝ in (1.5 cm) seam allowance.

8 Layer the seam.

9 Turn the fabric and ruffle through to the right side.

WRONG SIDE OF FABRIC

WRONG SIDE OF FABRIC

RIGHT SIDE OF FABRIC

SEWING AROUND A CORNER

Difficulty level ★★★★☆

It can be difficult to sew a ruffle to a corner and achieve a sharp point. It is easier to fit the gathers into a tight curve, which can be done as the ruffle is being applied to the corner.

1 Pull up the gathers to fit along one side of the fabric seam and pin in place.

2 Fit the gathers into a tight curve at the corner.

3 Sew the ruffle in place.

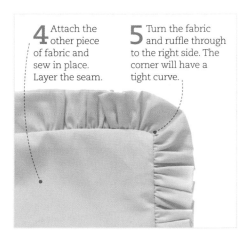

4 Attach the other piece of fabric and sew in place. Layer the seam.

5 Turn the fabric and ruffle through to the right side. The corner will have a tight curve.

SEWING A RUFFLE TO AN EDGE

Difficulty level ✳✳✳✳✳

If a ruffle is not in a seam then it will be attached to an edge. The edge of the seam will require neatening, which is often best done by using a binding method as it is more discreet. A self-bound edge, where the seam is wrapped on to itself, is suitable for fine, delicate fabrics. For thicker fabrics, use a bias binding to finish the edge.

▶ **SELF-BOUND FINISH**

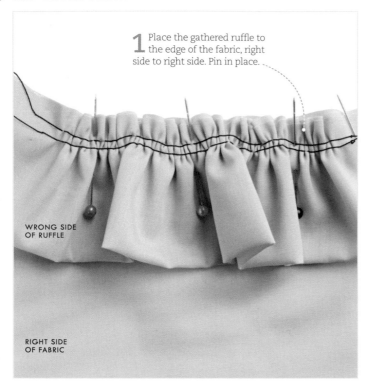

1 Place the gathered ruffle to the edge of the fabric, right side to right side. Pin in place.

WRONG SIDE OF RUFFLE

RIGHT SIDE OF FABRIC

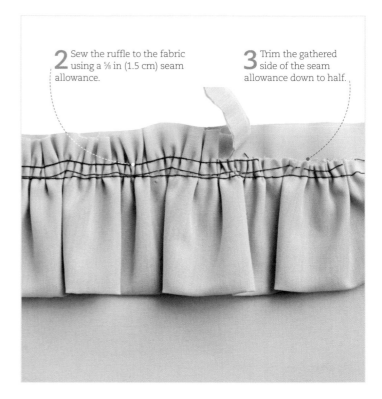

2 Sew the ruffle to the fabric using a ⅝ in (1.5 cm) seam allowance.

3 Trim the gathered side of the seam allowance down to half.

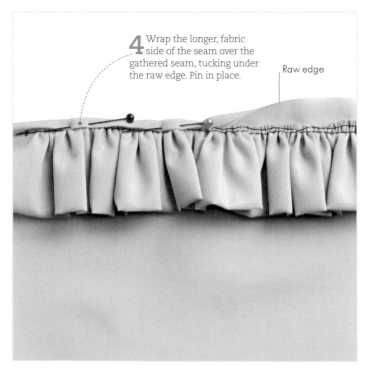

4 Wrap the longer, fabric side of the seam over the gathered seam, tucking under the raw edge. Pin in place.

Raw edge

WRONG SIDE OF FABRIC

5 Sew the wrapped seam to secure. Make sure it is attached to the seam only.

▶ **BIAS-BOUND FINISH**

1 Sew the gathered ruffle to the edge of the fabric, right side to right side, using a ⅝ in (1.5 cm) seam allowance (see steps 1 and 2, opposite).

2 Use ¾ in (2 cm) wide bias binding. Sew the crease in the bias over the ruffle stitches.

3 Trim back both sides of the seam allowance.

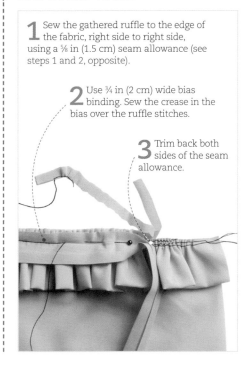

4 Wrap the bias over to the wrong side of the seam. Pin in place.

WRONG SIDE OF FABRIC

5 Sew the other side of the bias close to the fold.

RIGHT SIDE OF FABRIC

ATTACHING A DOUBLE RUFFLE TO AN EDGE

Difficulty level ✹✹✹✹✹

This is a very neat way to attach a double ruffle to an edge as the seam is hidden. The ruffle is sewn first to the wrong side of the work and then folded on to the right side.

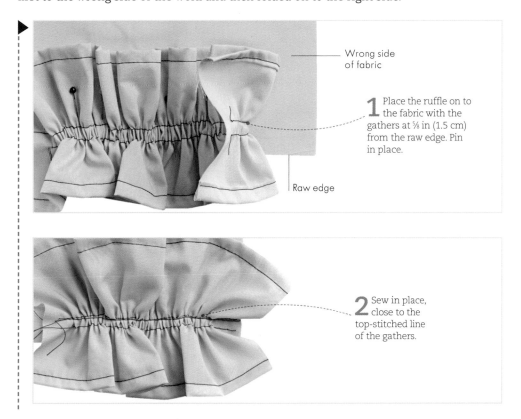

Wrong side of fabric

1 Place the ruffle on to the fabric with the gathers at ⅝ in (1.5 cm) from the raw edge. Pin in place.

Raw edge

2 Sew in place, close to the top-stitched line of the gathers.

3 Turn the ruffle to the right side of the fabric. Trim away half the seam allowance behind the ruffle.

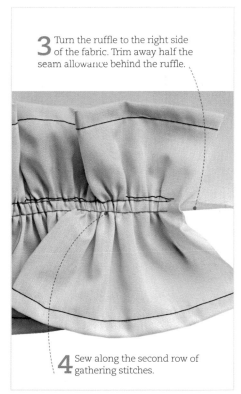

4 Sew along the second row of gathering stitches.

BIAS-BOUND HEMS **p.272**

CIRCULAR RUFFLE

Difficulty level ★★★★✴

A ruffle can be cut using a circular shape. The advantage is that there are no gathers because the center part of the circle is cut out to make a seam. The fullness occurs as the inner edge of the circle is stretched and attached. For a circular ruffle you will need a pattern.

MAKING THE PATTERN FOR A CIRCULAR RUFFLE

1 You'll need pattern paper to cut your circle and a compass created from a pencil with a piece of string tied on to it.

2 Draw an inner circle, the circumference of which will be the length of the seam into which the ruffle is to be attached. You can join several ruffles together to achieve this measurement.

3 Draw a smaller circle ⅝in (1.5cm) inside the inner circle. This is the seam allowance for the edge where the ruffle will be attached.

4 From the seamline, measure out the depth of the ruffle, then draw to make another circle.

5 Cut out the larger circle, then cut out the inner circle. Cut through the pattern, from the outer edge to the inner edge.

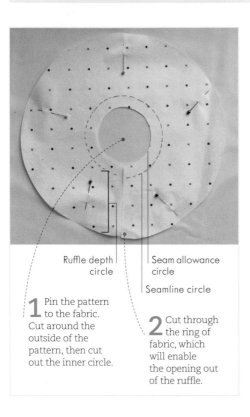

Ruffle depth circle
Seam allowance circle
Seamline circle

1 Pin the pattern to the fabric. Cut around the outside of the pattern, then cut out the inner circle.

2 Cut through the ring of fabric, which will enable the opening out of the ruffle.

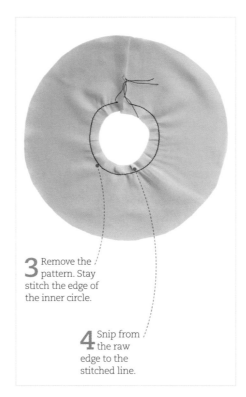

3 Remove the pattern. Stay stitch the edge of the inner circle.

4 Snip from the raw edge to the stitched line.

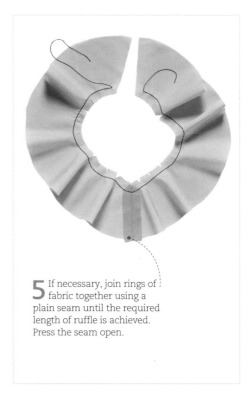

5 If necessary, join rings of fabric together using a plain seam until the required length of ruffle is achieved. Press the seam open.

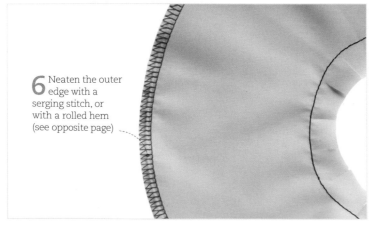

6 Neaten the outer edge with a serging stitch, or with a rolled hem (see opposite page)

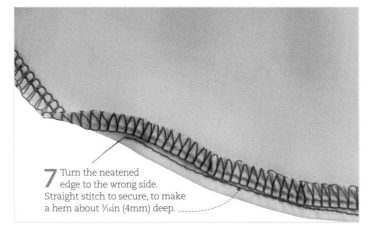

7 Turn the neatened edge to the wrong side. Straight stitch to secure, to make a hem about 3⁄16in (4mm) deep.

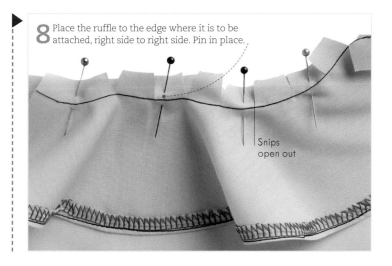

8 Place the ruffle to the edge where it is to be attached, right side to right side. Pin in place.

Snips open out

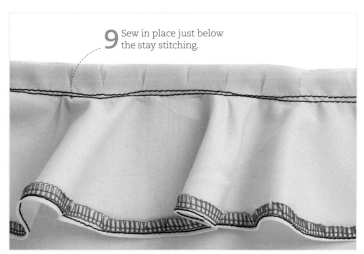

9 Sew in place just below the stay stitching.

NEATENING THE RUFFLE EDGE WITH A ROLLED HEM

An alternative way to neaten the outer edge is to use the sewing machine with the rolled hem foot and a straight stitch.

Another alternative is a rolled hem on the sewing machine using the rolled hem foot and a zigzag stitch.

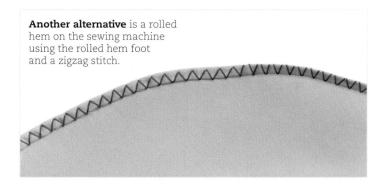

DOUBLE CIRCULAR RUFFLE

Difficulty level ★★★★★

On very lightweight fabrics such as chiffon or silk, it is advisable to make a double-layer ruffle as it will hang better. With this method there is no edge to neaten.

1 Cut two circular ruffles (see opposite) and join them together, right side to right side. Pin to secure.

2 Sew the outer edges together with a ⅝in (1.5cm) seam allowance. Continue sewing along the short ends.

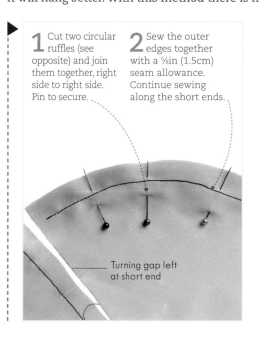

Turning gap left at short end

3 Trim down one half of the seam allowance.

4 Cut out V shapes to reduce the bulk.

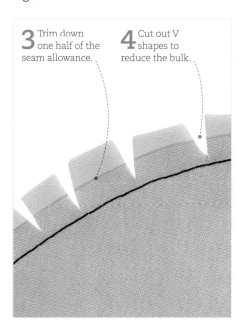

5 Turn through to the right side, pushing out the corners. Press.

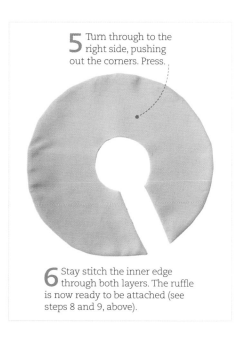

6 Stay stitch the inner edge through both layers. The ruffle is now ready to be attached (see steps 8 and 9, above).

STITCHING CORNERS AND CURVES **pp.102–103** • REDUCING SEAM BULK **pp.108–109**

FACINGS AND NECKLINES

Edges on garments are often neatened by means of a facing. This is a shaped piece of fabric, which may be stiffened with interfacing, attached to the inside of a neckline—or to an armhole or at a waist edge—for a strong finish.

FACINGS AND NECKLINES

The simplest way to finish the neck or armhole of a garment is to apply a facing. The neckline can be any shape to have a facing applied, from a curve to a square to a V, and many more. Some facings and necklines can add interest to the center back or center front of a garment.

DIRECTORY OF NECKLINES

ROUND NECKLINE
(p.156)

SQUARE NECKLINE
(p.156)

V-NECK
(p.156)

SWEETHEART NECKLINE (p.156)

SLASHED NECKLINE
(p.157)

BOUND NECK EDGE
(p.160)

PIPED NECKLINE
(p.154)

SLASHED NECKLINE WITH PLACKETS (p.163)

V-NECK WITH BANDING (p.165)

APPLYING INTERFACING TO A FACING

Difficulty level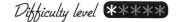

All facings require interfacing. The interfacing is to give structure to the facing and to hold it in shape. A fusible interfacing is the best choice and it should be cut on the same grain as the facing. Choose an interfacing that is lighter in weight than the main fabric.

▶ **INTERFACING FOR HEAVY FABRIC**

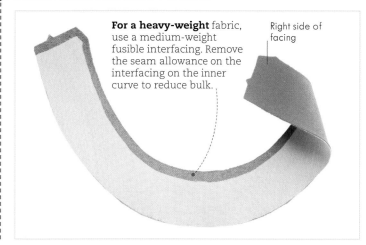

For a heavy-weight fabric, use a medium-weight fusible interfacing. Remove the seam allowance on the interfacing on the inner curve to reduce bulk.

Right side of facing

▶ **INTERFACING FOR LIGHT FABRIC**

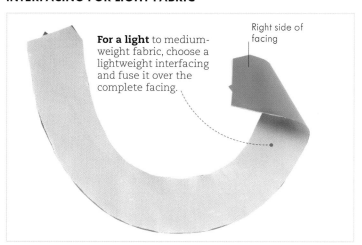

For a light to medium-weight fabric, choose a lightweight interfacing and fuse it over the complete facing.

Right side of facing

CONSTRUCTION OF A FACING

Difficulty level ✱✱✱✱

The facing may be in two or three pieces in order to fit around a neck or armhole edge. The facing sections need to be joined together prior to being attached. The photographs here show an interfaced neck facing in three pieces.

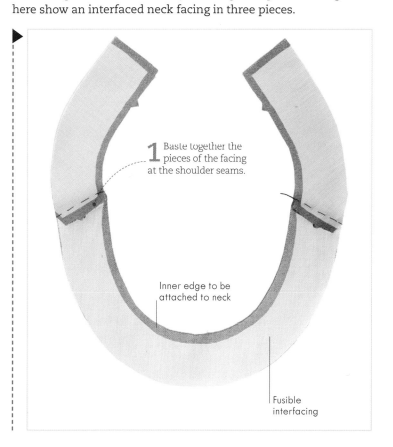

1 Baste together the pieces of the facing at the shoulder seams.

Inner edge to be attached to neck

Fusible interfacing

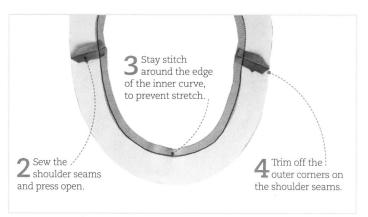

3 Stay stitch around the edge of the inner curve, to prevent stretch.

2 Sew the shoulder seams and press open.

4 Trim off the outer corners on the shoulder seams.

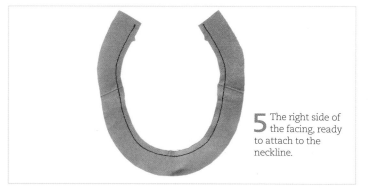

5 The right side of the facing, ready to attach to the neckline.

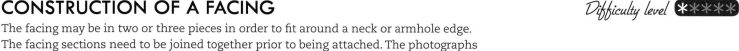

STITCHES MADE WITH A MACHINE pp.92–93

NEATENING THE EDGE OF A FACING

Difficulty level ❋❋✳✳✳

The outer edge of a facing will require neatening to prevent it from fraying, and there are several ways to do this. Binding the lower edge of a facing with a bias strip makes the garment a little more luxurious and can add a designer touch inside the garment. Alternatively, the edge can be sewn or pinked (see opposite page).

▶ **HOW TO CUT BIAS STRIPS**

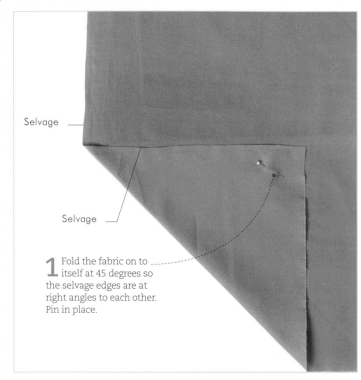

Selvage

Selvage

1 Fold the fabric on to itself at 45 degrees so the selvage edges are at right angles to each other. Pin in place.

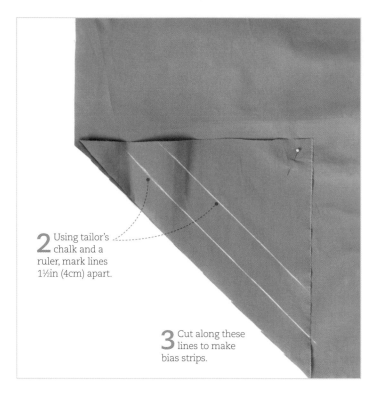

2 Using tailor's chalk and a ruler, mark lines 1½in (4cm) apart.

3 Cut along these lines to make bias strips.

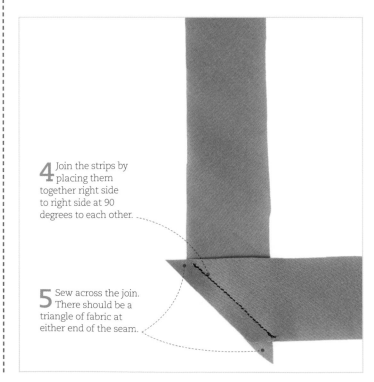

4 Join the strips by placing them together right side to right side at 90 degrees to each other.

5 Sew across the join. There should be a triangle of fabric at either end of the seam.

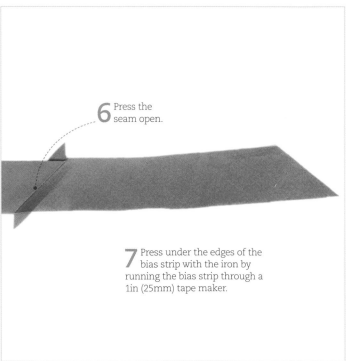

6 Press the seam open.

7 Press under the edges of the bias strip with the iron by running the bias strip through a 1in (25mm) tape maker.

TECHNIQUES

▶ NEATENING AN EDGE WITH A BIAS STRIP

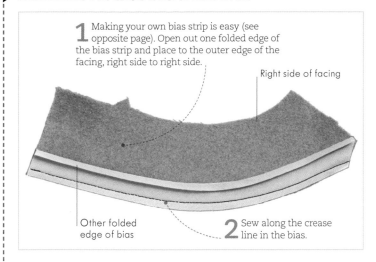

1 Making your own bias strip is easy (see opposite page). Open out one folded edge of the bias strip and place to the outer edge of the facing, right side to right side.

Right side of facing

Other folded edge of bias

2 Sew along the crease line in the bias.

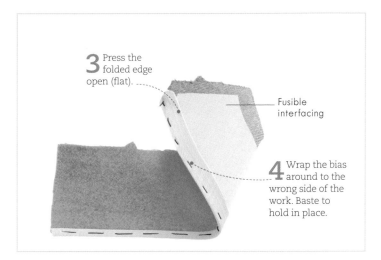

3 Press the folded edge open (flat).

Fusible interfacing

4 Wrap the bias around to the wrong side of the work. Baste to hold in place.

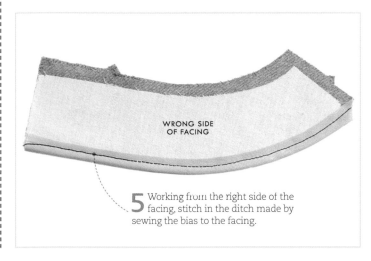

WRONG SIDE OF FACING

5 Working from the right side of the facing, stitch in the ditch made by sewing the bias to the facing.

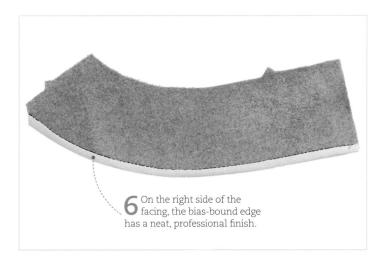

6 On the right side of the facing, the bias-bound edge has a neat, professional finish.

OTHER NEATENING METHODS

Difficulty level

The following techniques are alternative popular ways to neaten the edge of a facing. The one you choose depends upon the garment being made and the fabric used.

▶ SERGED

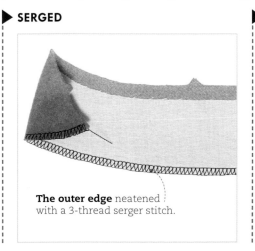

The outer edge neatened with a 3-thread serger stitch.

▶ PINKED

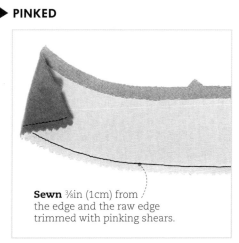

Sewn ⅜in (1cm) from the edge and the raw edge trimmed with pinking shears.

▶ ZIGZAG

The outer edge neatened with a zigzag stitch.

BASTING STITCHES **p.89** • STITCHES MADE WITH A MACHINE **pp.92–93**

ATTACHING A NECK FACING

This technique applies to all shapes of neckline, from round to square to sweetheart.

Difficulty level ★★★★★

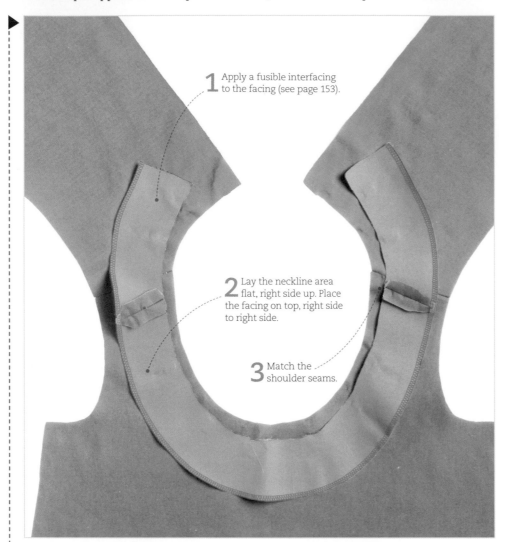

1 Apply a fusible interfacing to the facing (see page 153).

2 Lay the neckline area flat, right side up. Place the facing on top, right side to right side.

3 Match the shoulder seams.

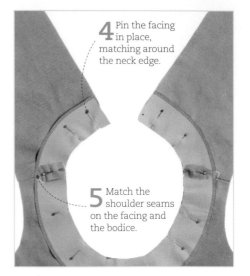

4 Pin the facing in place, matching around the neck edge.

5 Match the shoulder seams on the facing and the bodice.

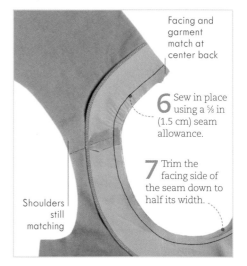

Facing and garment match at center back

6 Sew in place using a ⅝ in (1.5 cm) seam allowance.

7 Trim the facing side of the seam down to half its width.

Shoulders still matching

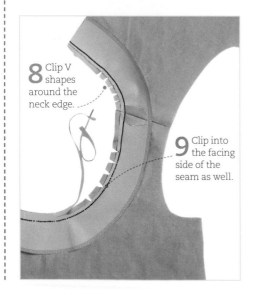

8 Clip V shapes around the neck edge.

9 Clip into the facing side of the seam as well.

10 Press the seam allowance toward the facing.

11 Understitch by sewing the seam allowance down on to the facing about ³⁄₁₆ in (5 mm) from the sewn line.

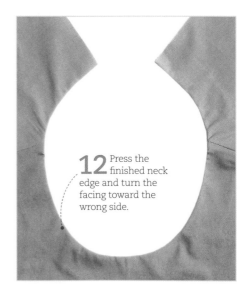

12 Press the finished neck edge and turn the facing toward the wrong side.

HOW TO APPLY A FUSIBLE INTERFACING p.54 • **PATTERN MARKING pp.82–83** • **STITCHES MADE WITH A MACHINE pp.92–93**

FACING A SLASHED V-NECKLINE

A slashed V-neckline occurs at either the center front or the center back neck edge. It enables a close-fitting neckline to open sufficiently to go over the head.

Difficulty level ★★★★★

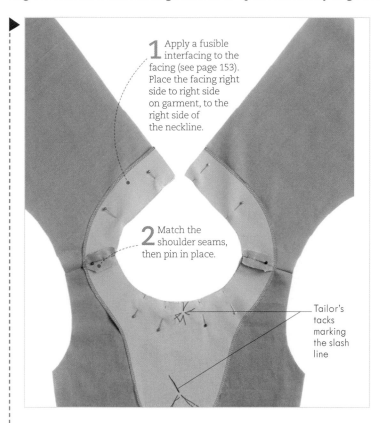

1 Apply a fusible interfacing to the facing (see page 153). Place the facing right side to right side on garment, to the right side of the neckline.

2 Match the shoulder seams, then pin in place.

Tailor's tacks marking the slash line

3 Sew the facing at the neck edge, pivoting to sew along both sides of the slash between the tailor's tacks. Take one stitch horizontally at the bottom edge of the slash line.

4 Trim the facing side of the seam down to half.

5 Clip V shapes at the neck edge to reduce the bulk.

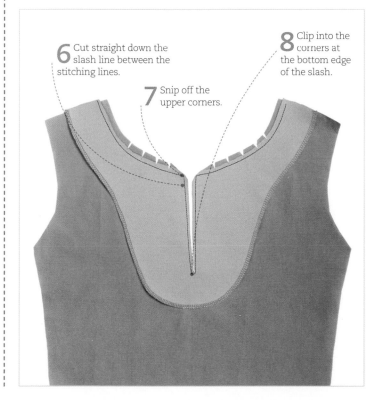

6 Cut straight down the slash line between the stitching lines.

7 Snip off the upper corners.

8 Clip into the corners at the bottom edge of the slash.

9 Turn the facing to the inside of the neckline and press.

TECHNIQUES

ARMHOLE FACING

Difficulty level ★★✱✱✱

On sleeveless garments, a facing is an excellent way of neatening an armhole because it is not bulky. Also, as the facing is made in the same fabric as the garment, it does not show.

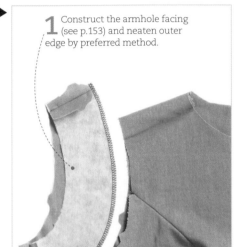

1 Construct the armhole facing (see p.153) and neaten outer edge by preferred method.

Armhole

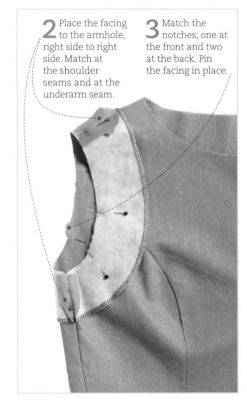

2 Place the facing to the armhole, right side to right side. Match at the shoulder seams and at the underarm seam.

3 Match the notches, one at the front and two at the back. Pin the facing in place.

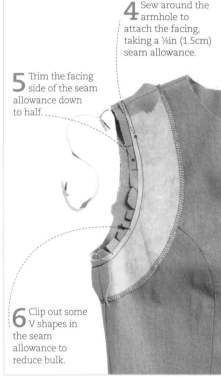

4 Sew around the armhole to attach the facing, taking a ⅝in (1.5cm) seam allowance.

5 Trim the facing side of the seam allowance down to half.

6 Clip out some V shapes in the seam allowance to reduce bulk.

7 Turn the facing into position on the wrong side. Understitch by pressing the seam allowance on to the facing and sewing down.

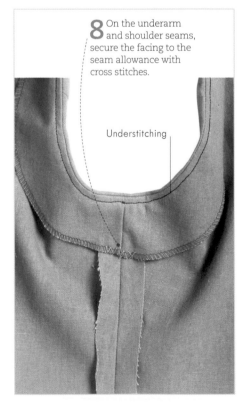

8 On the underarm and shoulder seams, secure the facing to the seam allowance with cross stitches.

Understitching

9 Press the stitched edge. On the right side, the armhole will have a neat finish.

◀
◀ **HOW TO APPLY A FUSIBLE INTERFACING p.54**

COMBINATION NECK AND ARMHOLE FACING

Difficulty level ★★★★★

This type of facing neatens the neck and the armhole edge at the same time. It needs to be stitched in place before the center back seam or the side seams are constructed.

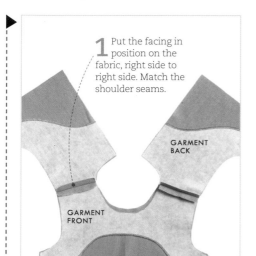

1 Put the facing in position on the fabric, right side to right side. Match the shoulder seams.

GARMENT BACK

GARMENT FRONT

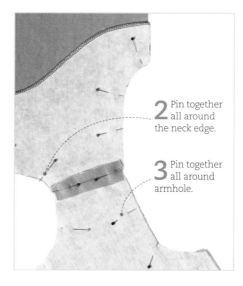

2 Pin together all around the neck edge.

3 Pin together all around armhole.

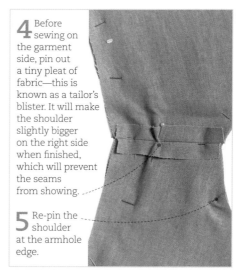

4 Before sewing on the garment side, pin out a tiny pleat of fabric—this is known as a tailor's blister. It will make the shoulder slightly bigger on the right side when finished, which will prevent the seams from showing.

5 Re-pin the shoulder at the armhole edge.

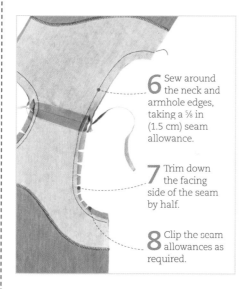

6 Sew around the neck and armhole edges, taking a ⅝ in (1.5 cm) seam allowance.

7 Trim down the facing side of the seam by half.

8 Clip the seam allowances as required.

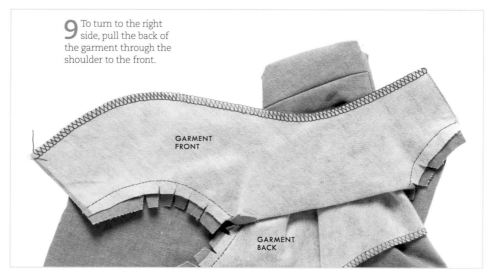

9 To turn to the right side, pull the back of the garment through the shoulder to the front.

GARMENT FRONT

GARMENT BACK

10 Press the completed neck and armhole facing on the right side.

11 To join the side seams, place the facing and sides together, right side to right side. Match the seam at the underarm.

12 Sew the facing and side together in one continuous seam. Press the seam open.

13 The faced neckline and armholes from the right side.

REDUCING SEAM BULK **pp.108–109** ● APPLYING INTERFACING TO A FACING **p.153**

EXTENDED FACING

Difficulty level ❋❋❋❋❋

A facing is not always a separate unit. Many garments, especially blouses, feature what is known as extended facing, which is where the facing is an extension of the front of the garment, cut out at the same time.

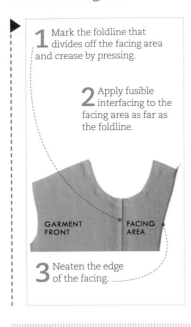

1 Mark the foldline that divides off the facing area and crease by pressing.

2 Apply fusible interfacing to the facing area as far as the foldline.

3 Neaten the edge of the facing.

GARMENT FRONT / FACING AREA

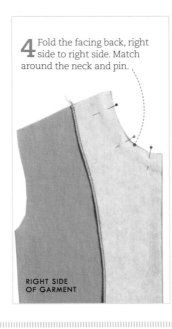

4 Fold the facing back, right side to right side. Match around the neck and pin.

RIGHT SIDE OF GARMENT

5 Sew around the neck edge to join the facing to the garment.

6 Trim the facing side of the seam and clip the seam allowance.

7 Turn through to the right side and press.

BOUND NECK EDGE

Difficulty level ❋❋❋❋❋

Binding is an excellent way to finish a raw neck edge. It has the added advantage of being a method that can be used if you are short of fabric or you would like a contrast or decorative finish. You can use bought bias tape or a bias strip cut from the same or a contrasting fabric (see p.154). A double bias strip is used on fine fabrics.

▶ **BIAS-BOUND NECK EDGE VERSION 1**

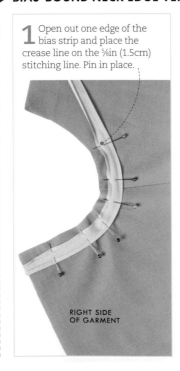

1 Open out one edge of the bias strip and place the crease line on the ⅝in (1.5cm) stitching line. Pin in place.

RIGHT SIDE OF GARMENT

2 Sew in place along the crease line.

3 Trim away the surplus fabric from the seam allowance.

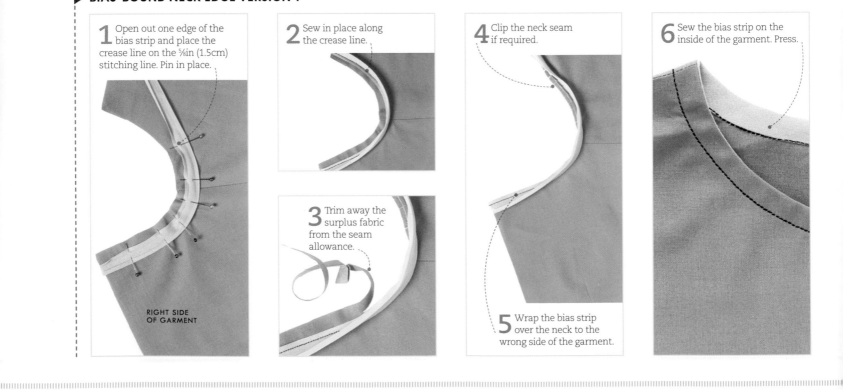

4 Clip the neck seam if required.

5 Wrap the bias strip over the neck to the wrong side of the garment.

6 Sew the bias strip on the inside of the garment. Press.

▶ BIAS-BOUND NECK EDGE VERSION 2

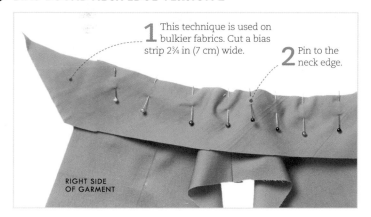

1 This technique is used on bulkier fabrics. Cut a bias strip 2¾ in (7 cm) wide.

2 Pin to the neck edge.

RIGHT SIDE OF GARMENT

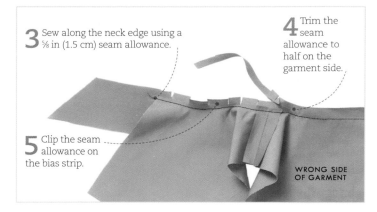

3 Sew along the neck edge using a ⅝ in (1.5 cm) seam allowance.

4 Trim the seam allowance to half on the garment side.

5 Clip the seam allowance on the bias strip.

WRONG SIDE OF GARMENT

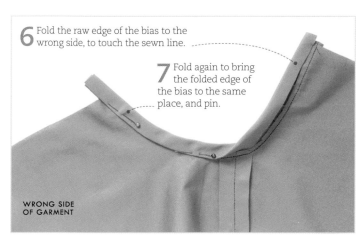

6 Fold the raw edge of the bias to the wrong side, to touch the sewn line.

7 Fold again to bring the folded edge of the bias to the same place, and pin.

WRONG SIDE OF GARMENT

8 Sew permanently in position using a flat fell stitch.

RIGHT SIDE OF GARMENT

▶ DOUBLE BIAS-BOUND NECK EDGE

1 Cut a bias strip 2⅜ in (6 cm) wide. Press in half.

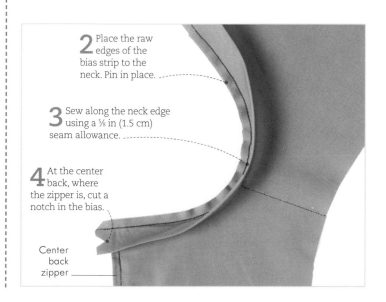

2 Place the raw edges of the bias strip to the neck. Pin in place.

3 Sew along the neck edge using a ⅝ in (1.5 cm) seam allowance.

4 At the center back, where the zipper is, cut a notch in the bias.

Center back zipper

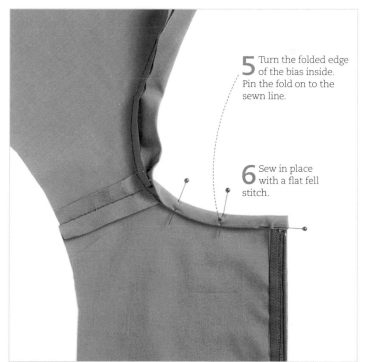

5 Turn the folded edge of the bias inside. Pin the fold on to the sewn line.

6 Sew in place with a flat fell stitch.

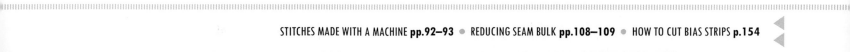

STITCHES MADE WITH A MACHINE **pp.92–93** ● REDUCING SEAM BULK **pp.108–109** ● HOW TO CUT BIAS STRIPS **p.154**

PIPED NECK EDGE

Difficulty level ★★✦✦✦

This technique features a piping around the neck as well as a facing. A piped neckline looks very good on special-occasion wear.

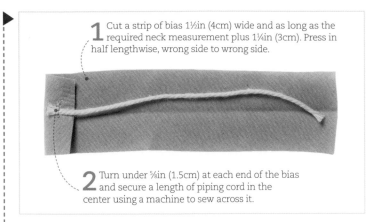

1 Cut a strip of bias 1½in (4cm) wide and as long as the required neck measurement plus 1¼in (3cm). Press in half lengthwise, wrong side to wrong side.

2 Turn under ⅝in (1.5cm) at each end of the bias and secure a length of piping cord in the center using a machine to sew across it.

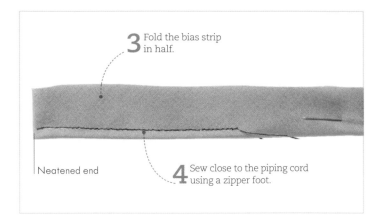

3 Fold the bias strip in half.

Neatened end

4 Sew close to the piping cord using a zipper foot.

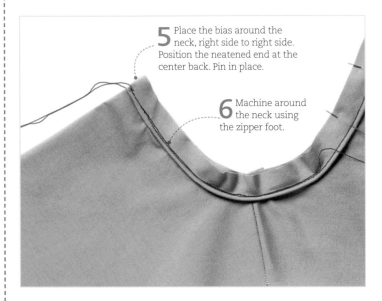

5 Place the bias around the neck, right side to right side. Position the neatened end at the center back. Pin in place.

6 Machine around the neck using the zipper foot.

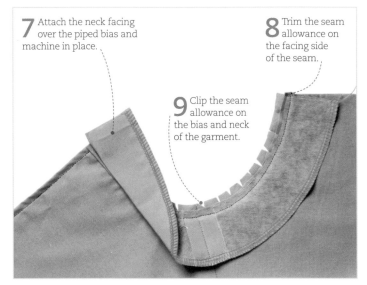

7 Attach the neck facing over the piped bias and machine in place.

8 Trim the seam allowance on the facing side of the seam.

9 Clip the seam allowance on the bias and neck of the garment.

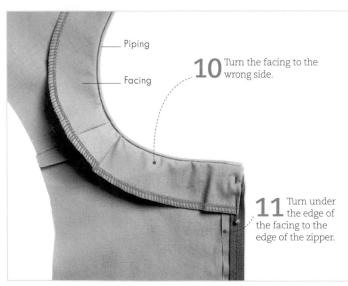

Piping

Facing

10 Turn the facing to the wrong side.

11 Turn under the edge of the facing to the edge of the zipper.

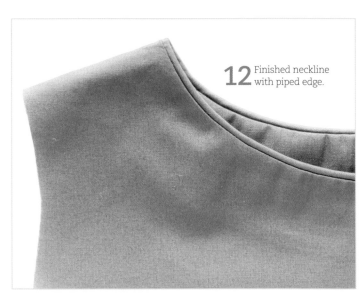

12 Finished neckline with piped edge.

TECHNIQUES

PLACKETS

A placket is an opening that stops partway down a bodice. It is made by applying two separate bands of fabric to the bodice. Care must be taken to ensure that the pattern pieces are accurately marked. A placket opening is popular on sportswear.

1 Cut two placket bands and apply fusible interfacing.

2 On the center front of the bodice, use trace basting to mark the sewing lines on either side of the opening.

3 Stay stitch along the lines.

4 Slash the seam allowance into the corners. Mark the stop points with tailor's tacks.

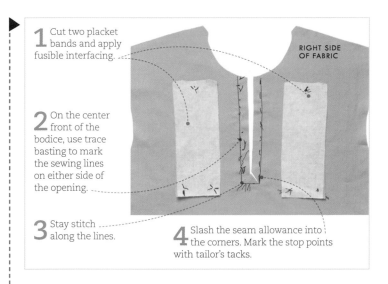

RIGHT SIDE OF FABRIC

5 Sew one placket to one side of the opening, right side to right side. Stop sewing at the given point.

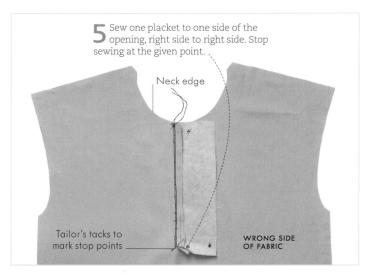

Neck edge

Tailor's tacks to mark stop points

WRONG SIDE OF FABRIC

6 Repeat with the other placket, sewing it on to the other side of the opening.

7 Trim the placket side of the seam down on both plackets.

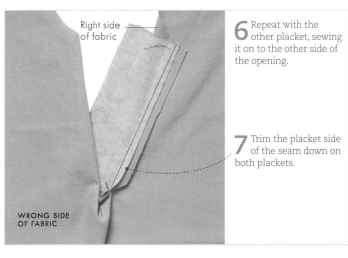

Right side of fabric

WRONG SIDE OF FABRIC

8 Fold each placket in half on to itself. Turn under the raw edge and pin to the sewn line.

9 At the bottom edge, the right hand placket is under the left hand placket.

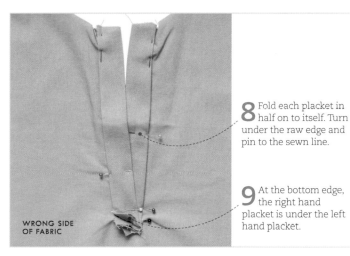

WRONG SIDE OF FABRIC

10 Hand sew the turned-under edge of each placket.

11 Sew the plackets together at the bottom edge. Bottom of placket can then be pinked or zigzagged.

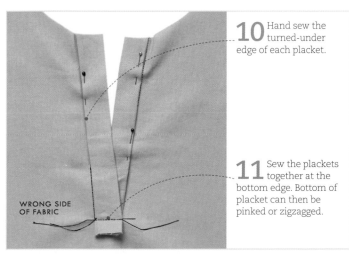

WRONG SIDE OF FABRIC

12 Turn to the right side and press.

RIGHT SIDE OF FABRIC

STITCHES MADE WITH A MACHINE **pp.92–93** ● REDUCING SEAM BULK **pp.108–109** ● HOW TO CUT BIAS STRIPS **p.154**

TECHNIQUES

NECKLINES IN STRETCH KNITS

Difficulty level ✷✷✷✷✷

When working with a stretch knit fabric, the neckline can be finished with a single banding or a more decorative double banding. The banding is usually attached with a 4-thread serger stitch, which enables the neck to stretch over the head. If you do not have a serger, you can use a 3-step zigzag stitch on the sewing machine.

▶ SINGLE BANDING WITH SERGER

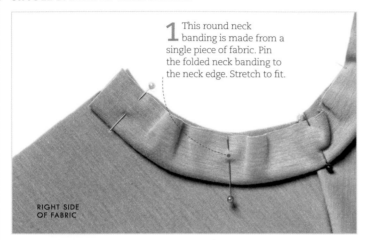

1 This round neck banding is made from a single piece of fabric. Pin the folded neck banding to the neck edge. Stretch to fit.

RIGHT SIDE OF FABRIC

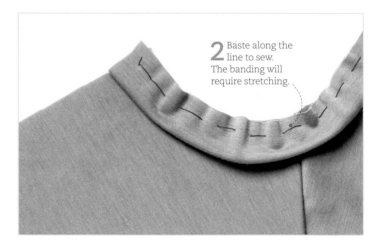

2 Baste along the line to sew. The banding will require stretching.

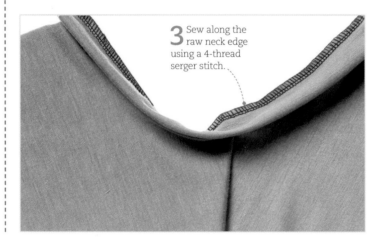

3 Sew along the raw neck edge using a 4-thread serger stitch.

4 When the garment is constructed, this is how the neckline will look on the right side.

▶ DOUBLE BANDING WITH SERGER

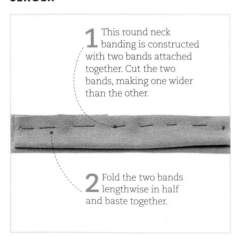

1 This round neck banding is constructed with two bands attached together. Cut the two bands, making one wider than the other.

2 Fold the two bands lengthwise in half and baste together.

3 Attach to the neckline as for a single band (see above), with the wider banding against the neck.

▶ ATTACHING BANDING WITH A SEWING MACHINE

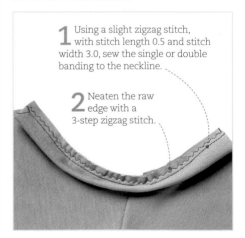

1 Using a slight zigzag stitch, with stitch length 0.5 and stitch width 3.0, sew the single or double banding to the neckline.

2 Neaten the raw edge with a 3-step zigzag stitch.

► BANDING FOR A V NECK

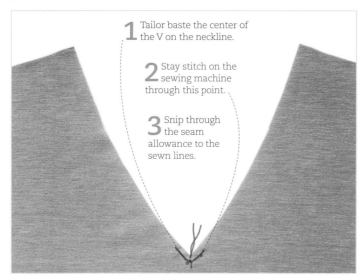

1 Tailor baste the center of the V on the neckline.

2 Stay stitch on the sewing machine through this point.

3 Snip through the seam allowance to the sewn lines.

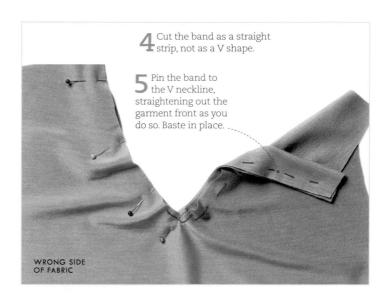

4 Cut the band as a straight strip, not as a V shape.

5 Pin the band to the V neckline, straightening out the garment front as you do so. Baste in place.

WRONG SIDE OF FABRIC

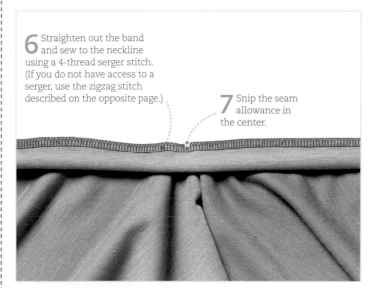

6 Straighten out the band and sew to the neckline using a 4-thread serger stitch. (If you do not have access to a serger, use the zigzag stitch described on the opposite page.)

7 Snip the seam allowance in the center.

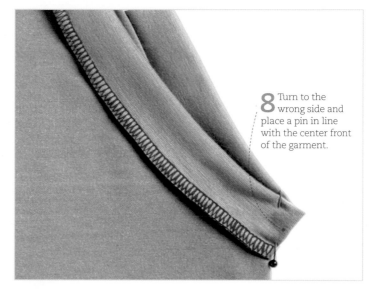

8 Turn to the wrong side and place a pin in line with the center front of the garment.

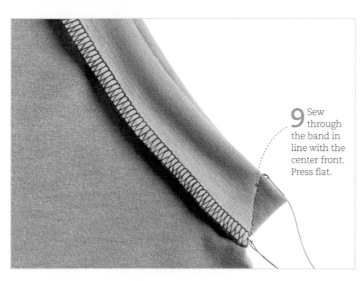

9 Sew through the band in line with the center front. Press flat.

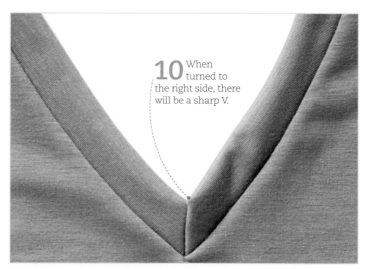

10 When turned to the right side, there will be a sharp V.

A-LINE **SHIFT DRESS**

Difficulty level ★★★★★

With its simple, easy silhouette, this dress will suit all figures. This is a great project for practicing garment construction—you'll use lots of key techniques such as making darts, pockets, and attaching a zipper and facings. Use a wool fabric for a winter dress, or a light cotton or linen fabric for a summer one.

TECHNIQUES USED Attaching a neck facing **p.156**, Inserting a set-in sleeve **p.211**, Separate in-seam pocket **p.248**, Concealed or invisible zipper **p.290**

YOU WILL NEED

- Pattern templates on pp.370–373. Choose your size using the Women's Sizing chart on p.370.
- 100 x 60in (250cm x 150cm) light- to medium-weight dressmaking fabric, such as cotton, linen, crepe, silk, fine wool suitings, scuba, or medium-weight polyester
- 20in (50cm) lightweight fusible interfacing
- 22in (56cm) concealed zipper
- Concealed zipper foot

Front   Back

PIECES TO CUT

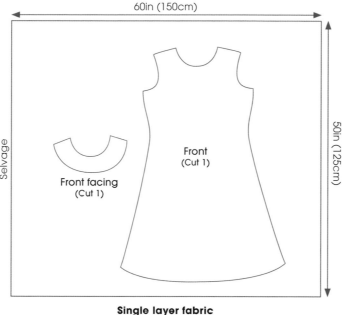

Single layer fabric

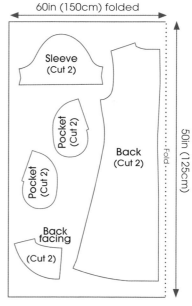

Double layer fabric

▶ MAKE THE DARTS

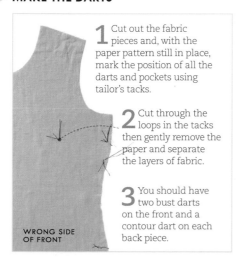

1 Cut out the fabric pieces and, with the paper pattern still in place, mark the position of all the darts and pockets using tailor's tacks.

2 Cut through the loops in the tacks then gently remove the paper and separate the layers of fabric.

3 You should have two bust darts on the front and a contour dart on each back piece.

WRONG SIDE OF FRONT

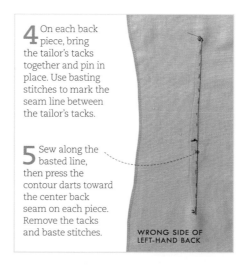

4 On each back piece, bring the tailor's tacks together and pin in place. Use basting stitches to mark the seam line between the tailor's tacks.

5 Sew along the basted line, then press the contour darts toward the center back seam on each piece. Remove the tacks and baste stitches.

WRONG SIDE OF LEFT-HAND BACK

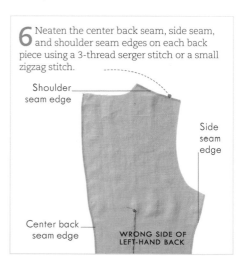

6 Neaten the center back seam, side seam, and shoulder seam edges on each back piece using a 3-thread serger stitch or a small zigzag stitch.

Shoulder seam edge

Side seam edge

Center back seam edge

WRONG SIDE OF LEFT-HAND BACK

7 On the front piece, bring the tailor's tacks for the bust darts together and pin in place. Baste to mark the seam line, then sew. Remove the tacks and baste stitches.

8 Press both bust darts toward the waist.

9 Neaten the side seams and shoulder seams using a 3-thread serger stitch or a small zigzag stitch.

WRONG SIDE OF FRONT

Pocket positions marked

INSERT THE CONCEALED ZIPPER

1 Fuse a ¾ x 24in (2 x 60cm) strip of interfacing on the wrong side of both center back seam allowances to match the zipper placement.

2 Baste the center back seam allowance on the right-hand back piece. Pin the zipper in place on the right side.

3 Undo the zipper and sew it to the seam allowance along the basted line using a concealed zipper foot.

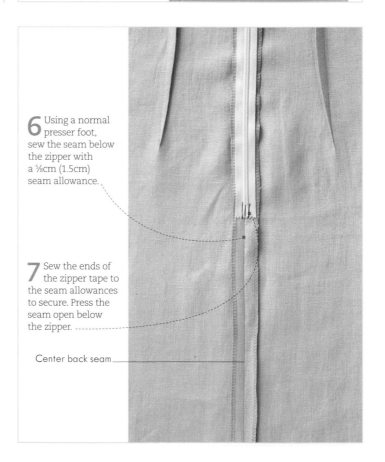

Open the zipper fully before sewing

Basted line

RIGHT SIDE OF RIGHT-HAND BACK

4 Zip up the zipper. Baste the center back seam allowance on the left-hand back. Pin the other side of the zipper in place on the right side.

Zipper attached to right side of left-hand back

5 Undo the zipper and sew in place along the basted line using a concealed zipper foot.

WRONG SIDE OF RIGHT-HAND BACK

6 Using a normal presser foot, sew the seam below the zipper with a ⅝cm (1.5cm) seam allowance.

7 Sew the ends of the zipper tape to the seam allowances to secure. Press the seam open below the zipper.

Center back seam

SEWING MACHINE ACCESSORIES **pp.32–33** • HOW TO APPLY A FUSIBLE INTERFACING **p.54** • BASTING STITCHES **p.89** • SEAM NEATENING **p.95** • PLAIN DART **p.113**

▶ INSERT THE IN-SEAM POCKETS

1 Neaten the straight edge of all four pocket pieces using a 3-thread serger stitch or a small zigzag stitch.

2 Line up the pocket pieces with the tailor's tacks on the front and back pieces, right side to right side.

3 Sew all four pocket pieces in position on the front and back pieces, using a ½in (1.2cm) seam allowance. Sew between the tailor's tacks.

4 Open out the pocket and press the seam toward the pocket.

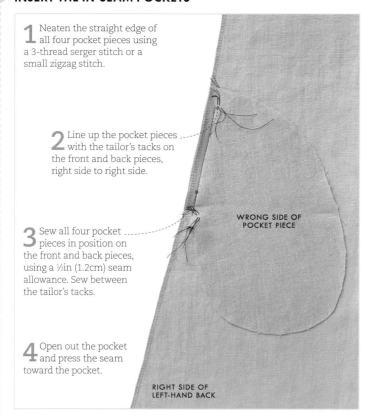

WRONG SIDE OF POCKET PIECE

RIGHT SIDE OF LEFT-HAND BACK

5 Place the front piece to the back piece, right side to right side, matching seams above and below the pocket.

6 Sew the side seams using a ⅝in (1.5cm) seam allowance, stopping just past the tailor's tacks.

7 Sew around the curved part of the pocket to join the two pieces.

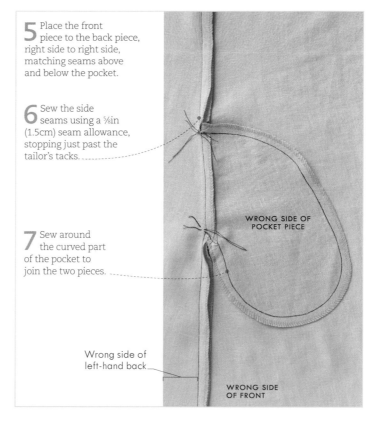

WRONG SIDE OF POCKET PIECE

Wrong side of left-hand back

WRONG SIDE OF FRONT

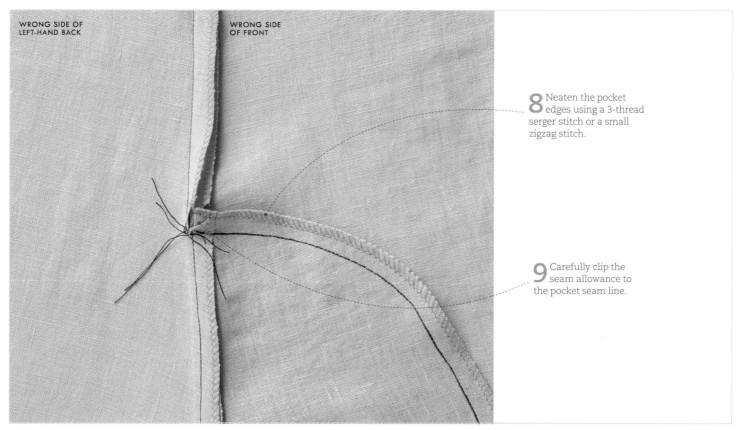

WRONG SIDE OF LEFT-HAND BACK

WRONG SIDE OF FRONT

8 Neaten the pocket edges using a 3-thread serger stitch or a small zigzag stitch.

9 Carefully clip the seam allowance to the pocket seam line.

SEPARATE IN-SEAM POCKET **p.248** ● CONCEALED OR INVISIBLE ZIPPER **p.290**

▶ **ATTACH THE NECK FACING**

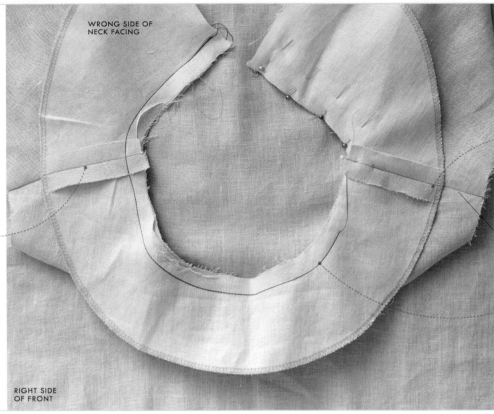

1 Apply interfacing to the neck facing pieces.

WRONG SIDE OF NECK FACING

3 Place the facing to the neck of the dress, right side to right side, matching the shoulder seams. Pin in place.

Shoulder seam

2 Sew the neck facing pieces together at the shoulder seams using a ⅝in (1.5cm) seam allowance. Neaten the edges and press the seams open.

4 Sew the neck facing in place using a ⅝in (1.5cm) seam allowance.

RIGHT SIDE OF FRONT

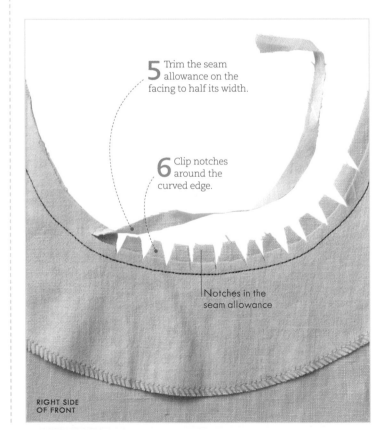

5 Trim the seam allowance on the facing to half its width.

6 Clip notches around the curved edge.

Notches in the seam allowance

RIGHT SIDE OF FRONT

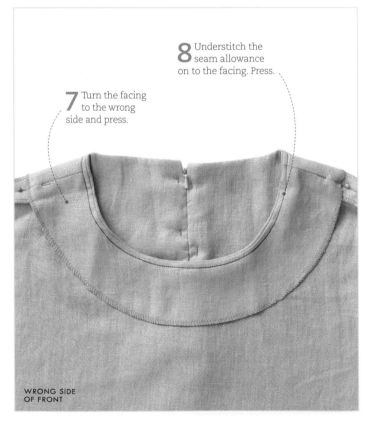

8 Understitch the seam allowance on to the facing. Press.

7 Turn the facing to the wrong side and press.

WRONG SIDE OF FRONT

▶ ATTACH THE SLEEVES

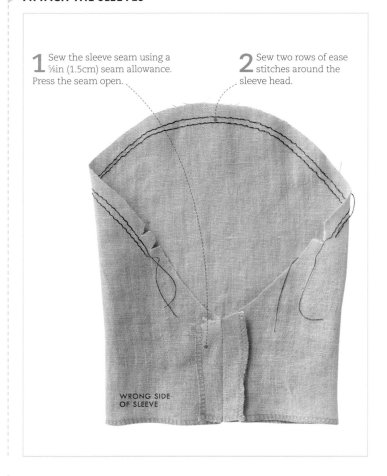

1 Sew the sleeve seam using a ⅝in (1.5cm) seam allowance. Press the seam open.

2 Sew two rows of ease stitches around the sleeve head.

WRONG SIDE OF SLEEVE

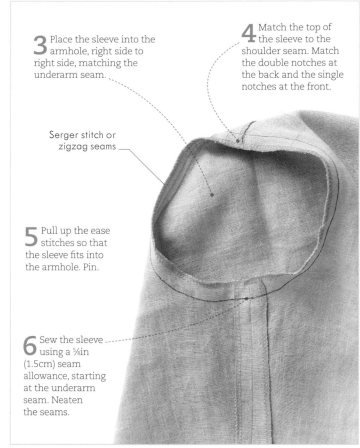

3 Place the sleeve into the armhole, right side to right side, matching the underarm seam.

4 Match the top of the sleeve to the shoulder seam. Match the double notches at the back and the single notches at the front.

Serger stitch or zigzag seams

5 Pull up the ease stitches so that the sleeve fits into the armhole. Pin.

6 Sew the sleeve using a ⅝in (1.5cm) seam allowance, starting at the underarm seam. Neaten the seams.

▶ SEW THE HEM

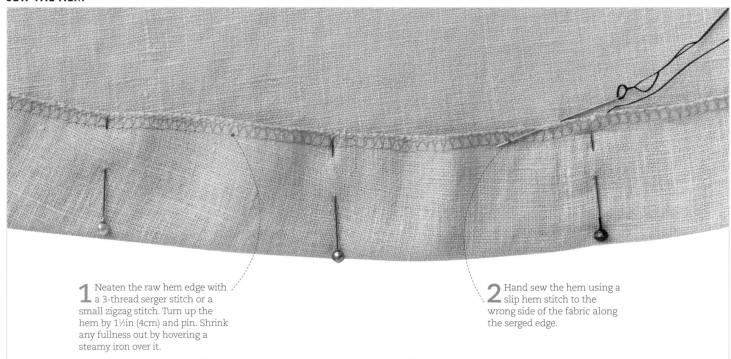

1 Neaten the raw hem edge with a 3-thread serger stitch or a small zigzag stitch. Turn up the hem by 1½in (4cm) and pin. Shrink any fullness out by hovering a steamy iron over it.

2 Hand sew the hem using a slip hem stitch to the wrong side of the fabric along the serged edge.

INSERTING A SET-IN SLEEVE **p.211** ● CURVED HEM FINISH **p.265**

COLLARS

Collars frame the face and neck, and are always a focal point on any garment. There are three main types: flat, standing, and turnover. To construct a symmetrical collar, careful and accurate marking and stitching are essential.

COLLARS

All collars consist of a minimum of two pieces, the upper collar (which will be on the outside) and the under collar. Interfacing, which is required to give the collar shape and structure, is often applied to the upper collar to give a smoother appearance to the fabric.

DIRECTORY OF COLLARS

FLAT COLLAR (p.175 and pp.176–177)

STAND COLLAR (p.178)

SHAWL COLLAR (p.179)

BLOUSE COLLAR WITH REVERS (p.180)

TWO-PIECE SHIRT COLLAR (pp.180–181)

HOW TO APPLY A FUSIBLE INTERFACING **p.54** ● PATTERN MARKING **pp.82–83** ● STITCHES MADE WITH A MACHINE **pp.92–93**

FLAT COLLAR

A flat collar is the easiest of all the collars to construct, and the techniques used are the same for most other shapes of flat collar and facings.

▶ **1** Cut out the fabric for the collar accurately. Make sure the two halves match.

2 Cut out a fusible interfacing, being sure to cut on the same grain as the collar. Apply the interfacing to the upper collar.

3 Insert tailor's tacks at the center front point of the collar where indicated by a dot on the pattern piece.

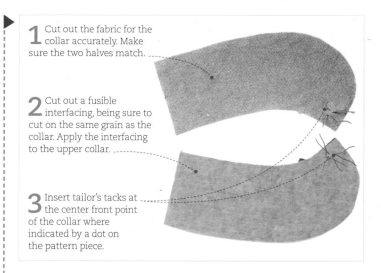

4 Pin the upper collar and under collar together, right side to right side. Match any notches and make sure the cut edges match.

5 Sew ⅝in (1.5cm) along the raw outer curved edge to the lower edge of the collar. Make sure the stitches at the center front go through the tailor's tack. If you have problems sewing a curve, mark the fabric first with chalk.

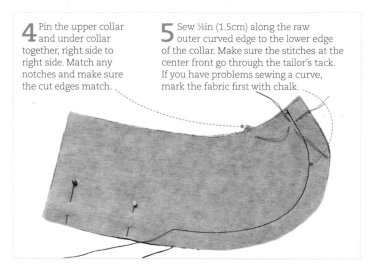

6 Trim the under collar seam allowance to half of its width, which will reduce the bulk.

7 Trim around the curve with pinking shears, reducing both layers. This will allow the fabric to turn.

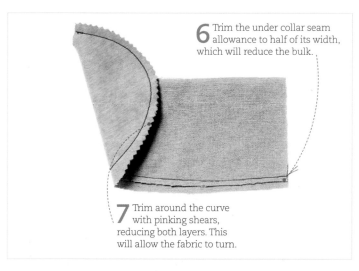

8 Clip the curve on the collar using small cuts at 90 degrees to the sewn line, clipping through the pinked seam.

9 Press the seam allowance of the upper collar on to the collar.

10 While the collar is still warm from the steam iron, turn to the right side.

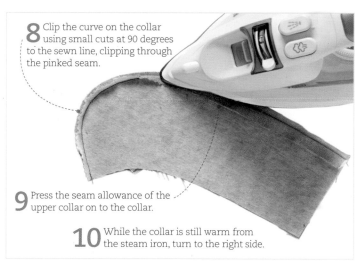

11 Working from the inside of the collar, push all the seam allowance toward the under collar and sew it to the under collar. This is called understitching and will hold the collar in shape.

12 Understitch as far through the curve as you can.

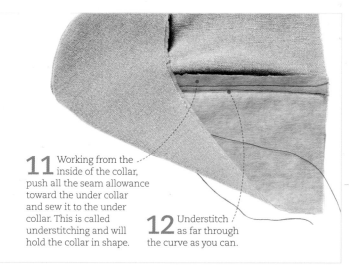

13 Press the curved edge flat, making sure the seam is pushed out completely on the right side.

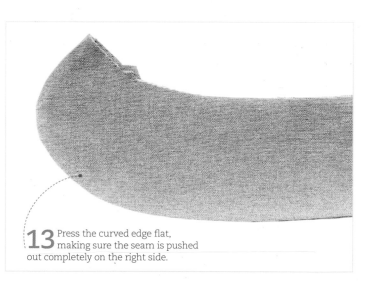

TECHNIQUES

ATTACHING A FLAT COLLAR

Difficulty level ★★★★✩

A flat collar can be attached to the neckline by means of a facing. Depending upon the style of the garment, the facing may go all around the neck, which is usually found on garments with center back openings, or just be at the front. The collar with no back facing has to be attached to the garment in stages.

▶ FLAT ROUND COLLAR WITH NO BACK FACING

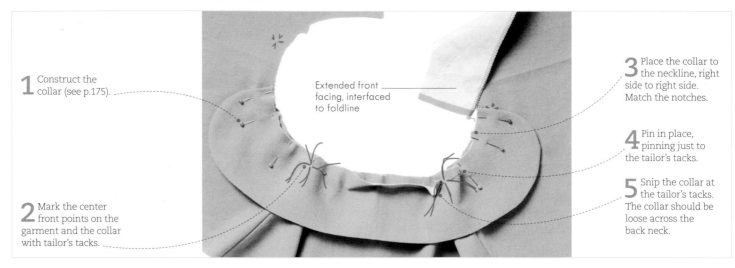

1 Construct the collar (see p.175).

Extended front facing, interfaced to foldline

2 Mark the center front points on the garment and the collar with tailor's tacks.

3 Place the collar to the neckline, right side to right side. Match the notches.

4 Pin in place, pinning just to the tailor's tacks.

5 Snip the collar at the tailor's tacks. The collar should be loose across the back neck.

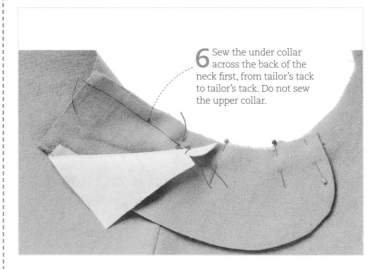

6 Sew the under collar across the back of the neck first, from tailor's tack to tailor's tack. Do not sew the upper collar.

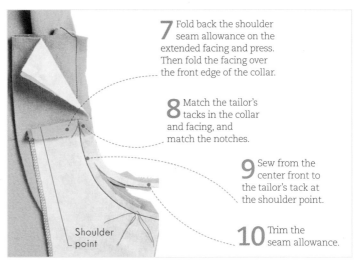

7 Fold back the shoulder seam allowance on the extended facing and press. Then fold the facing over the front edge of the collar.

8 Match the tailor's tacks in the collar and facing, and match the notches.

9 Sew from the center front to the tailor's tack at the shoulder point.

10 Trim the seam allowance.

Shoulder point

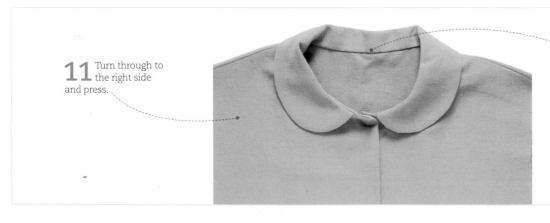

11 Turn through to the right side and press.

12 At the center back, turn under the seam allowance on the upper collar and hand sew across the back neck with a flat fell or blind hem stitch.

▶ **FLAT ROUND COLLAR WITH A FULL FACING**

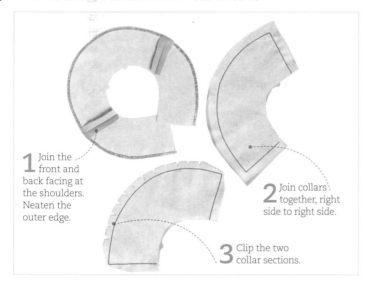

1 Join the front and back facing at the shoulders. Neaten the outer edge.

2 Join collars together, right side to right side.

3 Clip the two collar sections.

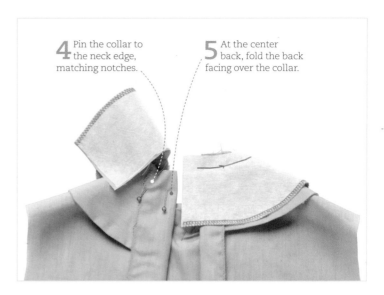

4 Pin the collar to the neck edge, matching notches.

5 At the center back, fold the back facing over the collar.

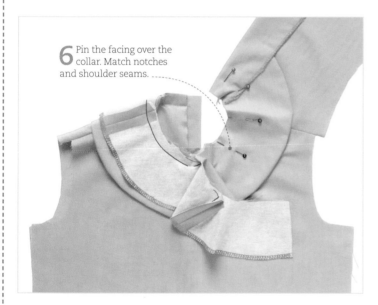

6 Pin the facing over the collar. Match notches and shoulder seams.

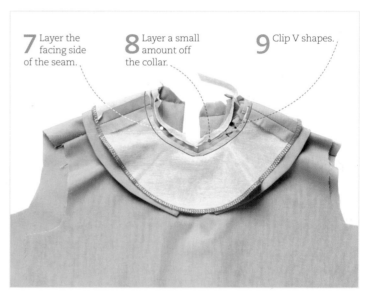

7 Layer the facing side of the seam.

8 Layer a small amount off the collar.

9 Clip V shapes.

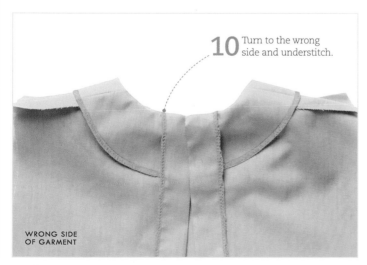

10 Turn to the wrong side and understitch.

WRONG SIDE OF GARMENT

11 Turn to the right side and press.

SEAM NEATENING **p.95** ● REDUCING SEAM BULK **pp.108–109** ● STITCH FINISHES **p.109** ● GROWN-ON FACING **p.160**

TECHNIQUES

MANDARIN COLLAR

Difficulty level **★★★★☆**

This collar stands upright around the neck. It is normally cut from a straight piece of fabric, with shaping at the center front edges. For a very close-fitting collar, the collar is cut with a slight curve.

1 Apply a fusible interfacing to the upper collar (see p.175). Insert any tailor's tacks as indicated on the pattern.

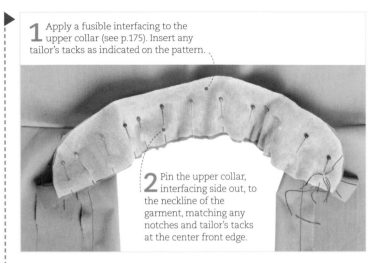

2 Pin the upper collar, interfacing side out, to the neckline of the garment, matching any notches and tailor's tacks at the center front edge.

3 Sew the upper collar to the neckline using a ⅝in (1.5cm) seam allowance. Make sure to stop at the tailor's tack at the front edge.

4 Reduce the seam allowance on the upper collar by half.

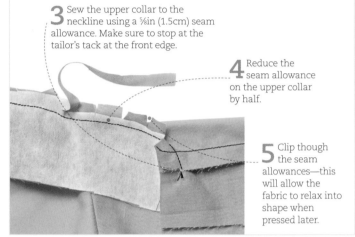

5 Clip though the seam allowances—this will allow the fabric to relax into shape when pressed later.

6 Working from the wrong side of the garment, turn in the center front edge as indicated by the pattern. This will leave the front edge of the collar sticking out from the garment.

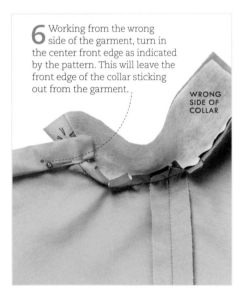

WRONG SIDE OF COLLAR

7 Pin the under collar to the upper collar, right side to right side, along the top edge.

8 Sew the two pieces together using a ⅝in (1.5cm) seam allowance.

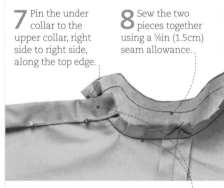

9 At the center front, the reduced neck seam allowance needs to be pointing up into the collar, so that the seam line attaching the two collar sections together goes over it. Be sure the seam is in line with the center front of the garment.

10 Reduce the seam allowance to half its width on the under collar side of the seam (the non-interfaced side).

11 Clip V shapes out of the seam allowance to reduce the bulk. Be careful not to cut through the stitches.

12 Press the seam as it has been sewn, and while warm turn to the right side.

13 Turn under the lower edge seam allowance on the under collar and baste in place around the neck edge.

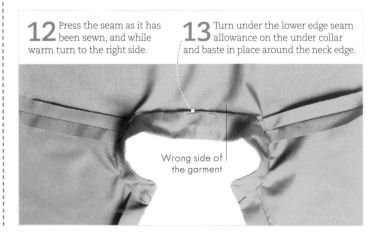

Wrong side of the garment

14 Make sure the two leading front edges of the collar are symmetrical.

15 Use a flat fell stitch to secure the under collar at the neck edge.

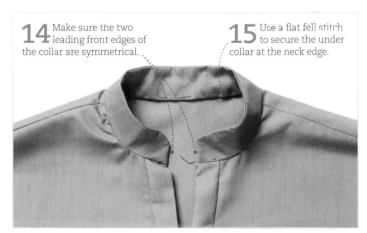

HOW TO APPLY A FUSIBLE INTERFACING p.54 ● PATTERN MARKING pp.82–83

SHAWL COLLAR

A shawl collar, which is a deep V-neck shape that combines both collar and lapels in one, gives a flattering neckline that is often found on blouses and jackets. Although the collar looks complicated, it is straightforward to make. The under collar is usually part of the front of the garment.

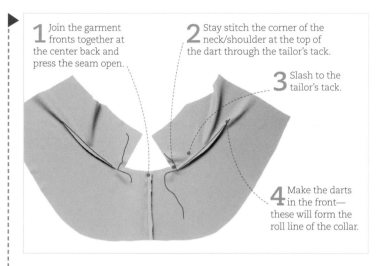

1 Join the garment fronts together at the center back and press the seam open.

2 Stay stitch the corner of the neck/shoulder at the top of the dart through the tailor's tack.

3 Slash to the tailor's tack.

4 Make the darts in the front—these will form the roll line of the collar.

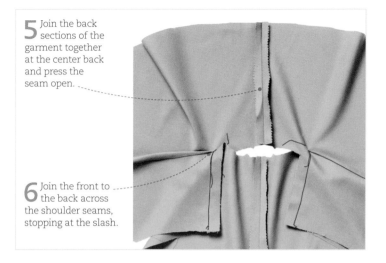

5 Join the back sections of the garment together at the center back and press the seam open.

6 Join the front to the back across the shoulder seams, stopping at the slash.

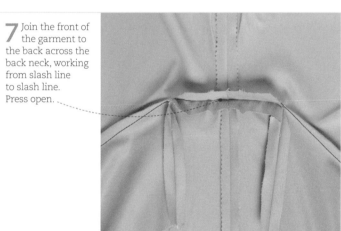

7 Join the front of the garment to the back across the back neck, working from slash line to slash line. Press open.

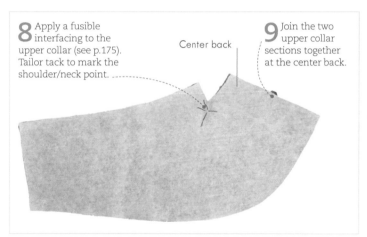

8 Apply a fusible interfacing to the upper collar (see p.175). Tailor tack to mark the shoulder/neck point.

Center back

9 Join the two upper collar sections together at the center back.

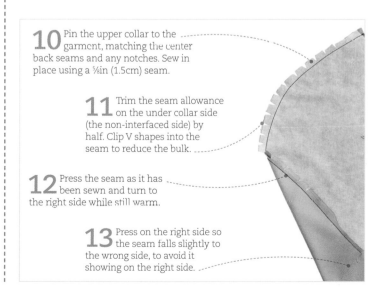

10 Pin the upper collar to the garment, matching the center back seams and any notches. Sew in place using a ⅝in (1.5cm) seam.

11 Trim the seam allowance on the under collar side (the non-interfaced side) by half. Clip V shapes into the seam to reduce the bulk.

12 Press the seam as it has been sewn and turn to the right side while still warm.

13 Press on the right side so the seam falls slightly to the wrong side, to avoid it showing on the right side.

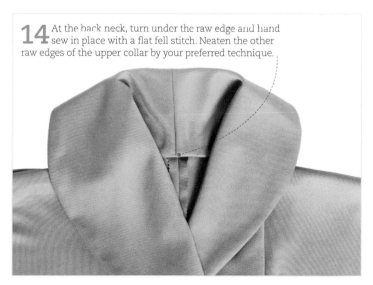

14 At the back neck, turn under the raw edge and hand sew in place with a flat fell stitch. Neaten the other raw edges of the upper collar by your preferred technique.

TECHNIQUES

BLOUSE COLLAR WITH LAPEL

Difficulty level ★★✱✱✱

A blouse collar can have rounded or pointed center front edges, depending on the style of blouse chosen. A blouse collar forms a V neckline with a lapel. When constructing the collar, before fusing the interfacing to the upper collar, trim the corners of the interfacing to reduce bulk.

1 Construct the collar by placing the fabric right side to right side. Mark any pattern markings with tailor's tacks. Sew at ⅝in (1.5cm).

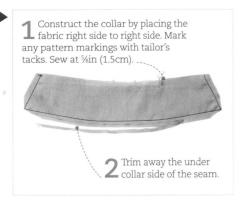

2 Trim away the under collar side of the seam.

3 Clip across the corners.

Back neck

Interfacing removed from corners

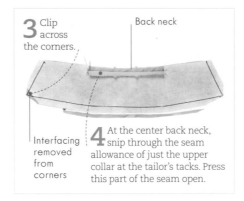

4 At the center back neck, snip through the seam allowance of just the upper collar at the tailor's tacks. Press this part of the seam open.

Sharp corners

5 Turn the collar through to the right side and press. The seam allowance on the back neck is pressed under between the clips.

6 Place the collar to the neck, matching the tailor's tacks. Pin to secure.

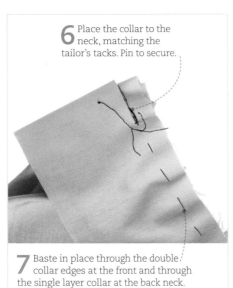

7 Baste in place through the double collar edges at the front and through the single layer collar at the back neck.

8 Place the front facing over the front part of the collar, matching notches and tailor's tacks.

9 Sew in place, stitching across the back neck at the same time. Match at the shoulder seams.

Sharp point in stitching at center front

10 Trim and layer the seam. Turn to the right side and press.

11 Turn under the raw edge of the upper collar at the back neck and baste in place, then hand sew with a flat fell or blind hem stitch.

Lapel

12 Press the collar and lapel.

TWO-PIECE SHIRT COLLAR

Difficulty level ★★★✱✱

A traditional-style shirt has a collar that consists of two pieces: a collar and a stand, both of which require interfacing. The stand fits close around the neck and the collar is attached to the stand. This type of collar is found on men's and ladies' shirts. On a man's shirt, the stand accommodates the tie.

1 Cut the upper and under collar. Apply interfacing to the upper collar.

2 Sew the upper and under collar together, right side to right side, sewing around the sides and the outside edge. Sew a sharp point by pivoting at the corners.

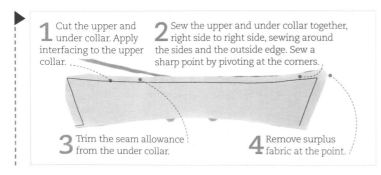

3 Trim the seam allowance from the under collar.

4 Remove surplus fabric at the point.

5 Press the seam open, pressing the upper collar seam allowance down on to the collar. Clip as required.

6 The fabric at the point should not be bulky. If it is, remove more.

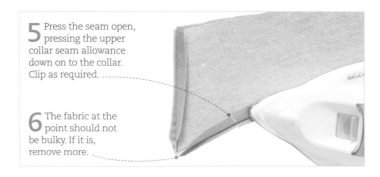

HOW TO APPLY A FUSIBLE INTERFACING **p.54** ● PATTERN MARKING **pp.82–83** ● HAND SEWING **pp.90–91**

7 Turn the collar to the right side and press.

8 Top-stitch the sides and outside edge using the edge of the machine foot as a guide.

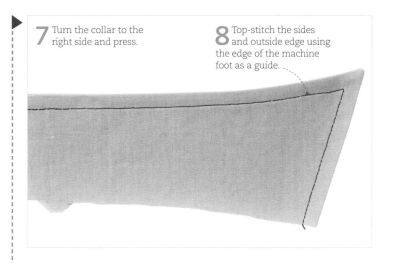

9 Construct the stand, applying interfacing to one side.

Collar fits between the tailor's tacks

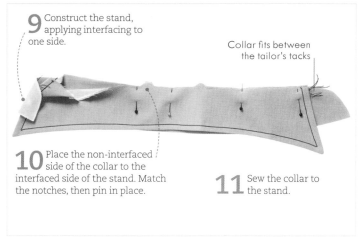

10 Place the non-interfaced side of the collar to the interfaced side of the stand. Match the notches, then pin in place.

11 Sew the collar to the stand.

12 Place the stand to the shirt neck, matching the notches, and pin in place.

13 Baste the stand to the neckline. The seam allowance on the stand extends at the center front.

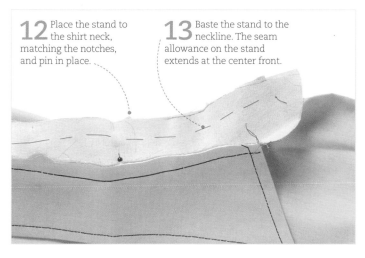

14 Pin the non-interfaced side of the collar stand to the neck edge, so that there is a collar stand on either side of the shirt.

15 Baste the collar stand to the neckline.

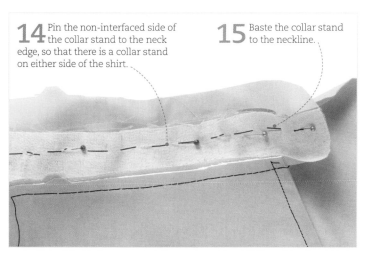

16 Reposition the stand so that the front edges come together right side to right side.

17 Sew along the neck edge and around the center front curve to the collar.

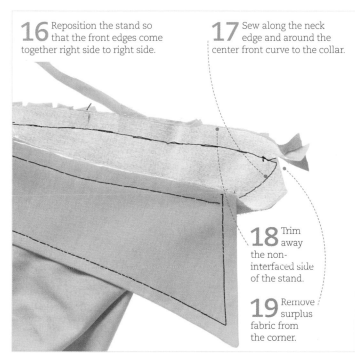

18 Trim away the non-interfaced side of the stand.

19 Remove surplus fabric from the corner.

20 Turn and press.

21 Bring the raw edge of the stand to the collar and turn under. Pin in place.

22 Secure this edge with a flat fell stitch.

23 Top-stitch the stand, if required. The stand fits snugly under the collar at the center front.

STITCHES MADE WITH A MACHINE **pp.92–93** ● STITCHING CORNERS AND CURVES **pp.102–103** ● REDUCING SEAM BULK **pp.108–109**

WAISTLINES, BELTS, AND TIE-BACKS

Bodice and skirt sections are often joined together at the waist. However, on some garments, a "waist" needs to be created to take a piece of elastic. A waist may be enhanced by making a matching belt. Curtain tie-backs are also covered in this section.

TECHNIQUES

WAISTLINES

Waistlines can be formed where a bodice and skirt join together or at the waist edge of a skirt or pair of pants. Some waistlines are attached separately to the garment to create a feature and others are more discreet. They may be shaped to follow the contours of the body.

DIRECTORY OF WAISTLINES

FITTED WAISTLINE
(p.185)

GATHERED WAISTLINE
(p.185)

WAISTLINE WITH A CASING (p.186–187)

APPLIED CASING
(p.187)

MOCK CASING USING ELASTIC (p.188)

ALTERNATIVE CASING USING A SEAM ALLOWANCE (p.189)

PARTIAL CASING
(p.189)

WAISTLINE WITH A FACING
(p.190)

STRAIGHT WAISTBAND
(p.192–193)

HOW TO MAKE A PLAIN SEAM **p.94** ● SEAM NEATENING **p.95**

JOINING A FITTED SKIRT TO A BODICE

Many dresses feature a straight fitted skirt attached to a fitted dress bodice. When joining them together, it is important that the darts or seamlines on the bodice line up with those on the skirt.

1 Be sure the darts on the skirt section are pressed toward the center. Stay stitch the waistline.

WRONG SIDE OF SKIRT

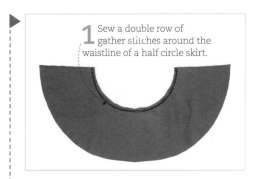

2 Press the seam allowance on the bodice open.

3 Place the skirt to the bodice, lining up the darts and the bodice seams and baste stitch. Pin the bodice and skirt together.

4 Sew the bodice to the skirt using a ⅝in (1.5cm) seam allowance and press.

5 Neaten the skirt/bodice seam using either a 3-thread serger stitch or a zigzag stitch.

6 Press the seam up toward the bodice.

WRONG SIDE OF GARMENT

7 On the right side, the seams and darts match at the waist.

RIGHT SIDE OF GARMENT

JOINING A GATHERED SKIRT TO A BODICE

When attaching a gathered skirt to a fitted bodice, the gathers must be distributed evenly around the waist. If there are seams on the gathered skirt, these must be matched to the bodice seams and darts.

1 Sew a double row of gather stitches around the waistline of a half circle skirt.

2 Pull up the gathers to fit the bodice waist.

3 Pin the gathered skirt to the bodice, making sure the bodice darts face toward the center.

4 Sew the gathered skirt to the bodice using a ⅝in (1.5cm) seam allowance. Neaten the seam using either a 3-thread serger stitch or a zigzag stitch.

WRONG SIDE OF GARMENT

5 Press the seam up toward the bodice. On the right side the skirt seam is gathered into a smooth bodice seam.

RIGHT SIDE OF GARMENT

PLAIN DART **p.113** • HOW TO MAKE AND FIT GATHERS **p.135**

TECHNIQUES

MAKING A CASING AT THE WAIST EDGE

Difficulty level ❋❋❋❋❋

An elastic waist is featured on both skirts and pants and also at the waist on casual jackets.
The casing can be made by using a deep waist seam or by attaching a facing. The facing will
form a complete circle that will be attached to the waist edge.

▶ **USING A DEEP WAIST SEAM AS A CASING**

1 Turn under a ⅝in (1.5cm) seam allowance to the wrong side and press.

2 Turn again by 1¼in (3cm). Pin in place.

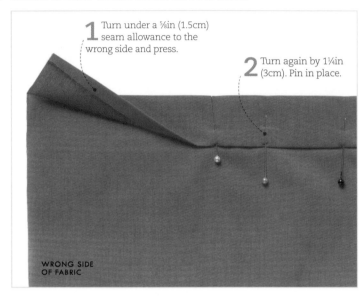

WRONG SIDE OF FABRIC

3 Sew ¹⁄₁₆in (2mm) from the top folded edge.

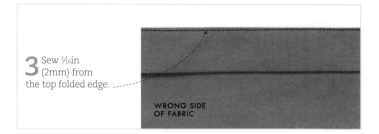

WRONG SIDE OF FABRIC

4 Sew the lower edge of the fold ¹⁄₁₆in (2mm) from the edge. Leave a 1in (3cm) gap to insert the elastic through.

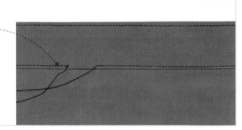

5 Cut a piece of non-roll elastic the length required to go around the waist comfortably.

6 Pin one end of the elastic to the fabric just below the opening.

7 Pin a safety pin to the other end and thread through the casing.

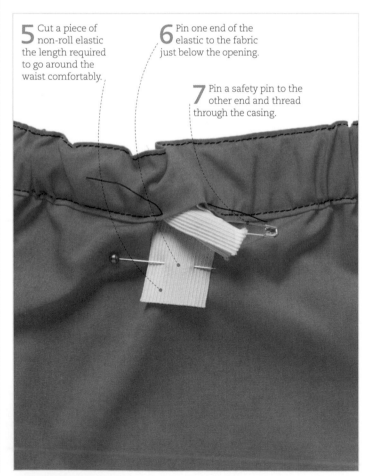

8 Pull the two ends of the elastic together and machine to join in a square shape with an X for strength.

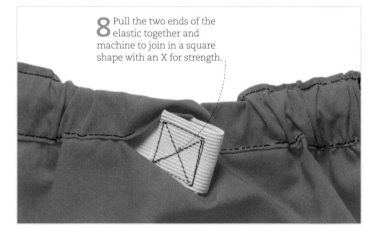

9 Push the elastic into the casing and sew across the gap.

▶ USING A FACING AS A CASING

1 Cut the facing, and join the facing sections together at the side seams. Press open. Do not join the remaining seam, but press back the seam allowances.

2 Pin the facing to the raw edge of the garment.

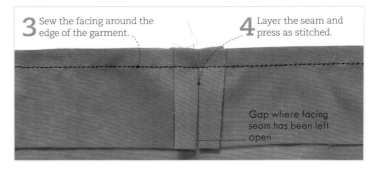

3 Sew the facing around the edge of the garment.

4 Layer the seam and press as stitched.

Gap where facing seam has been left open

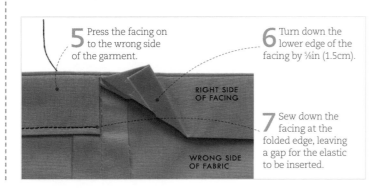

5 Press the facing on to the wrong side of the garment.

RIGHT SIDE OF FACING

WRONG SIDE OF FABRIC

6 Turn down the lower edge of the facing by ⅝in (1.5cm).

7 Sew down the facing at the folded edge, leaving a gap for the elastic to be inserted.

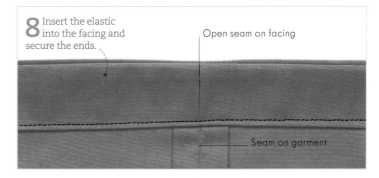

8 Insert the elastic into the facing and secure the ends.

Open seam on facing

Seam on garment

APPLIED CASINGS

Difficulty level ✱✱✱✱✱

Some elastic waists will require the application of extra fabric to make a casing into which the elastic can be inserted. The casing may be applied to the inside or the outside of the garment. A quick way is to make the casing with bias binding. The casing can also be made from the same fabric as the garment or from a facing.

▶ INTERNAL CASING

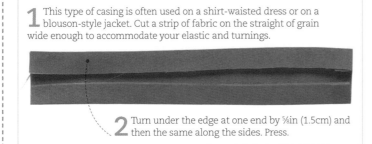

1 This type of casing is often used on a shirt-waisted dress or on a blouson-style jacket. Cut a strip of fabric on the straight of grain wide enough to accommodate your elastic and turnings.

2 Turn under the edge at one end by ⅝in (1.5cm) and then the same along the sides. Press.

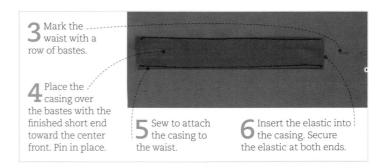

3 Mark the waist with a row of bastes.

4 Place the casing over the bastes with the finished short end toward the center front. Pin in place.

5 Sew to attach the casing to the waist.

6 Insert the elastic into the casing. Secure the elastic at both ends.

▶ INTERNAL CASING USING BIAS BINDING

1 Be sure to use bias binding that will be wide enough to insert an elastic through after it has been sewn down. Apply the bias to the waistline and sew at ⅟₁₆in (2mm) from either edge.

2 Insert the elastic and knot the ends.

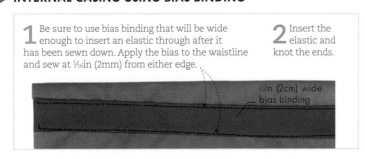

¾in (2cm) wide bias binding

▶ EXTERNAL CASING

1 Cut a strip of straight grain fabric 1⅜in (3.5cm) wide x the waist measurement on the garment. Turn under all raw edges by ³⁄₁₆in (5mm) and press.

2 Place this casing over the garment waistline, with the short ends to the center front.

3 Sew in place along the long edges. Insert elastic to fit the waist.

CONSTRUCTION OF A FACING **p.153** ● HOW TO CUT BIAS STRIPS **p.154**

TECHNIQUES

MOCK CASINGS

Difficulty level ★★★★☆

There are several ways to construct mock casings. The simplest is to sew on elastic at the waist. An alternative, if a bodice and skirt have a waist seam joining them together, is to insert elastic between the seam allowances. On many garments, there is elastic at the back only, in a partial casing, and a waistband interfacing at the front.

▶ **STITCHING ON ELASTIC TO MAKE A WAISTLINE**

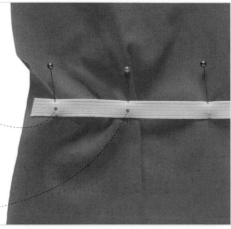

1 Cut a piece of elastic to the required length. Mark the waistline on the garment with a row of basting stitches.

2 Secure the elastic at one end with a pin.

3 Stretch the elastic across the fabric, pinning at regular intervals. The fabric will be loose under the elastic.

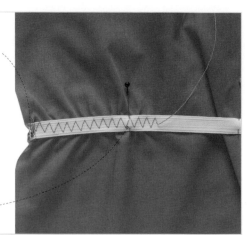

4 Secure the elastic at one end with a few machine stitches.

5 Place under the sewing machine and join the elastic to the fabric using a 3-step zigzag stitch, stretching the fabric and elastic together as you do so.

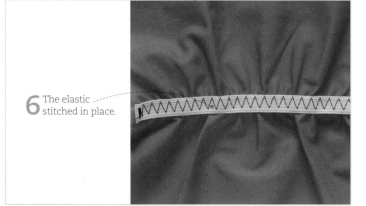

6 The elastic stitched in place.

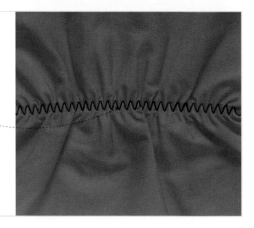

7 On the right side there is a neat elasticated waistline.

▶ **CASING IN A WAIST SEAM ALLOWANCE**

1 Join the fabric together using a ¾in (2cm) seam allowance.

2 Sew again ⅝in (1.5cm) from this line, ³⁄₁₆in (5mm) from the raw edge.

3 Neaten the edge of the seam using a 3-thread serger stitch or a zigzag stitch.

4 Insert elastic into the casing that you have made, with the help of a safety pin.

SERGER pp.34–35 ● **HOW TO APPLY A FUSIBLE INTERFACING p.54** ● **BASTING STITCHES p.89**

▶ ALTERNATIVE CASING USING A SEAM ALLOWANCE

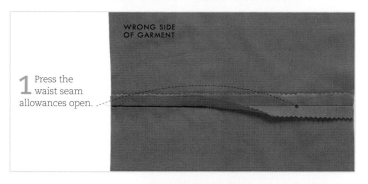

1 Press the waist seam allowances open.

WRONG SIDE OF GARMENT

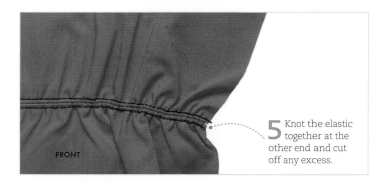

2 Top-stitch the seam allowances open, stitching ⅜in (1cm) from the seam, to make a channel either side of the seam. Use a zigzag stitch if you don't have a serger.

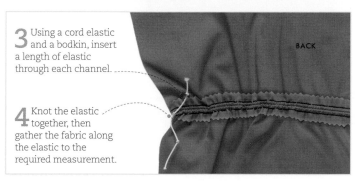

3 Using a cord elastic and a bodkin, insert a length of elastic through each channel.

4 Knot the elastic together, then gather the fabric along the elastic to the required measurement.

BACK

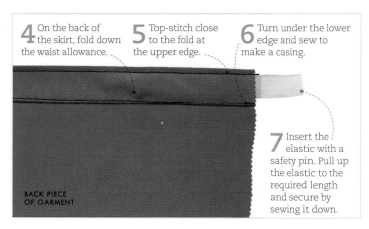

5 Knot the elastic together at the other end and cut off any excess.

FRONT

▶ PARTIAL CASING

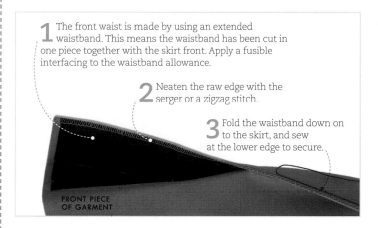

1 The front waist is made by using an extended waistband. This means the waistband has been cut in one piece together with the skirt front. Apply a fusible interfacing to the waistband allowance.

2 Neaten the raw edge with the serger or a zigzag stitch.

3 Fold the waistband down on to the skirt, and sew at the lower edge to secure.

FRONT PIECE OF GARMENT

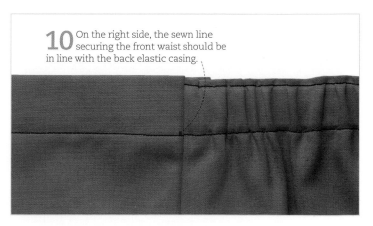

4 On the back of the skirt, fold down the waist allowance.

5 Top-stitch close to the fold at the upper edge.

6 Turn under the lower edge and sew to make a casing.

7 Insert the elastic with a safety pin. Pull up the elastic to the required length and secure by sewing it down.

BACK PIECE OF GARMENT

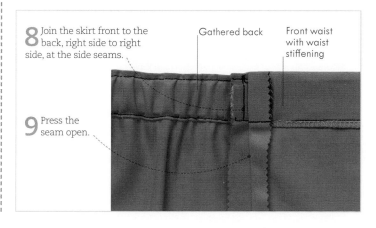

8 Join the skirt front to the back, right side to right side, at the side seams.

9 Press the seam open.

Gathered back

Front waist with waist stiffening

10 On the right side, the sewn line securing the front waist should be in line with the back elastic casing.

TECHNIQUES

A WAIST WITH A FACING

Difficulty level ★★☆☆☆

Many waistlines on skirts and pants are finished with a facing, which will follow the contours of the waist but will have had the dart shaping removed to make it smooth. A faced waistline always sits comfortably to the body. The facing is attached after all the main sections of the skirt or pants have been constructed.

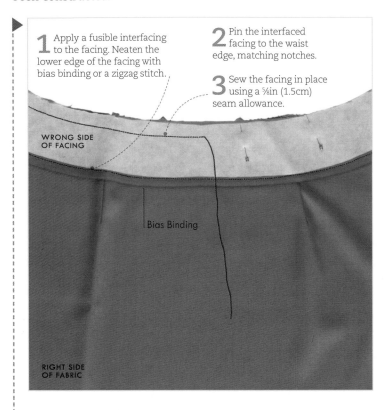

1 Apply a fusible interfacing to the facing. Neaten the lower edge of the facing with bias binding or a zigzag stitch.

2 Pin the interfaced facing to the waist edge, matching notches.

3 Sew the facing in place using a ⅝in (1.5cm) seam allowance.

WRONG SIDE OF FACING

Bias Binding

RIGHT SIDE OF FABRIC

4 Layer the seam allowance on the facing side of the seam to reduce it by half.

5 Clip the seam allowance by using straight cuts at 90 degrees to the stitching line.

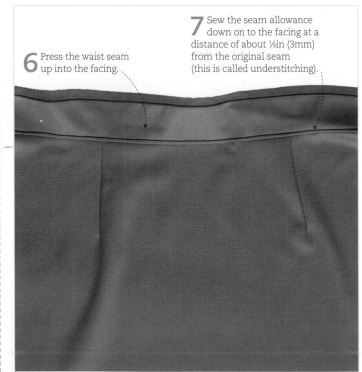

6 Press the waist seam up into the facing.

7 Sew the seam allowance down on to the facing at a distance of about ⅛in (3mm) from the original seam (this is called understitching).

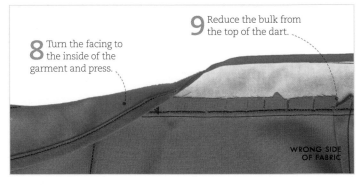

8 Turn the facing to the inside of the garment and press.

9 Reduce the bulk from the top of the dart.

WRONG SIDE OF FABRIC

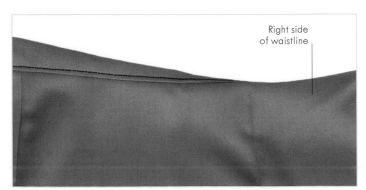

Right side of waistline

PETERSHAM-FACED WAIST

Difficulty level ✱✱✱✱✱

Petersham is an alternative finish to a facing if you do not have enough fabric to cut a facing. Available in black and white, it is a stiff, ridged tape that is 1in (2.5cm) wide and curved—the tighter curve is the top edge. Like a facing, petersham is attached to the waist after the skirt or pants have been constructed.

1 Stay stitch around the waist ½in (1.3cm) from the raw edge.

2 Trim back the raw edge to ¼in (6mm).

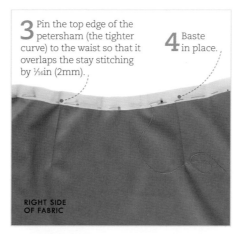

3 Pin the top edge of the petersham (the tighter curve) to the waist so that it overlaps the stay stitching by ⅟₁₆in (2mm).

4 Baste in place.

RIGHT SIDE OF FABRIC

5 Sew the petersham in place, sewing about ⅟₁₆in (2mm) from the edge of the petersham. Do not worry if the other edge looks wavy.

WRONG SIDE OF FABRIC

6 Turn over and roll the petersham to the inside of the waist.

7 Press the petersham flat to the fabric, making a neat pressed edge along the top of the seam.

FINISHING THE EDGE OF A WAISTBAND

Difficulty level ✱✱✱✱✱

One long edge of the waistband will be sewn to the garment waist. The other edge will need to be finished, to prevent fraying and reduce bulk inside.

▶ **TURNING UNDER**

This method is suitable for fine fabrics only. Turn under ⅝in (1.5cm) along the edge of the waistband and press in place. After the waistband has been attached to the garment, hand sew the pressed-under edge in place.

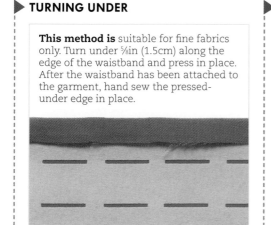

▶ **SERGER STITCHING**

This method is suitable for heavier fabrics as it is left flat inside the garment after construction. Neaten one long edge of the waistband with a 3-thread serger stitch.

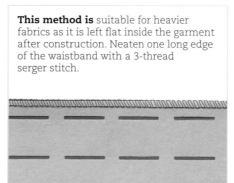

▶ **BIAS BINDING**

This method is ideal for fabrics that fray badly and can add a feature inside the garment. It is left flat inside the garment after construction. Apply a ¾in (2cm) bias binding to one long edge of the waistband.

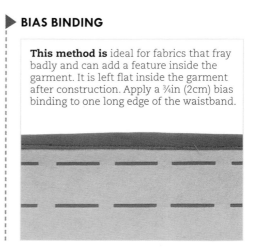

STITCHES MADE WITH A MACHINE **pp.92–93** ● LAYERING A SEAM **p.108** ● STITCH FINISHES **p.109** ● NEATENING THE EDGE OF A FACING **p.154**

TECHNIQUES

ATTACHING A STRAIGHT WAISTBAND

Difficulty level ✱✱✱✱✱

A waistband is designed to fit snugly but not tight to the waist. Whether it is shaped or straight or slightly curved, it will be constructed and attached in a similar way. Every waistband will require a fusible interfacing to give it structure and support. Special waistband interfacings are available, usually featuring slot lines that will guide you where to fold the fabric. Make sure the slots on the outer edge correspond to a ⅝in (1.5cm) seam allowance. If waistband fusible interfacing is not available, you can use a medium-weight fusible interfacing.

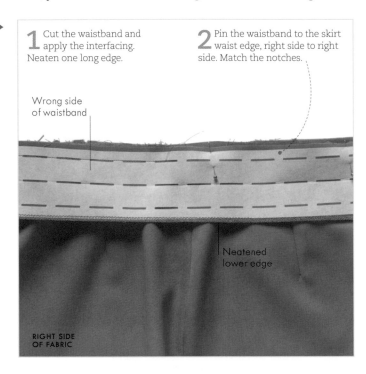

1 Cut the waistband and apply the interfacing. Neaten one long edge.

Wrong side of waistband

RIGHT SIDE OF FABRIC

2 Pin the waistband to the skirt waist edge, right side to right side. Match the notches.

Neatened lower edge

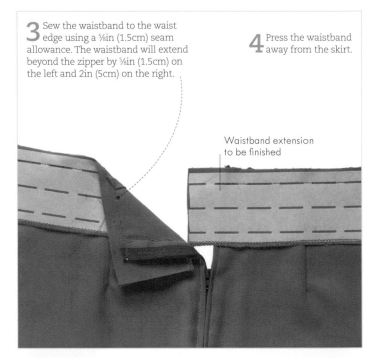

3 Sew the waistband to the waist edge using a ⅝in (1.5cm) seam allowance. The waistband will extend beyond the zipper by ⅝in (1.5cm) on the left and 2in (5cm) on the right.

Waistband extension to be finished

4 Press the waistband away from the skirt.

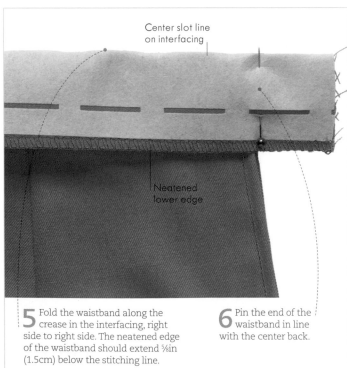

Center slot line on interfacing

Neatened lower edge

5 Fold the waistband along the crease in the interfacing, right side to right side. The neatened edge of the waistband should extend ⅝in (1.5cm) below the stitching line.

6 Pin the end of the waistband in line with the center back.

7 On the right-hand back at the waist, fold the waistband in half, right side to right side. Trim and clip seam, press, turn and press again.

8 Extend the waist/skirt seam line through the waistband and through the end. Trim and clip seam, press, turn and press again.

9 Turn the ends of the waistband to the right side. The extension on the waistband should be on the right-hand back.

10 Add your chosen fasteners.

11 To complete the waistband, sew through the band to the skirt seam. This is known as "stitching in the ditch."

12 The finished straight waistband.

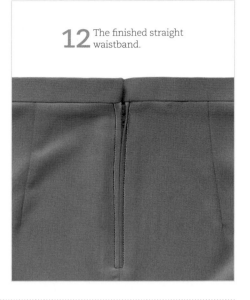

RIBBON-FACED WAISTBAND

Difficulty level ✷✷✷✷✷

On a bulky fabric, you can replace the inner side of the waistband with a ribbon. This will not affect the structure and stability of the waistband, but will produce a less bulky finish. Use a grosgrain ribbon that is 1in (2.5cm) wide. Grosgrain ribbon looks like petersham (see p.191), but is ribbed and much softer.

1 Apply interfacing to the waistband as usual.

2 Press the waistband in half, wrong side to wrong side, to give a defined crease.

3 Working from the right side of the waistband, place the ribbon along one side of the crease approx. ⅛in (3mm) from the crease.

4 Sew in place along the upper edge only.

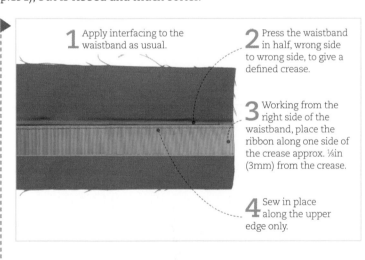

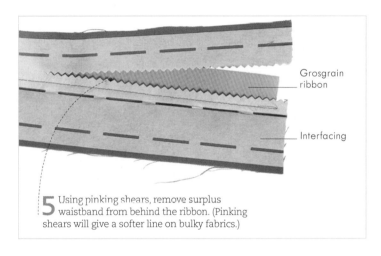

Grosgrain ribbon

Interfacing

5 Using pinking shears, remove surplus waistband from behind the ribbon. (Pinking shears will give a softer line on bulky fabrics.)

6 Attach the waistband to the skirt as for a normal waistband (see opposite page).

7 Fold the ribbon side to the inside of the waistband and press.

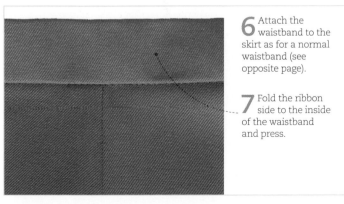

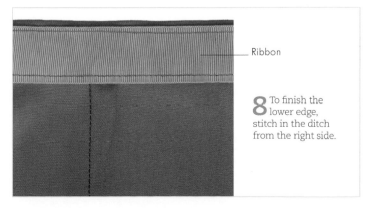

Ribbon

8 To finish the lower edge, stitch in the ditch from the right side.

FASTENERS pp.284–293

WRAP **SKIRT**

Difficulty level ★★★★☆

This modern take on the classic wrap skirt is every bit as chic as it is utilitarian with its stylish, contemporary tabs. For year-round style, you could make it in linen, denim, or corduroy—but allow extra fabric and cut on a nap layout for fabrics with pile, such as corduroy or suedette.

TECHNIQUES USED Layering a seam **p.108**, Understitching **p.109**, Attaching a straight waistband **pp.192–93**, Machine-sewn hems **p.266**

YOU WILL NEED

● Pattern templates on pp.374–377. Choose your size using the Women's Sizing chart on p.368.

● 110 x 45in (275 x 115cm) or 70 x 60in (175 x 150cm) medium-weight dressmaking fabric, such as denim, linen, corduroy, heavy cupro, or suedette. (Requirements for sizes 2–12; see pp.374–377 for other sizes).

● 20in (50cm) lightweight fusible interfacing

● 6 snap fasteners

● 1 button

● Matching thread

PIECES TO CUT

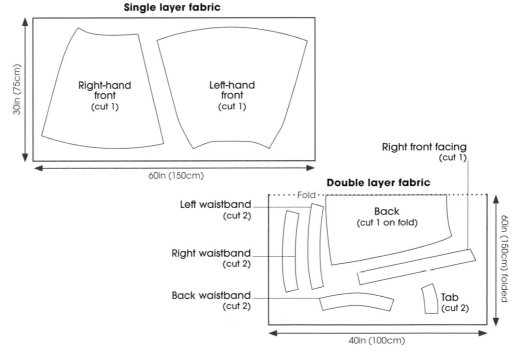

Single layer fabric

Right-hand front (cut 1)

Left-hand front (cut 1)

30in (75cm)

60in (150cm)

Right front facing (cut 1)

Double layer fabric

Fold

Left waistband (cut 2)

Right waistband (cut 2)

Back waistband (cut 2)

Back (cut 1 on fold)

Tab (cut 2)

60in (150cm) folded

40in (100cm)

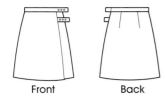

Front   Back

▶ APPLY THE INTERFACING

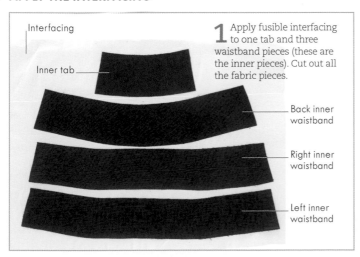

Interfacing

Inner tab

Back inner waistband

Right inner waistband

Left inner waistband

1 Apply fusible interfacing to one tab and three waistband pieces (these are the inner pieces). Cut out all the fabric pieces.

▶ ADD THE DARTS

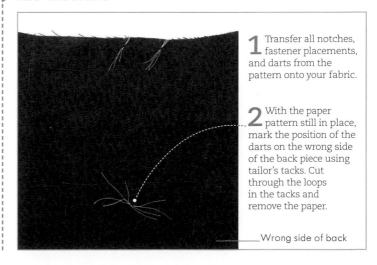

1 Transfer all notches, fastener placements, and darts from the pattern onto your fabric.

2 With the paper pattern still in place, mark the position of the darts on the wrong side of the back piece using tailor's tacks. Cut through the loops in the tacks and remove the paper.

Wrong side of back

PROJECT

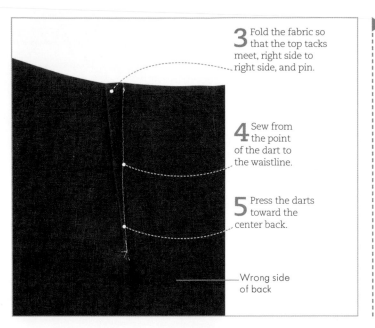

3 Fold the fabric so that the top tacks meet, right side to right side, and pin.

4 Sew from the point of the dart to the waistline.

5 Press the darts toward the center back.

Wrong side of back

SEW THE SIDE SEAMS

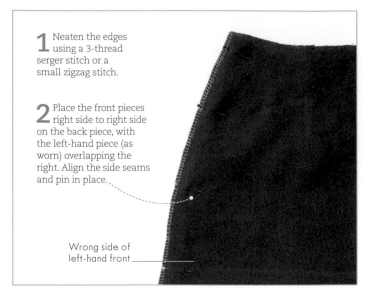

1 Neaten the edges using a 3-thread serger stitch or a small zigzag stitch.

2 Place the front pieces right side to right side on the back piece, with the left-hand piece (as worn) overlapping the right. Align the side seams and pin in place.

Wrong side of left-hand front

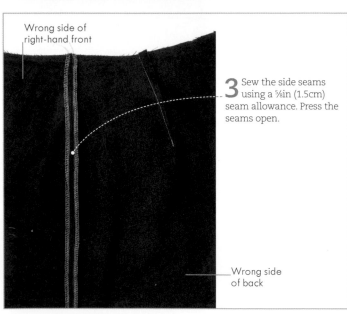

Wrong side of right-hand front

3 Sew the side seams using a ⅝in (1.5cm) seam allowance. Press the seams open.

Wrong side of back

HEM THE LEFT FRONT EDGE

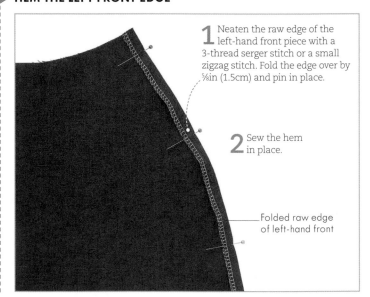

1 Neaten the raw edge of the left-hand front piece with a 3-thread serger stitch or a small zigzag stitch. Fold the edge over by ⅝in (1.5cm) and pin in place.

2 Sew the hem in place.

Folded raw edge of left-hand front

PREPARE THE TAB

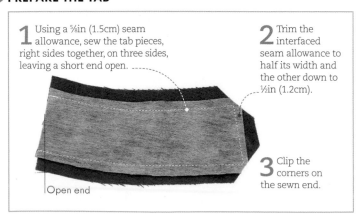

1 Using a ⅝in (1.5cm) seam allowance, sew the tab pieces, right sides together, on three sides, leaving a short end open.

2 Trim the interfaced seam allowance to half its width and the other down to ½in (1.2cm).

3 Clip the corners on the sewn end.

Open end

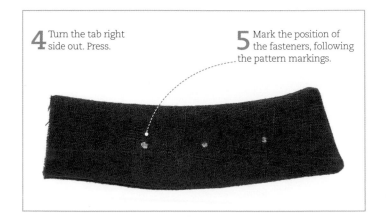

4 Turn the tab right side out. Press.

5 Mark the position of the fasteners, following the pattern markings.

MARKING AIDS **p.19** ● SERGER **pp.34–35** ● SEAM NEATENING **p.95** ● REDUCING SEAM BULK **pp.108–109** ● PLAIN DART **p.113**

▶ **ATTACH THE TAB AND FACING**

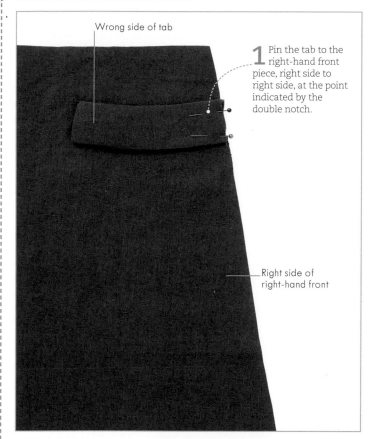

Wrong side of tab

1 Pin the tab to the right-hand front piece, right side to right side, at the point indicated by the double notch.

Right side of right-hand front

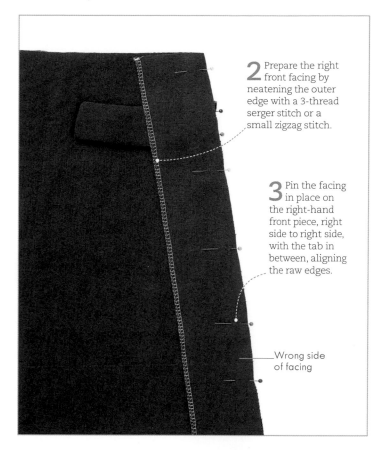

2 Prepare the right front facing by neatening the outer edge with a 3-thread serger stitch or a small zigzag stitch.

3 Pin the facing in place on the right-hand front piece, right side to right side, with the tab in between, aligning the raw edges.

Wrong side of facing

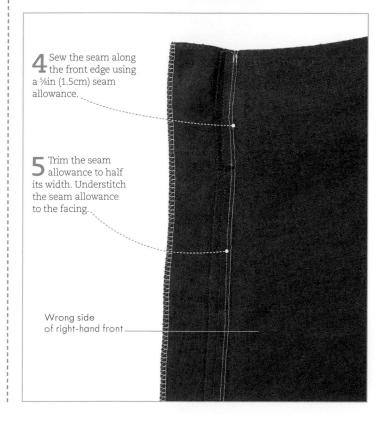

4 Sew the seam along the front edge using a ⅝in (1.5cm) seam allowance.

5 Trim the seam allowance to half its width. Understitch the seam allowance to the facing.

Wrong side of right-hand front

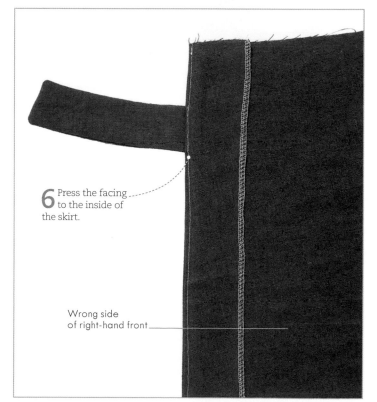

6 Press the facing to the inside of the skirt.

Wrong side of right-hand front

MACHINE-SEWN HEMS **p.226**

PROJECT

▶ **ASSEMBLE THE WAISTBAND**

1 Pin the outer waistband pieces together at the side seams, right side to right side.

2 Sew together using a ⅝in (1.5cm) seam allowance.

Right side of outer waistband piece

Right side of outer waistband piece

Right side of outer waistband piece

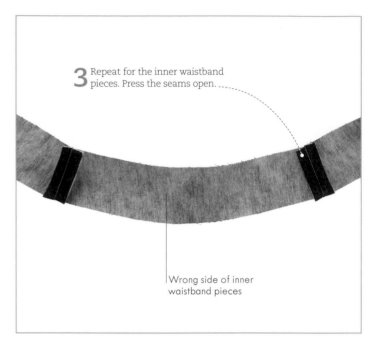

3 Repeat for the inner waistband pieces. Press the seams open.

Wrong side of inner waistband pieces

4 Pin the inner and outer waistband pieces together, right side to right side, along the top concave curve, around the right front flap, and down the left front end.

5 Mark the notch on the right front flap with a pin.

Pin marks stop point

Right front flap

Wrong side of outer waistband

6 Sew in place using a ⅝in (1.5cm) seam allowance, starting at the left front end and ending after rounding the flap, stopping at the first notch.

7 Make small snips along the seam allowance to help release tension along the concave seam.

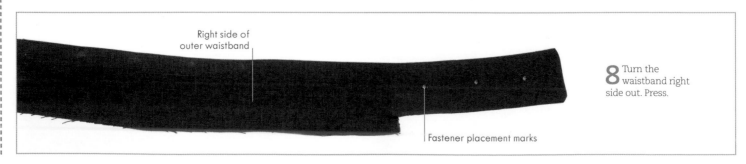

Right side of outer waistband

8 Turn the waistband right side out. Press.

Fastener placement marks

▶ FINISH THE SKIRT

1 Lay the skirt out flat, right side facing. Pin the waistband to the skirt's waistline, right side of the outer waistband facing the right side of the skirt, raw edges aligned, and matching side seams.

Raw edges aligned

2 Sew in place, clip into the curves of the seam allowance, and press the seam up into the waistband.

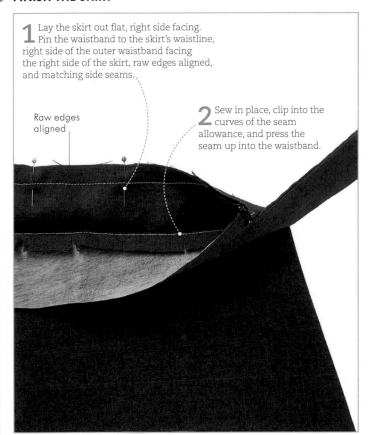

3 Press the unsewn waistline edge of the inner waistband in by ⅝in (1.5cm) and pin in place at the inside of the waistline. Blind hem stitch to secure.

4 Make a buttonhole on the left front waistband at the point indicated by the pattern markings.

Wrong side of left front

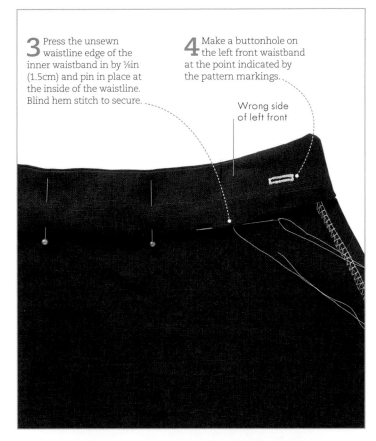

5 Attach a button to the inner waistband on the right front piece at the point indicated on the pattern markings.

6 Attach snap fasteners to the tab and to the extended end of the outer right waistband, and to the corresponding positions on the left underskirt.

▶ SEW THE HEM

1 Using a 3-thread serger stitch or a small zigzag stitch, neaten the raw edge of the hem.

2 Turn up the hem by 1in (2.5cm), or the amount required for your desired length. Press and pin.

3 Hand sew the hem using a blind hem stitch to the wrong side of the fabric along the serged edge. Alternatively, sew in place by machine.

HAND-SEWN HEMS **pp.264–265** ● MACHINE-SEWN HEMS **p.266** ● MACHINE-MADE BUTTONHOLES **p.306**

TECHNIQUES

BELTS

A belt in a fabric that matches the garment can add the perfect finishing touch. Whether it be a soft tie belt or a stiff structured belt, it will be best if it has an interfacing of some kind—the firmer and more structured the belt, the firmer the interfacing should be. A belt will also need belt loops to support it and prevent it from drooping.

DIRECTORY OF BELTS AND TIE-BACKS

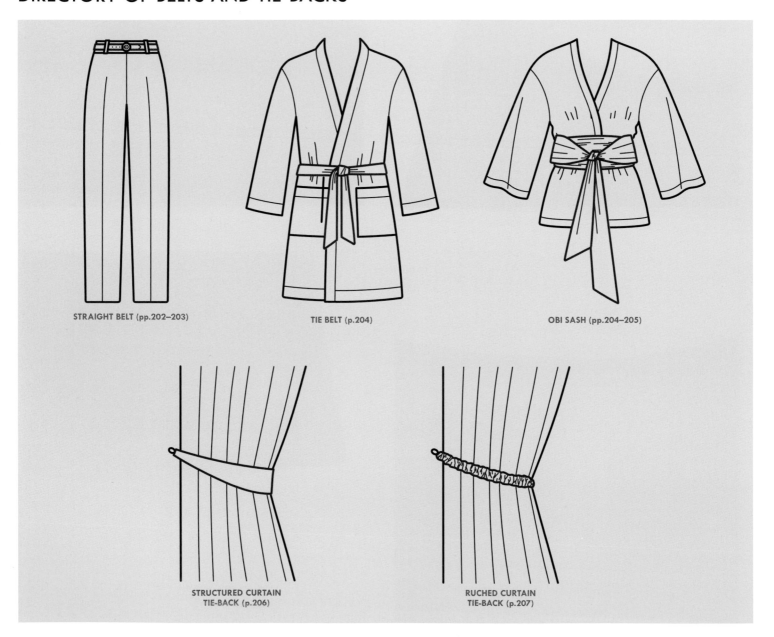

STRAIGHT BELT (pp.202–203)

TIE BELT (p.204)

OBI SASH (pp.204–205)

STRUCTURED CURTAIN
TIE-BACK (p.206)

RUCHED CURTAIN
TIE-BACK (p.207)

BELT LOOPS

Belt loops can be made from fabric strips and stitched to the garment, or they can be made more simply from thread loops fashioned by hand stitching. Fabric loops are designed to support a heavier belt.

▶ HAND-STITCHED BELT LOOPS

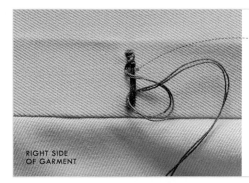

1 Work the belt loop prior to the waistband being finished on the inside. Using double buttonhole thread, work several strands of thread long enough to slot a belt through.

RIGHT SIDE OF GARMENT

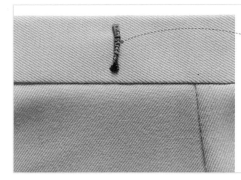

2 Use a buttonhole stitch and work the stitches across the loops.

3 When the loops are covered with buttonhole stitches, take the thread to the reverse and finish securely.

▶ MACHINE-STITCHED BELT LOOPS

1 Cut the fabric strips 1¼in (3cm) wide and long enough to allow for the depth of the belt plus turnings of ⅝in (1.5cm) at each end.

2 Press the long edges of the fabric loops to the center, wrong side to wrong side.

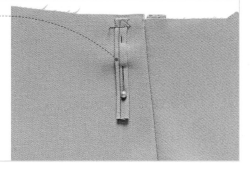

3 Press the loops in half lengthwise.

4 Sew along the center of each loop, securing the folded edges.

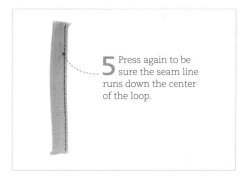

5 Press again to be sure the seam line runs down the center of the loop.

6 Starting at each side seam and then at regular intervals between, place the loops to the waist of the garment, on the right side. Sew to secure at the waist inside the seam allowance.

7 Apply the waistband to the garment, stitching across the loops as you do so.

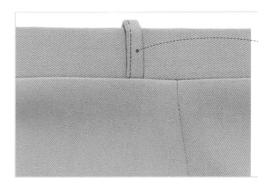

8 Press the waistband in half lengthwise to give a center crease.

9 Bring the loops up on to the waistband.

10 Secure the end of each loop to the inner edge of the waistband using a small, close zigzag stitch.

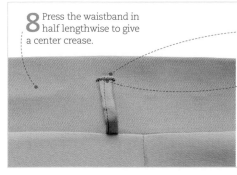

11 When the waistband is completed, the loop will sit on it with no visible stitches.

STITCHES MADE WITH A MACHINE **pp.92—93**

TECHNIQUES

REINFORCED STRAIGHT BELT

Difficulty level ★★★★☆

This is a straightforward way to make a belt to match a garment. It can be of any width as it is reinforced with a very firm fusible interfacing, such as a craft interfacing. If one layer of interfacing is not firm enough, try adding another layer. The interfacing should be cut along its length to avoid joins. To ensure that it is cut straight, use a rotary cutter on a self-healing mat.

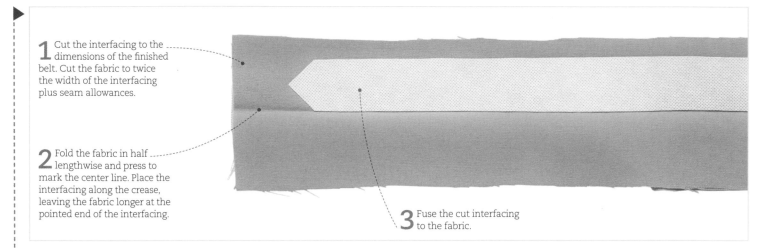

1 Cut the interfacing to the dimensions of the finished belt. Cut the fabric to twice the width of the interfacing plus seam allowances.

2 Fold the fabric in half lengthwise and press to mark the center line. Place the interfacing along the crease, leaving the fabric longer at the pointed end of the interfacing.

3 Fuse the cut interfacing to the fabric.

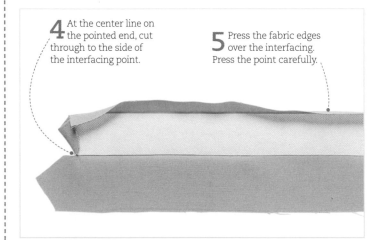

4 At the center line on the pointed end, cut through to the side of the interfacing point.

5 Press the fabric edges over the interfacing. Press the point carefully.

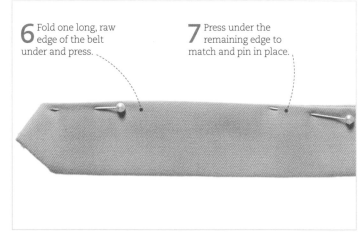

6 Fold one long, raw edge of the belt under and press.

7 Press under the remaining edge to match and pin in place.

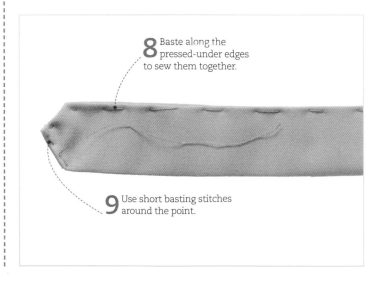

8 Baste along the pressed-under edges to sew them together.

9 Use short basting stitches around the point.

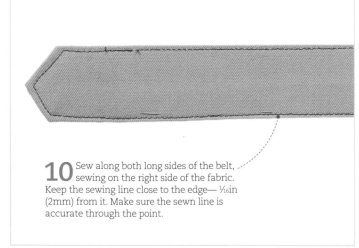

10 Sew along both long sides of the belt, sewing on the right side of the fabric. Keep the sewing line close to the edge— 1/16in (2mm) from it. Make sure the sewn line is accurate through the point.

11 Measure the positioning of the grommets toward the pointed end of the belt.

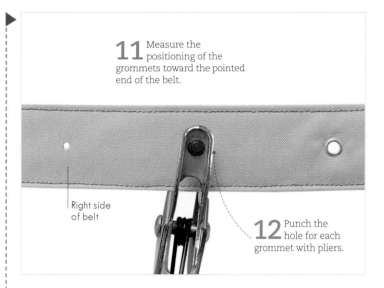

Right side of belt

12 Punch the hole for each grommet with pliers.

13 Insert a ³⁄₁₆in (4mm) grommet into the hole, working from the right side of the belt.

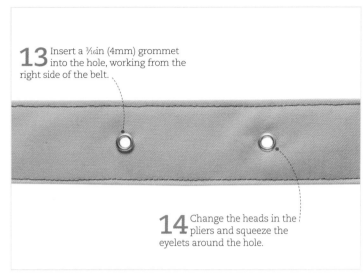

14 Change the heads in the pliers and squeeze the eyelets around the hole.

15 Insert one grommet at the other end of the belt about 2in (5cm) from the end, placing it centrally on the right side of the belt.

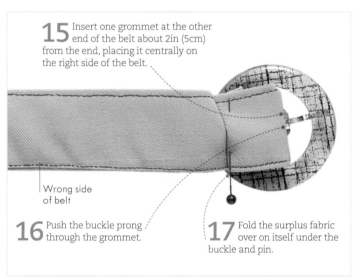

Wrong side of belt

16 Push the buckle prong through the grommet.

17 Fold the surplus fabric over on itself under the buckle and pin.

18 Sew down by machine or by hand, then turn the belt over.

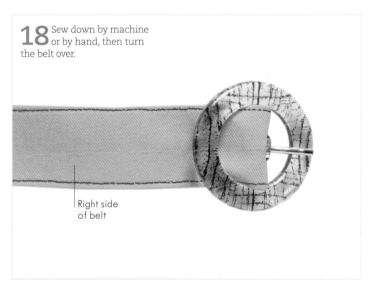

Right side of belt

19 When the belt is placed around the waist, check that the fit is correct. Add extra grommets if required.

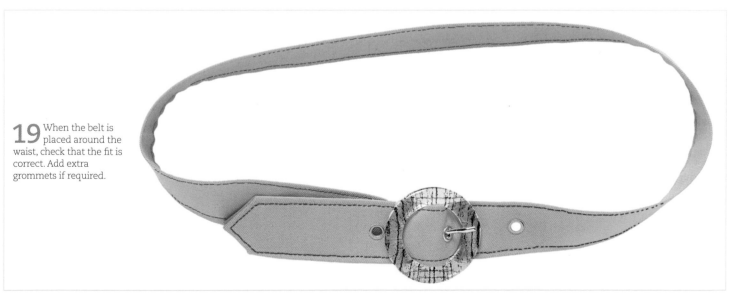

TECHNIQUES

TIE BELT

Difficulty level ★★★★★

A tie belt is the easiest of all the belts to make. It can be any width and made of most fabrics, from cottons for summer dresses to satin and silks for bridal wear. Most tie belts will require a light- to medium-weight interfacing for support. A fusible interfacing is the best choice as it will stay in place when tied repeatedly. If a very long tie belt is required, the belt can be joined at the center back.

1 Cut fabric for the belt, with a point at each end. Cut a fusible interfacing the same length, but half the width.

2 Place the interfacing on one half of the fabric on the wrong side and press to fuse.

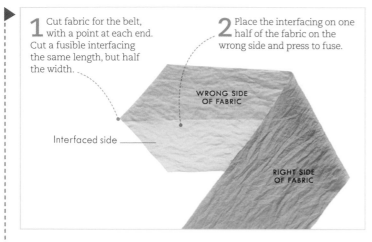

Interfaced side

WRONG SIDE OF FABRIC

RIGHT SIDE OF FABRIC

3 Fold the belt in half, right side to right side so the fusible is showing. Pin.

4 Sew along all the raw edges using a ⅝in (1.5cm) seam allowance. Remember to leave a gap of approx. 3in (8cm) at the center back to turn the belt through.

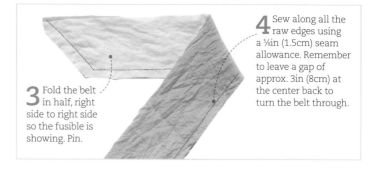

5 Layer the seam by removing half of the seam allowance on the fused side.

6 Remove the bulk from the corners.

7 Press the seam as stitched, then turn through while the fabric is still warm.

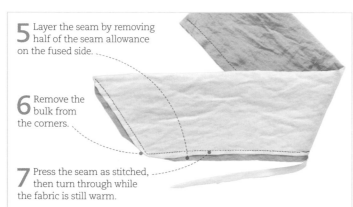

8 Once the belt has been turned to the right side, press the seam carefully so that it is on the very edge.

9 Press the points carefully.

10 Hand sew the gap at the center back closed with a flat fell or blind hem stitch.

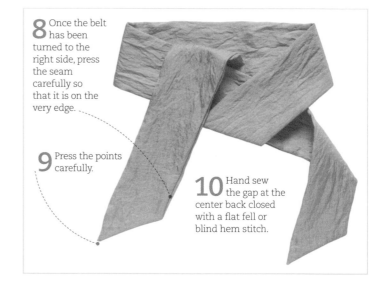

OBI SASH

Difficulty level ★★★☆☆

An obi sash is a variation of the traditional sash that is worn with a kimono. This type of sash has a stiffened center piece with softer ties that cross at the back and then wrap to the front and tie. If you are using a firm fabric such as silk dupioni, satin, or heavy cotton, interfacing will not be required for the ties.

1 Make the ties first. Cut long strips of fabric of the required length and width.

2 Fold the ties lengthwise in half, right side to right side, and pin.

3 Sew the long, raw edges together. Sew across the angled end.

4 Trim the pointed corners.

5 Turn the tie ends to the right side and press.

HOW TO APPLY A FUSIBLE INTERFACING p.54 ● **HAND SEWING pp.90–91**

6 Next make the center section. Cut out two shaped pieces of fabric and a matching piece of very firm fusible interfacing.

Interfacing

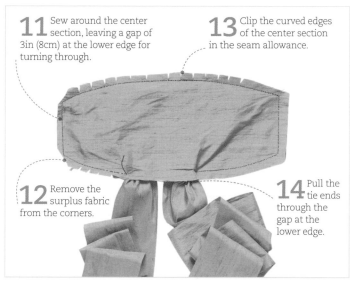

RIGHT SIDE OF FABRIC

7 Fuse the interfacing to the wrong side of one piece of fabric. If one layer of interfacing does not make the fabric stiff enough, add another layer.

8 Center the tie ends to the short ends of the stiffened center piece on the right side. Sew to secure, using a ⅜in (1cm) seam allowance.

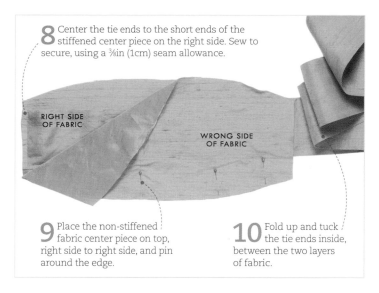

RIGHT SIDE OF FABRIC

WRONG SIDE OF FABRIC

9 Place the non-stiffened fabric center piece on top, right side to right side, and pin around the edge.

10 Fold up and tuck the tie ends inside, between the two layers of fabric.

11 Sew around the center section, leaving a gap of 3in (8cm) at the lower edge for turning through.

13 Clip the curved edges of the center section in the seam allowance.

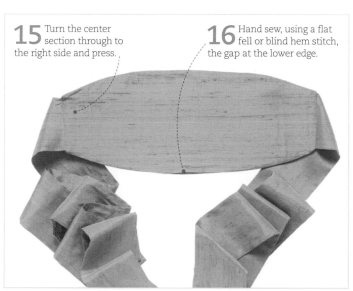

12 Remove the surplus fabric from the corners.

14 Pull the tie ends through the gap at the lower edge.

15 Turn the center section through to the right side and press.

16 Hand sew, using a flat fell or blind hem stitch, the gap at the lower edge.

17 The finished obi sash.

STITCHES MADE WITH A MACHINE pp.92–93 • **HOW TO MAKE A PLAIN SEAM p.94** • **REDUCING SEAM BULK pp.108–109**

CURTAIN TIE-BACKS

Difficulty level ✶✶✩✩✩

Tie-backs are used to hold the drape of a curtain in position. Some are structured, with an interfacing, and follow a predetermined shape, while others are softer and more decorative. The construction of a tie-back is similar to that of a tie belt.

▶ **STRUCTURED TIE-BACK**

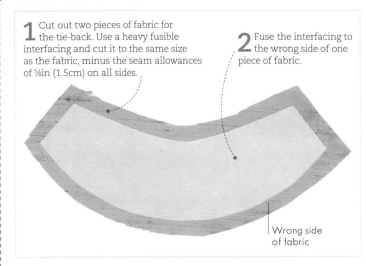

1 Cut out two pieces of fabric for the tie-back. Use a heavy fusible interfacing and cut it to the same size as the fabric, minus the seam allowances of ⅝in (1.5cm) on all sides.

2 Fuse the interfacing to the wrong side of one piece of fabric.

Wrong side of fabric

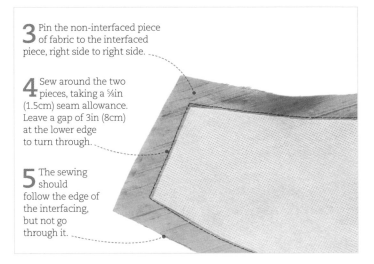

3 Pin the non-interfaced piece of fabric to the interfaced piece, right side to right side.

4 Sew around the two pieces, taking a ⅝in (1.5cm) seam allowance. Leave a gap of 3in (8cm) at the lower edge to turn through.

5 The sewing should follow the edge of the interfacing, but not go through it.

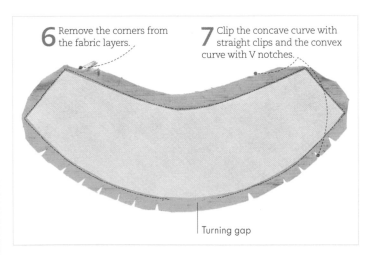

6 Remove the corners from the fabric layers.

7 Clip the concave curve with straight clips and the convex curve with V notches.

Turning gap

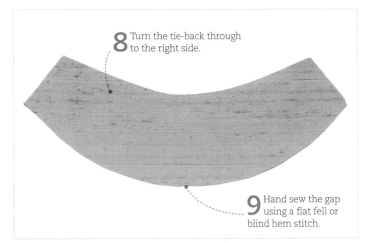

8 Turn the tie-back through to the right side.

9 Hand sew the gap using a flat fell or blind hem stitch.

10 On the two short ends of the tie-back, sew on a curtain ring, using polyester all-purpose thread. Use a buttonhole stitch to secure it.

USEFUL EXTRAS pp.20–21 ● **HOW TO APPLY A FUSIBLE INTERFACING p.54** ● **HAND SEWING pp.90–91** ● **REDUCING SEAM BULK pp.108–109**

▶ DECORATIVE RUCHED TIE-BACK

1 Cut a piece of batting 10in (25cm) wide and to the required tie-back length.

2 Roll up the batting like a sausage, but not too tight, and pin in place.

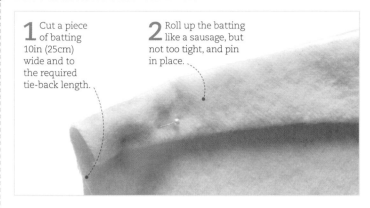

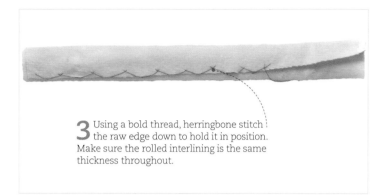

3 Using a bold thread, herringbone stitch the raw edge down to hold it in position. Make sure the rolled interlining is the same thickness throughout.

4 For the outer decorative layer, cut a piece of fabric 5in (12cm) wide and three times the required length.

5 Fold lengthwise in half, right side to right side.

6 Sew the long raw edges together using a ⅜in (1cm) seam allowance.

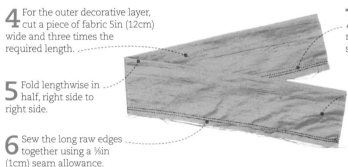

7 Sew again, between the seam line and the raw edge. The double seams are for strength.

8 Turn the decorative top layer fabric through to the right side and press.

9 Tie the thread ends from the herringbone stitch on the batting to a loop turner.

10 Using the loop turner, pull the batting sausage through the decorative layer. This is difficult as it will stick. Work the decorative fabric gently down the batting.

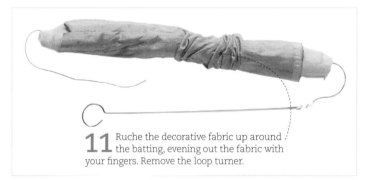

11 Ruche the decorative fabric up around the batting, evening out the fabric with your fingers. Remove the loop turner.

12 Hand sew about every 1¼in (3cm) to secure the ruching on the tie-back.

13 Sew on a curtain ring at each end, using a buttonhole stitch to secure the rings.

INTERLININGS **p.324**

SLEEVES AND SLEEVE FINISHES

Sleeves come in all shapes and lengths. They should always hang properly from the end of the wearer's shoulder, without wrinkles. The lower end of the sleeve is normally finished by means of a cuff or a facing.

SLEEVES

A few sleeves, such as the dolman, are cut as part of the garment, but most sleeves, including set-in and raglan, are made separately and then inserted into the armhole. Whichever type of sleeve is being inserted, always place it to the armhole and not the armhole to the sleeve—in other words, always work with the sleeve facing you.

DIRECTORY OF SLEEVES

SET-IN SLEEVE (p.211)

PUFF SLEEVE (p.212)

FLAT SLEEVE (p.213)

RAGLAN SLEEVE (p.213)

KIMONO SLEEVE (p.214)

DOLMAN SLEEVE (p.215)

DOLMAN SLEEVE WITH A GUSSET (p.215)

STITCHES MADE WITH A MACHINE **pp.92–93** ● HOW TO MAKE A PLAIN SEAM **p.94**

INSERTING A SET-IN SLEEVE

Difficulty level ✳✳✳✳✳

A set-in sleeve should feature a smooth sleeve head that fits on the end of your shoulder accurately. This is achieved by the use of ease stitches, which are long stitches used to tighten the fabric but not gather it.

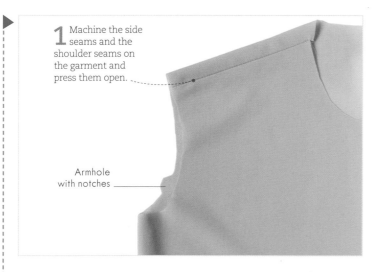

1 Machine the side seams and the shoulder seams on the garment and press them open.

Armhole with notches

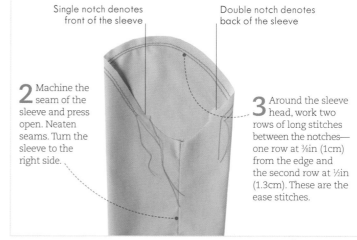

Single notch denotes front of the sleeve

Double notch denotes back of the sleeve

2 Machine the seam of the sleeve and press open. Neaten seams. Turn the sleeve to the right side.

3 Around the sleeve head, work two rows of long stitches between the notches—one row at ⅜in (1cm) from the edge and the second row at ½in (1.3cm). These are the ease stitches.

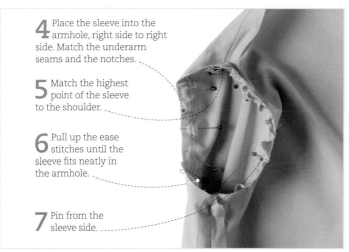

4 Place the sleeve into the armhole, right side to right side. Match the underarm seams and the notches.

5 Match the highest point of the sleeve to the shoulder.

6 Pull up the ease stitches until the sleeve fits neatly in the armhole.

7 Pin from the sleeve side.

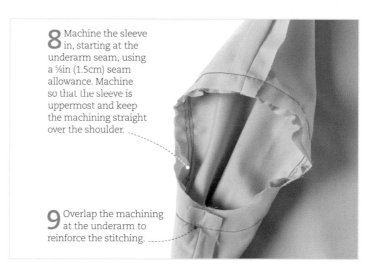

8 Machine the sleeve in, starting at the underarm seam, using a ⅝in (1.5cm) seam allowance. Machine so that the sleeve is uppermost and keep the machining straight over the shoulder.

9 Overlap the machining at the underarm to reinforce the stitching.

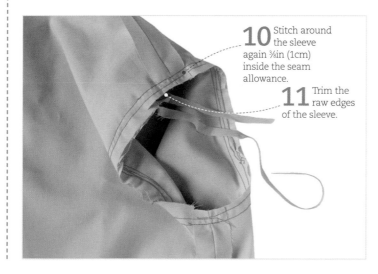

10 Stitch around the sleeve again ⅜in (1cm) inside the seam allowance.

11 Trim the raw edges of the sleeve.

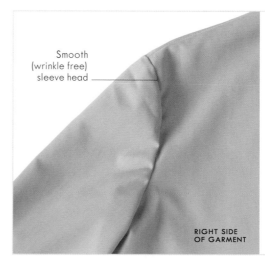

Smooth (wrinkle free) sleeve head

12 Neaten the seam with a zigzag or serger stitch, then turn the sleeve through the armhole.

RIGHT SIDE OF GARMENT

SEAM NEATENING p.95 ● REDUCING SEAM BULK pp.108–109

PUFF SLEEVE

Difficulty level  ✶✶✶✶✶

A sleeve that has a gathered sleeve head is referred to as a puff sleeve or gathered sleeve. It is one of the easiest sleeves to insert because the gathers take up any spare fabric.

1 Sew the sleeve, right side to right side, using a ⅝ in (1.5 cm) seam allowance. Press the seam open.

2 Between the sleeve notches, insert two rows of gather stitches, one row at ⅜ in (1 cm) from the raw edge and the second row at ½ in (1.3 cm).

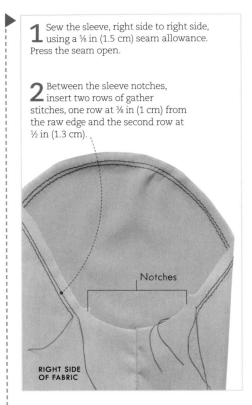

Notches

RIGHT SIDE OF FABRIC

3 Place the sleeve into the armhole, right side to right side.

4 Match the notches and the underarm seams.

5 Pull up the gathers to make the sleeve head fit the armhole.

6 Pin from the sleeve side.

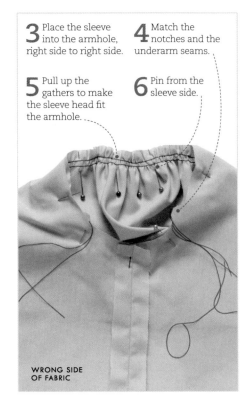

WRONG SIDE OF FABRIC

7 Working with the sleeve upper-most, sew the sleeve to the armhole. Use a ⅝ in (1.5 cm) seam allowance. Overlap the seam at underarm to reinforce. Keep seam allowances open and flat.

8 Sew around the sleeve seam again between the seam and the raw edge.

9 Trim away the surplus fabric by ³⁄₁₆ in (5 mm).

10 Neaten the seam.

11 Turn right side out— all the gathers will be at the top of the sleeve.

STITCHES MADE WITH A MACHINE **pp.92—93** ● SEAM NEATENING **p.95**

FLAT SLEEVE CONSTRUCTION

On shirts and children's clothes, sleeves are inserted flat prior to the side seams being constructed. This technique can be difficult on firmly woven fabrics, because no ease stitches are used.

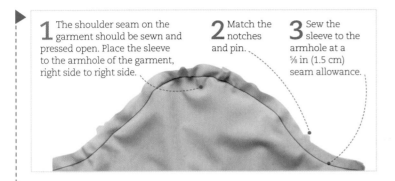

1 The shoulder seam on the garment should be sewn and pressed open. Place the sleeve to the armhole of the garment, right side to right side.

2 Match the notches and pin.

3 Sew the sleeve to the armhole at a ⅝ in (1.5 cm) seam allowance.

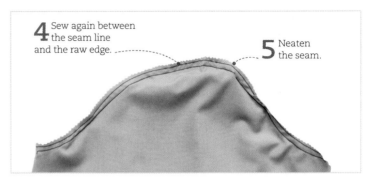

4 Sew again between the seam line and the raw edge.

5 Neaten the seam.

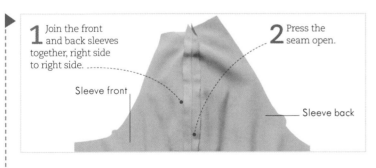

6 Press the sleeve seam toward the sleeve.

7 Fold the garment and sleeve right side to right side. Match the underarm seams.

8 Sew together with a ⅝ in (1.5 cm) seam allowance.

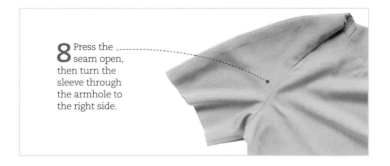

9 Press the seam open, then turn the sleeve through the armhole, right side out.

RAGLAN SLEEVE

A raglan sleeve can be constructed as a one-piece sleeve or a two-piece sleeve. The armhole seam on a raglan sleeve runs diagonally from the armhole to the neck.

1 Join the front and back sleeves together, right side to right side.

2 Press the seam open.

Sleeve front

Sleeve back

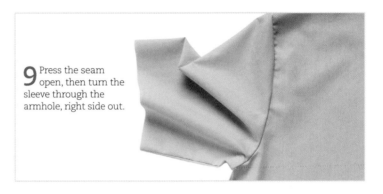

3 Pin the sleeve to the front and back of the garment, matching the notches.

4 Sew together using a ⅝ in (1.5 cm) seam allowance.

5 Press the seams open.

Sleeve   Back   Sleeve

6 Bring the front and the back of the garment together, right side to right side.

7 Sew the side seam of the garment and continue stitching down the sleeve.

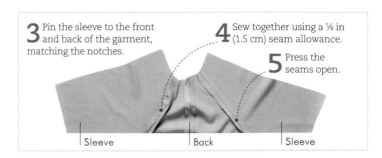

8 Press the seam open, then turn the sleeve through the armhole to the right side.

REDUCING SEAM BULK pp.108–109 • **HOW TO MAKE AND FIT GATHERS p.135**

KIMONO SLEEVE

Difficulty level ★★☆☆☆

A kimono sleeve is a very large, deep sleeve that is inserted on to a garment prior to its construction. Some kimono sleeves are cut with a curve and others are cut straight, but they are made the same way.

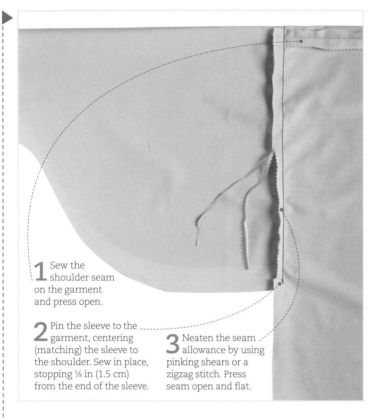

1 Sew the shoulder seam on the garment and press open.

2 Pin the sleeve to the garment, centering (matching) the sleeve to the shoulder. Sew in place, stopping ⅝ in (1.5 cm) from the end of the sleeve.

3 Neaten the seam allowance by using pinking shears or a zigzag stitch. Press seam open and flat.

4 Sew the side seam of the garment, starting where the sleeve seam stops.

5 Push the sleeve seam allowance toward the garment and sew the sleeve seam.

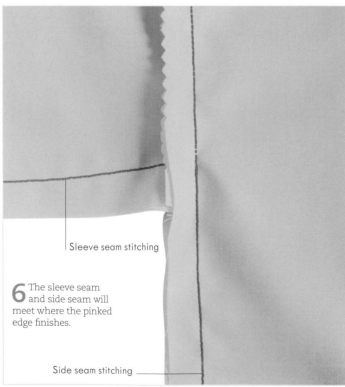

Sleeve seam stitching

6 The sleeve seam and side seam will meet where the pinked edge finishes.

Side seam stitching

7 Turn the sleeve through to the right side. The sleeve to garment side should be square. Finish the sleeve opening with a single hem.

PATTERN MARKING **pp.82–83** ● STITCHES MADE WITH A MACHINE **pp.92–93** ● HOW TO MAKE A PLAIN SEAM **p.94**

DOLMAN SLEEVE

Difficulty level ✱✱✱✱✱

A dolman sleeve is cut as an extension to a garment. As the armhole is very loose, it is ideal for a coat or jacket. The dolman sleeve often has a raglan shoulder pad to define the shoulder end.

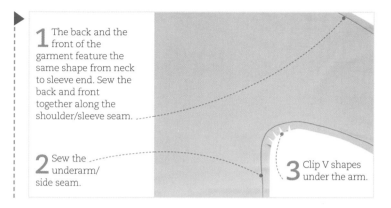

1 The back and the front of the garment feature the same shape from neck to sleeve end. Sew the back and front together along the shoulder/sleeve seam.

2 Sew the underarm/side seam.

3 Clip V shapes under the arm.

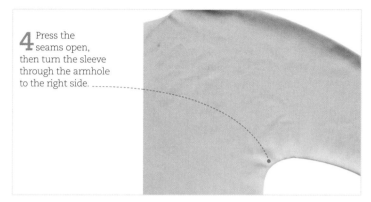

4 Press the seams open, then turn the sleeve through the armhole to the right side.

DOLMAN SLEEVE WITH A GUSSET

Difficulty level ✱✱✱✱✱

A dolman sleeve can be cut through, to give a tight sleeve. However a tight dolman sleeve will require an underarm gusset to allow movement. The gusset requires accurate sewing and marking if it is to be inserted correctly.

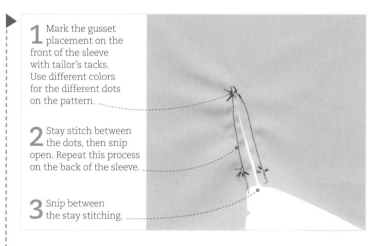

1 Mark the gusset placement on the front of the sleeve with tailor's tacks. Use different colors for the different dots on the pattern.

2 Stay stitch between the dots, then snip open. Repeat this process on the back of the sleeve.

3 Snip between the stay stitching.

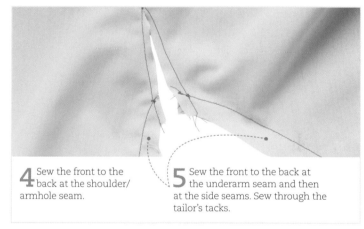

4 Sew the front to the back at the shoulder/armhole seam.

5 Sew the front to the back at the underarm seam and then at the side seams. Sew through the tailor's tacks.

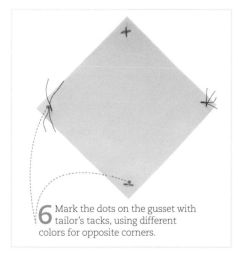

6 Mark the dots on the gusset with tailor's tacks, using different colors for opposite corners.

7 Place the gusset into the opening in the sleeve, matching the colored tailor's tacks.

8 Sew from one tailor's tack to the next. Do not pivot at corners.

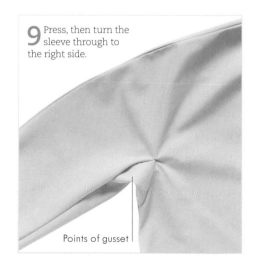

9 Press, then turn the sleeve through to the right side.

Points of gusset

UNISEX **DRESSING GOWN**

Difficulty level ✺✺✹✹✹

Perfect for him or for her to wear on lazy Sundays, this fabulous gown looks luxurious but is straightforward to make. Optional hem and cuff panels allow you to make long or short variations, and it will drape beautifully in lightweight fabrics such as cotton lawn, silk, or viscose.

TECHNIQUES USED Tie belt **p.204**, Kimono sleeve **p.214**, Attaching a patch pocket **p.242**

YOU WILL NEED

- Pattern templates on pp.378–383. Choose your size using the Unisex Sizing chart on p.368.

- For long version (pictured): 130 x 60in (3.3m x 150cm) main fabric and 102 x 60in (2.6m x 150cm) contrast fabric in lightweight fabrics, such as cotton lawn, cotton silk, woven viscose, silk habutai, or lightweight linen. (See pp.378–383 for full fabric requirements for both long and short versions.)

- Loop turner

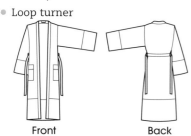

Front   Back

PIECES TO CUT

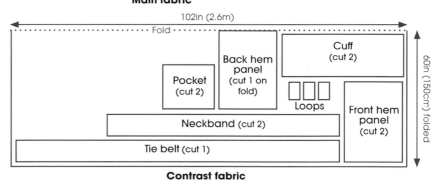

Main fabric

Contrast fabric

ASSEMBLE AND SEW ON THE POCKETS

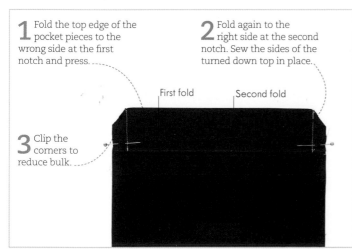

1 Fold the top edge of the pocket pieces to the wrong side at the first notch and press.

2 Fold again to the right side at the second notch. Sew the sides of the turned down top in place.

First fold   Second fold

3 Clip the corners to reduce bulk.

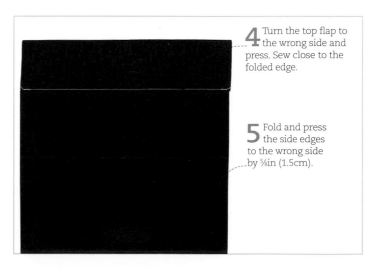

4 Turn the top flap to the wrong side and press. Sew close to the folded edge.

5 Fold and press the side edges to the wrong side by ⅝in (1.5cm).

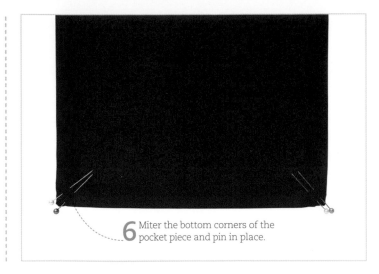

6 Miter the bottom corners of the pocket piece and pin in place.

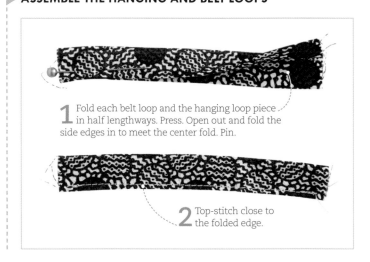

Diagonal stitch

7 Position the pockets on the right side of the front pieces according to the pattern markings. Top-stitch the sides and along the bottom, as close to the edge as possible.

8 Reinforce the top corners with a diagonal stitch.

▶ JOIN THE EXTENSION PANELS (LONG VERSION)

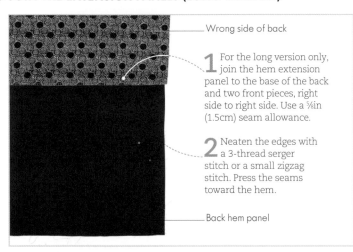

Wrong side of back

1 For the long version only, join the hem extension panel to the base of the back and two front pieces, right side to right side. Use a ⅝in (1.5cm) seam allowance.

2 Neaten the edges with a 3-thread serger stitch or a small zigzag stitch. Press the seams toward the hem.

Back hem panel

▶ ASSEMBLE THE HANGING AND BELT LOOPS

1 Fold each belt loop and the hanging loop piece in half lengthways. Press. Open out and fold the side edges in to meet the center fold. Pin.

2 Top-stitch close to the folded edge.

▶ SEW THE SHOULDER SEAMS

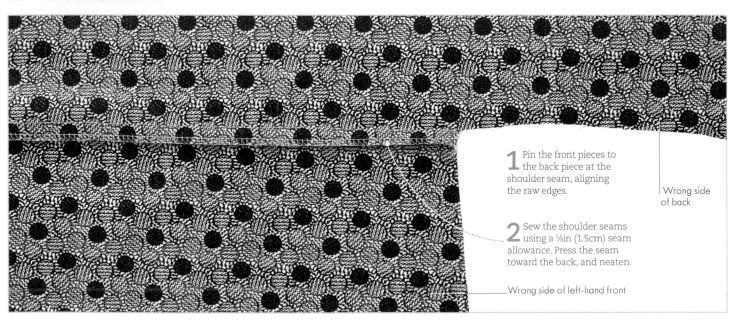

1 Pin the front pieces to the back piece at the shoulder seam, aligning the raw edges.

Wrong side of back

2 Sew the shoulder seams using a ⅝in (1.5cm) seam allowance. Press the seam toward the back, and neaten.

Wrong side of left-hand front

SEAM NEATENING **p.95** ● BELT LOOPS **p.201** ● KIMONO SLEEVE **p.214**

▶ ATTACH THE SLEEVES

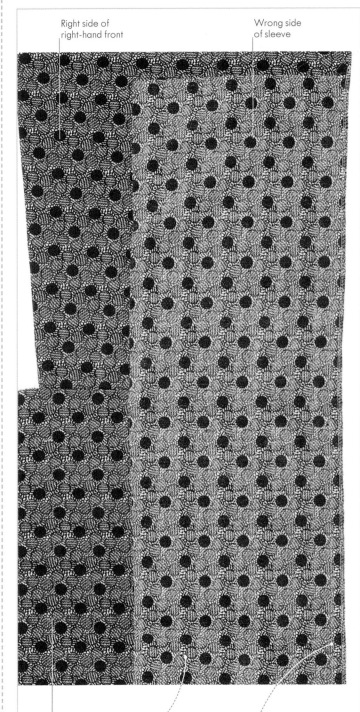

Right side of
right-hand front

Wrong side
of sleeve

Right side of back

1 Pin the sleeve, flat,
right side to right
side, to the side seam.
Align the sleeve between
the two notches on the
side seam, and match
the central notch with
the shoulder seam.

2 Sew in place using
a ⅝in (1.5cm) seam
allowance. Press the
seam toward the
sleeve.

3 Repeat steps
1–2 for the
other sleeve.

▶ SEW THE SIDE SEAMS

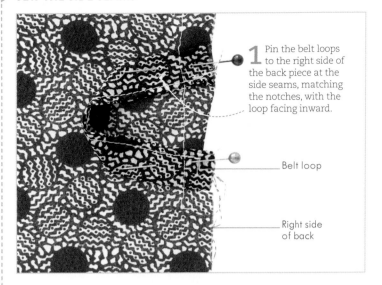

1 Pin the belt loops
to the right side of
the back piece at the
side seams, matching
the notches, with the
loop facing inward.

Belt loop

Right side
of back

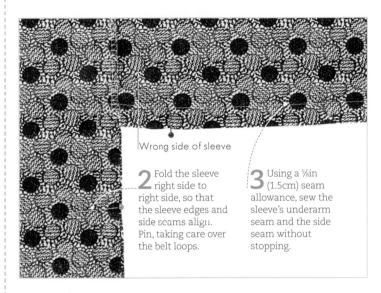

Wrong side of sleeve

2 Fold the sleeve
right side to
right side, so that
the sleeve edges and
side seams align.
Pin, taking care over
the belt loops.

3 Using a ⅝in
(1.5cm) seam
allowance, sew the
sleeve's underarm
seam and the side
seam without
stopping.

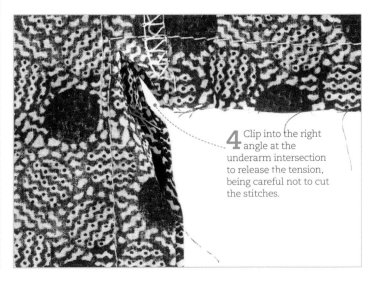

4 Clip into the right
angle at the
underarm intersection
to release the tension,
being careful not to cut
the stitches.

REINFORCING POCKET CORNERS **p.242** ● MITERED CORNERS **p.269**

▶ **ATTACH THE CUFF**

1 For the cuffed version, join the side edges of the cuff extension panels to make a tube, using a ⅝in (1.5cm) seam allowance. Press the seam open.

Side edges joined to make a tube

2 Fold the cuff piece in half, wrong side to wrong side. Align the raw edge of the cuff to the raw edge of the sleeve, right side to right side. Match the underarm seam to the cuff seam.

Cuff seam aligned with underarm seam

3 Sew, then neaten the seam using a 3-thread serger stitch or a small zigzag stitch.

4 Fold the cuff out to the right side and press in place.

▶ **ASSEMBLE AND ATTACH THE NECKBAND**

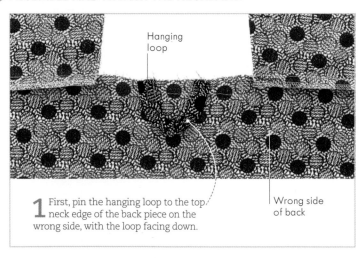

Hanging loop

Wrong side of back

1 First, pin the hanging loop to the top neck edge of the back piece on the wrong side, with the loop facing down.

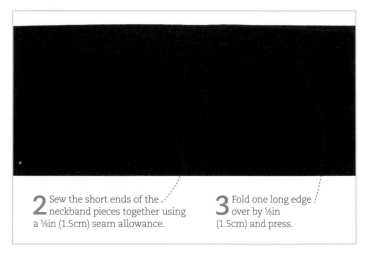

2 Sew the short ends of the neckband pieces together using a ⅝in (1.5cm) seam allowance.

3 Fold one long edge over by ⅝in (1.5cm) and press.

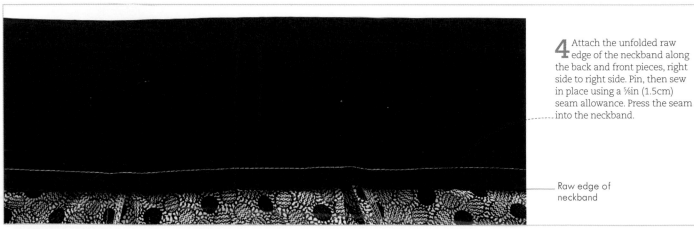

4 Attach the unfolded raw edge of the neckband along the back and front pieces, right side to right side. Pin, then sew in place using a ⅝in (1.5cm) seam allowance. Press the seam into the neckband.

Raw edge of neckband

USEFUL EXTRAS p.20 • **HAND SEWING pp.90–91** • **SEAM NEATENING p.95** • **TOP-STITCHING p.109** • **TIE BELT p.204**

5 Fold and press the unsewn edge of the neckband in to the wrong side, so that it meets the seamline. Pin in place.

Wrong side of front

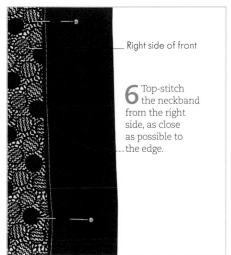

Right side of front

6 Top-stitch the neckband from the right side, as close as possible to the edge.

▶ FINISH THE SLEEVES AND HEM

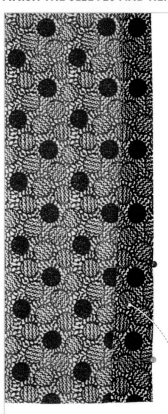

1 For the short sleeve version, make a double-turn hem by folding and pressing the hem by ¼in (6mm) and again by ½in (1.2cm)—or the amount required for your desired length. Sew ⅜in (1cm) from the folded edge.

2 To finish the bottom hem, make a double-turn hem by folding and pressing the hem by ¼in (6mm) and again by ½in (1.2cm)—or the amount required for your desired length. Sew ⅜in (1cm) from the folded edge.

▶ ASSEMBLE THE TIE BELT

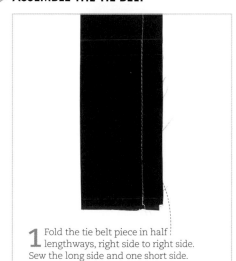

1 Fold the tie belt piece in half lengthways, right side to right side. Sew the long side and one short side. Leave one side open to turn through.

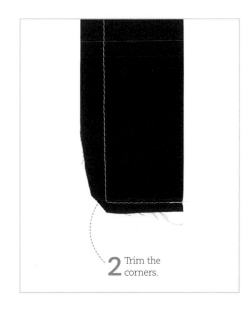

2 Trim the corners.

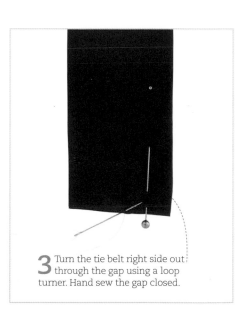

3 Turn the tie belt right side out through the gap using a loop turner. Hand sew the gap closed.

DOUBLE-TURN HEM **p.266**

SLEEVE EDGE **FINISHES**

The lower edge of a sleeve has to be finished according to the style of the garment being made. Some sleeves are finished tight into the arm or wrist, while others may have a more decorative or functional finish.

DIRECTORY OF SLEEVE EDGE FINISHES

SLEEVE EDGE WITH SELF HEM (p.223)

SLEEVE EDGE WITH A BIAS-BOUND HEM (p.223)

ELASTIC SLEEVE EDGE WITH A HEADING (p.224)

ELASTIC SLEEVE EDGE (p.225)

SLEEVE EDGE WITH RUFFLE (p.226)

FACED SLEEVE EDGE (p.227)

SLEEVE HEMS

Difficulty level **★★☆☆☆**

The simplest way to finish a sleeve is to make a small hem, which can be part of the sleeve or additional fabric that is attached to turn up. A self hem is where the edge of the sleeve is turned up on to itself. If there is insufficient fabric to turn up, a bias binding can be used to create the hem. You can use purchased bias binding or make your own bias strips.

▶ SELF HEM

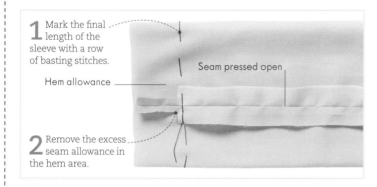

1 Mark the final length of the sleeve with a row of basting stitches.

Hem allowance

Seam pressed open

2 Remove the excess seam allowance in the hem area.

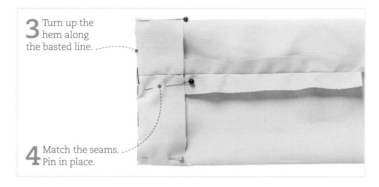

3 Turn up the hem along the basted line.

4 Match the seams. Pin in place.

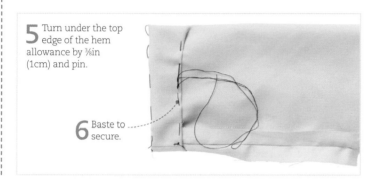

5 Turn under the top edge of the hem allowance by ⅜in (1cm) and pin.

6 Baste to secure.

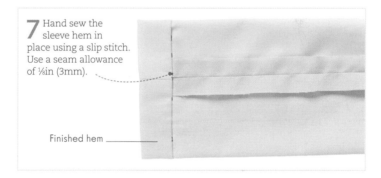

7 Hand sew the sleeve hem in place using a slip stitch. Use a seam allowance of ⅛in (3mm).

Finished hem

▶ BIAS-BOUND HEM

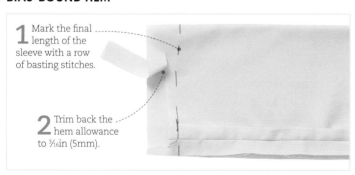

1 Mark the final length of the sleeve with a row of basting stitches.

2 Trim back the hem allowance to ³⁄₁₆in (5mm).

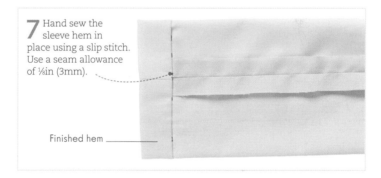

3 Cut a strip of ¾in (2cm) wide bias binding to the required length. Attach the bias to the sleeve, right side to right side.

4 Turn under the end of the bias, placing the fold of the bias to the sleeve seam.

5 Sew in place using a ³⁄₁₆in (5mm) seam allowance.

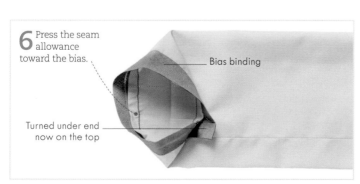

6 Press the seam allowance toward the bias.

Bias binding

Turned under end now on the top

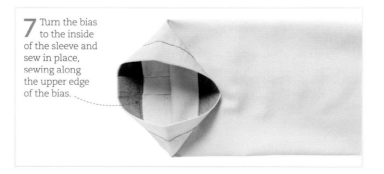

7 Turn the bias to the inside of the sleeve and sew in place, sewing along the upper edge of the bias.

REDUCING SEAM BULK pp.108–109 ● **HOW TO CUT BIAS STRIPS p.154**

TECHNIQUES

A CASING ON A SLEEVE EDGE

Difficulty level

A casing is often used on the edge of a sleeve to insert elastic into, which will allow you to gather the sleeve in a specific place. The casing may be extended, which means it is part of the sleeve, or it may be applied separately. The photographs below show an applied casing of bias binding.

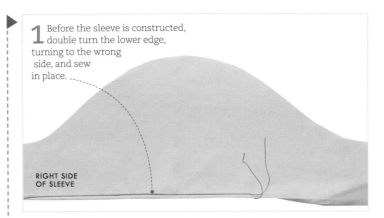

1 Before the sleeve is constructed, double turn the lower edge, turning to the wrong side, and sew in place.

RIGHT SIDE OF SLEEVE

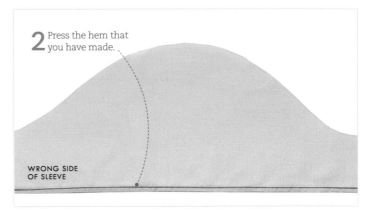

2 Press the hem that you have made.

WRONG SIDE OF SLEEVE

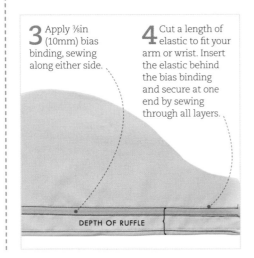

3 Apply ⅜in (10mm) bias binding, sewing along either side.

4 Cut a length of elastic to fit your arm or wrist. Insert the elastic behind the bias binding and secure at one end by sewing through all layers.

DEPTH OF RUFFLE

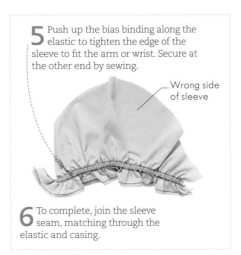

5 Push up the bias binding along the elastic to tighten the edge of the sleeve to fit the arm or wrist. Secure at the other end by sewing.

Wrong side of sleeve

6 To complete, join the sleeve seam, matching through the elastic and casing.

7 Press the seam open, then turn the sleeve through the armhole to the right side. You can adjust the ruffles if they are not evenly placed.

ELASTIC EDGE WITH A HEADING

Difficulty level

This is an alternative method for making a ruffle or heading at the end of a sleeve, using a casing that is part of the sleeve.

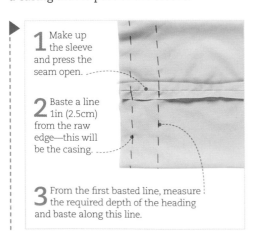

1 Make up the sleeve and press the seam open.

2 Baste a line 1in (2.5cm) from the raw edge—this will be the casing.

3 From the first basted line, measure the required depth of the heading and baste along this line.

4 Turn up the raw edge of the fabric to the wrong side of the sleeve along the second line of bastes.

5 Turn the fabric under to make a casing along the first basting line.

6 Sew two rows ⅜in (1cm) apart for the elastic, leaving a gap in the top line where the elastic will be inserted.

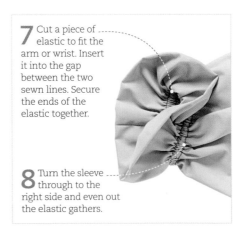

7 Cut a piece of elastic to fit the arm or wrist. Insert it into the gap between the two sewn lines. Secure the ends of the elastic together.

8 Turn the sleeve through to the right side and even out the elastic gathers.

ELASTIC SLEEVE EDGE

Difficulty level ★★☆☆☆

The ends of sleeves on workwear and children's clothes are often elastic to produce a neat and functional finish. Elastic that is ½in (12mm) or 1in (25mm) wide will be most suitable.

1 Make up the sleeve and press the seam open.

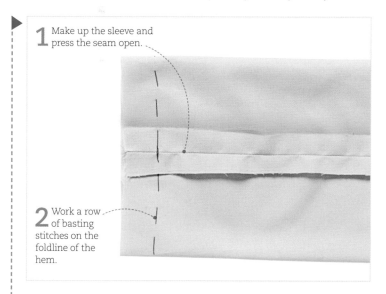

2 Work a row of basting stitches on the foldline of the hem.

3 Turn up ¼in (6mm) at the raw edge and press.

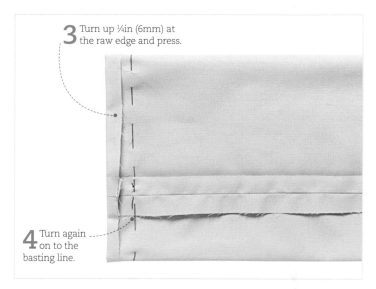

4 Turn again on to the basting line.

5 Sew to hold the turn-up in place, ¹⁄₁₆in (2mm) from the folded edge. Leave a 1in (3cm) gap next to the seam allowance through which you will insert the elastic.

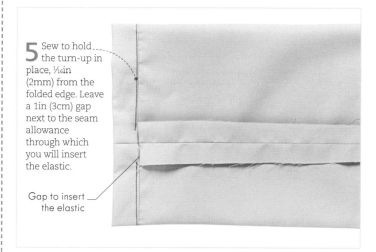

Gap to insert the elastic

6 Sew the bottom of the sleeve ¹⁄₁₆in (2mm) from the edge, to give a neat finish. This will also help prevent the elastic from twisting.

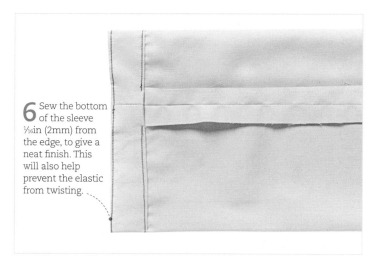

7 Cut a piece of elastic to fit the arm or wrist and insert it into the sleeve end between the two rows of machining.

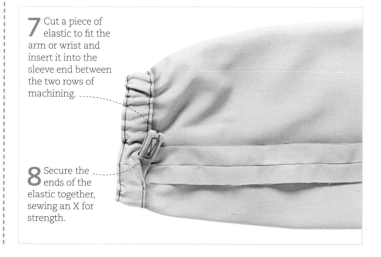

8 Secure the ends of the elastic together, sewing an X for strength.

9 Turn the sleeve through the armhole and check that the elasticated edge is even.

MACHINED HEMS p.266

TECHNIQUES

SLEEVE EDGE WITH RUFFLE

Difficulty level ★★☆☆☆

A ruffle at the end of a sleeve is a very feminine finish. It is used on a set-in sleeve that may or may not have a gathered sleeve head.

1 First, cut out the ruffle according to your pattern.

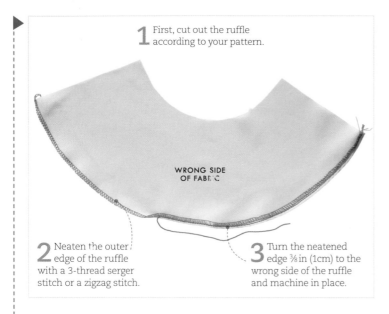

WRONG SIDE OF FABRIC

2 Neaten the outer edge of the ruffle with a 3-thread serger stitch or a zigzag stitch.

3 Turn the neatened edge ⅜in (1cm) to the wrong side of the ruffle and machine in place.

4 Join the short ends of the ruffle together, right side to right side, using a ⅝in (1.5cm) seam allowance.

5 Neaten the seam edge using your preferred method, then press the seam open.

6 Place the ruffle at the end of the sleeve, right side to right side, matching seams and notches.

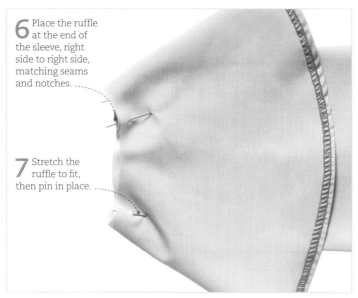

7 Stretch the ruffle to fit, then pin in place.

8 Sew the ruffle to the sleeve around the sleeve edge, using a ⅝in (1.5cm) seam allowance.

9 Neaten the seam allowance then press it toward the ruffle.

WRONG SIDE OF FABRIC

10 Turn the sleeve through the armhole to the right side.

PRESSING AIDS **pp.28–29** • HOW TO APPLY A FUSIBLE INTERFACING **p.54** • HOW TO MAKE A PLAIN SEAM **p.94**

FACED SLEEVE EDGE

Adding a facing to the end of a sleeve produces a very clean and bulk-free finish. This technique is particularly suitable for dress sleeves and sleeves on unlined jackets.

Difficulty level ★★☆☆☆

1 Apply a fusible interfacing to the facing.

WRONG SIDE OF FABRIC

2 Join the short ends of the facing together, right side to right side, then press the seam open.

3 Turn up one long edge of the facing by ⅜in (1cm) and pin in place.

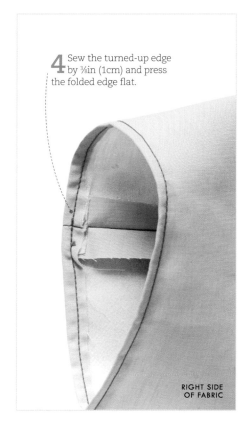

4 Sew the turned-up edge by ⅜in (1cm) and press the folded edge flat.

RIGHT SIDE OF FABRIC

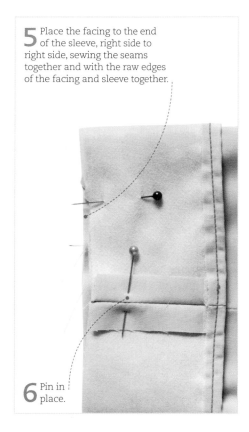

5 Place the facing to the end of the sleeve, right side to right side, sewing the seams together and with the raw edges of the facing and sleeve together.

6 Pin in place.

7 Trim the facing seam allowance down to half its width.

8 Press the whole seam allowance toward the facing. Use a seam roll to help the pressing.

9 Understitch the seam allowance to the facing.

10 Turn the facing through to the inside of the sleeve.

Completed facing

11 Press the sleeve edge on the right side.

SEAM NEATENING **p.95** ● REDUCING SEAM BULK **pp.108–109** ● STITCH FINISHES **p.109**

CUFFS AND OPENINGS

A cuff and an opening are ways of producing a sleeve finish that will fit neatly around the wrist. The opening enables the hand to fit through the end of the sleeve, and it allows the sleeve to be rolled up. There are various types of cuffs—single or double, and with pointed or curved edges. All cuffs are interfaced, with the interfacing attached to the upper cuff. The upper cuff is sewn to the sleeve.

DIRECTORY OF CUFFS AND OPENINGS

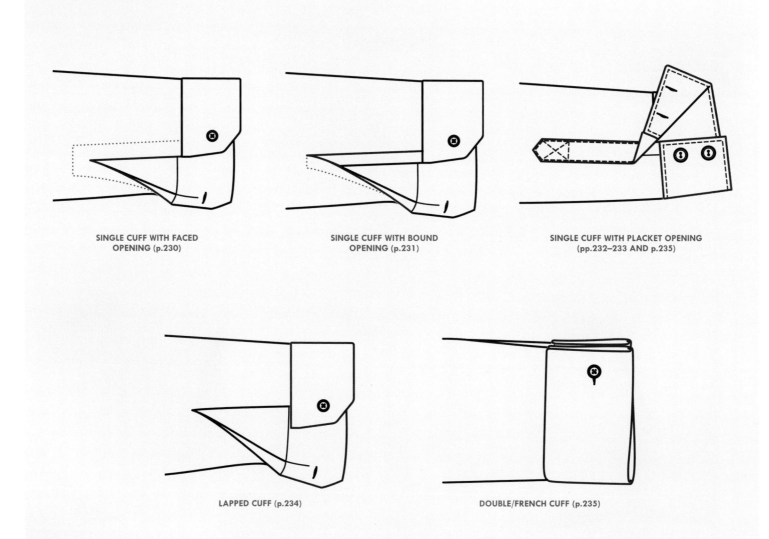

SINGLE CUFF WITH FACED
OPENING (p.230)

SINGLE CUFF WITH BOUND
OPENING (p.231)

SINGLE CUFF WITH PLACKET OPENING
(pp.232–233 AND p.235)

LAPPED CUFF (p.234)

DOUBLE/FRENCH CUFF (p.235)

HOW TO APPLY A FUSIBLE INTERFACING **p.54** • BASTING STITCHES **p.89**

ONE-PIECE CUFF

Difficulty level ✷✷✷✷

A one-piece cuff is cut out from the fabric in one piece, and in most cases only half of it is interfaced. The exception is the one-piece double cuff (see p.235).

1 Apply fusible interfacing to the half of the cuff that will be the upper cuff.

WRONG SIDE OF FABRIC

2 Turn under a seam allowance on the non-interfaced side and baste to secure.

3 Layer the seam by trimming the excess.

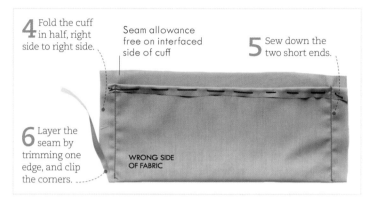

4 Fold the cuff in half, right side to right side.

Seam allowance free on interfaced side of cuff

5 Sew down the two short ends.

6 Layer the seam by trimming one edge, and clip the corners.

WRONG SIDE OF FABRIC

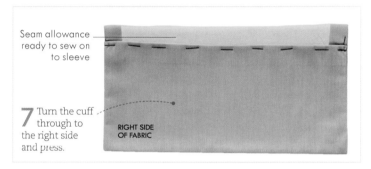

Seam allowance ready to sew on to sleeve

7 Turn the cuff through to the right side and press.

RIGHT SIDE OF FABRIC

TWO-PIECE CUFF

Difficulty level ✷✷✷✷

Some cuffs are cut in two pieces: an upper cuff and an under cuff. The upper cuff piece is interfaced.

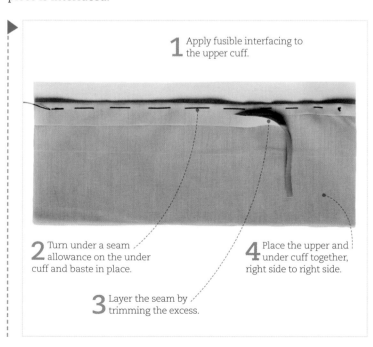

1 Apply fusible interfacing to the upper cuff.

2 Turn under a seam allowance on the under cuff and baste in place.

3 Layer the seam by trimming the excess.

4 Place the upper and under cuff together, right side to right side.

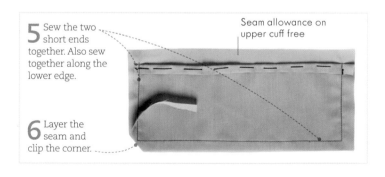

5 Sew the two short ends together. Also sew together along the lower edge.

Seam allowance on upper cuff free

6 Layer the seam and clip the corner.

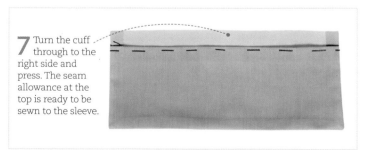

7 Turn the cuff through to the right side and press. The seam allowance at the top is ready to be sewn to the sleeve.

TECHNIQUES

FACED OPENING

Difficulty level ✶✶✶✶

Adding a facing to the area of the sleeve where the opening is to be is a neat method of finishing. This type of opening is appropriate to use with a one-piece cuff.

1 Turn under the long edges and one short edge on the facing by about ⅛ in (3 mm). Sew to secure.

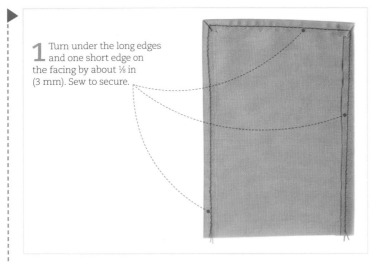

2 Place the right side of the facing to the right side of the sleeve at the appropriate sleeve markings.

3 Sew vertically up the center of the facing. Take one stitch across the top and then sew straight down the other side. Keep a distance of about ¼ in (6 mm) between the sewn lines at the raw edge.

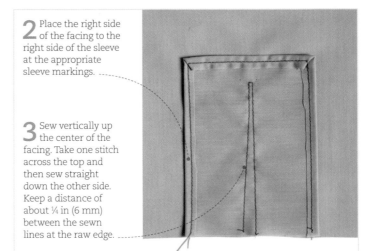

4 Snip between the sewn lines.

5 Snip with small scissors into the corners.

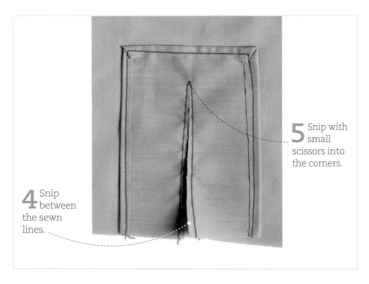

6 Turn the facing to the wrong side of the sleeve and press.

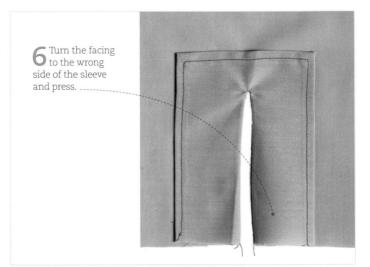

7 The finished opening on the right side.

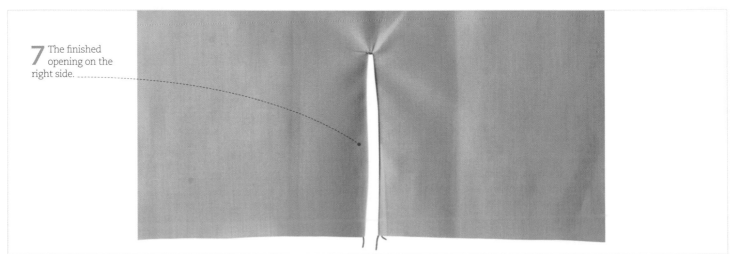

BOUND OPENING

On a fabric that frays badly or a sleeve that may get a great deal of wear, a strong bound opening is a good idea. It involves binding a slash in the sleeve with a matching bias strip.

Difficulty level ✱✱✱✱✱

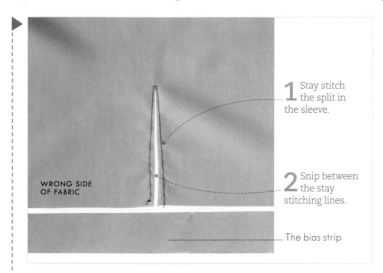

WRONG SIDE OF FABRIC

1 Stay stitch the split in the sleeve.

2 Snip between the stay stitching lines.

The bias strip

WRONG SIDE OF FABRIC

3 Working on the right side of the sleeve, pin the bias strip along the stay stitched lines. To sew around the top of the split, open the split out into a straight line.

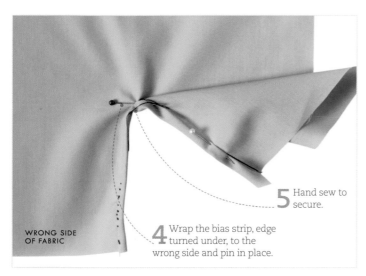

WRONG SIDE OF FABRIC

5 Hand sew to secure.

4 Wrap the bias strip, edge turned under, to the wrong side and pin in place.

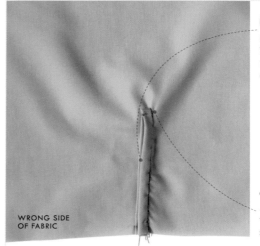

WRONG SIDE OF FABRIC

6 Allow the bias strip to close. One side of the bias strip will fold under and the other will extend.

7 Secure the top fold in the bias with a double stitch.

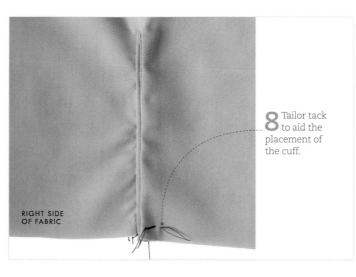

RIGHT SIDE OF FABRIC

8 Tailor tack to aid the placement of the cuff.

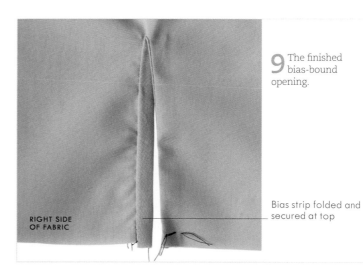

RIGHT SIDE OF FABRIC

9 The finished bias-bound opening.

Bias strip folded and secured at top

MACHINE-SEWN HEMS **p.266**

TECHNIQUES

SHIRT SLEEVE PLACKET

Difficulty level ✦✦✦✦✧

This is the opening that is found on the sleeves of men's shirts and tailored ladies' shirts. It looks complicated, but is straightforward if you take it one step at a time.

1 Cut out the placket and mark the pattern dots with tailor's tacks. Only these four tailor's tacks are required.

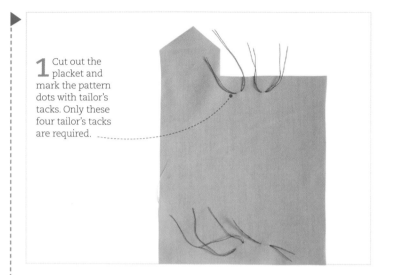

2 Place the placket to the shirt sleeve, right side of the placket to the wrong side of the sleeve, sewing the tailor's tacks.

3 Pin in place.

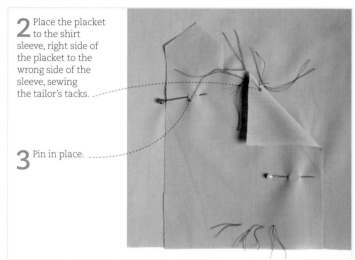

4 Sew a rectangular box, joining the tailor's tacks together. Make sure the rows of stitches are parallel. Remove tailor's tacks.

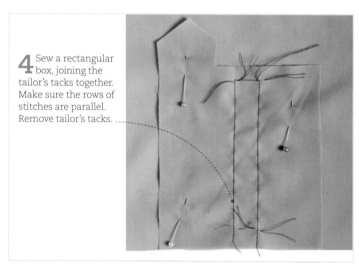

5 Snip though the placket and sleeve straight down the center, between the rows of seams.

6 Snip into the corners of the rectangle.

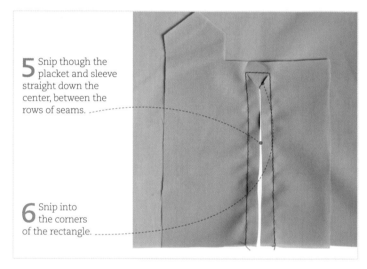

7 Open up the placket to the right side of the fabric and press. You will have a rectangular gap with sharp corners.

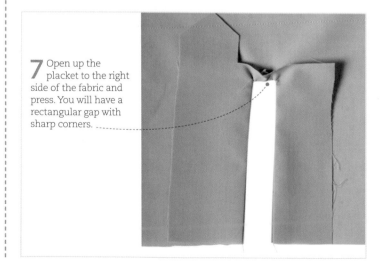

8 Fold back the long edge of the shorter side of the placket.

9 Place the folded edge on top of the sewn line and pin in place.

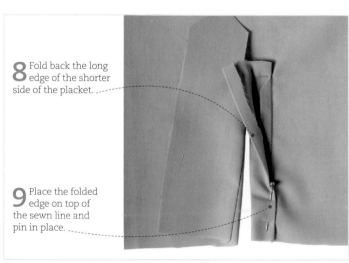

10 Sew the folded edge with a ¹⁄₁₆ in (2 mm) seam allowance. Stop the sewing at the top of the gap.

11 Fold the other side of the placket across the shorter side.

12 Press under the long edge. Fold back so that the pressed-under edge is on the sewn line. Pin in place.

13 Fold under the top pointed end, following the cut edge, and press.

14 Sew the long folded edge in place. Make sure the underside of the placket is not caught by the stitches.

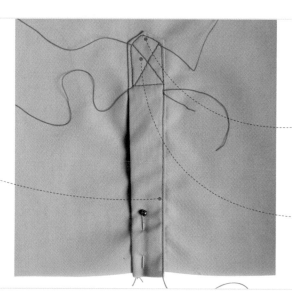

15 Continue sewing around the point.

16 Stitch an X through the point.

17 Pull all the ends of the threads through to the reverse and tie off.

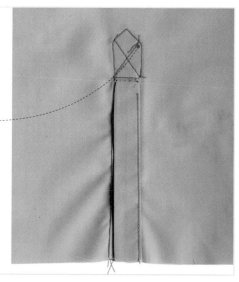

18 On the right side, the completed placket will be neatly stitched.

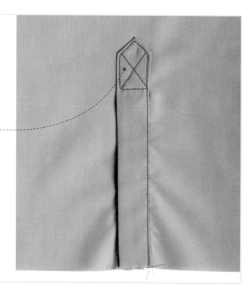

MACHINED HEMS p.266

TECHNIQUES

ATTACHING A CUFF

Difficulty level ★★★★☆

There are various types of cuff that can be attached to sleeve openings. The one-piece overlapped cuff works well with a bound or faced opening. A two-piece barrel cuff is usually on a sleeve with a placket opening, but works equally well on a bound opening. The double cuff, or French cuff, is for men's dress shirts and tailored shirts for both ladies and men, and may be cut in one or two sections. It is usually found with a placket or bound opening.

▶ OVERLAPPED CUFF

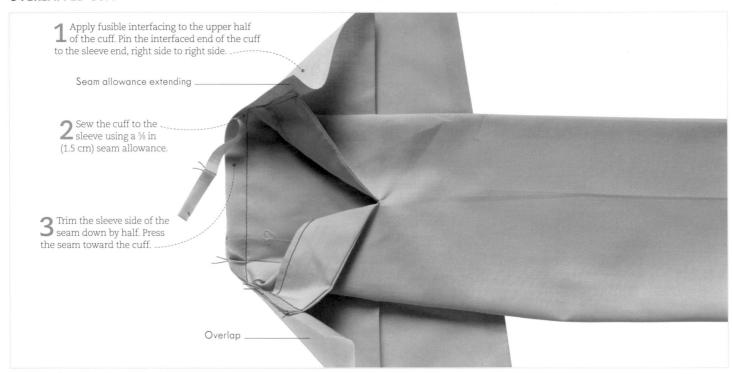

1 Apply fusible interfacing to the upper half of the cuff. Pin the interfaced end of the cuff to the sleeve end, right side to right side.

Seam allowance extending

2 Sew the cuff to the sleeve using a ⅝ in (1.5 cm) seam allowance.

3 Trim the sleeve side of the seam down by half. Press the seam toward the cuff.

Overlap

4 Fold the non-interfaced edge of the cuff over to the wrong side by ⅝ in (1.5 cm) and press along the non-attached edge.

5 Fold the cuff to itself, right side to right side, so the folded side of the cuff comes to the sleeve-to-cuff seamline.

6 Sew the one short end in line with the opening.

7 Sew the other short end along from the sleeve-to-cuff seam and then down the cuff.

8 Remove the corners. Press the seams open.

9 Turn the cuff to the right side. Push the corners out to points.

10 On the inside, hand sew the folded edge (using a flat fell or blind hem stitch) to finish.

11 Make a buttonhole on the upper side of the cuff.

12 Sew a button on the underside of the cuff.

HOW TO APPLY A FUSIBLE INTERFACING p.54 ● **REDUCING SEAM BULK pp.108–109** ● **STITCH FINISHES p.109**

▶ BARREL CUFF

1 Apply fusible interfacing to the upper cuff. Place it to the sleeve end, right side to right side, with a seam allowance extending at either end. Pin in place.

— Upper cuff

2 Sew using a ⅝in (1.5cm) seam allowance.

3 Place the right side of the under cuff to the right side of the upper cuff. Sew together around three sides, sewing in line with the sleeve opening.

— Under cuff

4 Trim down the under cuff side of the seam.

5 Remove bulk from the corners. Press.

— Upper cuff

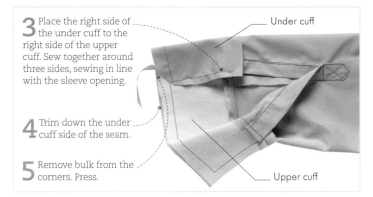

6 Turn the cuff to the right side and press.

7 Turn under the raw edge of the under cuff and place to the end of the sleeve. With this type of sleeve, the edge of the cuff is sewn in place.

8 Add buttonholes to the upper cuff and attach buttons to the under cuff.

▶ DOUBLE/FRENCH CUFF

1 Apply interfacing to the whole of the cuff. Attach the cuff to the sleeve end, right side to right side, using a ⅝in (1.5cm) seam allowance.

2 Fold the cuff back on to itself, right side to right side.

3 Sew the two sides in line with the sleeve opening.

4 Trim the bulk from the seams and corners.

5 Press, then turn the cuff through to the right side.

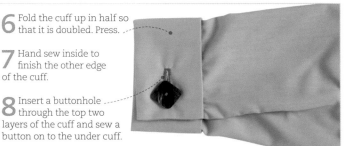

6 Fold the cuff up in half so that it is doubled. Press.

7 Hand sew inside to finish the other edge of the cuff.

8 Insert a buttonhole through the top two layers of the cuff and sew a button on to the under cuff.

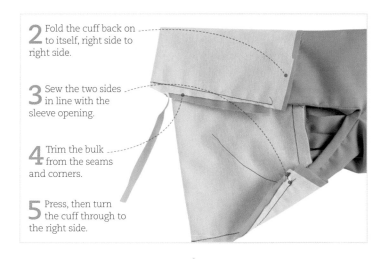

BUTTONHOLES **pp.304–311**

POCKETS

Pockets can be functional or just for show, and are essential on some items of clothing. Making a pocket requires a little patience, but the finished result is well worth it.

POCKETS

Pockets come in lots of shapes and formats. Some, such as patch pockets, paper bag pockets, and jetted pockets with a flap, are external and can be decorative, while others, including front hip pockets, are more discreet and hidden from view. They can be made from the same fabric as the garment or from a contrasting fabric. Whether casual or tailored, all pockets are functional.

DIRECTORY OF POCKETS

PATCH POCKET
(pp.239–242)

PAPER BAG POCKET
(p.243)

WELT POCKET
(p.244)

**WELT POCKET ON
TROUSER BACK (p.245)**

**JETTED POCKET
WITH A FLAP (pp.246–247)**

IN-SEAM POCKET
(pp.248–249)

FRONT HIP POCKET
(p.250)

CHINO POCKET
(p.251)

KANGAROO POCKET
(p.252)

UNLINED PATCH POCKET

Difficulty level ✱✱✱✱✱

An unlined patch pocket is one of the most popular types of pocket. It can be found on garments of all kinds and be made from a wide variety of fabrics. On lightweight fabrics, such as used for a shirt pocket, interfacing is not required, but on medium and heavier fabrics, it is advisable to apply a fusible interfacing.

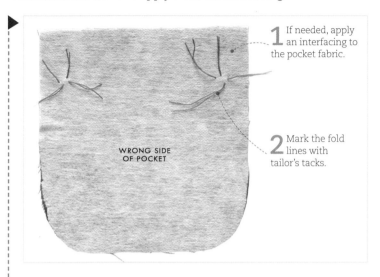

1 If needed, apply an interfacing to the pocket fabric.

2 Mark the fold lines with tailor's tacks.

WRONG SIDE OF POCKET

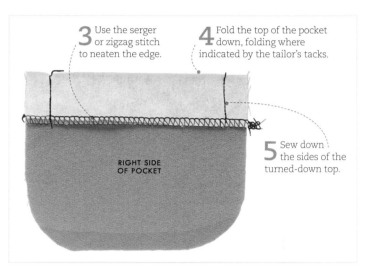

3 Use the serger or zigzag stitch to neaten the edge.

4 Fold the top of the pocket down, folding where indicated by the tailor's tacks.

5 Sew down the sides of the turned-down top.

RIGHT SIDE OF POCKET

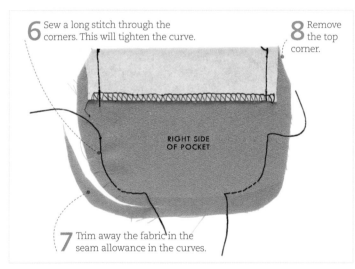

6 Sew a long stitch through the corners. This will tighten the curve.

8 Remove the top corner.

7 Trim away the fabric in the seam allowance in the curves.

RIGHT SIDE OF POCKET

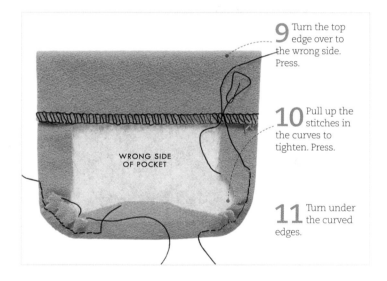

9 Turn the top edge over to the wrong side. Press.

10 Pull up the stitches in the curves to tighten. Press.

11 Turn under the curved edges.

WRONG SIDE OF POCKET

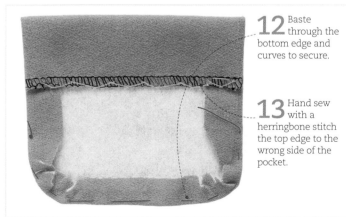

12 Baste through the bottom edge and curves to secure.

13 Hand sew with a herringbone stitch the top edge to the wrong side of the pocket.

14 Press. The pocket is now ready to attach.

RIGHT SIDE OF POCKET

SEAM NEATENING **p.95** ● REDUCING SEAM BULK **pp.108–109**

SELF-LINED PATCH POCKET

Difficulty level ✱✱✱✱✱

If a patch pocket is to be self-lined, it needs to be cut with the top edge of the pocket on a fold. Like an unlined pocket, if you are using a lightweight fabric, an interfacing may not be required, whereas for medium-weight fabrics, a fusible interfacing is advisable. A self-lined patch pocket is not suitable for heavy fabrics.

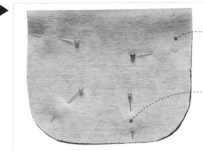

1 Cut the pocket fabric and apply a fusible interfacing, if needed.

2 Fold the pocket in half, right side to right side. Pin to secure.

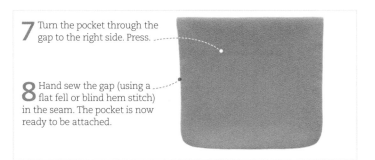

3 Sew around the three open sides of the pocket. Leave a gap of 1in (3cm) for turning through.

4 Remove bulk from the corners by trimming.

5 Trim one side of the seam allowance down to half its width.

6 Use pinking shears to trim the corners.

7 Turn the pocket through the gap to the right side. Press.

8 Hand sew the gap (using a flat fell or blind hem stitch) in the seam. The pocket is now ready to be attached.

LINED PATCH POCKET

Difficulty level ✱✱✱✱✱

If a self-lined patch pocket is likely to be too bulky, then a lined pocket is the answer. It is advisable to interface the pocket fabric.

1 Cut the pocket fabric and apply interfacing. Cut the lining fabric. The lining will be shorter than the pocket fabric.

2 Place the lining top edge to the upper edge of the pocket and sew together. Leave a 1in (3cm) gap in the seam for turning through.

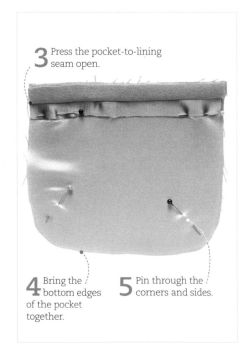

3 Press the pocket-to-lining seam open.

4 Bring the bottom edges of the pocket together.

5 Pin through the corners and sides.

6 Sew around the other three open sides of the pocket to attach the lining to the pocket fabric.

7 Remove the corners.

8 Use pinking shears to trim the curves.

9 Turn through the gap left in the seam to the right side. Press.

10 Hand sew the gap using a flat fell or blind hem stitch.

11 The lined patch pocket is ready to be attached.

SQUARE PATCH POCKET

Difficulty level ★★☆☆☆

It is possible to have a patch pocket with square corners. This requires mitering the corners to reduce the bulk. Use a fusible interfacing on medium-weight fabrics.

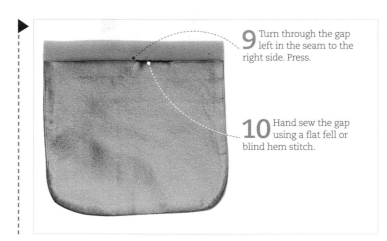

1 Cut the pocket and apply interfacing, if needed. Neaten the upper edge of the pocket with serger or zigzag stitches.

2 Fold over the upper edge and sew down the sides.

3 Fold in the other three edges and press to crease.

4 Remove the top corners.

5 Fold in the bottom corners, then fold across these to give creases for the miters.

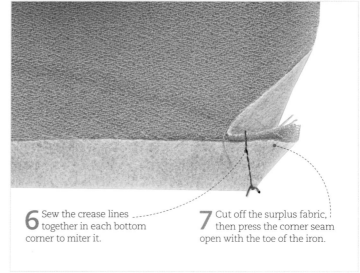

6 Sew the crease lines together in each bottom corner to miter it.

7 Cut off the surplus fabric, then press the corner seam open with the toe of the iron.

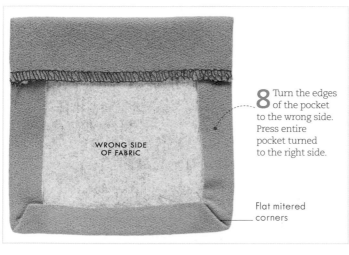

WRONG SIDE OF FABRIC

Flat mitered corners

8 Turn the edges of the pocket to the wrong side. Press entire pocket turned to the right side.

9 The finished pocket is now ready to be attached.

MITERED CORNERS **p.269**

ATTACHING A PATCH POCKET

Difficulty level

To attach a pocket well, accurate pattern marking is essential. It is best to do this by means of tailor's tacks or even trace basting. If you are using a checker or striped fabric, the pocket fabric must align with the checkers or stripes on the garment.

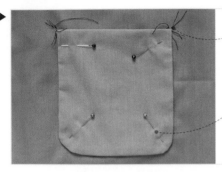

1 Mark the pocket placement lines on the garment with tailor's tacks.

2 Take the completed pocket and place it to the fabric, matching the corners with the tailor's tacks. Pin in position.

3 To make sure the pocket remains in the correct position, baste around the edge along the sides and bottom. Keep the basting stitches close to the finished edge of the pocket.

4 Sew approx ½in (1mm) from the edge of the pocket.

5 Remove the basting stitches. Press.

6 Alternatively, the pocket can be hand sewn in place, using a slip hem stitch into the underside of the pocket seam. Do not pull on the thread too tightly or the pocket will wrinkle.

REINFORCING POCKET CORNERS

Difficulty level

On any patch pocket, it is essential to reinforce the upper corners as these take all the strain when the pocket is being used. There are several ways to do this, some of which are quite decorative.

▶ REVERSE STITCH

1 Reinforce the corner with a reverse stitch. Make sure the stitches lie on top of one another.

2 Pull the threads to the reverse to tie off.

▶ DIAGONAL STITCH

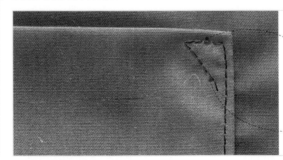

1 This is a technique used primarily on shirts. When sewing the pocket in place, sew along horizontally for four stitches.

2 Turn and sew diagonally back to the side, to create a triangular shape in the corner.

▶ ZIGZAG STITCH

1 Using a small zigzag stitch, width 1.0 and length 1.0, sew diagonally across the corner.

2 Make a feature of this stitch by using a thread in a contrasting color.

▶ PARALLEL ZIGZAG STITCH

1 Place a patch on the wrong side of the garment, behind the pocket corner, to sew into for strength.

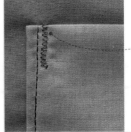

2 Using a small zigzag stitch, width 1.0 and length 1.0, sew a short vertical line next to the straight stitching.

PAPER BAG POCKET

This pocket is so-named because it resembles a paper bag. It is found on men's and women's casual wear. The pocket is attached to the garment with a gusset, which is a straight strip of fabric. A paper bag pocket is best made in a light or medium-weight fabric.

Difficulty level ★★★✷✷

1 First neaten the upper edge of the pocket. Fold it over twice, making a double hem. Sew along the edge close to the fold.

2 Place the gusset to the outer edge of the pocket, right side to right side.

3 Fold under the ends of the gusset and match the ends to the edge of the pocket.

4 Sew the gusset to the pocket along the sides and bottom.

5 Clip the seam allowance in the curves.

6 Turn under the raw edge of the gusset. Miter the corners. Baste to secure.

7 Place the basted edge to the garment. Match the edge to the tailor-tack markings on the garment. Pin.

8 Sew the edge of the gusset to the garment. Sew close to the folded edge.

9 Remove the basting.

10 At the top edge, pleat the gusset under the pocket and place the top corner of the pocket and gusset together.

11 Sew diagonally across the upper corners through the pocket, gusset, and garment. Leave the lower curved edges loose.

STITCHING CORNERS AND CURVES **pp.102–103** ● REDUCING SEAM BULK **pp.108–109**

TECHNIQUES

WELT POCKET

Difficulty level ★★★☆☆

A welt pocket features a small, straight flap that faces upward on a garment, with the pocket opening behind the flap. This kind of pocket is found on waistcoats and is the usual breast pocket on men's jackets, as well as being used on coats.

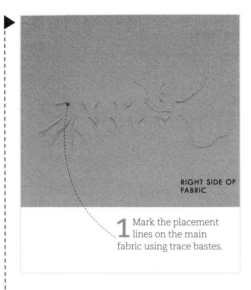

1 Mark the placement lines on the main fabric using trace bastes.

RIGHT SIDE OF FABRIC

2 Apply fusible interfacing to the welt. Fold it in half, right side to right side, matching the tailor's tacks.

3 Sew the two short ends, following the shape of the welt.

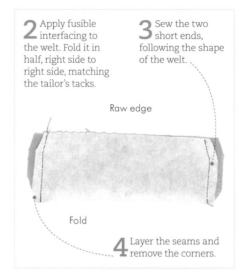

Raw edge

Fold

4 Layer the seams and remove the corners.

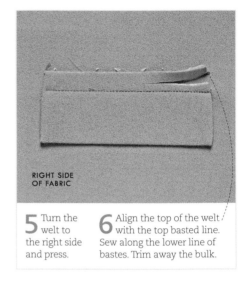

5 Turn the welt to the right side and press.

6 Align the top of the welt with the top basted line. Sew along the lower line of bastes. Trim away the bulk.

RIGHT SIDE OF FABRIC

7 Place the lining pocket over the welt, right side to right side. Match the pattern markings.

8 Baste the lining in place over the welt.

9 Sew the lining over the welt. The upper row of stitches will be shorter than the lower row, producing angled sides.

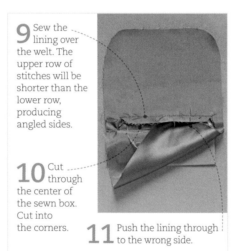

10 Cut through the center of the sewn box. Cut into the corners.

11 Push the lining through to the wrong side.

12 Pull the remaining lining through from the wrong side.

13 On the reverse, bring the lining together and sew around the edge to make the pocket bag.

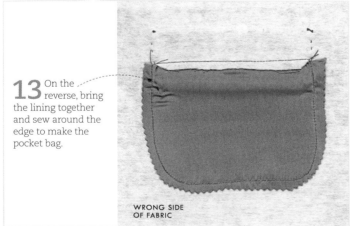

WRONG SIDE OF FABRIC

14 The finished welt pocket on the right side.

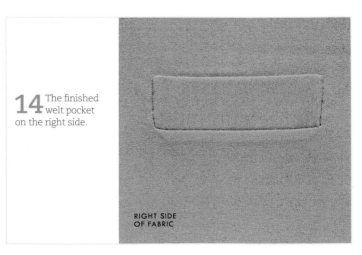

RIGHT SIDE OF FABRIC

HOW TO APPLY A FUSIBLE INTERFACING p.54 • **PATTERN MARKING pp.82–83** • **BASTING STITCHES p.89**

WELT POCKET ON PANT BACK

A welt pocket on the back of a pair of pants features a slim, elegant welt. For this reason, its construction is slightly different and you will need to reinforce the finished welt with stitches on the right side.

Difficulty level ✱✱✱✱✱

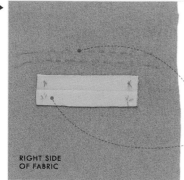

1 Reinforce the wrong side of the pocket area with fusible interfacing (not shown on these samples).

2 On the right side, mark parallel seam lines for the welt according to your pattern with baste stitches.

3 Apply fusible interfacing to the welt. Use tailor's tacks to transfer the dot markings on the welt pattern.

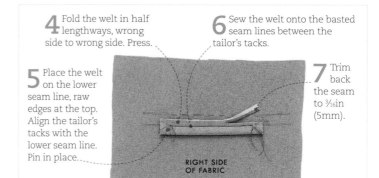

4 Fold the welt in half lengthways, wrong side to wrong side. Press.

5 Place the welt on the lower seam line, raw edges at the top. Align the tailor's tacks with the lower seam line. Pin in place.

6 Sew the welt onto the basted seam lines between the tailor's tacks.

7 Trim back the seam to 3/16in (5mm).

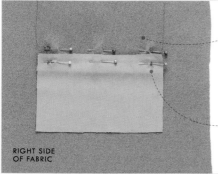

8 Place the pocket fabric on the upper seam line. Pin in place.

9 Place the pocket lining on the lower seam line over the welt. Pin in place.

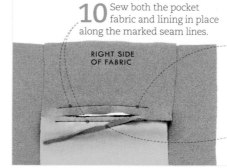

10 Sew both the pocket fabric and lining in place along the marked seam lines.

11 The two rows must be parallel and exactly the same length as the sewn welt. Do not sew across the short ends.

12 Trim away the bulk from both seams.

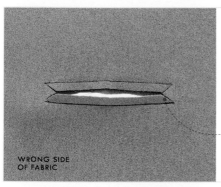

13 On the wrong side, cut through the center of the welt.

14 Cut into the corners as shown.

15 Pull both pocket pieces and the welt through to the wrong side.

16 Make sure the triangles at the short ends are also on the wrong side.

17 Press in place with the welt over the triangles.

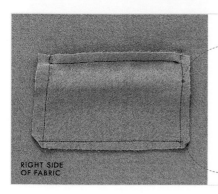

18 Fold the pocket fabric down onto the pocket lining. Sew the two pocket sections together on three sides to make a pocket sack or bag. Make sure you catch in the triangle end of the cut and the end of the welts.

19 Trim the corners to reduce bulk.

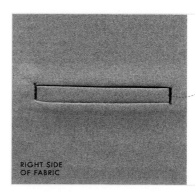

20 On the right side, set the machine to a zigzag stitch, width 2.5 and length 0.5, and sew across the short ends of the welt to reinforce.

STITCHES MADE WITH A MACHINE **pp.92–93** ● REDUCING SEAM BULK **pp.108–09**

TECHNIQUES

JETTED POCKET WITH A FLAP

This type of pocket is found on tailored jackets and coats and men's wear. It is straightforward to make. The main components are the welts (the strips that make the edges of the pocket), the flap, and the lining that makes the pocket bag.

Difficulty level ★★★★✲

1 First make the upper welt. Apply fusible interfacing to the wrong side.

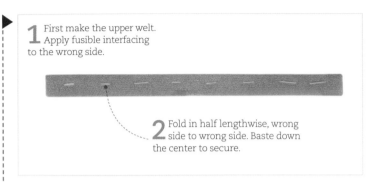

2 Fold in half lengthwise, wrong side to wrong side. Baste down the center to secure.

3 Next, make the pocket flap. Apply fusible interfacing to the wrong side of the fabric.

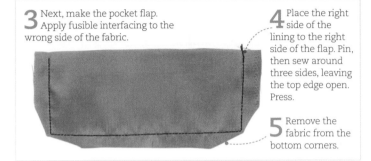

4 Place the right side of the lining to the right side of the flap. Pin, then sew around three sides, leaving the top edge open. Press.

5 Remove the fabric from the bottom corners.

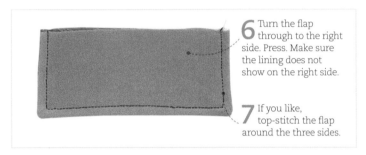

6 Turn the flap through to the right side. Press. Make sure the lining does not show on the right side.

7 If you like, top-stitch the flap around the three sides.

8 On the welt, trim the raw edge of the seam allowance down to half its width.

9 Place the welt to the right side of the pocket. Align the raw edges. Make sure the welt overhangs the flap by equal amounts at each end.

10 Sew together through the center of the welt.

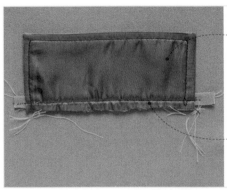

11 Place the right side of the welt and flap to the right side of the garment. Match the ends of the flap to the upper tailor's tacks on the garment. Pin in place.

12 Sew to the garment along the line that is holding the welt and flap together.

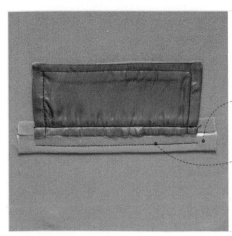

13 Make up the lower welt in the same fabric as the upper welt.

14 Place the lower welt to the garment below the upper welt and flap.

15 Sew in place. Make sure the two rows of stitches are exactly the same length. Also make sure the sewn lines are parallel.

16 Take the lining and press in half, right side to right side, matching the tailor's tacks, to produce a center crease.

17 Place the right side of the lining over the welt and flaps, sewing the tailor's tacks. The crease line should be sitting between the two welts. Pin in place.

HOW TO APPLY A FUSIBLE INTERFACING p.54 • **PATTERN MARKING pp.82–83** • **BASTING STITCHES p.89** • **STITCHES MADE WITH A MACHINE pp.92–93** • **REDUCING SEAM BULK pp.108–109**

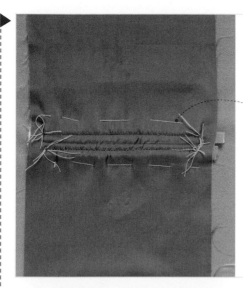

18 Baste the lining in position. Keep the basting stitches about ⅝ in (1.5 cm) from the tailor's tacks that mark the welts.

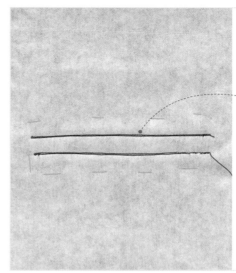

19 Working from the wrong side, sew the lining in place by sewing over the lines that are holding the welts in place. The two rows of stitches should be exactly the same length. Secure at both ends.

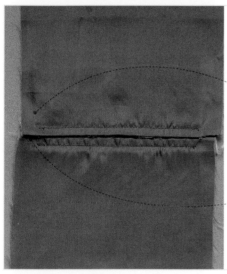

20 Turn to the right side and remove the basting.

21 Snip through just the lining along the pressed crease line. Cut through to the edge of the lining.

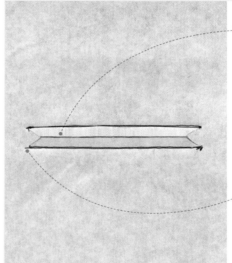

22 On the reverse, cut through the fabric of the garment. The cut line should cut through just the fabric and not the welts or flaps.

23 Cut into the corners right to the sewn lines.

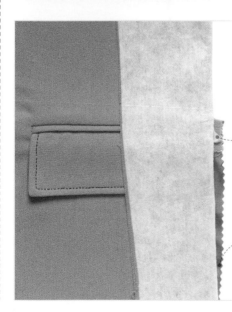

24 Pull the lining through the cut to the wrong side. Push through the ends of the welts. The pocket flap will turn down.

25 To make the pocket, pull the ends of the welts out away from the cut lines. A small triangle of fabric should be on top of these welts.

26 Sew across the welts and the triangle and around the pocket. Use pinking shears to neaten the seams on the lining.

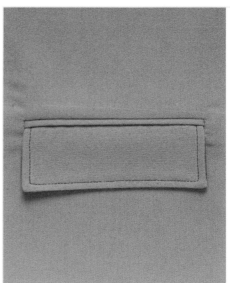

27 Press everything in place, using a pressing cloth if necessary.

JETTED POCKET pp.338—339

IN-SEAM POCKET

In pants and skirts, the pocket is sometimes disguised in the seam line. There are two ways of making an in-seam pocket, either by adding a separate pocket shape or by the pocket shape being cut as part of the main fabric.

Difficulty level ★★☆☆☆

▶ **SEPARATE IN-SEAM POCKET**

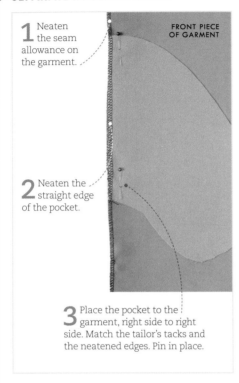

1 Neaten the seam allowance on the garment.

FRONT PIECE OF GARMENT

2 Neaten the straight edge of the pocket.

3 Place the pocket to the garment, right side to right side. Match the tailor's tacks and the neatened edges. Pin in place.

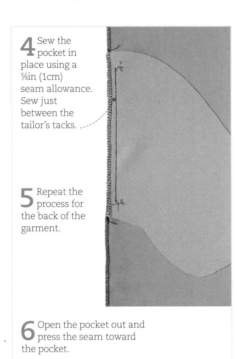

4 Sew the pocket in place using a ⅜in (1cm) seam allowance. Sew just between the tailor's tacks.

5 Repeat the process for the back of the garment.

6 Open the pocket out and press the seam toward the pocket.

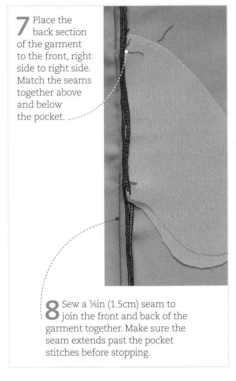

7 Place the back section of the garment to the front, right side to right side. Match the seams together above and below the pocket.

8 Sew a ⅝in (1.5cm) seam to join the front and back of the garment together. Make sure the seam extends past the pocket stitches before stopping.

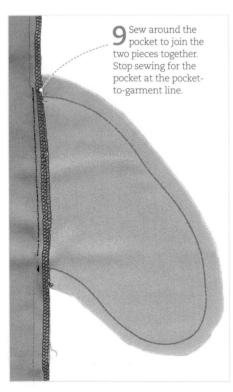

9 Sew around the pocket to join the two pieces together. Stop sewing for the pocket at the pocket-to-garment line.

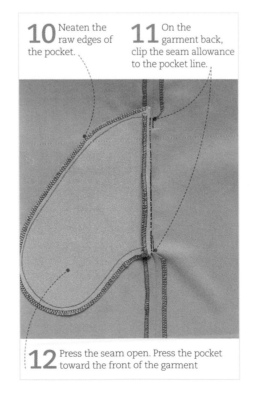

10 Neaten the raw edges of the pocket.

11 On the garment back, clip the seam allowance to the pocket line.

12 Press the seam open. Press the pocket toward the front of the garment

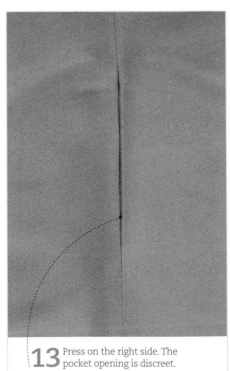

13 Press on the right side. The pocket opening is discreet.

▶ ALL-IN-ONE IN-SEAM POCKET

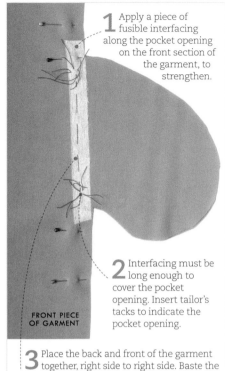

1 Apply a piece of fusible interfacing along the pocket opening on the front section of the garment, to strengthen.

2 Interfacing must be long enough to cover the pocket opening. Insert tailor's tacks to indicate the pocket opening.

FRONT PIECE OF GARMENT

3 Place the back and front of the garment together, right side to right side. Baste the pocket opening closed over the interfacing, sewing between the tailor's tacks.

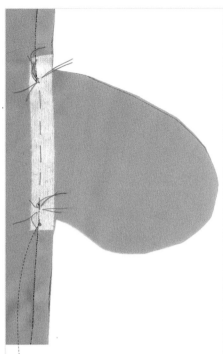

4 Sew the back and front together with a ⅝in (1.5cm) seam allowance, above and below the pocket opening. Stop sewing at the tailor's tack points.

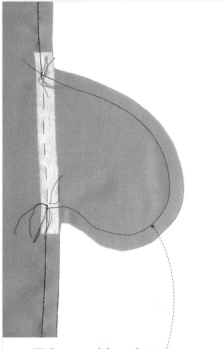

5 Sew around the pocket to join the two pieces. Start and finish the stitching at the tailor's tack points.

6 Clip the seam allowances above and below the pocket extension.

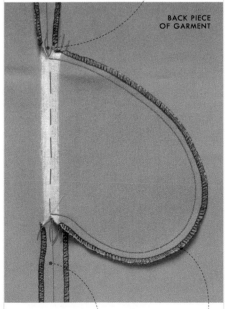

BACK PIECE OF GARMENT

7 Press the seams open. Neaten the edges of the seam allowances.

8 Neaten the raw edges of the seam allowances on the pocket together.

9 Remove the basting on the interfacing. Press the pocket toward the front.

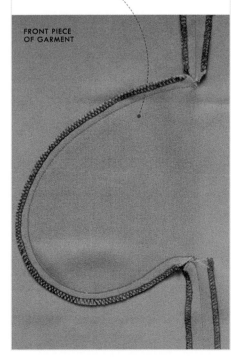

FRONT PIECE OF GARMENT

10 This is how the all-in-one pocket looks on the right side.

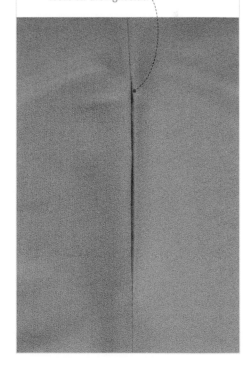

SEAM NEATENING **p.95** ● REDUCING SEAM BULK **pp.108–109**

FRONT HIP POCKET

Difficulty level ❋❋❋❋❋

On many pants and casual skirts, the pocket is placed on the hipline. It can be low on the hipline or cut quite high as on jeans. The construction is the same for all types of hip pockets. When inserted at an angle, hip pockets can slim the figure.

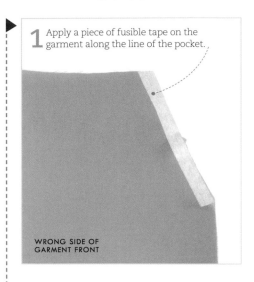

1 Apply a piece of fusible tape on the garment along the line of the pocket.

WRONG SIDE OF GARMENT FRONT

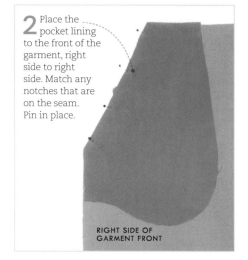

2 Place the pocket lining to the front of the garment, right side to right side. Match any notches that are on the seam. Pin in place.

RIGHT SIDE OF GARMENT FRONT

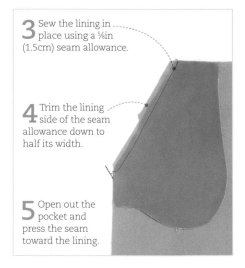

3 Sew the lining in place using a ⅝in (1.5cm) seam allowance.

4 Trim the lining side of the seam allowance down to half its width.

5 Open out the pocket and press the seam toward the lining.

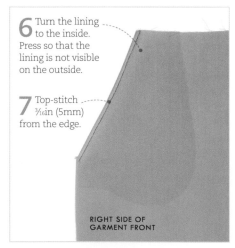

6 Turn the lining to the inside. Press so that the lining is not visible on the outside.

7 Top-stitch ³⁄₁₆in (5mm) from the edge.

RIGHT SIDE OF GARMENT FRONT

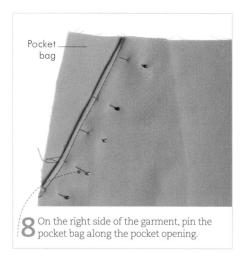

Pocket bag

8 On the right side of the garment, pin the pocket bag along the pocket opening.

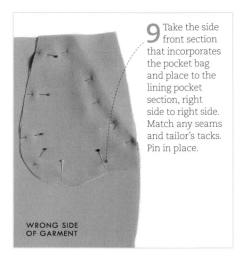

9 Take the side front section that incorporates the pocket bag and place to the lining pocket section, right side to right side. Match any seams and tailor's tacks. Pin in place.

WRONG SIDE OF GARMENT

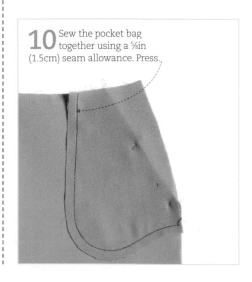

10 Sew the pocket bag together using a ⅝in (1.5cm) seam allowance. Press.

11 Neaten the raw edges of the seam allowance around the pocket.

12 Neaten the side seam allowance, sewing from the top down. Make sure that the fabric lies flat where it joins to the side seam.

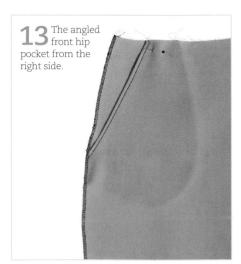

13 The angled front hip pocket from the right side.

HOW TO APPLY A FUSIBLE INTERFACING p.54 ● **STITCHES MADE WITH A MACHINE pp.92–93** ● **HOW TO MAKE A PLAIN SEAM p.94**

CHINO POCKET

Difficulty level ★★★★✶

This is the style of pocket found on the front of chino pants and jeans, but it can also be applied to skirts. The pocket is sometimes curved in shape rather than angular, as shown here. This pocket features a facing, which gives it a neat finish at the opening edge.

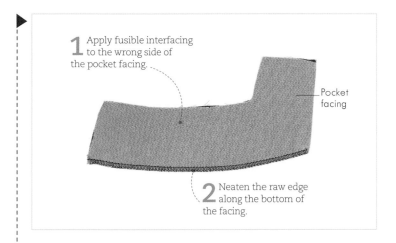

1 Apply fusible interfacing to the wrong side of the pocket facing.

Pocket facing

2 Neaten the raw edge along the bottom of the facing.

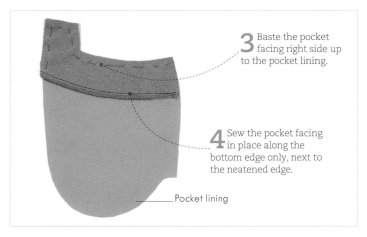

3 Baste the pocket facing right side up to the pocket lining.

4 Sew the pocket facing in place along the bottom edge only, next to the neatened edge.

Pocket lining

5 Place the pocket facing and lining right side to right side on the pant or skirt front. Sew together along the top edge.

6 Clip into the corner and along the top of the seam.

7 Trim the pocket side of the seam to half its width.

WRONG SIDE OF FACING AND POCKET LINING

RIGHT SIDE OF GARMENT FRONT

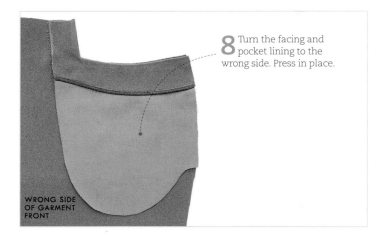

8 Turn the facing and pocket lining to the wrong side. Press in place.

WRONG SIDE OF GARMENT FRONT

9 On the right side of the garment, top-stitch using a 3.0 stitch length.

RIGHT SIDE OF GARMENT FRONT

10 On the wrong side of the skirt front, place the pocket fabric over the facing and lining.

11 Stitch around the pocket sack to join the lining to the pocket fabric.

Pocket fabric

WRONG SIDE OF GARMENT FRONT

12 Sew the side seam together, through the skirt and pocket, using a serger or zigzag stitch. The seam is left loose in order to allow extra room for the pocket.

SEWING CORNERS AND CURVES pp.102–03 ● STITCH FINISHES p.109

KANGAROO POCKET

Difficulty level ★★☆☆☆

This is a variation on a patch pocket. It is a large pocket that is often found on aprons and the front of hooded sweatshirts. A half version of this pocket also features on casual jackets.

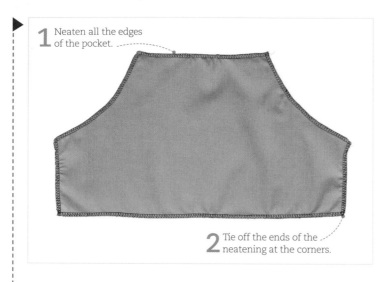

1 Neaten all the edges of the pocket.

2 Tie off the ends of the neatening at the corners.

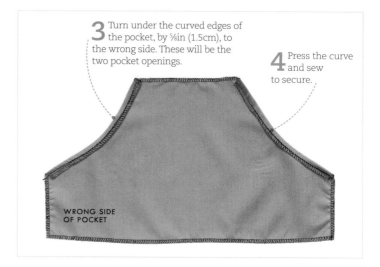

3 Turn under the curved edges of the pocket, by ⅝in (1.5cm), to the wrong side. These will be the two pocket openings.

4 Press the curve and sew to secure.

WRONG SIDE OF POCKET

5 Turn under all the remaining edges of the pocket to the wrong side. If the fabric is bulky, miter the corners. Press in place.

WRONG SIDE OF POCKET

6 Place the pocket to the garment, wrong side of the pocket to right side of the garment. Make sure the pocket is sitting flat and straight. Pin in place.

RIGHT SIDE OF FABRIC

RIGHT SIDE OF POCKET

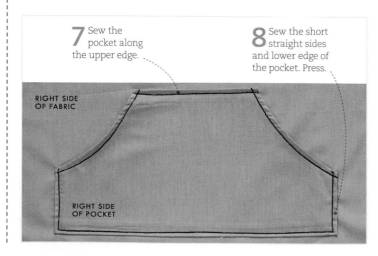

7 Sew the pocket along the upper edge.

8 Sew the short straight sides and lower edge of the pocket. Press.

RIGHT SIDE OF FABRIC

RIGHT SIDE OF POCKET

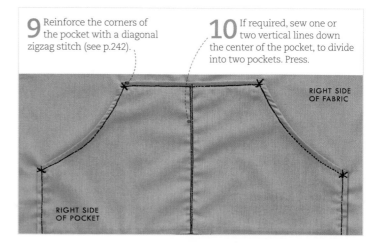

9 Reinforce the corners of the pocket with a diagonal zigzag stitch (see p.242).

10 If required, sew one or two vertical lines down the center of the pocket, to divide into two pockets. Press.

RIGHT SIDE OF FABRIC

RIGHT SIDE OF POCKET

HOW TO APPLY A FUSIBLE INTERFACING p.54 ● **PATTERN MARKING pp.82–83** ● **BASTING STITCHES p.89** ● **STITCHES MADE WITH A MACHINE pp.92–93**

MAKING A POCKET FLAP

On some styles of garment, there is no pocket, just a flap for decorative purposes. The flap is sewn where the pocket would be, but there is no opening under the flap. This is to reduce the bulk that would arise from having the rest of the pocket.

1 The flap consists of two pieces—a piece of lining and a piece of interfaced fabric. Place the two pieces together, right side to right side.

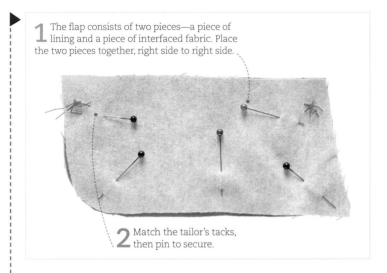

2 Match the tailor's tacks, then pin to secure.

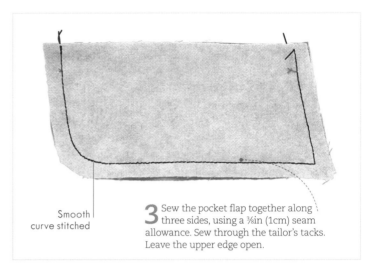

Smooth curve stitched

3 Sew the pocket flap together along three sides, using a ⅜in (1cm) seam allowance. Sew through the tailor's tacks. Leave the upper edge open.

4 Layer the seam allowance, trimming away the lining side.

5 Remove the fabric from the point.

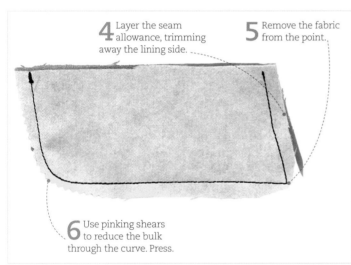

6 Use pinking shears to reduce the bulk through the curve. Press.

7 Turn the flap through to the right side. Push out the point.

8 Press the lining toward the back so that it does not show. Press a smooth curve.

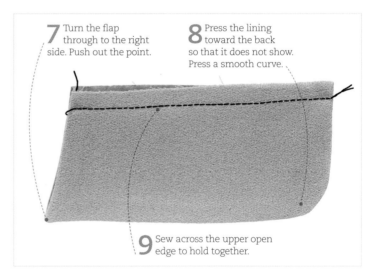

9 Sew across the upper open edge to hold together.

10 Place the flap to the garment, right side to right side. Match the edges of the flaps to the tailor's tacks on the garment.

11 Sew in place over the sewn line, holding the gap at the upper edge together.

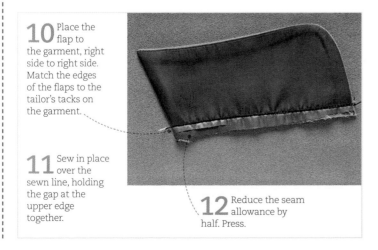

12 Reduce the seam allowance by half. Press.

13 Press the flap into place. Do not pull too tight.

14 Top-stitch across the upper edge to secure.

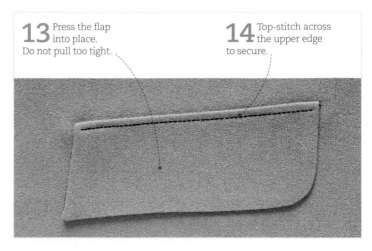

CHILD'S **REVERSIBLE JACKET**

Difficulty level ★★★★★

This reversible jacket is the perfect opportunity for using fun craft cottons and coordinating prints. For practicality, choose a washable fabric. Light cottons would be great for spring and summer, while thicker fabrics such as corduroy or denim will provide added warmth in cooler months.

TECHNIQUES USED Attaching a patch pocket **p.242**, Flat sleeve construction **p.213**, Snaps **p.320**

YOU WILL NEED

● Pattern templates on pp.384–385. Choose your size using the Children's Sizing chart on p.368.

● For Fabric A and Fabric B: 60 x 45in (150 x 115cm) or 40 x 60in (100 x 150cm) light- to medium-weight dressmaking fabric. (Quantity for size 6–7 years; see pp.384–385 for fabric quantities for other sizes).

● 20 x 36in (50 x 90cm) lightweight fusible interfacing

● 6 snap fasteners

● Matching thread

Front   Back

PIECES TO CUT

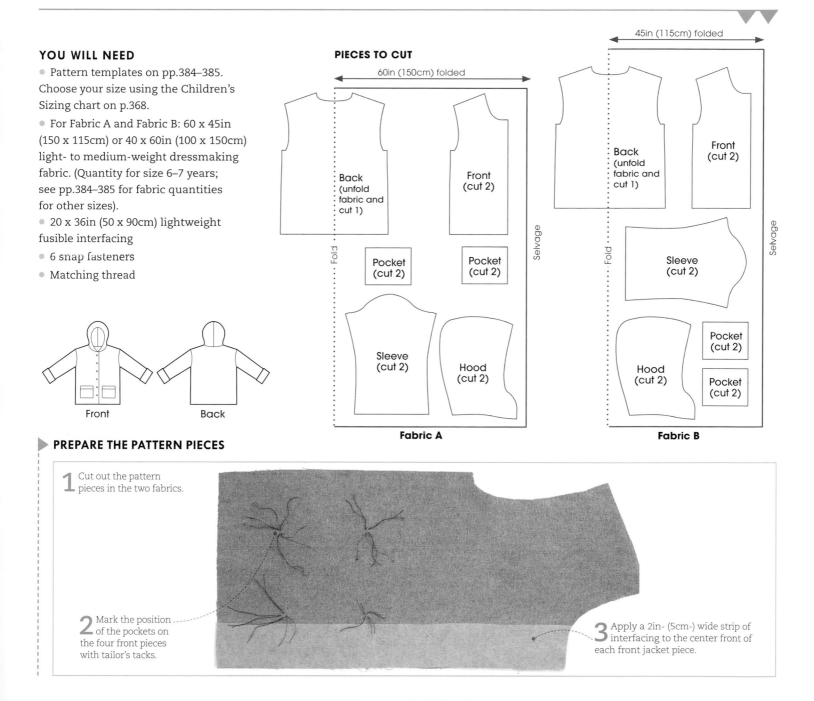

45in (115cm) folded

60in (150cm) folded

Fold / Selvage

Back (unfold fabric and cut 1)
Front (cut 2)
Pocket (cut 2)
Pocket (cut 2)
Sleeve (cut 2)
Hood (cut 2)

Fabric A

Back (unfold fabric and cut 1)
Front (cut 2)
Sleeve (cut 2)
Hood (cut 2)
Pocket (cut 2)
Pocket (cut 2)

Fabric B

▶ PREPARE THE PATTERN PIECES

1 Cut out the pattern pieces in the two fabrics.

2 Mark the position of the pockets on the four front pieces with tailor's tacks.

3 Apply a 2in- (5cm-) wide strip of interfacing to the center front of each front jacket piece.

PROJECT

▶ ASSEMBLE AND ATTACH THE POCKETS

1 Place two different fabric pocket pieces together, right side to right side.

Gap for turning

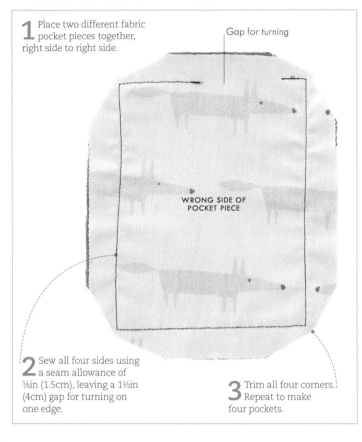

WRONG SIDE OF POCKET PIECE

2 Sew all four sides using a seam allowance of ⅝in (1.5cm), leaving a 1½in (4cm) gap for turning on one edge.

3 Trim all four corners. Repeat to make four pockets.

4 Turn the pockets to the right side and press. Hand sew the gap closed and fold down the top edge by 1¼in (3cm).

5 Using the tailor's tacks to position the pocket, top-stitch it to the jacket front, ¼in 6mm from the edge.

6 Bar baste the flaps down. Repeat to attach one pocket to each front piece.

▶ INSERT THE SLEEVES

1 Sew the front pieces to the back piece at the shoulder seams using a ⅝in (1.5cm) seam allowance. Press the seams open.

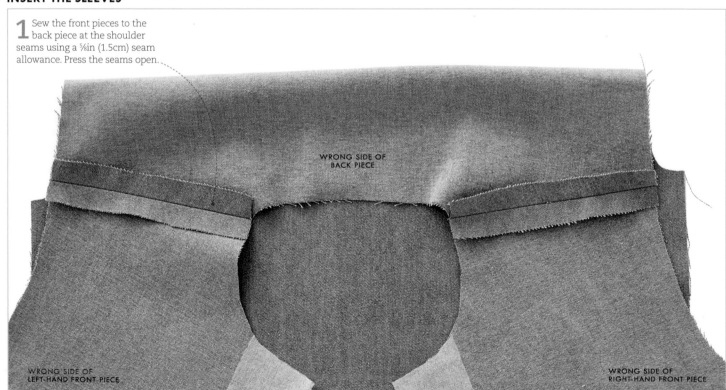

WRONG SIDE OF BACK PIECE

WRONG SIDE OF LEFT-HAND FRONT PIECE

WRONG SIDE OF RIGHT-HAND FRONT PIECE

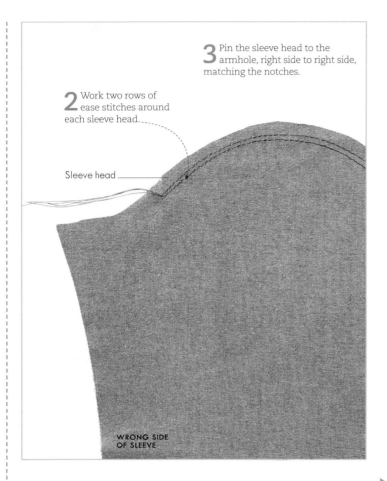

2 Work two rows of ease stitches around each sleeve head.

Sleeve head

3 Pin the sleeve head to the armhole, right side to right side, matching the notches.

WRONG SIDE OF SLEEVE

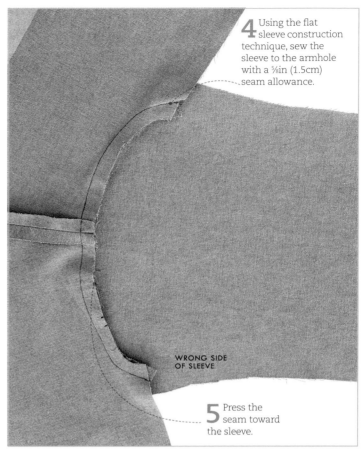

4 Using the flat sleeve construction technique, sew the sleeve to the armhole with a ⅝in (1.5cm) seam allowance.

WRONG SIDE OF SLEEVE

5 Press the seam toward the sleeve.

6 Fold the garment and sleeve, right side to right side, bringing the side seams together. Align the underarm seam.

Underarm seam

7 Using a ⅝in (1.5cm) seam allowance, sew the side seam and then continue along the sleeve.

8 Press the seam open and clip around the underarm.

Side seam

▶ **ATTACH THE HOOD**

1 With right sides together, sew the hood pieces together using a ⅝in (1.5cm) seam allowance.

2 Clip the seam and press it open.

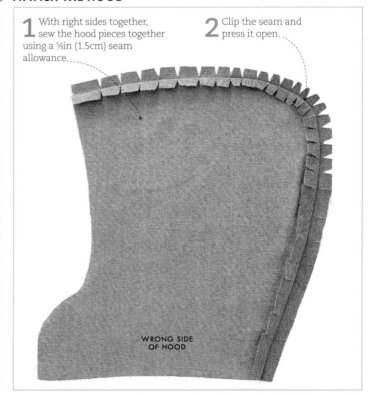

WRONG SIDE OF HOOD

FLAT SLEEVE CONSTRUCTION **p.213** ● ATTACHING A PATCH POCKET **p.242**

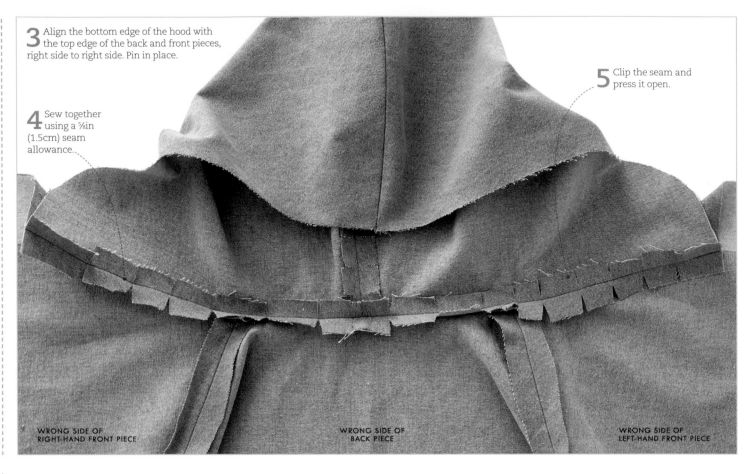

3 Align the bottom edge of the hood with the top edge of the back and front pieces, right side to right side. Pin in place.

4 Sew together using a ⅝in (1.5cm) seam allowance.

5 Clip the seam and press it open.

WRONG SIDE OF
RIGHT-HAND FRONT PIECE

WRONG SIDE OF
BACK PIECE

WRONG SIDE OF
LEFT-HAND FRONT PIECE

▶ ASSEMBLE THE JACKET

1 Construct the jacket in the second fabric, following the instructions above.

Hood

Center front

Pockets

2 Place the two jackets together right side to right side, inserting one inside the other.

3 Sew around all the outer edges, from one side seam, up the center front, around the hood, to the other side seam.

4 Leave a 6in (15cm) gap in the center back hem for turning.

5 Clip the seams.

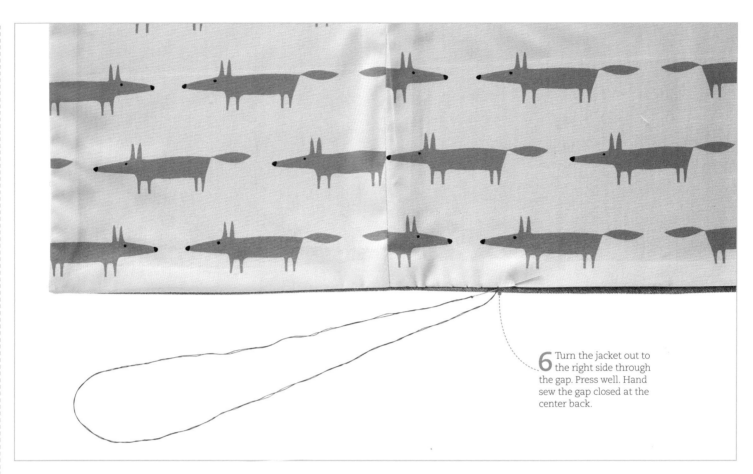

6 Turn the jacket out to the right side through the gap. Press well. Hand sew the gap closed at the center back.

▶ **ATTACH THE FASTENERS AND FINISH EDGES**

1 Attach the snaps in the positions marked on the pattern and following the manufacturer's instructions.

2 Top-stitch all around the jacket center front, hood, and hems, ¼in (6mm) from the edge, using a contrasting thread, if desired.

7 Turn in the hem allowances on the sleeves and hand sew the hem folds together.

SNAPS **p.320**

HEMS AND EDGES

The lower edge of a garment—or of a curtain or other home goods—is normally finished with a hem. This is to give not only a neat finish, but also to provide weight at the lower edge so that the garment or curtain hangs well.

HEMS AND EDGES

The edge of a piece of fabric can be finished with a hem—which is normally used on garments—or with a decorative edge, which is used for crafts and home goods as well as garments. Sometimes the style of what is being constructed dictates the finish that is used, and sometimes it is the fabric.

DIRECTORY OF HEMS

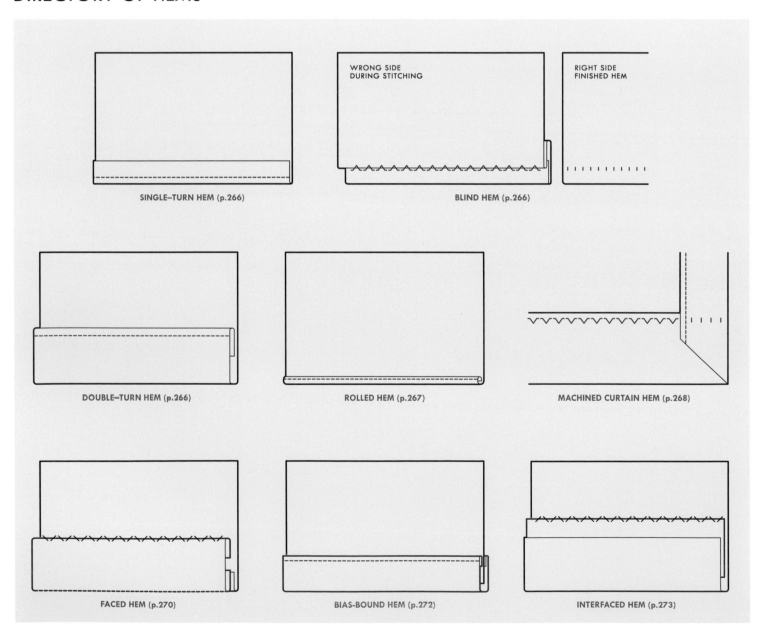

SINGLE-TURN HEM (p.266)

WRONG SIDE DURING STITCHING

RIGHT SIDE FINISHED HEM

BLIND HEM (p.266)

DOUBLE-TURN HEM (p.266)

ROLLED HEM (p.267)

MACHINED CURTAIN HEM (p.268)

FACED HEM (p.270)

BIAS-BOUND HEM (p.272)

INTERFACED HEM (p.273)

USEFUL EXTRAS **p.21** • BASTING STITCHES **p.89**

MARKING A HEMLINE

On a garment such as a skirt or a dress, it is important that the hemline is level all around. Even if the fabric has been cut straight, some styles of skirt—such as A-line or circular—will "drop," which means that the hem edge is longer in some places. This is due to the fabric stretching where it is not on the straight of the grain. Poor posture will also cause a hem to hang unevenly.

▶ USING A RULER

1 You'll need a helper for this method. Put on the skirt or dress (without shoes). With the end of the ruler on the floor, measure straight up on to the skirt.

2 Use pins to mark where the crease line of the hem should be. Mark the hemline all the way around to the same point on the ruler.

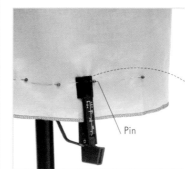

▶ USING A DRESS FORM

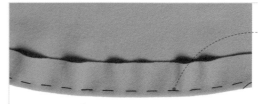

1 Adjust the dress form to your height and measurements. Place the skirt or dress on the dress form.

2 Using the hem marker on the stand, mark the crease line of the hem. The hem marker will hold the fabric either side of the hemline.

3 Slide a pin through the slot in the marker, then gently release the marker.

Pin

TURNING UP A STRAIGHT HEM

Difficulty level ✱✱✱✱✱

Once the crease line for the hem has been marked by the pins, you need to trim the hem allowance to a reasonable amount. Most straight hems are about 1½in (4cm) deep.

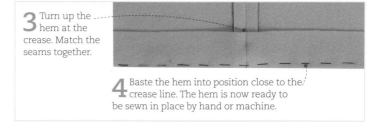

1 Gently press the crease line of the hem with the iron. Don't press too hard as you do not want a sharp crease.

2 Trim the seam allowance back to reduce the bulk. If wished, neaten the raw edge.

3 Turn up the hem at the crease. Match the seams together.

4 Baste the hem into position close to the crease line. The hem is now ready to be sewn in place by hand or machine.

TURNING UP A CURVED HEM

Difficulty level ✱✱✱✱✱

When the hem on a shaped skirt is turned up, it will be fuller at the upper edge. This fullness will need to be eased out before the hem is sewn.

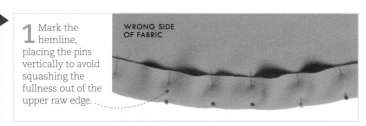

WRONG SIDE OF FABRIC

1 Mark the hemline, placing the pins vertically to avoid squashing the fullness out of the upper raw edge.

2 Baste the hem into position close to the crease line. Remove the pins.

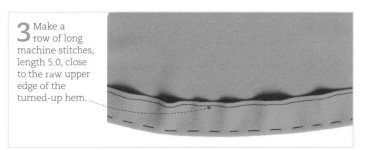

3 Make a row of long machine stitches, length 5.0, close to the raw upper edge of the turned-up hem.

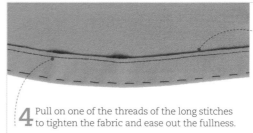

4 Pull on one of the threads of the long stitches to tighten the fabric and ease out the fullness.

5 Use the steam iron to shrink out the remainder of the fullness. The hem is now ready to be sewn in place by hand or machine.

HAND-SEWN HEMS **pp.264–265** ● MACHINE-SEWN HEMS **p.266**

TECHNIQUES

HAND-SEWN HEMS

Difficulty level ❋❋❋❋

One of the most popular ways to secure a hem edge is by hand. Hand sewing is discreet and, if a fine hand sewing needle is used, the stitches should not show on the right side of the work.

TIPS FOR SEWING HEMS BY HAND

1 Always use a single thread in the needle—a polyester all-purpose thread is ideal for hemming.

2 Once the raw edge of the hem allowance has been neatened by one of the methods below, secure it using a slip hem stitch. For this, take half of the stitch into the neatened edge and the other half into the wrong side of the garment fabric.

3 Start and finish the hand sewing with a double stitch, not a knot, because knots will catch and pull the hem down.

4 It is a good idea to take a small back stitch every 4in (10cm) or so to make sure that if the hem does come loose in one place, it will not all unravel.

▶ CLEAN FINISH

1 This is suitable for fine and lightweight fabrics. Lightly press the hem into position.

2 Turn the raw edge of the hem allowance to itself wrong side to wrong side and tack in place.

3 Open out the hem and machine the tacked edge.

4 Fold the hem back up and tack in place.

5 Roll the sewn edge back and sew underneath it.

6 Using a small slip hem stitch, secure the edge of the hem to the wrong side of the fabric. Roll the edge back into place.

7 Remove the basting and press lightly.

▶ SERGING FINISH

1 Using a 3-thread serger stitch, sew along the raw edge of the hem allowance.

2 Gently press the hem up into position and baste close to the crease.

3 Roll back the serged edge. Hand sew to the wrong side of the fabric using a slip hem stitch.

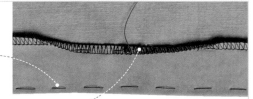

4 Press carefully to prevent the serging from being imprinted through to the right side.

▶ BIAS-BOUND FINISH

1 This is a good finish for fabrics that fray or that are bulky. Turn up the hem on to the wrong side of the garment and baste close to the crease line.

2 Pin the bias binding to the raw edge of the hem allowance.

3 Open out the crease in the bias and stitch along the crease line, keeping the raw edges level.

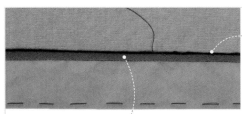

4 Turn down the bias over the raw edge and press.

5 Using a slip hem stitch, join the edge of the bias to the wrong side of the fabric. Remove the basting and press lightly.

▶ ZIGZAG FINISH

1 Use this to neaten the edge of the hem on fabrics that do not fray too badly. Set the sewing machine to a zigzag stitch, width 4.0 and length 3.0. Sew along the raw edge. Trim the fabric edge back to the zigzag stitch.

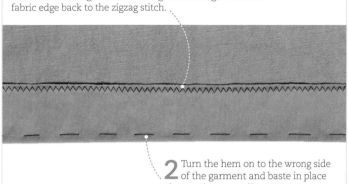

2 Turn the hem on to the wrong side of the garment and baste in place close to the crease line.

3 Fold back the zigzag-stitched edge. Using a slip hem stitch, sew the hem into place.

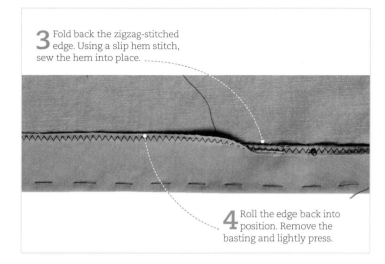

4 Roll the edge back into position. Remove the basting and lightly press.

▶ PINKED FINISH

1 Pinking shears can give an excellent hem finish on difficult fabrics such as rayon or georgette. Sew a row of straight stitches along the raw edge, ⅜in (1cm) from the edge. Pink the raw edge.

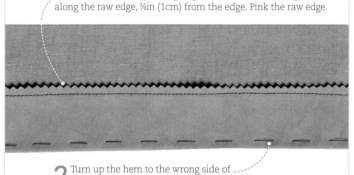

2 Turn up the hem to the wrong side of the garment and baste in place close to the crease line.

3 Fold back the edge along the sewn line and hand sew the hem in place with a slip hem stitch.

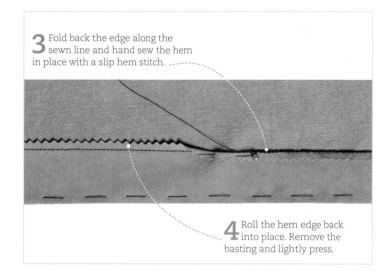

4 Roll the hem edge back into place. Remove the basting and lightly press.

▶ CURVED HEM FINISH

1 With a curved hem on a cotton or firm fabric, it is important that any fullness does not bulge on to the right side. Prior to turning up the hem into position, zigzag the raw edge, using stitch width 4.0 and stitch length 3.0.

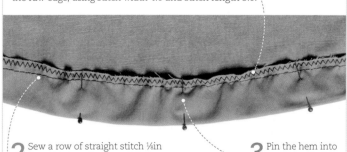

2 Sew a row of straight stitch ⅛in (3mm) below the row of zigzag stitch, using stitch length 5.0.

3 Pin the hem into position, placing the pins vertically.

4 Baste the hem into position close to the crease line.

5 Pull on the straight stitches to tighten the fabric.

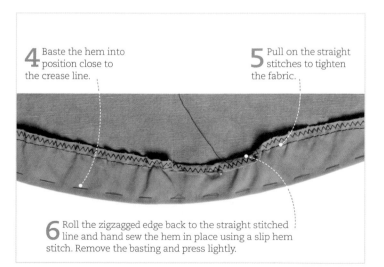

6 Roll the zigzagged edge back to the straight stitched line and hand sew the hem in place using a slip hem stitch. Remove the basting and press lightly.

STITCHES MADE WITH A MACHINE **pp.92–93** ● TURNING UP A CURVED HEM **p.263**

MACHINE-SEWN HEMS

Difficulty level ✱✱✱✱

On many occasions, the hem or edge of a garment or other item is turned up and secured using the sewing machine. It can be sewn with a straight stitch, a zigzag stitch, or a blind hem stitch. Hems can also be made on the serger.

▶ SINGLE TURN HEM

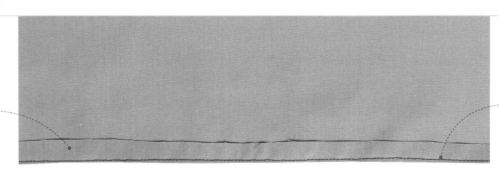

1 This is a popular technique. Turn up the hem to the wrong side of the work. Press in place.

2 Sew with a straight stitch close to the hem edge.

▶ BLIND HEM STITCH

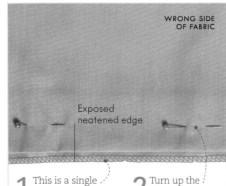

WRONG SIDE OF FABRIC

Exposed neatened edge

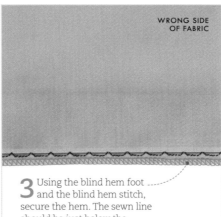

WRONG SIDE OF FABRIC

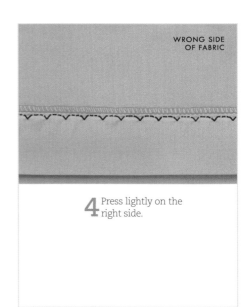

WRONG SIDE OF FABRIC

1 This is a single turn hem that is secured using the blind hem stitch on the machine. Neaten the raw edge of the fabric (here a serged finish has been used).

2 Turn up the hem, then fold the hem to the right side of the fabric leaving a little hem exposed at the bottom edge. Pin, but not too close to the fold.

3 Using the blind hem foot and the blind hem stitch, secure the hem. The sewn line should be just below the neatened edge.

4 Press lightly on the right side.

▶ DOUBLE TURN HEM

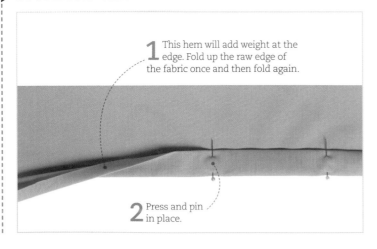

1 This hem will add weight at the edge. Fold up the raw edge of the fabric once and then fold again.

2 Press and pin in place.

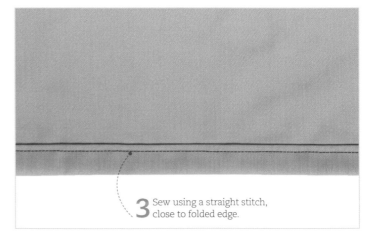

3 Sew using a straight stitch, close to folded edge.

SEWING-MACHINE ACCESSORIES **p.32** ● SERGER **pp.34—35**

HEMS ON DIFFICULT FABRICS

Difficulty level ✱✱✱✱✱

Some very fine fabrics or fabrics that fray badly require more thought when a hem is to be made. This technique works very well on delicate fabrics.

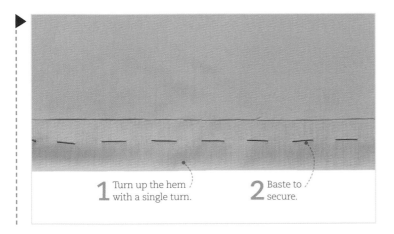

1 Turn up the hem with a single turn.   **2** Baste to secure.

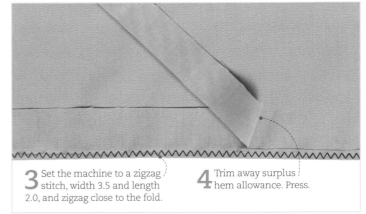

3 Set the machine to a zigzag stitch, width 3.5 and length 2.0, and zigzag close to the fold.   **4** Trim away surplus hem allowance. Press.

ROLLED HEMS

Difficulty level ✱✱✱✱✱

A rolled hem is used on lightweight fabrics. It is often found on home goods as well as garments. To make it, the fabric is rolled to the wrong side by using the rolled hem foot on the sewing machine.

▶ STRAIGHT-STITCHED ROLLED HEM

Use the rolled hem foot on the sewing machine and a straight stitch.

▶ ZIGZAG-STITCHED ROLLED HEM

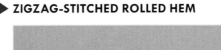

Use the rolled hem foot on the sewing machine and a zigzag stitch.

▶ SERGER ROLLED HEM

You will need to alter the settings on the serger to make this hem (consult the instruction book). Use a 3-thread stitch, with a bulky thread on the upper looper.

▶ MANUAL ROLLED HEM

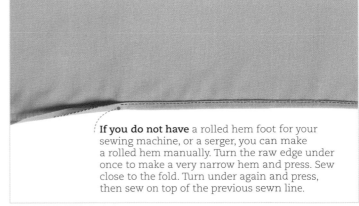

If you do not have a rolled hem foot for your sewing machine, or a serger, you can make a rolled hem manually. Turn the raw edge under once to make a very narrow hem and press. Sew close to the fold. Turn under again and press, then sew on top of the previous sewn line.

TECHNIQUES

MACHINE-SEWN CURTAIN HEMS

Difficulty level ✱✱✱✱

Curtains have hems at the bottom edge as well as at the sides. The hem at the bottom is treated differently from the side hems, although both types of hems are folded twice. The hems can be sewn using machine or hand methods.

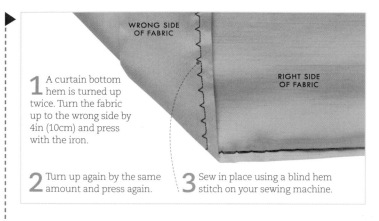

1 A curtain bottom hem is turned up twice. Turn the fabric up to the wrong side by 4in (10cm) and press with the iron.

WRONG SIDE OF FABRIC

RIGHT SIDE OF FABRIC

2 Turn up again by the same amount and press again.

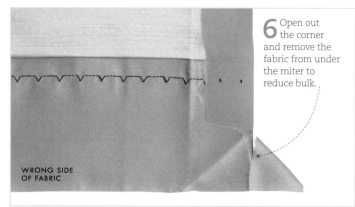

3 Sew in place using a blind hem stitch on your sewing machine.

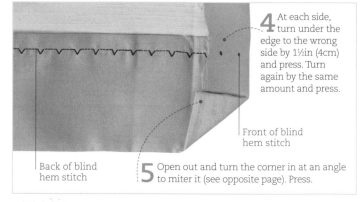

4 At each side, turn under the edge to the wrong side by 1½in (4cm) and press. Turn again by the same amount and press.

Front of blind hem stitch

Back of blind hem stitch

5 Open out and turn the corner in at an angle to miter it (see opposite page). Press.

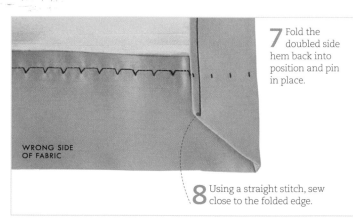

6 Open out the corner and remove the fabric from under the miter to reduce bulk.

WRONG SIDE OF FABRIC

7 Fold the doubled side hem back into position and pin in place.

WRONG SIDE OF FABRIC

8 Using a straight stitch, sew close to the folded edge.

HAND-SEWN CURTAIN HEMS

Difficulty level ✱✱✱✱

Hand sewing is used on heavier curtain fabrics or where you do not want a machine stitch to show on the right side. Everything is pressed in place first.

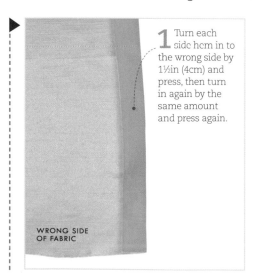

1 Turn each side hem in to the wrong side by 1½in (4cm) and press, then turn in again by the same amount and press again.

WRONG SIDE OF FABRIC

2 Turn up the bottom hem to the wrong side by 4in (10cm) and press, then turn up again by the same amount and press again.

3 Where the bottom hem and side hem meet, press under the hem at an angle to miter it (see opposite page).

4 Open out all the crease lines and reduce some of the bulk.

5 Fold everything back into place and pin.

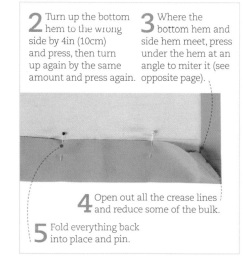

6 Use a herringbone stitch to sew the bottom hem in place. Take shallow stitches that run along the folded edge.

7 Repeat the process down the side hems.

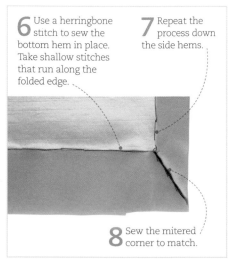

8 Sew the mitered corner to match.

MITERED CORNERS

At the bottom corners of curtains, where the bottom and side hems meet, the fabric is folded at an angle. This is called a miter. By pressing the miter with the iron and then unfolding it, you can use the crease lines that have been formed as a guide for removing surplus fabric to reduce bulk. For lined curtains, where the lining is constructed separately, the side and bottom hems are sewn in place. The same mitering technique is used for both curtains and linings.

Difficulty level ✳✳✳✳

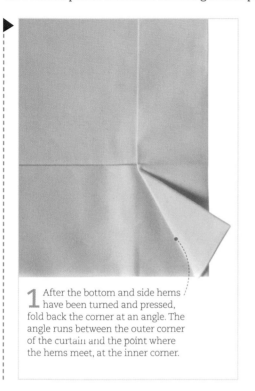

1 After the bottom and side hems have been turned and pressed, fold back the corner at an angle. The angle runs between the outer corner of the curtain and the point where the hems meet, at the inner corner.

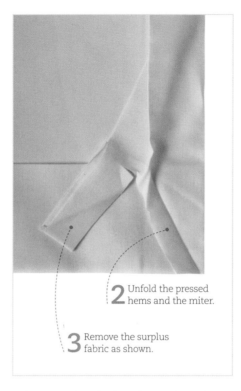

2 Unfold the pressed hems and the miter.

3 Remove the surplus fabric as shown.

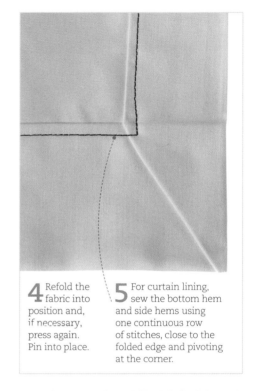

4 Refold the fabric into position and, if necessary, press again. Pin into place.

5 For curtain lining, sew the bottom hem and side hems using one continuous row of stitches, close to the folded edge and pivoting at the corner.

WEIGHTING CURTAINS

A weight is often inserted into the bottom hem of a curtain at the corners, to hold the curtain in place and make it hang properly. Specialist weights can be purchased, although a heavy coin can work just as well.

Difficulty level ✳✳✳✳

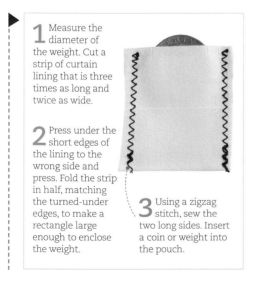

1 Measure the diameter of the weight. Cut a strip of curtain lining that is three times as long and twice as wide.

2 Press under the short edges of the lining to the wrong side and press. Fold the strip in half, matching the turned-under edges, to make a rectangle large enough to enclose the weight.

3 Using a zigzag stitch, sew the two long sides. Insert a coin or weight into the pouch.

4 Zigzag stitch across the open side.

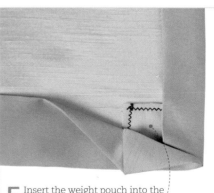

5 Insert the weight pouch into the bottom corner of the curtain.

6 When sewing the hems for the side and bottom, place stitches through the weight pouch to hold it in place.

SEWING CORNERS AND CURVES **pp.102–103** ● MACHINE-SEWN HEMS **p.266**

TECHNIQUES

HEMS ON STRETCH KNITS

Difficulty level

When making a garment with a stretch knit, the hem will need to stretch as well. There are two methods for sewing the hem on stretch knits, and the one you use depends on whether or not the fabric will run when it is cut.

▶ FABRIC THAT RUNS

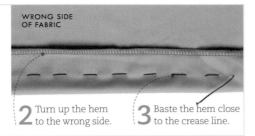

1 Neaten the raw edge using a 3-thread serger stitch. If no serger is available, use a zigzag stitch on the sewing machine.

WRONG SIDE OF FABRIC

2 Turn up the hem to the wrong side.

3 Baste the hem close to the crease line.

4 Insert a twin needle into the sewing machine and thread the machine with two threads.

5 Working from the right side of the garment, sew the hem in place.

▶ FABRIC THAT DOES NOT RUN

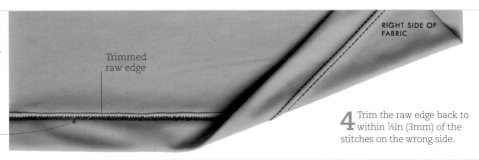

1 Insert the twin needle into the machine and thread the machine with two threads.

2 Turn up the hem to the wrong side and baste to hold in place.

3 Sew the hem in position.

Trimmed raw edge

RIGHT SIDE OF FABRIC

4 Trim the raw edge back to within ⅛in (3mm) of the stitches on the wrong side.

FACED HEM

Difficulty level ★★★☆☆

A faced hem is used on garments made from fabrics that may be too bulky to turn up without the hem showing, or on napped fabrics that may catch or ride up when they are worn. A faced hem is also used if there is not enough fabric to turn up to make a hem.

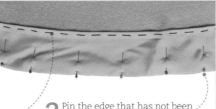

1 Cut a bias strip of lining fabric 4in (10cm) wide to make a facing. Join the strips together until there is enough to go all around the hem.

2 Baste under ⅜in (1cm) along one long edge.

3 Pin the edge that has not been turned under to the lower edge of the garment, right side to right side.

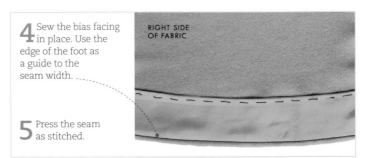

4 Sew the bias facing in place. Use the edge of the foot as a guide to the seam width.

RIGHT SIDE OF FABRIC

5 Press the seam as stitched.

6 Open out the bias facing. Press the seam down on to the bias.

7 Roll the bias facing to the wrong side of the garment. Make sure the seam is not on the crease line but shows on the wrong side.

8 Using a herringbone stitch, sew the folded edge of the bias strip in place.

WRONG SIDE OF FABRIC

HAND SEWING **pp.90–91** • STITCHES MADE WITH A MACHINE **pp.92–93** • SEWING CORNERS AND CURVES **pp.102–103** • HOW TO CUT BIAS STRIPS **p.154**

DECORATIVE FACED HEM

Difficulty level ★★★✱✱

If the edge of a garment, blind, cushion, or other item is to have a decorative effect, such as points or scallops (as shown here), a faced hem is used.

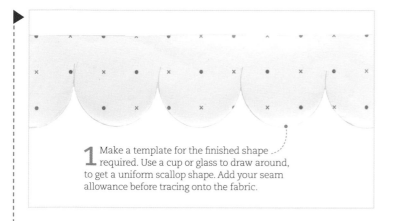

1 Make a template for the finished shape required. Use a cup or glass to draw around, to get a uniform scallop shape. Add your seam allowance before tracing onto the fabric.

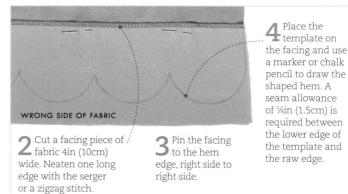

WRONG SIDE OF FABRIC

2 Cut a facing piece of fabric 4in (10cm) wide. Neaten one long edge with the serger or a zigzag stitch.

3 Pin the facing to the hem edge, right side to right side.

4 Place the template on the facing and use a marker or chalk pencil to draw the shaped hem. A seam allowance of ⅝in (1.5cm) is required between the lower edge of the template and the raw edge.

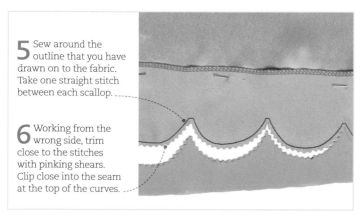

5 Sew around the outline that you have drawn on to the fabric. Take one straight stitch between each scallop.

6 Working from the wrong side, trim close to the stitches with pinking shears. Clip close into the seam at the top of the curves.

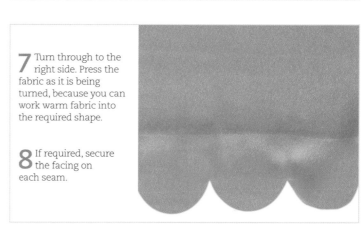

7 Turn through to the right side. Press the fabric as it is being turned, because you can work warm fabric into the required shape.

8 If required, secure the facing on each seam.

FUSED HEM

Difficulty level ★✱✱✱✱

A fused hem is useful for a fabric that is difficult to hand sew, as well as for an emergency hem repair. It uses a fusible web that has a fusible adhesive on both sides.

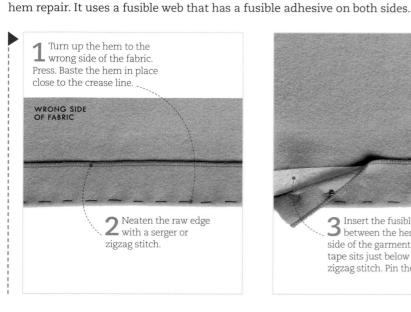

1 Turn up the hem to the wrong side of the fabric. Press. Baste the hem in place close to the crease line.

WRONG SIDE OF FABRIC

2 Neaten the raw edge with a serger or zigzag stitch.

3 Insert the fusible hemming tape between the hem and the wrong side of the garment. Make sure the tape sits just below the serger or zigzag stitch. Pin the tape in place.

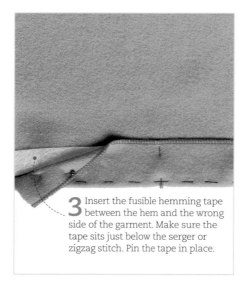

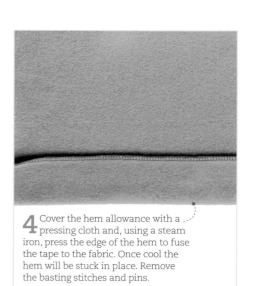

4 Cover the hem allowance with a pressing cloth and, using a steam iron, press the edge of the hem to fuse the tape to the fabric. Once cool the hem will be stuck in place. Remove the basting stitches and pins.

FUSIBLE TAPES p.325

BIAS-BOUND HEMS

Difficulty level

A bias-bound hem will give a narrow decorative edge to a garment or an item of home furnishing. It is particularly useful for curved shapes, to finish them neatly and securely. On a chunky or bulky fabric, a double bias is used so that it will be more substantial and hold its shape better. A double bias is also used on sheer fabrics as there will be no visible raw edges. The bias strip can be made from purchased bias binding or cut from a matching or contrasting fabric.

▶ SINGLE BIAS-BOUND HEM

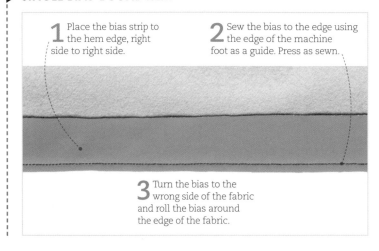

1 Place the bias strip to the hem edge, right side to right side.

2 Sew the bias to the edge using the edge of the machine foot as a guide. Press as sewn.

3 Turn the bias to the wrong side of the fabric and roll the bias around the edge of the fabric.

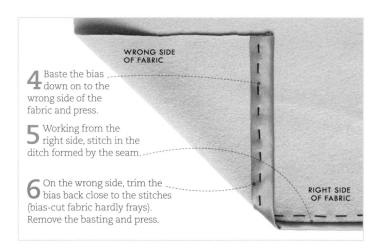

WRONG SIDE OF FABRIC

4 Baste the bias down on to the wrong side of the fabric and press.

5 Working from the right side, stitch in the ditch formed by the seam.

6 On the wrong side, trim the bias back close to the stitches (bias-cut fabric hardly frays). Remove the basting and press.

RIGHT SIDE OF FABRIC

▶ DOUBLE BIAS-BOUND HEM

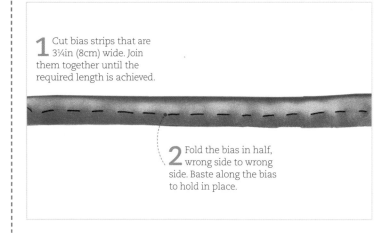

1 Cut bias strips that are 3¼in (8cm) wide. Join them together until the required length is achieved.

2 Fold the bias in half, wrong side to wrong side. Baste along the bias to hold in place.

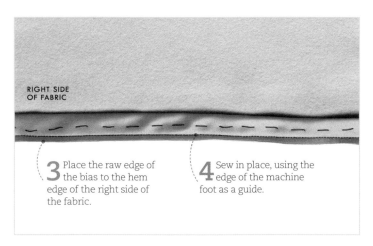

RIGHT SIDE OF FABRIC

3 Place the raw edge of the bias to the hem edge of the right side of the fabric.

4 Sew in place, using the edge of the machine foot as a guide.

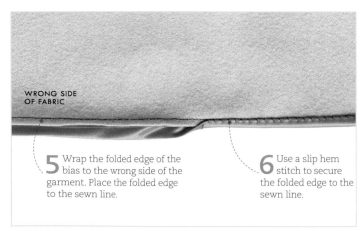

WRONG SIDE OF FABRIC

5 Wrap the folded edge of the bias to the wrong side of the garment. Place the folded edge to the sewn line.

6 Use a slip hem stitch to secure the folded edge to the sewn line.

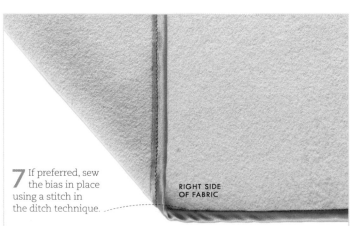

7 If preferred, sew the bias in place using a stitch in the ditch technique.

RIGHT SIDE OF FABRIC

HOW TO APPLY A NON-FUSIBLE INTERFACING p.55 ● **BASTING STITCHES p.89** ● **HAND SEWING pp.90–91**

TECHNIQUES

INTERFACED HEMS

On tailored garments, such as jackets and winter skirts, an interfaced hem can be used. It is only suitable for straight hems as it produces a heavy, structured edge. A sew-in woven interfacing cut on the bias grain is used for this technique.

Difficulty level

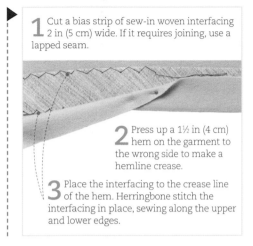

1 Cut a bias strip of sew-in woven interfacing 2 in (5 cm) wide. If it requires joining, use a lapped seam.

2 Press up a 1½ in (4 cm) hem on the garment to the wrong side to make a hemline crease.

3 Place the interfacing to the crease line of the hem. Herringbone stitch the interfacing in place, sewing along the upper and lower edges.

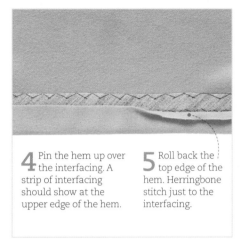

4 Pin the hem up over the interfacing. A strip of interfacing should show at the upper edge of the hem.

5 Roll back the top edge of the hem. Herringbone stitch just to the interfacing.

6 Roll back the hem into position. Press. On the right side, no stitches will be visible.

HORSEHAIR BRAID HEMS

On special-occasion wear, a horsehair braid is used in the hem edge as it will hold the edge out and give a look of fullness. Although once made from horsehair, the braid is now made from nylon. It is available in various widths. The braid is stretchy, so try not to stretch it when applying.

Difficulty level ✳✳✳✳✳

▶ USING A NARROW HORSEHAIR BRAID

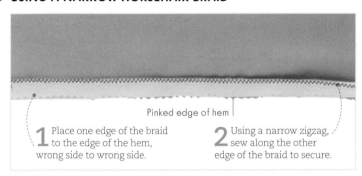

Pinked edge of hem

1 Place one edge of the braid to the edge of the hem, wrong side to wrong side.

2 Using a narrow zigzag, sew along the other edge of the braid to secure.

3 Fold the braid on to the wrong side of the fabric along the zigzag stitching. Press into position.

4 Sew with a straight stitch, through the center of the hem and braid. A row of stitches will show on the right side.

▶ USING A WIDE HORSEHAIR BRAID

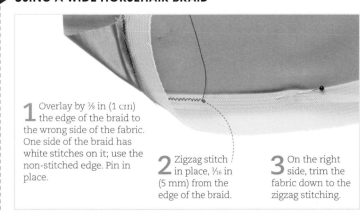

1 Overlay by ⅜ in (1 cm) the edge of the braid to the wrong side of the fabric. One side of the braid has white stitches on it; use the non-stitched edge. Pin in place.

2 Zigzag stitch in place, ³⁄₁₆ in (5 mm) from the edge of the braid.

3 On the right side, trim the fabric down to the zigzag stitching.

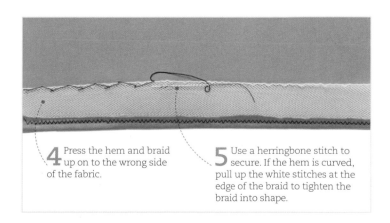

4 Press the hem and braid up on to the wrong side of the fabric.

5 Use a herringbone stitch to secure. If the hem is curved, pull up the white stitches at the edge of the braid to tighten the braid into shape.

STITCHES MADE WITH A MACHINE **pp.92–93** ● HOW TO CUT BIAS STRIPS **p.154**

HEMS WITH BANDING

Difficulty level ★★★★☆

Banding is a term applied to a much wider bias strip. Some banding is visible by the same amount at the hem or edge on both sides of the work, while other bandings are surface-mounted to the edge of a fabric, such as for a decorative effect on a blind or a table runner. Dealing with the corners on banding needs accurate marking and sewing. Most of the following techniques are used primarily on craft and home furnishing items.

▶ BANDING AT INNER CORNERS

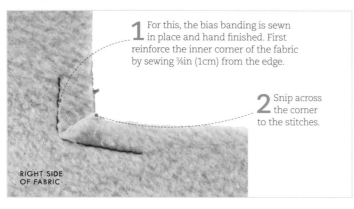

1 For this, the bias banding is sewn in place and hand finished. First reinforce the inner corner of the fabric by sewing ⅜in (1cm) from the edge.

2 Snip across the corner to the stitches.

RIGHT SIDE OF FABRIC

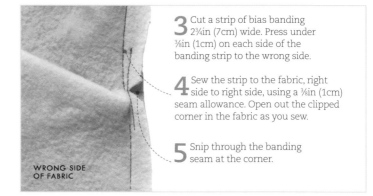

3 Cut a strip of bias banding 2¾in (7cm) wide. Press under ⅜in (1cm) on each side of the banding strip to the wrong side.

4 Sew the strip to the fabric, right side to right side, using a ⅜in (1cm) seam allowance. Open out the clipped corner in the fabric as you sew.

5 Snip through the banding seam at the corner.

WRONG SIDE OF FABRIC

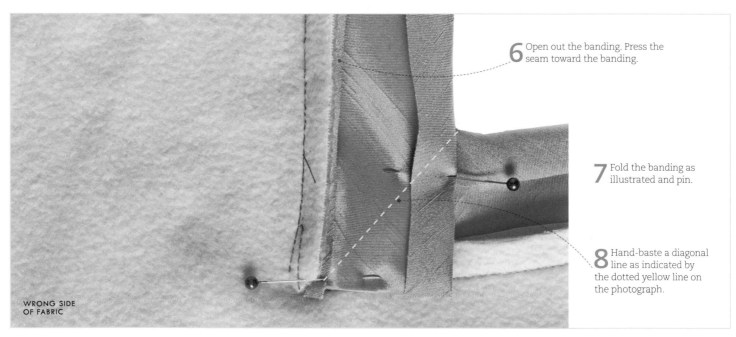

6 Open out the banding. Press the seam toward the banding.

7 Fold the banding as illustrated and pin.

8 Hand-baste a diagonal line as indicated by the dotted yellow line on the photograph.

WRONG SIDE OF FABRIC

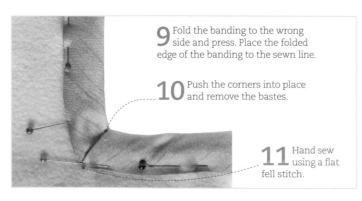

9 Fold the banding to the wrong side and press. Place the folded edge of the banding to the sewn line.

10 Push the corners into place and remove the bastes.

11 Hand sew using a flat fell stitch.

12 This is how banding looks on the right side. Press to finish.

PATTERN MARKING **pp.82–83** ● BASTING STITCHES **p.89** ● HAND SEWING **pp.90–91**

TECHNIQUES

▶ BANDING AT OUTER CORNERS

1 Cut a bias banding strip 2¾in (7cm) wide. Press under the long edges to the wrong side by ⅜in (1cm). Press the binding in half lengthwise, wrong side to wrong side.

2 Place the banding to the fabric, right side to right side. You can pin it in place if you like. Sew along the crease line, stopping ⅜in (1cm) from corner of fabric.

⅜in (1cm) from corner base fabric

Center foldline

WRONG SIDE OF BIAS BANDING

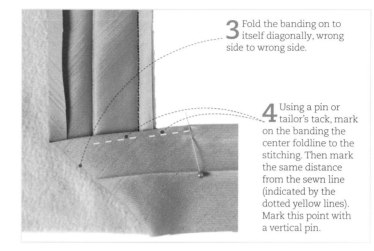

3 Fold the banding on to itself diagonally, wrong side to wrong side.

4 Using a pin or tailor's tack, mark on the banding the center foldline to the stitching. Then mark the same distance from the sewn line (indicated by the dotted yellow lines). Mark this point with a vertical pin.

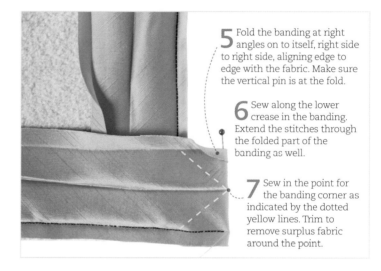

5 Fold the banding at right angles on to itself, right side to right side, aligning edge to edge with the fabric. Make sure the vertical pin is at the fold.

6 Sew along the lower crease in the banding. Extend the stitches through the folded part of the banding as well.

7 Sew in the point for the banding corner as indicated by the dotted yellow lines. Trim to remove surplus fabric around the point.

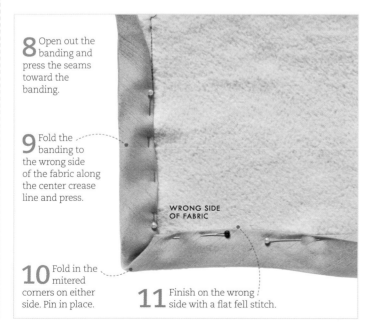

8 Open out the banding and press the seams toward the banding.

9 Fold the banding to the wrong side of the fabric along the center crease line and press.

10 Fold in the mitered corners on either side. Pin in place.

11 Finish on the wrong side with a flat fell stitch.

WRONG SIDE OF FABRIC

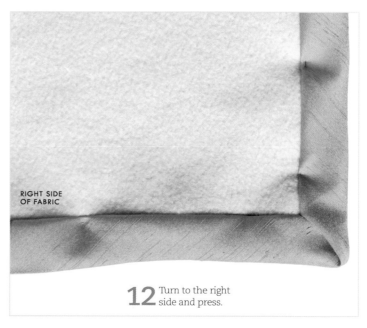

RIGHT SIDE OF FABRIC

12 Turn to the right side and press.

▶ SURFACE-MOUNTED BANDING AT OUTER CORNERS

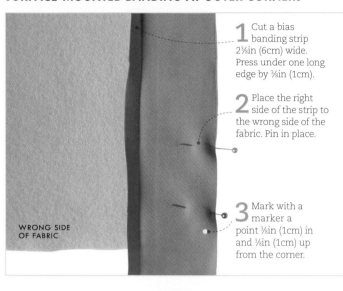

1 Cut a bias banding strip 2⅜in (6cm) wide. Press under one long edge by ⅜in (1cm).

2 Place the right side of the strip to the wrong side of the fabric. Pin in place.

3 Mark with a marker a point ⅜in (1cm) in and ⅜in (1cm) up from the corner.

WRONG SIDE OF FABRIC

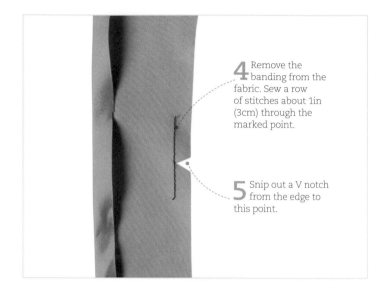

4 Remove the banding from the fabric. Sew a row of stitches about 1in (3cm) through the marked point.

5 Snip out a V notch from the edge to this point.

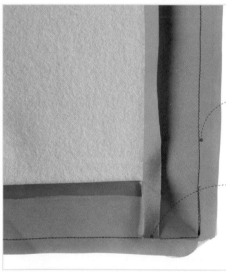

6 Place the banding back to the wrong side of the fabric. Pin in place.

7 Sew to secure, stretching out the banding as snipped to open it, and pivoting through the corner.

8 Fold the banding strip at an angle with the fold touching the sewn line. Keep the outer edge of the strip folded in place. Press to form crease lines.

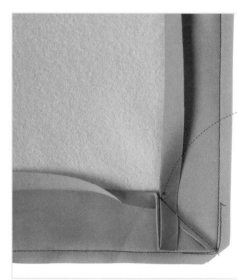

9 Sew along the crease lines. Be careful to keep edges folded as pressed in step 1.

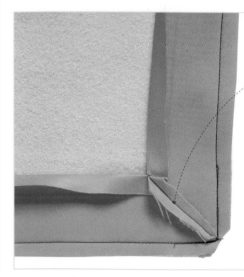

10 Remove the surplus fabric and press the seam open. Make sure the folds meet exactly.

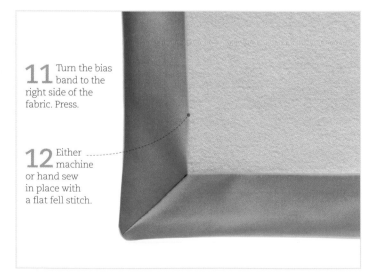

11 Turn the bias band to the right side of the fabric. Press.

12 Either machine or hand sew in place with a flat fell stitch.

MARKING AIDS **p.19** ● HAND SEWING **pp.90–91** ● STITCHES MADE WITH A MACHINE **pp.92–93**

▶ SURFACE-MOUNTED BANDING AT INNER CORNERS

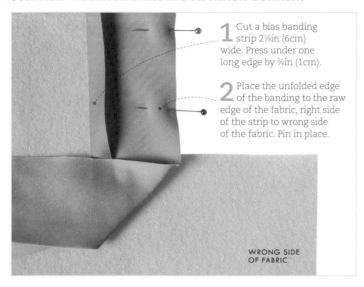

1 Cut a bias banding strip 2⅜in (6cm) wide. Press under one long edge by ⅜in (1cm).

2 Place the unfolded edge of the banding to the raw edge of the fabric, right side of the strip to wrong side of the fabric. Pin in place.

WRONG SIDE OF FABRIC

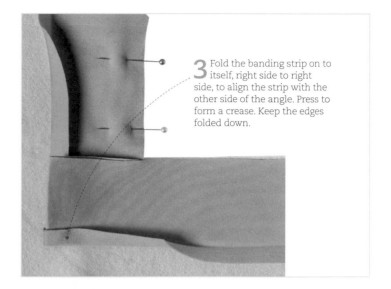

3 Fold the banding strip on to itself, right side to right side, to align the strip with the other side of the angle. Press to form a crease. Keep the edges folded down.

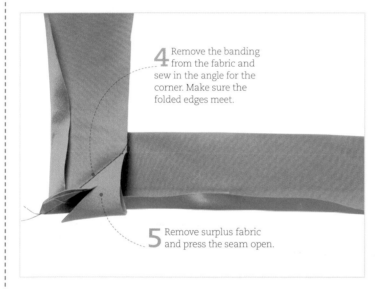

4 Remove the banding from the fabric and sew in the angle for the corner. Make sure the folded edges meet.

5 Remove surplus fabric and press the seam open.

6 Place the banding back in place on to the wrong side of the fabric. Pin in place, then sew to secure. Press.

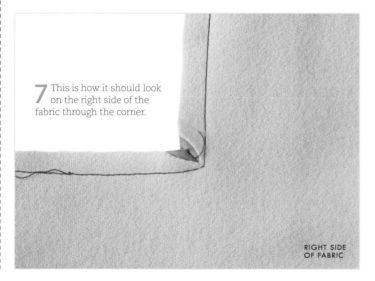

7 This is how it should look on the right side of the fabric through the corner.

RIGHT SIDE OF FABRIC

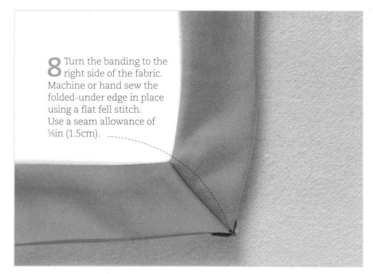

8 Turn the banding to the right side of the fabric. Machine or hand sew the folded-under edge in place using a flat fell stitch. Use a seam allowance of ⅝in (1.5cm).

HOW TO CUT BIAS STRIPS **p.154** ● MITERED CORNERS **p.269**

TECHNIQUES

APPLYING A FLAT TRIM

Difficulty level ✱✱✱✱✱

On some items a flat trim braid or ribbon is added for a decorative effect. This may be right on the hem or edge, or placed just above it. To achieve a neat finish, any corners should be mitered.

1 Pin the trim to the fabric, wrong side of the trim to right side of the fabric.

2 At the corner point where the trim is to be mitered, fold the trim back on itself and secure with a pin.

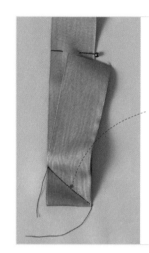

3 Sew across the trim at 45 degrees from the edge of the fold, through all layers.

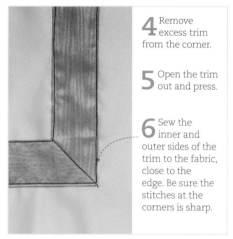

4 Remove excess trim from the corner.

5 Open the trim out and press.

6 Sew the inner and outer sides of the trim to the fabric, close to the edge. Be sure the stitches at the corners is sharp.

PIPED EDGES

Difficulty level ✱✱✱✱✱

A piped edge can look very effective on a garment, especially if it is made in a contrasting color or fabric. Piping is also an excellent way of finishing special-occasion wear as well as home goods. The piping may be single, double, or gathered.

▶ **SINGLE PIPING**

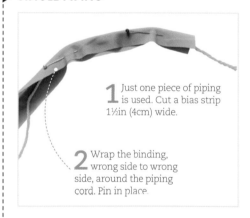

1 Just one piece of piping is used. Cut a bias strip 1½in (4cm) wide.

2 Wrap the binding, wrong side to wrong side, around the piping cord. Pin in place.

3 Sew along the binding close to the cord, using the zipper foot.

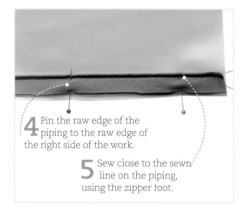

4 Pin the raw edge of the piping to the raw edge of the right side of the work.

5 Sew close to the sewn line on the piping, using the zipper foot.

6 Place the other side of the fabric over the piping, right side to right side.

7 Sew in place close to the piping, using the zipper foot.

— Piping

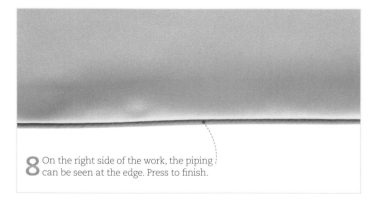

8 On the right side of the work, the piping can be seen at the edge. Press to finish.

◀ STITCHES MADE WITH A MACHINE **pp.92–93**

▶ DOUBLE PIPING

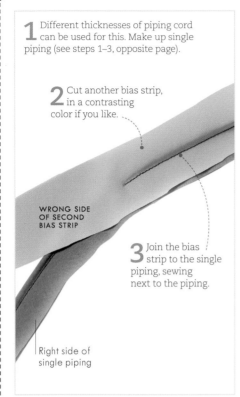

1 Different thicknesses of piping cord can be used for this. Make up single piping (see steps 1–3, opposite page).

2 Cut another bias strip, in a contrasting color if you like.

WRONG SIDE OF SECOND BIAS STRIP

3 Join the bias strip to the single piping, sewing next to the piping.

Right side of single piping

4 Place a second piping cord to the wrong side of the contrast strip.

5 Wrap the contrast strip around the cord and sew.

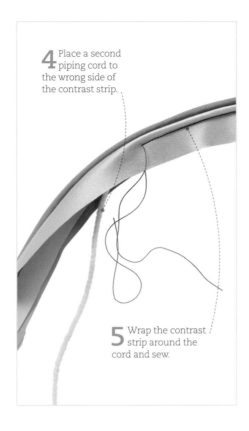

6 Attach to the edge of the work as for single piping (see steps 4–7, opposite page). On the right side, there is a double row of piping at the edge.

▶ GATHERED PIPING

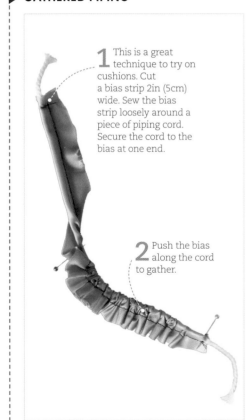

1 This is a great technique to try on cushions. Cut a bias strip 2in (5cm) wide. Sew the bias strip loosely around a piece of piping cord. Secure the cord to the bias at one end.

2 Push the bias along the cord to gather.

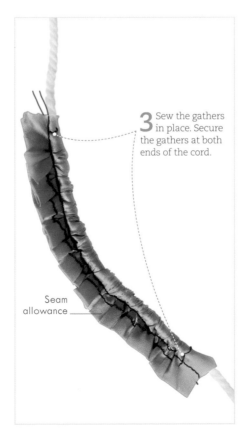

3 Sew the gathers in place. Secure the gathers at both ends of the cord.

Seam allowance

4 Attach to the edge of the work as for single piping (see steps 4–7, opposite page).

Gathered piping

HOW TO CUT BIAS STRIPS **p.154** ● MITERED CORNERS **p.269**

ATTACHING A LACE TRIM

Difficulty level ★★★★★

A lace edge can give a look of luxury to any garment. There are many ways of applying lace, depending on how the lace has been made. A heavy lace trim has a definite edge to be sewn on to the fabric. Lace edging has a decorative edge and an unfinished edge, whereas a galloon lace has decorative scallops on both edges.

▶ HEAVY LACE TRIM

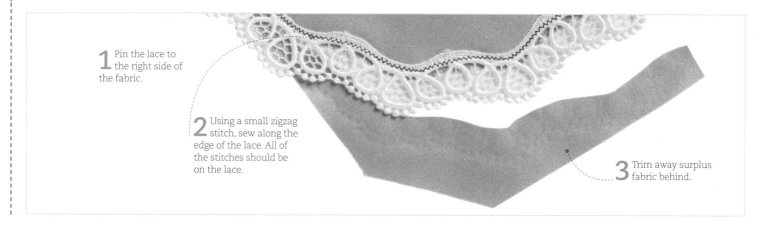

1 Pin the lace to the right side of the fabric.

2 Using a small zigzag stitch, sew along the edge of the lace. All of the stitches should be on the lace.

3 Trim away surplus fabric behind.

▶ LACE EDGING

1 Place the lace to the fabric, right side to right side. Align the raw edges.

2 Sew using a straight stitch.

3 Turn the raw edges to the wrong side of the fabric. Press in place on to the wrong side.

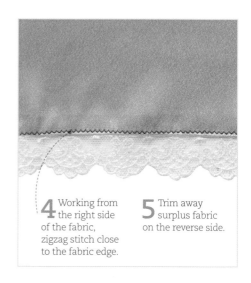

4 Working from the right side of the fabric, zigzag stitch close to the fabric edge.

5 Trim away surplus fabric on the reverse side.

▶ GALLOON LACE

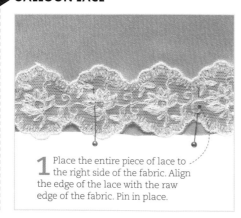

1 Place the entire piece of lace to the right side of the fabric. Align the edge of the lace with the raw edge of the fabric. Pin in place.

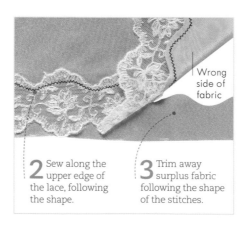

2 Sew along the upper edge of the lace, following the shape.

3 Trim away surplus fabric following the shape of the stitches.

Wrong side of fabric

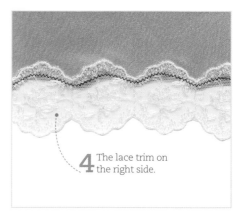

4 The lace trim on the right side.

TRIMMINGS, DECORATIONS, FRINGES, AND BRAIDS **p.27** ● SEWING-MACHINE ACCESSORIES **pp.32–33**

APPLYING OTHER TRIMS

There are many kinds of trims—ribbons, braids, beads, feathers, sequins, fringes, and so on—that can be applied to a fabric edge. If a trim is made on a narrow ribbon or braid it can often be inserted into a seam during construction. Other trims are attached after the garment or item has been completed.

Difficulty level ★★★★☆

▶ INSERTING A TRIM IN A SEAM

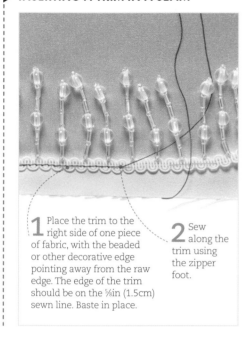

1 Place the trim to the right side of one piece of fabric, with the beaded or other decorative edge pointing away from the raw edge. The edge of the trim should be on the ⅝in (1.5cm) sewn line. Baste in place.

2 Sew along the trim using the zipper foot.

3 Place the other piece of fabric to the first one, right side to right side. Sew again to join them.

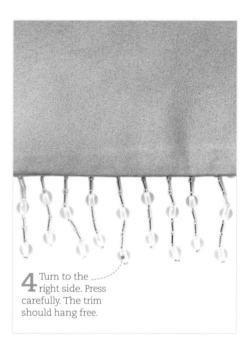

4 Turn to the right side. Press carefully. The trim should hang free.

▶ ATTACHING A TRIM TO AN EDGE

1 Pin the trim in position along the finished edge of the work. Be sure the trim is aligned to the edge. Baste in place.

2 Using the zipper foot, sew in place close to the upper edge, leaving the lower edge of the trim free.

▶ HAND STITCHING A TRIM

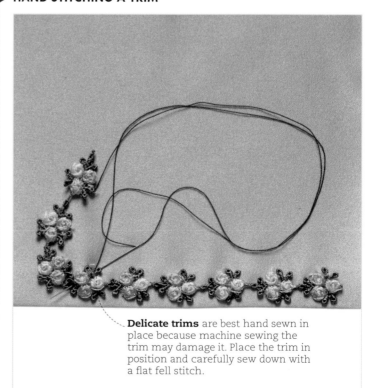

Delicate trims are best hand sewn in place because machine sewing the trim may damage it. Place the trim in position and carefully sew down with a flat fell stitch.

FASTENERS

There are many types of fastening available. Some of them are purely functional while others are more decorative as well as practical. A great many fastenings are hand sewn in place.

ZIPPERS

The zipper is probably the most used of all fastenings. There are a great many types available, in a variety of lengths, colors, and materials, but they all fall into one of five categories: skirt or pant zippers, metal or jeans zippers, invisible zippers, open-ended zippers, and decorative zippers. Before attaching any zipper, apply ¾in (2cm)-wide strips of fusible interfacing to the zipper seam allowances on the wrong side of the fabric.

DIRECTORY OF ZIPPERS

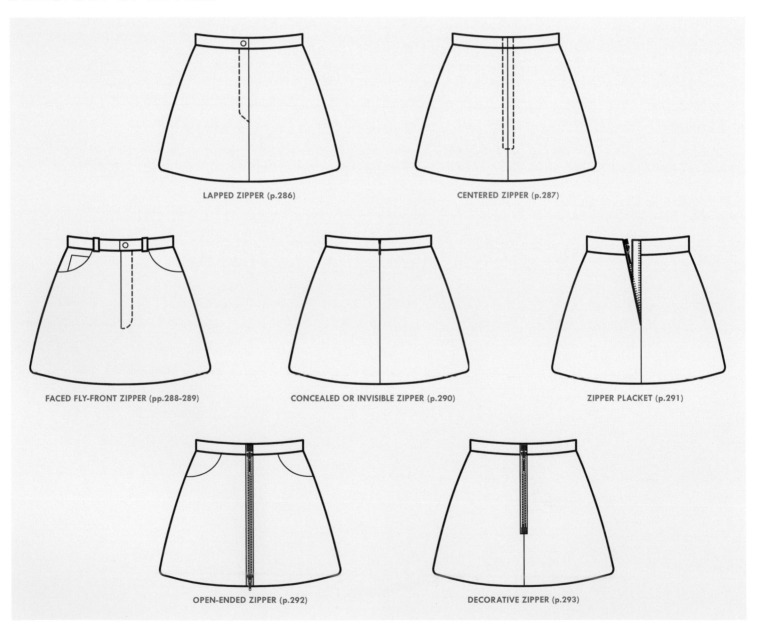

LAPPED ZIPPER (p.286)

CENTERED ZIPPER (p.287)

FACED FLY-FRONT ZIPPER (pp.288-289)

CONCEALED OR INVISIBLE ZIPPER (p.290)

ZIPPER PLACKET (p.291)

OPEN-ENDED ZIPPER (p.292)

DECORATIVE ZIPPER (p.293)

HOW TO SHORTEN A ZIPPER

Difficulty level ✳✳✳✳

Zippers do not always come in the length that you need, but it is easy to shorten them. Skirt or pant zippers and invisible zippers are all shortened by sewing across the teeth or coils, whereas an open-ended zipper is shortened at the top and not at the bottom.

▶ **SHORTENING A SKIRT/PANT OR INVISIBLE ZIPPER**

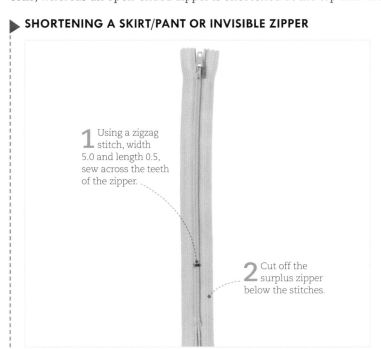

1 Using a zigzag stitch, width 5.0 and length 0.5, sew across the teeth of the zipper.

2 Cut off the surplus zipper below the stitches.

▶ **SHORTENING AN OPEN-ENDED ZIPPER**

1 Mark with a marker the place where the zipper is to be shortened.

2 Open the zipper past this point.

3 Using a zigzag stitch, width 3.0 and length 0.5, sew across each side of the opened zipper. Cut off the surplus.

MARKING FOR PLACING ZIPPERS

Difficulty level ✳✳✳✳

For a zipper to sit accurately in the seam, the seam allowances where the zipper will be inserted need to be marked. The upper seam allowance at the top of the zipper also needs marking to ensure that the zipper pull sits just fractionally below the sewn line.

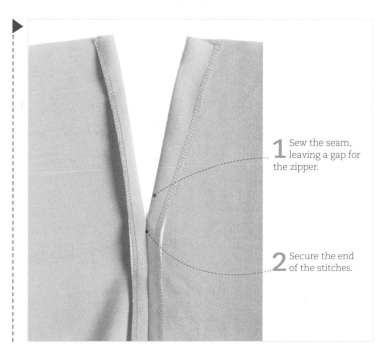

1 Sew the seam, leaving a gap for the zipper.

2 Secure the end of the stitches.

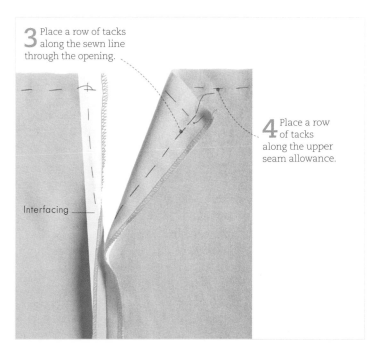

3 Place a row of tacks along the sewn line through the opening.

4 Place a row of tacks along the upper seam allowance.

Interfacing

REPAIRING A BROKEN ZIPPER **p.367**

LAPPED ZIPPER

Difficulty level ✱✱✱✱✱

A skirt zipper in a skirt or a dress is usually put in by means of a lapped technique or a centered zipper technique (see opposite page). For both of these techniques, you will require the zipper foot on the sewing machine. A lapped zipper features one side of the seam—the left-hand side—covering the teeth of the zipper to conceal them.

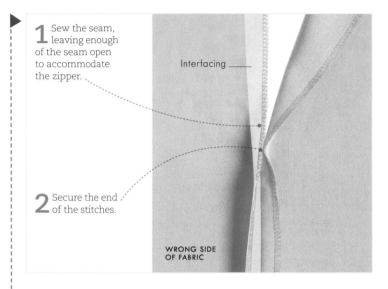

1 Sew the seam, leaving enough of the seam open to accommodate the zipper.

Interfacing

2 Secure the end of the stitches.

WRONG SIDE OF FABRIC

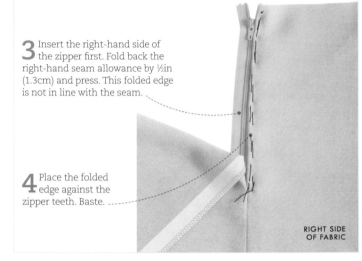

3 Insert the right-hand side of the zipper first. Fold back the right-hand seam allowance by ½in (1.3cm) and press. This folded edge is not in line with the seam.

4 Place the folded edge against the zipper teeth. Baste.

RIGHT SIDE OF FABRIC

5 Using the zipper foot, sew along the baste line to secure the zipper tape to the fabric. Sew from the bottom of the zipper to the top.

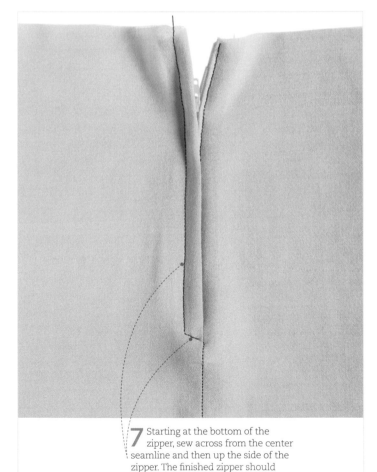

6 Fold back the left-hand seam allowance by ⅝in (1.5cm) and press. Place the folded edge over the sewn line of the other side. Pin and then hand-baste along foldline.

7 Starting at the bottom of the zipper, sew across from the center seamline and then up the side of the zipper. The finished zipper should have the teeth covered by the fabric.

CENTERED ZIPPER

With a centered zipper, the two folded edges of the seam allowances meet over the center of the teeth, to conceal the zipper completely.

1 Sew the seam, leaving a gap for the zipper.

2 Baste the rest of the seam allowance.

3 Press the seam open lightly.

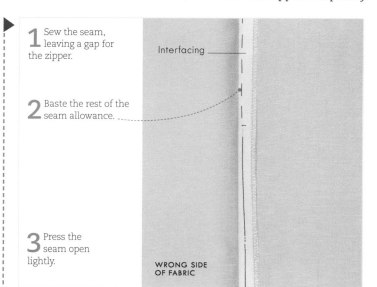

Interfacing

WRONG SIDE OF FABRIC

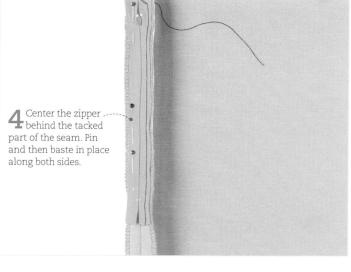

4 Center the zipper behind the tacked part of the seam. Pin and then baste in place along both sides.

5 On the wrong side, lift the seam allowance and the zipper tape away from the main fabric. Pin.

6 Sew the zipper tape to the seam allowance. Make sure both sides of the zipper tape are secured to the seam allowances. Sew through to the end of the zipper tape.

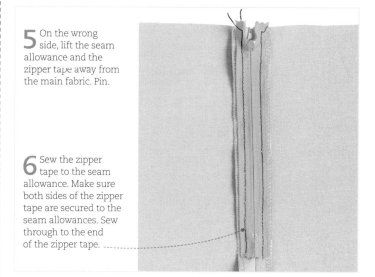

7 Working from the right side of the work, sew down one side, across the bottom, and up the other side of the zipper.

8 Remove the tacks and press.

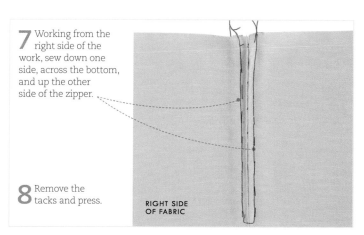

RIGHT SIDE OF FABRIC

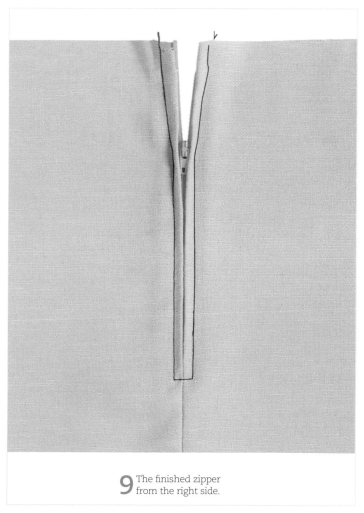

9 The finished zipper from the right side.

STITCHES MADE WITH A MACHINE **pp.92–93** ● HOW TO MAKE A PLAIN SEAM **p.94**

FACED FLY-FRONT ZIPPER

Difficulty level ✱✱✱✱✱

Whether it be for a classic pair of pants or a pair of jeans, a fly front is the most common technique for inserting a pant zipper. The zipper usually has a facing behind it to prevent the zipper teeth from catching.

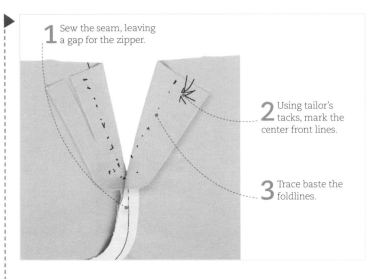

1 Sew the seam, leaving a gap for the zipper.

2 Using tailor's tacks, mark the center front lines.

3 Trace baste the foldlines.

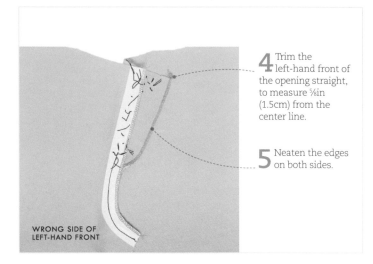

4 Trim the left-hand front of the opening straight, to measure ⅝in (1.5cm) from the center line.

5 Neaten the edges on both sides.

WRONG SIDE OF LEFT-HAND FRONT

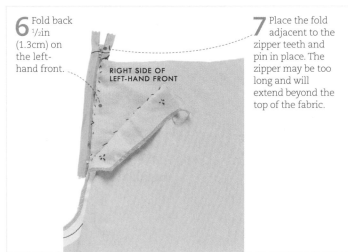

6 Fold back ½in (1.3cm) on the left-hand front.

RIGHT SIDE OF LEFT-HAND FRONT

7 Place the fold adjacent to the zipper teeth and pin in place. The zipper may be too long and will extend beyond the top of the fabric.

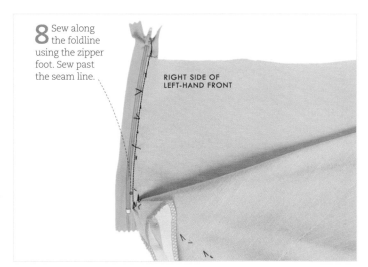

8 Sew along the foldline using the zipper foot. Sew past the seam line.

RIGHT SIDE OF LEFT-HAND FRONT

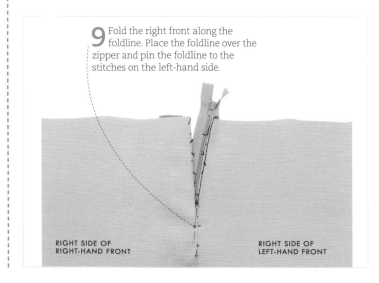

9 Fold the right front along the foldline. Place the foldline over the zipper and pin the foldline to the stitches on the left-hand side.

RIGHT SIDE OF RIGHT-HAND FRONT

RIGHT SIDE OF LEFT-HAND FRONT

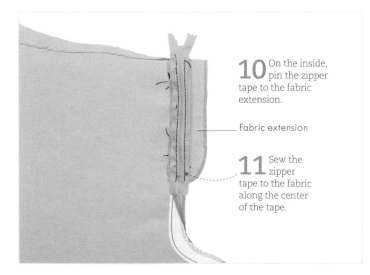

10 On the inside, pin the zipper tape to the fabric extension.

Fabric extension

11 Sew the zipper tape to the fabric along the center of the tape.

SEWING-MACHINE ACCESSORIES p.33 • **PATTERN MARKING pp.82–83** • **BASTING STITCHES p.89** • **ATTACHING A STRAIGHT WAISTBAND pp.192–193**

12 On the right side, top-stitch around the zipper. Start sewing at the center front. Sew a smooth curve.

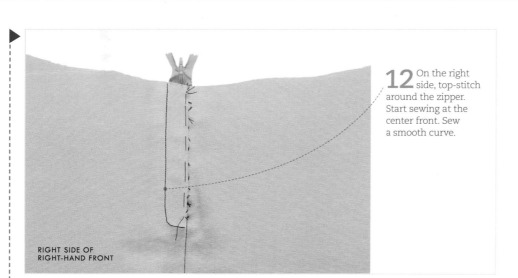

RIGHT SIDE OF RIGHT-HAND FRONT

13 Neaten all the edges of the fly-front facing, leaving the top edge raw.

13 On the wrong side, pin the facing to the seam allowance on the left-hand side. Ensure that the facing covers the zip fully.

15 Sew to the seam allowance on the left-hand side.

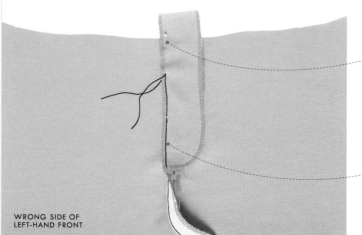

WRONG SIDE OF LEFT-HAND FRONT

16 Attach the waistband over the zipper and the facings. Trim the facing and zipper.

17 Secure the lower edge of the facing on the right-hand side to the right-hand seam allowance.

18 The waistband goes over the zipper and acts as the zipper stop. Attach a pant hook and eye.

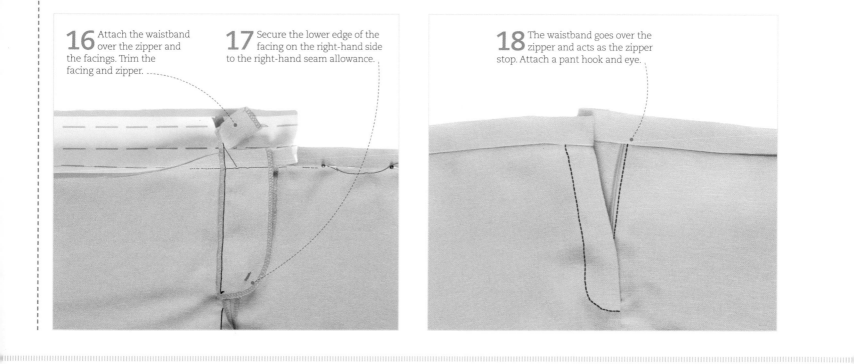
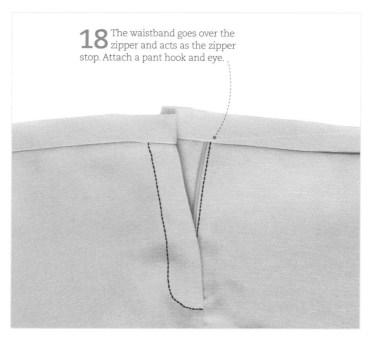

HOOKS AND EYES **p.319**

TECHNIQUES

CONCEALED OR INVISIBLE ZIPPER

Difficulty level

This type of zipper looks different from other zippers because the teeth are on the reverse and nothing except the pull is seen on the front. The zipper is inserted before the seam is sewn. A special concealed zipper foot is required.

RIGHT SIDE OF FABRIC

1 Mark the seam allowance with basting stitches.

2 On the left-hand back place the center of the zipper over the baste line, right side down. Pin in place.

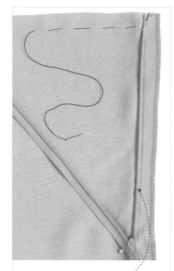

3 Undo the zipper. Using the concealed zipper foot, sew from the top of the zipper down as far as possible. Sew under the teeth. Stop when the foot hits the zipper pull.

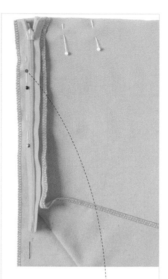

4 Zip up the zipper. Place the other piece of fabric to the zipper. Match along the upper edge. Pin the other side of the zipper tape in place.

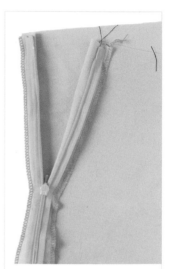

5 Open the zipper again. Using the concealed zipper foot, sew down the other side of the zipper to attach to the right-hand side. Remove any basting stitches.

Free end of zipper tape

6 Close the zipper. On the wrong side at the bottom of the zipper, the two rows of stitches that hold in the zipper should finish at the same place.

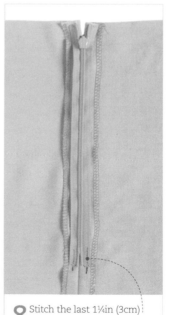

7 Sew the seam below the zipper. Use the normal foot for this. There will be a small gap of about ⅛in (3mm) between the seam line for the zipper and that for the seam.

8 Stitch the last 1¼in (3cm) of the zipper tape to just the seam allowances. This will stop the zipper pulling loose.

9 On the right side, the zipper is completely concealed, with just the pull visible at the top. Apply waistband or facing.

SEWING-MACHINE ACCESSORIES **p.33** ● PATTERN MARKING **pp.82–83** ● BASTING STITCHES **p.89**

ZIPPER PLACKET

The zipper placket, or zipper guard, can be placed behind any of the zippers that are covered in this chapter. This type of placket sits behind the zipper on the inside of the garment, and prevents the zipper from catching on you or on your clothes.

Difficulty level ★★★✦✦

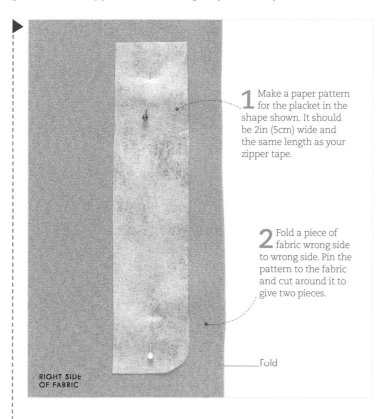

1 Make a paper pattern for the placket in the shape shown. It should be 2in (5cm) wide and the same length as your zipper tape.

2 Fold a piece of fabric wrong side to wrong side. Pin the pattern to the fabric and cut around it to give two pieces.

Fold

RIGHT SIDE OF FABRIC

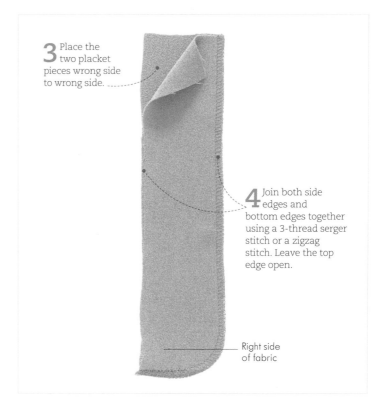

3 Place the two placket pieces wrong side to wrong side.

4 Join both side edges and bottom edges together using a 3-thread serger stitch or a zigzag stitch. Leave the top edge open.

Right side of fabric

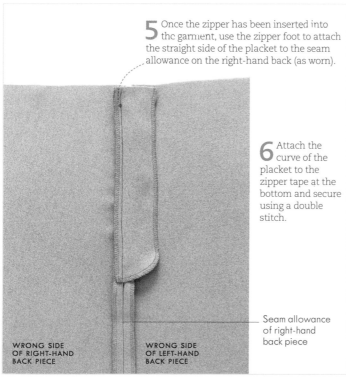

5 Once the zipper has been inserted into the garment, use the zipper foot to attach the straight side of the placket to the seam allowance on the right-hand back (as worn).

6 Attach the curve of the placket to the zipper tape at the bottom and secure using a double stitch.

Seam allowance of right-hand back piece

WRONG SIDE OF RIGHT-HAND BACK PIECE

WRONG SIDE OF LEFT-HAND BACK PIECE

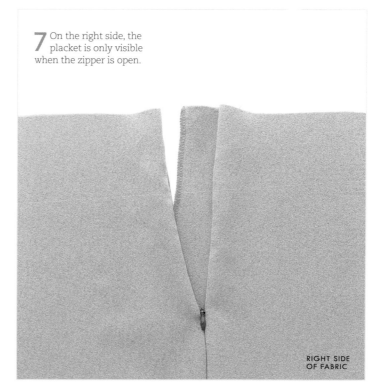

7 On the right side, the placket is only visible when the zipper is open.

RIGHT SIDE OF FABRIC

STITCHES MADE WITH A MACHINE pp.92—93

OPEN-ENDED ZIPPER

Difficulty level **★★**☆☆

The open-ended zipper is used on garments where the two halves need to be fully opened in order to put the garment on—for example, on a jacket or cardigan.

TECHNIQUES

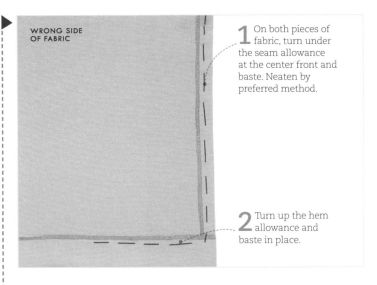
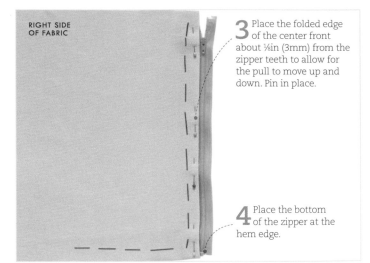

WRONG SIDE OF FABRIC

1 On both pieces of fabric, turn under the seam allowance at the center front and baste. Neaten by preferred method.

2 Turn up the hem allowance and baste in place.

RIGHT SIDE OF FABRIC

3 Place the folded edge of the center front about ⅛in (3mm) from the zipper teeth to allow for the pull to move up and down. Pin in place.

4 Place the bottom of the zipper at the hem edge.

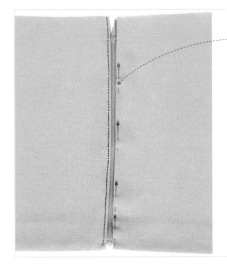

RIGHT SIDE OF FABRIC

5 Using the zipper foot, sew the zipper in place. Start with the zipper open. Sew 2in (5cm), then place the needle in the work, raise the zipper foot, and close the zipper.

6 Sew to the end of the zipper tape and secure.

7 Pin the other side of the zipper in place on the other piece of fabric. Make sure the fabric lines up top and bottom.

8 Undo the zipper and, using the zipper foot, sew in place as you did on the first side.

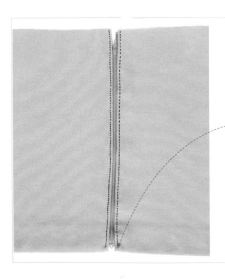

9 Once the zipper is sewn in place, check that the hems line up. If they do not, you will have to rip the seam and start again.

10 The zipper should open completely.

MARKING AIDS p.19 ● **SEWING-MACHINE ACCESSORIES p.33** ● **ORGANZA p.49** ● **BASTING STITCHES p.89**

A DECORATIVE ZIPPER

Some zippers are meant to be seen—they may have crystals in the teeth, or they may have decorative, colored teeth.

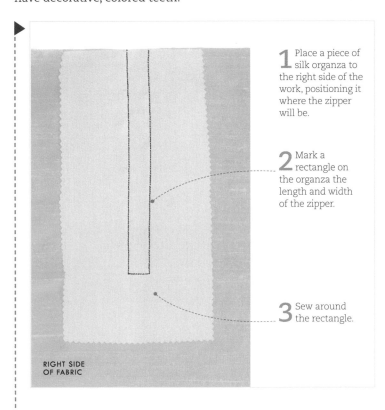

1 Place a piece of silk organza to the right side of the work, positioning it where the zipper will be.

2 Mark a rectangle on the organza the length and width of the zipper.

3 Sew around the rectangle.

RIGHT SIDE OF FABRIC

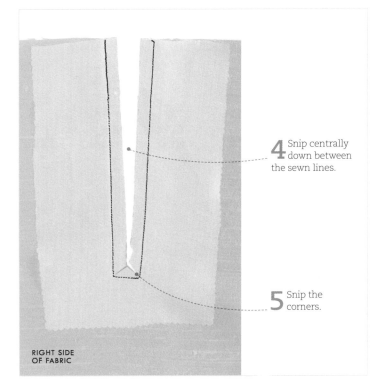

4 Snip centrally down between the sewn lines.

5 Snip the corners.

RIGHT SIDE OF FABRIC

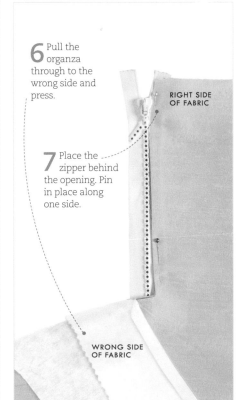

6 Pull the organza through to the wrong side and press.

7 Place the zipper behind the opening. Pin in place along one side.

RIGHT SIDE OF FABRIC

WRONG SIDE OF FABRIC

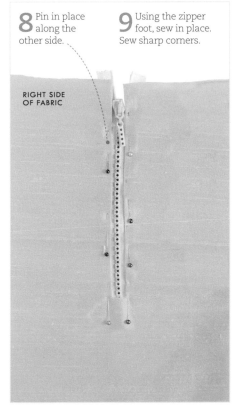

8 Pin in place along the other side.

9 Using the zipper foot, sew in place. Sew sharp corners.

RIGHT SIDE OF FABRIC

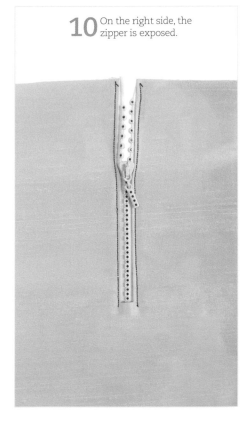

10 On the right side, the zipper is exposed.

TOILETRIES **BAG**

Difficulty level ★★★★★

Inserting a zipper is nothing to fear. The zipper on this lined toiletries bag is attached in the same way as an open-ended zipper to help it open wide, but is neatened with a zipper cover. With its flat bottom, the bag will sit beautifully on a dressing table or bathroom shelf.

TECHNIQUES USED How to apply a fusible interfacing **p.54**, Open-ended zipper **p.256**

YOU WILL NEED

- Pattern template on p.386
- 20 x 43in (50 x 110cm) quilting-weight cotton for outer fabric
- 20 x 43in (50 x 110cm) quilting-weight cotton for the lining
- 20 x 36in (50 x 90cm) woven cotton fusible interfacing
- 10 x 36in (25 x 90cm) medium-loft fusible fleece batting
- 10in (25cm) closed-end nylon dress zipper
- Matching thread
- Zipper foot

PIECES TO CUT

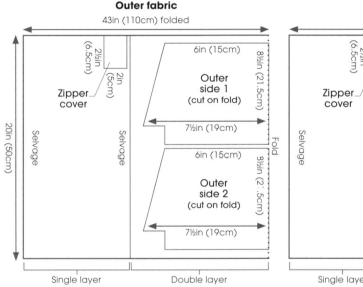

Outer fabric
43in (110cm) folded

2½in (6.5cm) — 2in (5cm)
Zipper cover
Outer side 1 (cut on fold)
6in (15cm)
8½in (21.5cm)
7½in (19cm)
Outer side 2 (cut on fold)
6in (15cm)
8½in (21.5cm)
7½in (19cm)
20in (50cm)
Selvage — Selvage — Fold
Single layer — Double layer

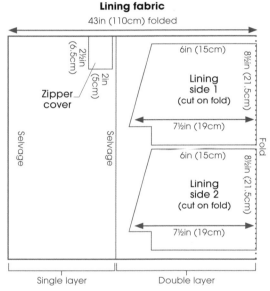

Lining fabric
43in (110cm) folded

2½in (6.5cm) — 2in (5cm)
Zipper cover
Lining side 1 (cut on fold)
6in (15cm)
8½in (21.5cm)
7½in (19cm)
Lining side 2 (cut on fold)
6in (15cm)
8½in (21.5cm)
7½in (19cm)
Selvage — Selvage — Fold
Single layer — Double layer

▶ PREPARE THE ZIP

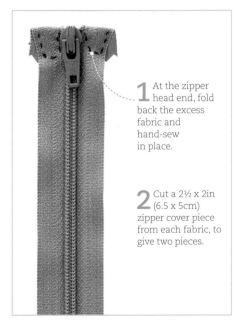

1 At the zipper head end, fold back the excess fabric and hand-sew in place.

2 Cut a 2½ x 2in (6.5 x 5cm) zipper cover piece from each fabric, to give two pieces.

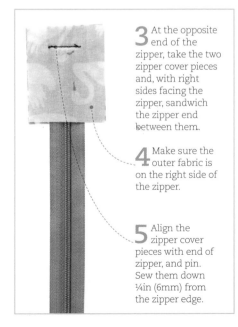

3 At the opposite end of the zipper, take the two zipper cover pieces and, with right sides facing the zipper, sandwich the zipper end between them.

4 Make sure the outer fabric is on the right side of the zipper.

5 Align the zipper cover pieces with end of zipper, and pin. Sew them down ¼in (6mm) from the zipper edge.

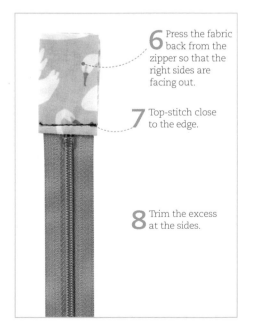

6 Press the fabric back from the zipper so that the right sides are facing out.

7 Top-stitch close to the edge.

8 Trim the excess at the sides.

▶ **ATTACH THE ZIPPER TO THE SIDES**

1 Cut four pieces of woven cotton interfacing using the template. Apply to the two outer pieces and two lining pieces according to the manufacturer's instructions. Leave to cool for 20 minutes.

2 Cut two pieces of fusible fleece batting using the template, then trim ¾in (18mm) on the top and ¼in (6mm) on all the other sides. Apply to the outer fabric only, positioning so that the top of the fleece is ¾in (18mm) below the top edge. Leave aside to cool for 20 minutes.

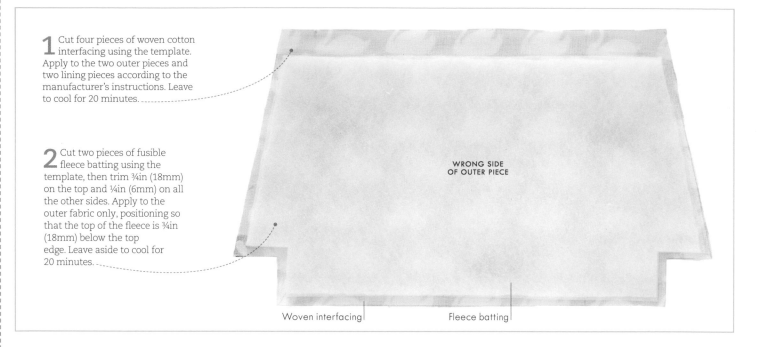

WRONG SIDE
OF OUTER PIECE

Woven interfacing

Fleece batting

3 Take one outer piece and, with right side facing up, pin the zipper (facing down) to the top edge, positioning the zipper head ½in (1.2cm) from the left-hand side edge.

½in (1.2cm)

Wrong side of zipper

RIGHT SIDE OF
OUTER PIECE 1

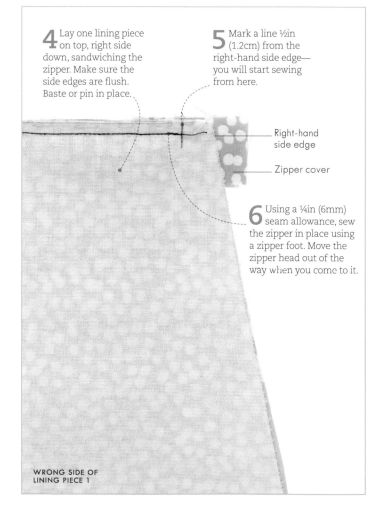

4 Lay one lining piece on top, right side down, sandwiching the zipper. Make sure the side edges are flush. Baste or pin in place.

5 Mark a line ½in (1.2cm) from the right-hand side edge— you will start sewing from here.

Right-hand
side edge

Zipper cover

6 Using a ¼in (6mm) seam allowance, sew the zipper in place using a zipper foot. Move the zipper head out of the way when you come to it.

WRONG SIDE OF
LINING PIECE 1

MEASURING TOOLS AND MARKING AIDS pp.18–19 ● **PRESSING AIDS pp.28–29** ● **SEWING MACHINE ACCESSORIES pp.32–33** ● **HOW TO APPLY A FUSIBLE INTERFACING p.54**

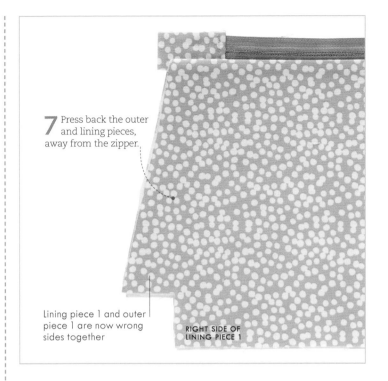

7 Press back the outer and lining pieces, away from the zipper.

Lining piece 1 and outer piece 1 are now wrong sides together

RIGHT SIDE OF LINING PIECE 1

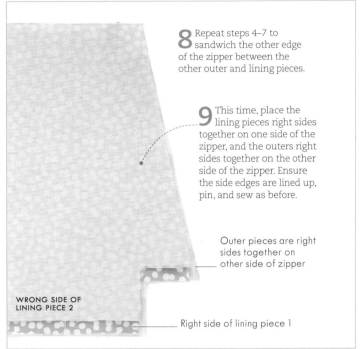

8 Repeat steps 4–7 to sandwich the other edge of the zipper between the other outer and lining pieces.

9 This time, place the lining pieces right sides together on one side of the zipper, and the outers right sides together on the other side of the zipper. Ensure the side edges are lined up, pin, and sew as before.

Outer pieces are right sides together on other side of zipper

WRONG SIDE OF LINING PIECE 2

Right side of lining piece 1

½in (1.2cm) from side edge

RIGHT SIDE OF OUTER PIECE 2

RIGHT SIDE OF OUTER PIECE 1

10 Fold both outers and linings away from the zipper and press well so that you have very crisp edges.

11 Top-stitch either side of the zipper, about ⅛in (3mm) from the fold, starting and stopping ½in (1.2cm) from both side edges. Press to set the stitches.

12 Using a hand needle, take the thread ends on the outer and linings from the right to wrong sides of the fabric to give a tidy finish.

STITCHES MADE WITH A MACHINE pp.92–93 ● **TOP-STITCHING p.109** ● **OPEN-ENDED ZIPPER p.292**

▶ **SEW THE SIDES TOGETHER**

1 Open up the zipper, then fold the pieces so that the outers are right sides facing and the linings are right sides facing, and pin down both sides.

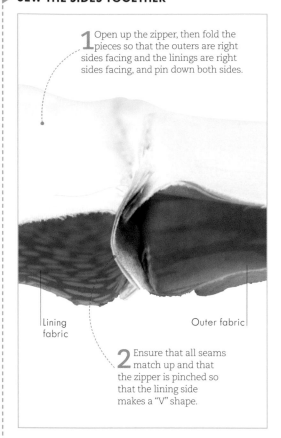

Lining fabric

Outer fabric

2 Ensure that all seams match up and that the zipper is pinched so that the lining side makes a "V" shape.

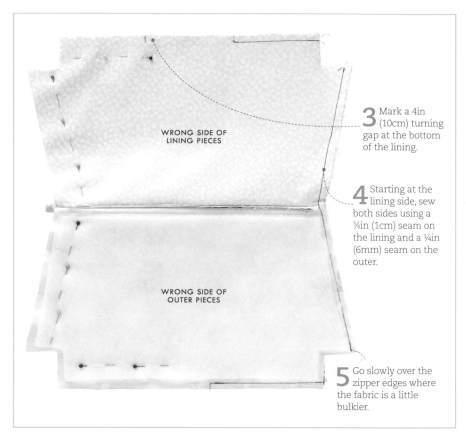

WRONG SIDE OF LINING PIECES

WRONG SIDE OF OUTER PIECES

3 Mark a 4in (10cm) turning gap at the bottom of the lining.

4 Starting at the lining side, sew both sides using a ⅜in (1cm) seam on the lining and a ¼in (6mm) seam on the outer.

5 Go slowly over the zipper edges where the fabric is a little bulkier.

WRONG SIDE OF LINING

Side seam

Bottom seam

6 Sew the side and bottom seams only, leaving the corner notches unsewn.

▶ **MAKE THE CORNER SEAMS**

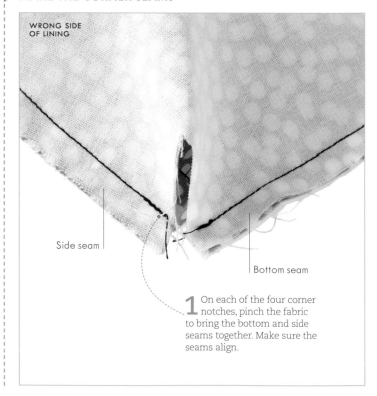

WRONG SIDE OF LINING

Side seam

Bottom seam

1 On each of the four corner notches, pinch the fabric to bring the bottom and side seams together. Make sure the seams align.

Raw edge of
corner notch

2 Pinch out the fabric so that
the raw edges of the corner
notch align to form a straight
edge. This brings the seams
uppermost to face you.

3 Fold the pinched corner to
one side and pin it together.

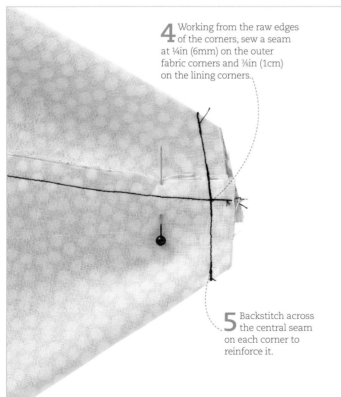

4 Working from the raw edges
of the corners, sew a seam
at ¼in (6mm) on the outer
fabric corners and ⅜in (1cm)
on the lining corners.

5 Backstitch across
the central seam
on each corner to
reinforce it.

▶ **TURN AND FINISH**

1 Trim the ends of
the zipper covers
and turn the bag right
side out.

2 Close the turning gap
by hand using a ladder
stitch. Press well.

HAND SEWING **pp.90–91** ● STITCHES MADE WITH A MACHINE **pp.92–93**

TECHNIQUES

BUTTONS

Buttons are one of the oldest forms of fastening. They come in many shapes and sizes, and can be made from a variety of materials including shell, bone, plastic, nylon, and metal. Buttons are sewn to the fabric either through holes on their face, or through a hole in a stalk called a shank, which is on the back. Buttons are normally sewn on by hand, although a two-hole button can be sewn on by machine.

DIRECTORY OF BUTTONS

TWO-HOLE BUTTON (p.301)

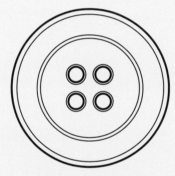

FOUR-HOLE BUTTON (p.301)

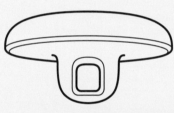

SHANKED BUTTON (p.302)

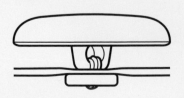

REINFORCED BUTTON (p.302)

OVERSIZED AND LAYERED BUTTON (p.302)

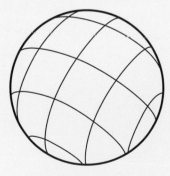

COVERED BUTTON (p.303)

SEWING ON A 2-HOLE BUTTON

This is the most popular type of button and requires a thread shank to be made when sewing in place. A toothpick will help you to sew on this type of button.

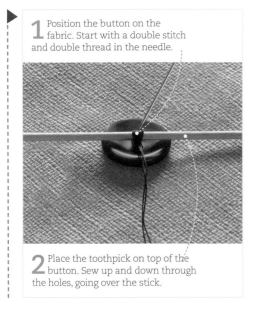

1 Position the button on the fabric. Start with a double stitch and double thread in the needle.

2 Place the toothpick on top of the button. Sew up and down through the holes, going over the stick.

3 Remove the toothpick.

4 Wrap the thread around the thread loops under the button to make a shank.

5 Take the thread through to the back of the fabric.

6 Buttonhole stitch over the loop of threads on the back of the work.

SEWING ON A 4-HOLE BUTTON

This is sewn in the same way as for a two-hole button except that the threads make an "X" over the button on the front.

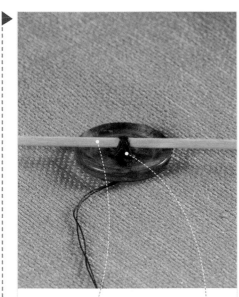

1 Position the button on the fabric. Place a toothpick on the button.

2 Using double thread, sew up and down through alternate sets of holes, over the toothpick. Make an "X" shape as you stitch.

3 Remove the toothpick.

4 Wrap the thread around the thread loops under the button to make the shank.

5 On the reverse of the fabric, buttonhole sew over the thread loops in an "X" shape.

SEWING ON A SHANKED BUTTON **p.302** ● REPAIRING FABRIC UNDER A BUTTON **p.363**

SEWING ON A SHANKED BUTTON

Difficulty level

When sewing this type of button in place, use a toothpick under the button to enable you to make a thread shank on the underside of the fabric.

1 Position the button on the fabric. Hold a tooth-pick on the other side of the fabric, behind the button.

2 Using double thread, sew the button to the fabric, through the shank.

3 Be sure each stitch goes through the fabric and around the toothpick beneath.

4 Remove the toothpick. Work buttonhole stitch over the looped thread shank.

SEWING ON A REINFORCED BUTTON

Difficulty level ★★★☆☆

A large, heavy button often features a second button sewn to it on the wrong side and sewn on with the same threads that secure the larger button. The smaller button helps support the weight of the larger button.

1 Position the large button on the right side of the fabric. Hold a smaller button beneath the fabric, in line with the large button.

2 Sew on the large button, sewing through to secure both buttons together.

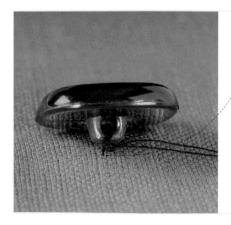

3 When the sewing is complete, wrap the thread around the thread loops beneath the larger button. Secure with a double stitch.

OVERSIZED AND LAYERED BUTTONS

Difficulty level ★★★★★

There are some huge buttons available, many of which are really more decorative than functional. By layering buttons of varying sizes together, you can make an unusual feature on a garment or home good.

1 First position the oversized button on the fabric.

2 Top with a smaller button and stitch the two together to the fabric.

3 Place a small one-hole button on the layered buttons and attach to the thread using a buttonhole stitch.

BUTTONS **p.26** • HOW TO APPLY A FUSIBLE INTERFACING **p.54** • SECURING THE THREAD **p.88**

TECHNIQUES

COVERED BUTTONS

Covered buttons are often found on expensive clothes and will add a professional finish to any jacket or other garment you make. A purchased button-making tool will enable you to create covered buttons very easily.

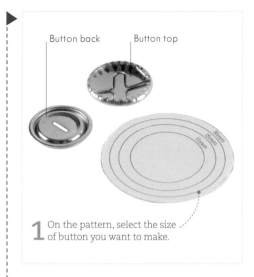

Button back   Button top

1 On the pattern, select the size of button you want to make.

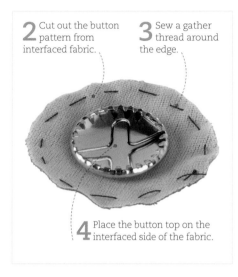

2 Cut out the button pattern from interfaced fabric.

3 Sew a gather thread around the edge.

4 Place the button top on the interfaced side of the fabric.

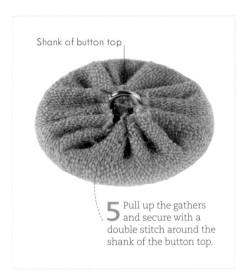

Shank of button top

5 Pull up the gathers and secure with a double stitch around the shank of the button top.

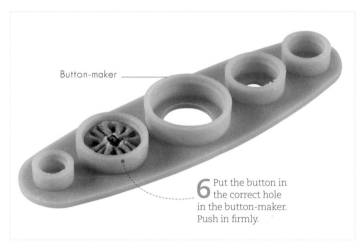

Button-maker

6 Put the button in the correct hole in the button-maker. Push in firmly.

7 Place the button back on top of the button.

8 Take the other side of the button-maker and press down on the button back until it clicks into position.

9 Remove the button from the button-maker and check to be sure that the back is firmly in place.

10 The finished covered button.

HAND SEWING **pp.90–91** ● HOW TO MAKE AND FIT GATHERS **p.135**

BUTTONHOLES

A buttonhole is essential if a button is to be truly functional, although for many oversize buttons, a snap fastener on the reverse is a better option, because the buttonhole would be too big and could cause the garment to stretch.

TECHNIQUES

DIRECTORY OF BUTTONHOLES AND BUTTON LOOPS

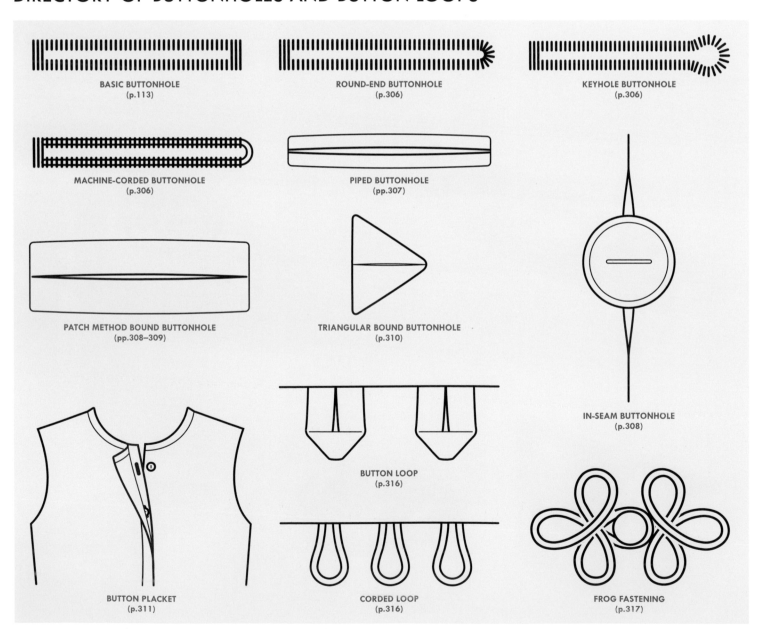

BASIC BUTTONHOLE
(p.113)

ROUND-END BUTTONHOLE
(p.306)

KEYHOLE BUTTONHOLE
(p.306)

MACHINE-CORDED BUTTONHOLE
(p.306)

PIPED BUTTONHOLE
(pp.307)

PATCH METHOD BOUND BUTTONHOLE
(pp.308–309)

TRIANGULAR BOUND BUTTONHOLE
(p.310)

IN-SEAM BUTTONHOLE
(p.308)

BUTTON PLACKET
(p.311)

BUTTON LOOP
(p.316)

CORDED LOOP
(p.316)

FROG FASTENING
(p.317)

MEASURING TOOLS **p.18** • SEWING-MACHINE ACCESSORIES **pp.32–33** • BASTING STITCHES **p.89** • STITCHES MADE WITH A MACHINE **pp.92–93**

STAGES OF A BUTTONHOLE

A sewing machine stitches a buttonhole in four stages. The stitch can be slightly varied in width and length to suit the garment or craft item, but it needs to be tight and close together.

1 Sew the first side of the buttonhole.

2 Sew a bar baste at one end.

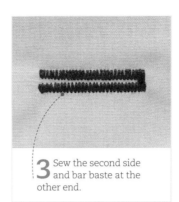

3 Sew the second side and bar baste at the other end.

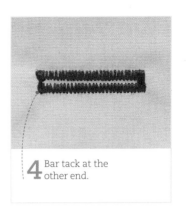

4 Bar tack at the other end.

POSITIONING BUTTONHOLES

Difficulty level ✱✱✱✱✱

Whether the buttonholes are to be stitched by machine or another type of buttonhole is to be made, the size of the button will need to be established in order to work out the position of the button on the fabric.

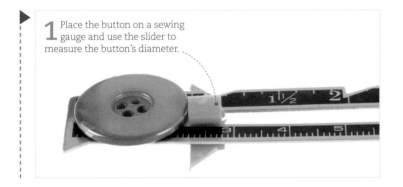

1 Place the button on a sewing gauge and use the slider to measure the button's diameter.

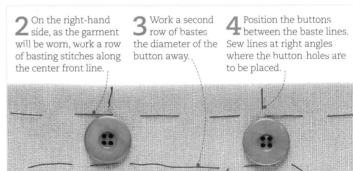

2 On the right-hand side, as the garment will be worn, work a row of basting stitches along the center front line.

3 Work a second row of bastes the diameter of the button away.

4 Position the buttons between the baste lines. Sew lines at right angles where the button holes are to be placed.

VERTICAL OR HORIZONTAL?

As a general rule, buttonholes are only vertical on a garment when there is a placket or a strip into which the buttonhole fits. All other buttonholes should be horizontal. Any strain on the buttonhole will then pull to the end and prevent the button from coming undone.

▶ **HORIZONTAL BUTTONHOLES**

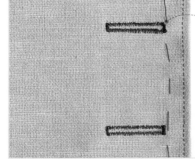

These are positioned with the end on the basted center line.

▶ **VERTICAL BUTTONHOLES**

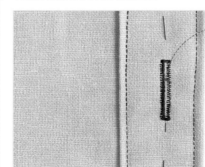

These are positioned with the buttonhole centered on the basted center line.

REPAIRING A DAMAGED BUTTONHOLE **p.363**

TECHNIQUES

MACHINE-MADE BUTTONHOLES

Difficulty level ✱✱✱✱✱

Modern sewing machines can sew various types of buttonhole, suitable for all kinds of garments. On many machines the button fits into a special foot, and a sensor on the machine determines the correct size of buttonhole. The width and length of the stitch can be altered to suit the fabric. Once the buttonhole has been stitched, always cut through with a buttonhole cutter, to ensure that the cut is clean.

▶ BASIC BUTTONHOLE

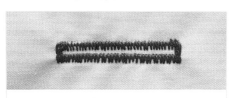

The most popular shape for a buttonhole is square on both ends.

▶ ROUND-END BUTTONHOLE

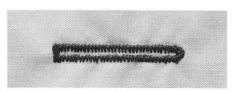

A buttonhole featuring one rounded end and one square end is used on lightweight jackets.

▶ KEYHOLE BUTTONHOLE

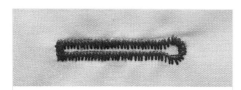

This is also called a tailor's buttonhole. It has a square end and a keyhole end, and is used on jackets and coats.

MACHINE-CORDED BUTTONHOLE

Difficulty level ✱✱✱✱✱

This buttonhole has a cord of heavier sewing thread running through it. You may have to consult your sewing machine manual for the positioning of the cord. This buttonhole is used for a bold buttonhole on a plain fabric.

1 Place the cord into the buttonhole foot as directed by your machine manual.

2 Work the buttonhole on the machine—the machine will sew the buttonhole over the cord.

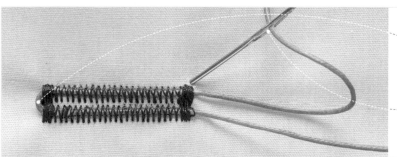

3 Gently pull on the ends of the cord to eliminate the loop.

4 Using a chenille needle size 18, thread the ends of the cord into a large needle.

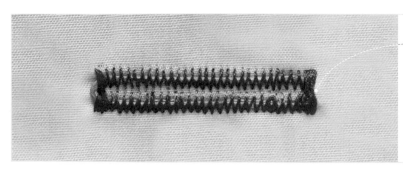

5 Take the cord to the back of the fabric. Secure by hand with a back or whip stitch.

◀ **CUTTING TOOLS p.16** ● **SEWING-MACHINE ACCESSORIES pp.32–33**

PIPED BUTTONHOLE

Difficulty level ✹✹✹✸✸

A buttonhole can also be made using piping cord. This is a type of buttonhole that is worked early in the construction of the garment. ³⁄₁₆in (5mm) piping cord needs to be used, otherwise the buttonhole will be too bulky.

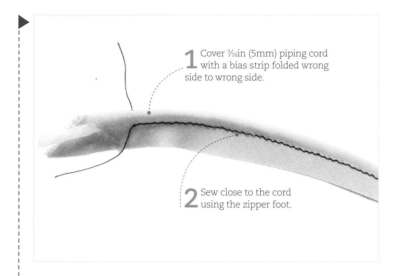

1 Cover ³⁄₁₆in (5mm) piping cord with a bias strip folded wrong side to wrong side.

2 Sew close to the cord using the zipper foot.

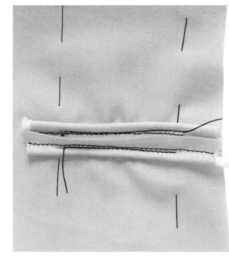

3 Cut a length of cord the width of the buttonhole plus ¾in (2cm) Place the cord against the buttonhole markings on the right side of the fabric, the raw edges of the cord to the center of the buttonhole markings.

4 Use the zipper foot to sew close to the cord. Stop sewing at the markings on the garment.

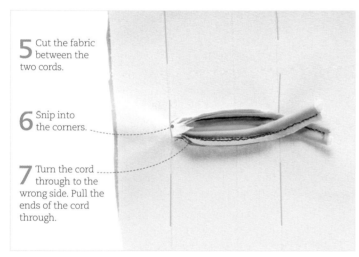

5 Cut the fabric between the two cords.

6 Snip into the corners.

7 Turn the cord through to the wrong side. Pull the ends of the cord through.

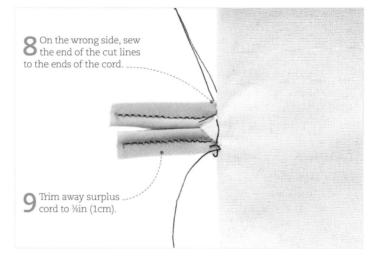

8 On the wrong side, sew the end of the cut lines to the ends of the cord.

9 Trim away surplus cord to ⅜in (1cm).

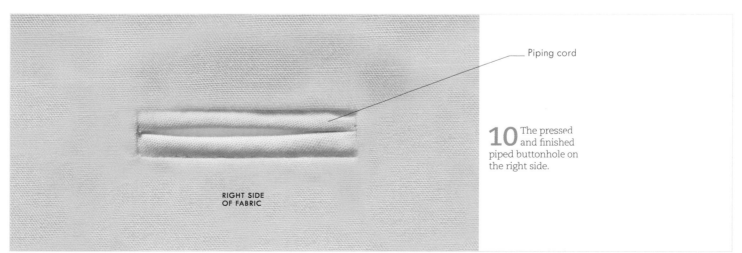

Piping cord

10 The pressed and finished piped buttonhole on the right side.

RIGHT SIDE
OF FABRIC

STITCHES MADE WITH A MACHINE **pp.92–93** ● HOW TO CUT BIAS STRIPS **p.154**

IN-SEAM BUTTONHOLE

Difficulty level **★★★★★**

This is a buttonhole formed in a seam allowance. It is found down decorative center fronts that feature seam detailing. It is a very discreet buttonhole.

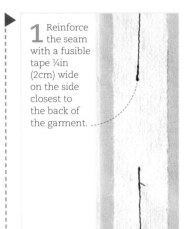

1 Reinforce the seam with a fusible tape ¾in (2cm) wide on the side closest to the back of the garment.

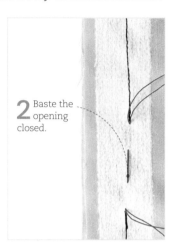

2 Baste the opening closed.

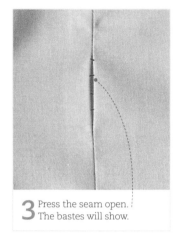

3 Press the seam open. The bastes will show.

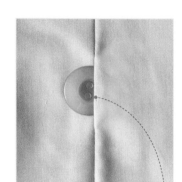

4 Remove the basting stitches to form the buttonhole.

PATCH METHOD BOUND BUTTONHOLE

Difficulty level **★★★★★**

Another method of creating a buttonhole is to use a patch of fabric stitched on to the main fabric. The technique is ideal for jackets and coats. A contrast fabric can be used for an attractive detail. This is known as a bound buttonhole.

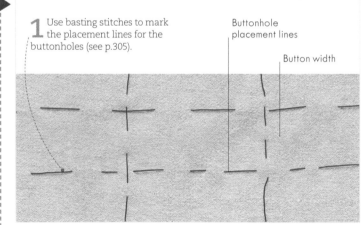

1 Use basting stitches to mark the placement lines for the buttonholes (see p.305).

Buttonhole placement lines

Button width

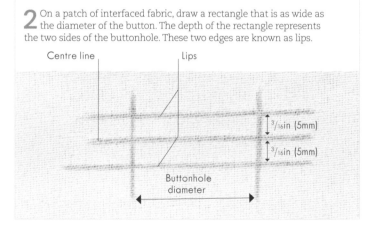

2 On a patch of interfaced fabric, draw a rectangle that is as wide as the diameter of the button. The depth of the rectangle represents the two sides of the buttonhole. These two edges are known as lips.

Centre line

Lips

³/₁₆in (5mm)

³/₁₆in (5mm)

Buttonhole diameter

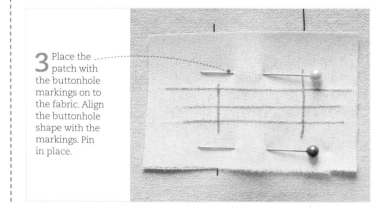

3 Place the patch with the buttonhole markings on to the fabric. Align the buttonhole shape with the markings. Pin in place.

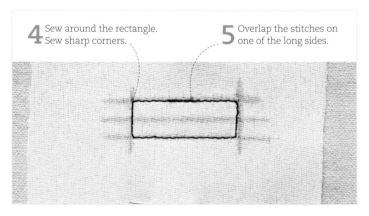

4 Sew around the rectangle. Sew sharp corners.

5 Overlap the stitches on one of the long sides.

◄ **HOW TO APPLY A FUSIBLE INTERFACING p.54** ● **HAND SEWING pp.90–91** ● **STITCHES MADE WITH A MACHINE pp.92–93** ● **SEWING CORNERS AND CURVES pp.102–103**

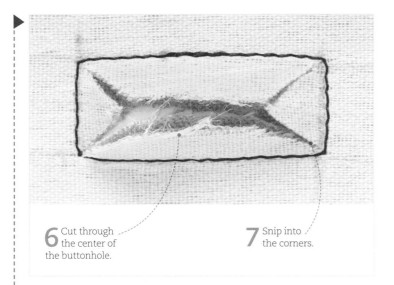

6 Cut through the center of the buttonhole.

7 Snip into the corners.

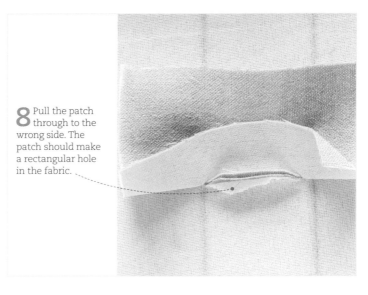

8 Pull the patch through to the wrong side. The patch should make a rectangular hole in the fabric.

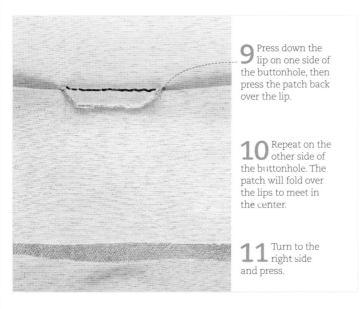

9 Press down the lip on one side of the buttonhole, then press the patch back over the lip.

10 Repeat on the other side of the buttonhole. The patch will fold over the lips to meet in the center.

11 Turn to the right side and press.

12 On the wrong side, sew the end of the cut lines over the folded patch.

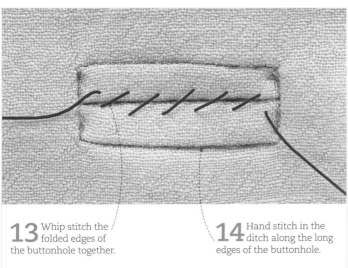

13 Whip stitch the folded edges of the buttonhole together.

14 Hand stitch in the ditch along the long edges of the buttonhole.

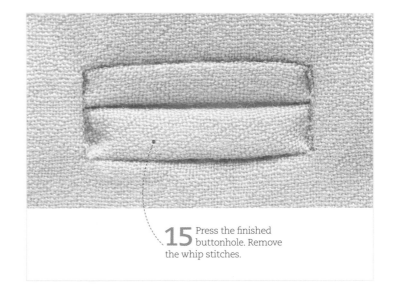

15 Press the finished buttonhole. Remove the whip stitches.

INTERFACINGS **pp.324–325**

TECHNIQUES

TRIANGULAR BUTTONHOLE

Difficulty level ★★★★★

A triangular buttonhole makes a nice feature on coats, jackets, waistcoats, or even bags, where you are using a large button. The method must be adapted from the bound buttonhole method to suit the triangle shape.

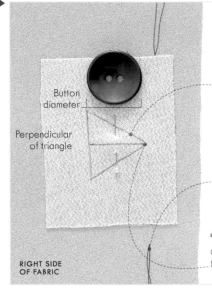

1 Apply interfacing to the wrong side of your garment or main fabric.

2 On a patch of interfaced fabric, draw your triangle shape. The perpendicular of the triangle must match the diameter of your button as the buttonhole will open through the center.

3 Mark the center front line on the right side of the garment with basting stitches.

4 Place the patch right side down, aligning one point of the triangle with the center front line. Pin in place.

RIGHT SIDE OF FABRIC

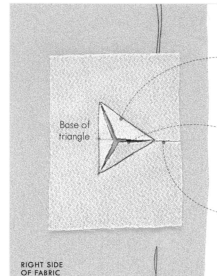

5 Sew around the shape, starting on a side not a corner to make it easier to pivot.

6 Cut through both layers of fabric inside the shape as shown, going right into the corners.

7 At the sharp point of the triangle, snip the outer patch fabric to the stitch line. This will help it turn.

RIGHT SIDE OF FABRIC

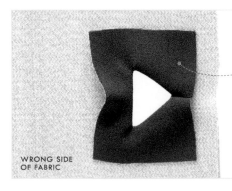

8 Push the buttonhole fabric through the hole to the wrong side.

WRONG SIDE OF FABRIC

9 Fold one half of the buttonhole fabric toward the center. Pin in place

WRONG SIDE OF FABRIC

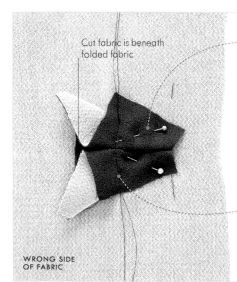

Cut fabric is beneath folded fabric

10 Fold the other half of the buttonhole fabric to the center line to meet the first fold. Pin in place.

11 On the right side, check that the buttonhole opening is straight and equal on both sides. Reposition if necessary.

12 Turn up the patch fabric at the base of the triangle and sew across the cut fabric underneath to join it to the patch. To secure, don't sew through to the right side of the main fabric.

WRONG SIDE OF FABRIC

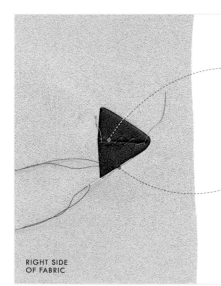

13 On the right side, whip stitch the folded edges of the buttonhole together.

14 Hand stitch in the ditch along all sides of the shape using a prick stitch. This holds the buttonhole flat.

15 Pess the finished buttonhole. Remove the whip stitches.

RIGHT SIDE OF FABRIC

HOW TO APPLY A FUSIBLE INTERFACING p.54 • **PATTERN MARKING pp.82–83** • **BASTING STITCHES p.89**

BUTTON PLACKET

A hidden button placket is a great addition to a shirt, a shirt dress, or a coat. By hiding the buttons completely from view, it creates a discreet fastening that can be placed anywhere on the garment without disrupting the line of the pattern.

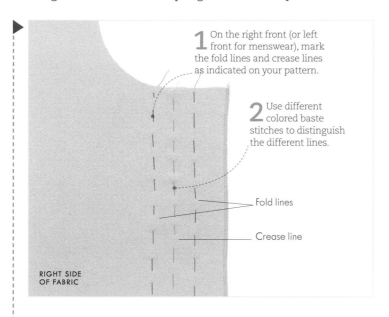

1 On the right front (or left front for menswear), mark the fold lines and crease lines as indicated on your pattern.

2 Use different colored baste stitches to distinguish the different lines.

Fold lines

Crease line

RIGHT SIDE OF FABRIC

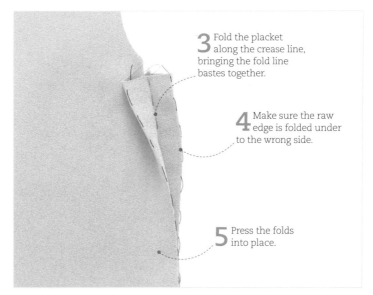

3 Fold the placket along the crease line, bringing the fold line bastes together.

4 Make sure the raw edge is folded under to the wrong side.

5 Press the folds into place.

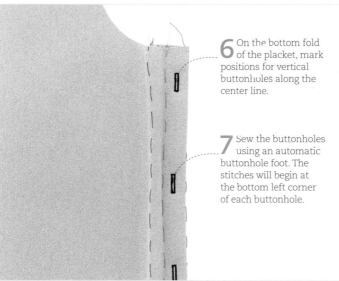

6 On the bottom fold of the placket, mark positions for vertical buttonholes along the center line.

7 Sew the buttonholes using an automatic buttonhole foot. The stitches will begin at the bottom left corner of each buttonhole.

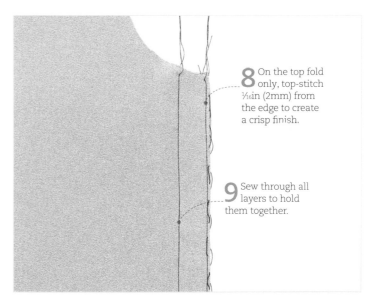

8 On the top fold only, top-stitch ⅟₁₆in (2mm) from the edge to create a crisp finish.

9 Sew through all layers to hold them together.

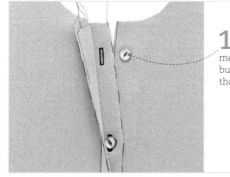

10 On the left front (or right front for menswear), attach the buttons so they align with the buttonholes.

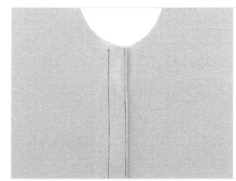

11 On the finished front, the buttons will be hidden from view behind the placket.

ENVELOPE **CUSHION**

Difficulty level ✱✱✱✱✱

This attractive cushion with matching covered buttons is quick and easy to make; an ideal project for beginners. It is made using just three pieces—one front and two back pieces—to create the envelope, and requires just 20in (50cm) of fabric using an economical cutting layout.

TECHNIQUES USED Pattern layout **pp.78–81**, Seam neatening **p.95**, Double-turn hem **p.266**, Machine-made buttonholes **p.306**

YOU WILL NEED

- 20 x 45in (50 x 115cm) medium-weight cotton or linen
- 3 pieces 3½ x 1½in (9 x 4cm) lightweight non-woven fusible interfacing
- 3 covered buttons, ⅞in (22mm) in diameter (see p.303 for technique)
- 16 x 16in (40 x 40cm) cushion pad
- Matching thread
- Buttonhole foot

PIECES TO CUT

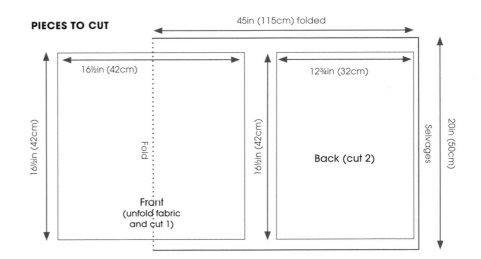

45in (115cm) folded

16½in (42cm)

16½in (42cm)

Fold

Front
(unfold fabric
and cut 1)

12¾in (32cm)

16½in (42cm)

Back (cut 2)

Selvages

20in (50cm)

▶ PIN AND CUT THE FABRIC

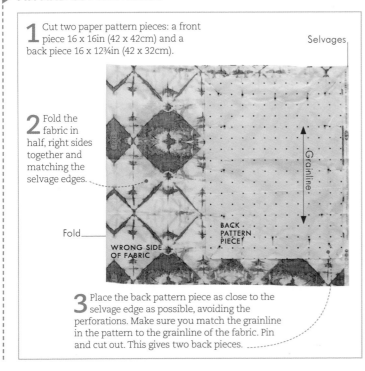

1 Cut two paper pattern pieces: a front piece 16 x 16in (42 x 42cm) and a back piece 16 x 12¾in (42 x 32cm).

Selvages

2 Fold the fabric in half, right sides together and matching the selvage edges.

Fold

BACK PATTERN PIECE

WRONG SIDE OF FABRIC

Grainline

3 Place the back pattern piece as close to the selvage edge as possible, avoiding the perforations. Make sure you match the grainline in the pattern to the grainline of the fabric. Pin and cut out. This gives two back pieces.

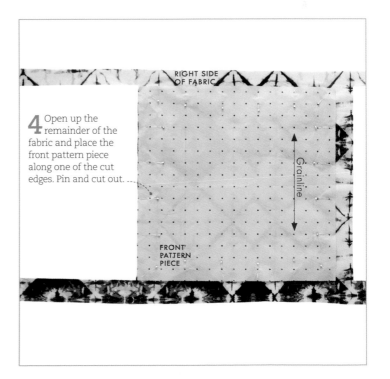

RIGHT SIDE OF FABRIC

4 Open up the remainder of the fabric and place the front pattern piece along one of the cut edges. Pin and cut out.

FRONT PATTERN PIECE

Grainline

PROJECT

▶ MAKE THE HEMS

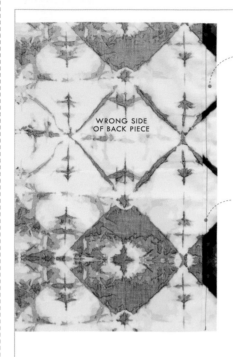

WRONG SIDE
OF BACK PIECE

1 On each of the back pieces, fold one long edge to the wrong side by ⅜in (1cm) and press. Fold by a further ¾in (2cm) to create a double-turn hem and press again. Pin in place.

2 Using an "edge" needle position setting on your machine, sew from top to bottom on the hemmed edges, remembering to reverse stitch at the start and finish. Line up the fold of the hem against the left hand side of the presser foot as your guideline.

▶ MAKE THE BUTTONHOLES

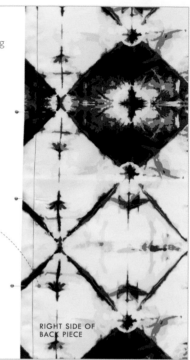

RIGHT SIDE OF
BACK PIECE

1 A ⅞in (22mm) button (used here) requires a 1¼in (3cm) buttonhole. Refer to your sewing machine manual for where to mark the start positions of the buttonholes.

2 For even spacing, place a pin at 9¾in (9.5cm), 17¾in (19.5cm), and 11¾in (29.5cm) from the bottom edge of one back piece to mark each of the three starting points.

3 If you want to position the buttons differently, or use buttons of a different size, sew a sample buttonhole on a scrap piece of fabric first. This will give you the size of the finished hole so you can position it accurately.

RIGHT SIDE
OF FABRIC

WRONG SIDE
OF FABRIC

4 Apply the three pieces of interfacing on the wrong side of the fabric, next to the hem, where you will sew the buttonholes. This will add strength to the fabric.

5 Mark the positions of the buttonholes with basting stitches, then remove the pins.

6 Adjust your machine to the correct settings and sew your buttonholes on the right side of the fabric. Ensure the needle starts accurately at the correct point.

7 Remove the baste stitches. Using a seam ripper or buttonhole chisel, carefully open up the center of each buttonhole.

RIGHT SIDE OF
BACK PIECE

CUTTING TOOLS **pp.16–17** ● HOW TO APPLY A FUSIBLE INTERFACING **p.54** ● BASTING STITCHES **p.89** ● SECURING THE THREAD **p.92**

▶ SEW THE CUSHION TOGETHER

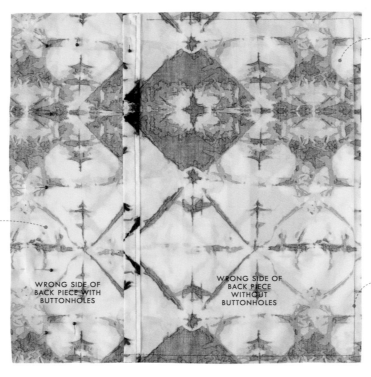

1 Place the front piece right side up on a table.

2 Place the back piece with the buttonholes right side down on top of the front, matching the outer raw edges.

3 Place the second back piece on top, right side down, matching the outer raw edges. The hemmed edges should lie in the center. Pin all around the four outside edges.

4 Starting just below a hemmed edge, sew all four sides of the cushion using a ⅜in (1cm) seam allowance, remembering to reverse stitch at the start and finish.

WRONG SIDE OF BACK PIECE WITH BUTTONHOLES

WRONG SIDE OF BACK PIECE WITHOUT BUTTONHOLES

▶ FINISHING TOUCHES

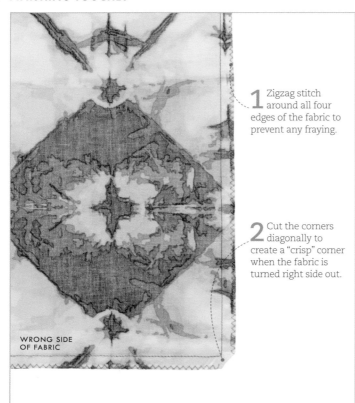

1 Zigzag stitch around all four edges of the fabric to prevent any fraying.

2 Cut the corners diagonally to create a "crisp" corner when the fabric is turned right side out.

WRONG SIDE OF FABRIC

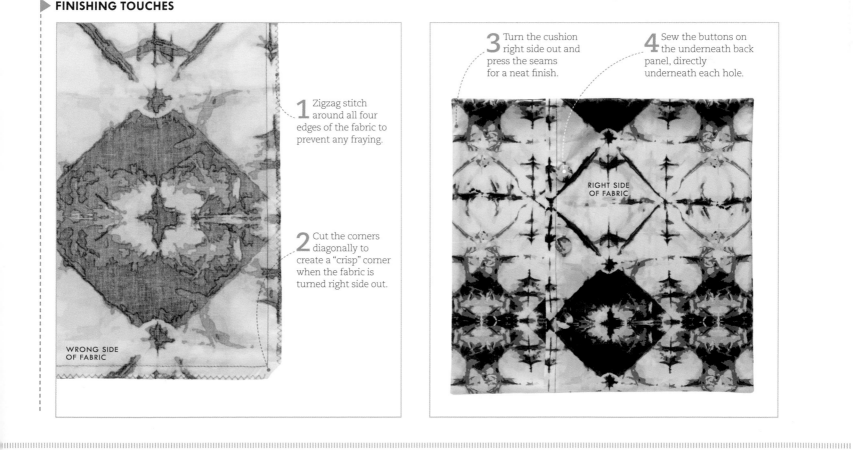

3 Turn the cushion right side out and press the seams for a neat finish.

4 Sew the buttons on the underneath back panel, directly underneath each hole.

RIGHT SIDE OF FABRIC

STITCHES MADE WITH A MACHINE **pp.92–93** • SEAM NEATENING **p.95** • DOUBLE-TURN HEM **p.266** • COVERED BUTTONS **p.303** • POSITIONING BUTTONHOLES **p.305**

TECHNIQUES

BUTTON **LOOPS**

A buttonhole is not the only way of using buttons. Buttons can also be fastened by means of a fabric loop, which is usually attached at the edge of a garment. Fabric loops are often found on the back of special-occasion wear, where multiple loops secure rows of small, often covered buttons. Loops, called frog fasteners, can also be made from decorative cord.

FABRIC BUTTON LOOP

Difficulty level ★★★★★

This button loop is formed from a bias strip. Choose a smooth fabric for the strip as it will be easier to turn through. A fabric loop is used with a round ball-type button.

▶

1 Cut a bias strip 1½in (4cm) wide. Fold lengthwise, right side to right side, and pin together.

2 Sew with a seam allowance of ⅝in (1.5cm), keeping the edge of the machine foot against the folded edge.

3 Sew another row ¹⁄₁₆in (2mm) away from the first stitches. This is for strength.

4 Trim the bias close to the stitches.

5 Turn the bias strip to the right side, using a loop turner.

6 Pin the prepared loop strip to the ironing board and press with a steam iron.

CORDED LOOP

Difficulty level ★★★★★

It is possible to make a very fine button loop that has a cord running through it. This type of loop is suitable for lightweight fabrics. Use a shanked button with a corded loop.

▶

1 Cut a bias strip 1½in (4cm) wide, and any length. Cut a piece of cord twice the length of the strip.

2 Wrap the cord in the bias strip, folded wrong side to wrong side. Pin. Make sure the bias strip is near to one end of the cord.

3 Sew along the bias strip, next to, but not too close to, the cord.

4 Sew another row ¹⁄₁₆in (2mm) away from the first stitches.

5 Trim away the bias strip close to the stitches.

6 Stitch through the cord and bias strip in the center of the cord and near the end of the bias strip.

7 At the center point, ease the fabric over the cord to turn it to the right side.

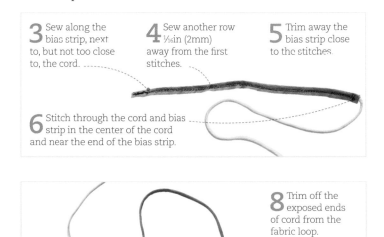

8 Trim off the exposed ends of cord from the fabric loop.

SPACING THE LOOPS

Once the loops have been made, the next step is to attach them to the garment. It is important that all the loops are the same size and positioned the same distance apart. To achieve this you will need to baste your fabric to mark the placement lines. The loops go on the right-hand front or the left-hand back of the work.

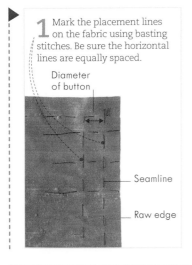

1 Mark the placement lines on the fabric using basting stitches. Be sure the horizontal lines are equally spaced.

Diameter of button

Seamline

Raw edge

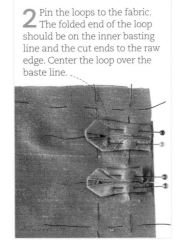

2 Pin the loops to the fabric. The folded end of the loop should be on the inner basting line and the cut ends to the raw edge. Center the loop over the baste line.

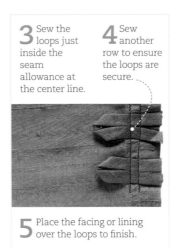

3 Sew the loops just inside the seam allowance at the center line.

4 Sew another row to ensure the loops are secure.

5 Place the facing or lining over the loops to finish.

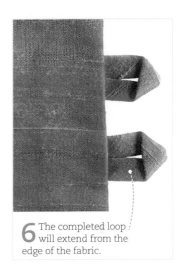

6 The completed loop will extend from the edge of the fabric.

FROG FASTENINGS

A loop made from a decorative cord is often found on garments with an Asian influence. These so-called frog fastenings can be purchased, although they are straightforward to make. A matching ball button can be made from cord as well, by twisting the cord over and under itself.

▶ **MAKING A FROG FASTENER**

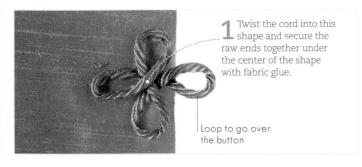

1 Twist the cord into this shape and secure the raw ends together under the center of the shape with fabric glue.

Loop to go over the button

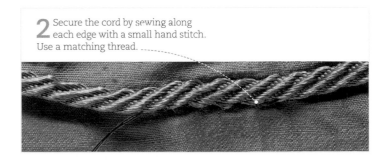

2 Secure the cord by sewing along each edge with a small hand stitch. Use a matching thread.

▶ **TYING A BALL BUTTON**

1 Start by making a loop in the cord.

2 Twist the cord to make another loop over the first loop. The end of the cord goes under the first side.

3 Take the cord over, under, over, and under all the other loops.

4 Pull the two ends to tighten into a ball button.

5 Sew the ends into a decorative pattern to match the frog fastener.

HOW TO CUT BIAS STRIPS **p.154** ● SEWING ON A SHANKED BUTTON **p.302**

OTHER **FASTENINGS**

There are many alternative ways to fasten garments, craft projects, and other items, some of which can be used instead of or in conjunction with other fasteners. These include hooks and eyes, snaps, tape fasteners, and laced eyelets.

DIRECTORY OF OTHER FASTENINGS

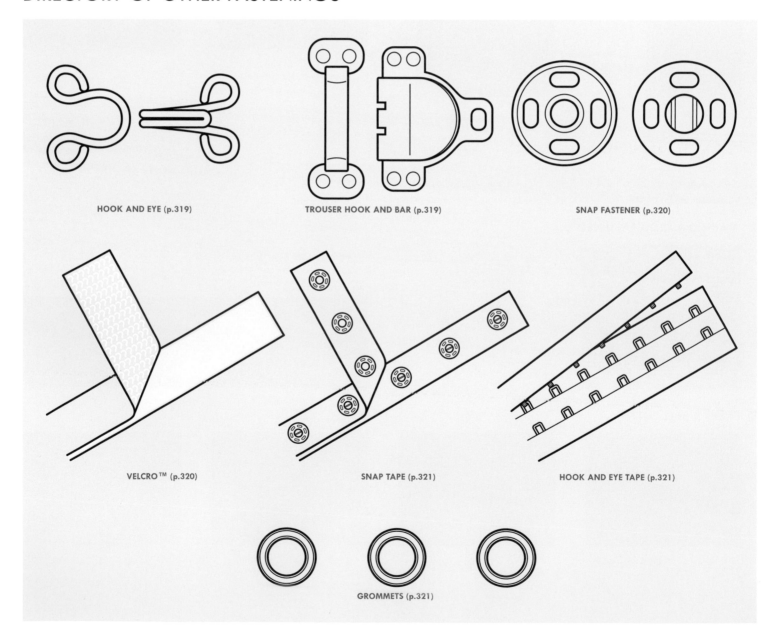

HOOK AND EYE (p.319)

TROUSER HOOK AND BAR (p.319)

SNAP FASTENER (p.320)

VELCRO™ (p.320)

SNAP TAPE (p.321)

HOOK AND EYE TAPE (p.321)

GROMMETS (p.321)

OTHER FASTENERS **p.26** ● BASTING STITCHES **p.89** ● HAND SEWING **pp.90—91**

HOOKS AND EYES

Difficulty level **✳✳**✳✳

There are a multitude of different types of hook and eye fasteners. Purchased hooks and eyes are made from metal and are normally silver or black in color. Different shaped hooks and eyes are used on different garments—large, broad hooks and eyes can be decorative and sewn to show on the outside, while the tiny fasteners are meant to be discreet. A hook that goes into a hand-worked eye produces a neat, close fastening.

▶ ATTACHING HOOKS AND EYES

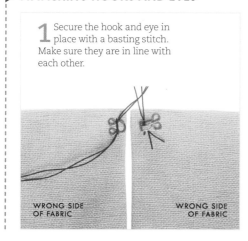

1 Secure the hook and eye in place with a basting stitch. Make sure they are in line with each other.

WRONG SIDE OF FABRIC   WRONG SIDE OF FABRIC

2 Sew around each circular end with a buttonhole stitch. Be careful not to sew through the fabric, as you don't want stitches to show on the outside of the garment.

3 Place a few over-stitches under the hook to stop it from moving.

▶ HAND-WORKED EYE

1 Using a double thread, work several small loops into the edge of the fabric.

RIGHT SIDE OF FABRIC

2 Buttonhole stitch over these loops.

RIGHT SIDE OF FABRIC

3 The completed loop will have a neat row of tight buttonhole stitches.

RIGHT SIDE OF FABRIC

▶ PANT HOOK AND EYE

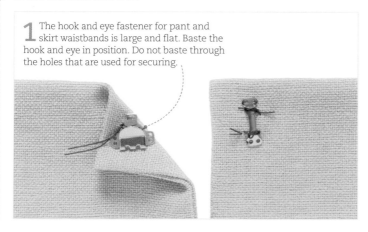

1 The hook and eye fastener for pant and skirt waistbands is large and flat. Baste the hook and eye in position. Do not baste through the holes that are used for securing.

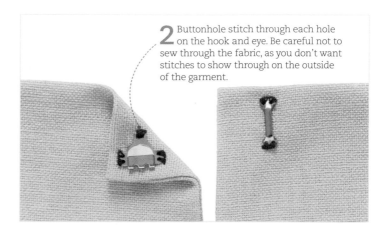

2 Buttonhole stitch through each hole on the hook and eye. Be careful not to sew through the fabric, as you don't want stitches to show through on the outside of the garment.

HOOK AND EYE TAPE **p.321** ▶

TECHNIQUES

SNAPS

Difficulty level ★★☆☆☆

A snap is a ball and socket fastener that is used to hold two overlapping edges closed. The ball side goes on top and the socket side underneath. Snaps can be round or square and can be made from metal or plastic.

▶ METAL SNAPS

1 Baste the ball and socket halves of the snap in place.

2 Secure permanently using a buttonhole stitch through each hole in the outer edge of the snap half.

3 Remove the bastes.

▶ PLASTIC SNAPS

A plastic snap may be white or clear plastic and is usually square in shape. Sew in place as for a metal snap (see left).

TAPE FASTENERS

Difficulty level ★★★☆☆

In addition to individual small fasteners, there are fasteners in the form of tapes that can be sewn or stuck on. Velcro™, a hook and loop tape, is available in many colors and types. Sewn-on Velcro™ is ideal for both clothing and soft furnishings, while the stick-on variety can be used to fix curtain valances and blinds to battens on windows. Plain cotton tape with snap fasteners is used primarily in home goods. Hook and eye tape is found in underwear or down the front of a shirt or jacket, where it can be very decorative.

▶ VELCRO™

1 Pin the Velcro™ in place. The loop side should be underneath and the hook side on top.

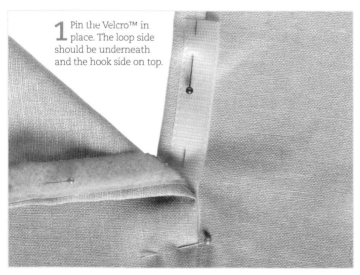

2 Sew around all the edges.

▶ SNAP TAPE

1 Pin the tape in position. Make sure the snaps align.

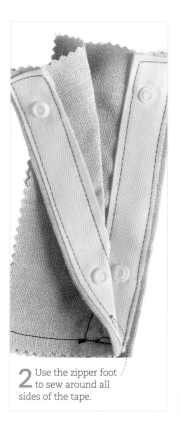

2 Use the zipper foot to sew around all sides of the tape.

▶ HOOK AND EYE TAPE

1 The eye side of the tape features a slot into which the fabric is inserted. Pin in place.

2 Sew along the edge using either a stretch stitch or a narrow 3-step zigzag stitch.

3 Wrap the hook side of the tape over the raw edge of the fabric. Pin in place.

4 Sew to match up with the eye side.

GROMMETS

Difficulty level ✴✴✴✴✴

A grommet fastening can be decorative and is often found on bridal wear and prom dresses. A piece of boning needs to be inserted into the fabric between the edge and the grommets, to give strength. You will require grommet pliers to punch the holes and then insert the grommets.

▶

1 Using the pliers, punch out the holes for the grommets at 1¼–1½in (3–4cm) intervals.

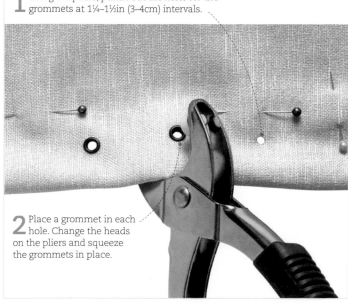

2 Place a grommet in each hole. Change the heads on the pliers and squeeze the grommets in place.

3 Insert a row of eyelets on either side of the back opening.

Boning channel

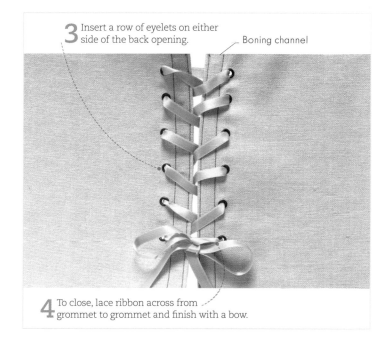

4 To close, lace ribbon across from grommet to grommet and finish with a bow.

HAND SEWING pp.90–91 • **STITCHES MADE WITH A MACHINE pp.92–93**

LININGS AND
INTERFACINGS

Interfacings provide shape and structure in a garment or in soft furnishings, while a lining will make any garment more comfortable to wear as well as hiding the inside seams and stitches from view.

TECHNIQUES

INTERLININGS AND INTERFACINGS

Interlinings are similar to interfacings, the difference being that an interfacing is an extra layer of fabric attached in a small area, while an interlining is attached to a whole garment or item. Interlinings and interfacings may be woven, knitted, or non-woven and can be applied with heat (fusible) or sewn-in. Always try to buy products recommended for domestic use. Be sure to cut all these fabrics on the straight of the grain even if they are non-woven.

INTERLININGS

These are fabrics that cover the inside of an entire garment. They are cut to the same pattern pieces and joined to the main fabric by means of basting stitches around the edges. The two layers are treated as one during construction.

▶ **MUSLIN**

This is a cotton muslin. Use with wools and cottons for jackets, skirts, and dresses.

▶ **SILK ORGANZA**

An interlining of silk organza will give shape and structure. Use on special-occasion wear and silk fabrics as well as wool in tailored skirts.

▶ **DRESS NET**

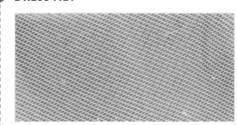

Net is used for bounce and rustle. Use in all special-occasion wear for effect and to prevent creasing.

INTERFACINGS

Difficulty level ✱✱✱✱✱

An interfacing may be fusible or non-fusible (sew-in) and is only attached to part of a garment or item. Sections of a garment normally interfaced include the collar and cuffs and the facings. In addition to fusible interfacings, there are also fusible tapes available, which are used to prevent a fabric from stretching and will support edges, and fusible webs that provide stiffening.

▶ **NON-FUSIBLE INTERFACINGS**

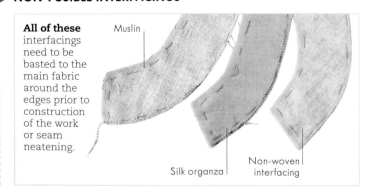

All of these interfacings need to be basted to the main fabric around the edges prior to construction of the work or seam neatening.

Muslin

Silk organza

Non-woven interfacing

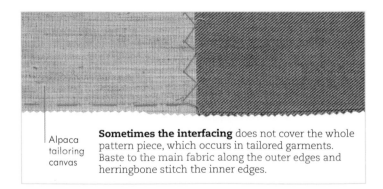

Alpaca tailoring canvas

Sometimes the interfacing does not cover the whole pattern piece, which occurs in tailored garments. Baste to the main fabric along the outer edges and herringbone stitch the inner edges.

▶ **INTERFACINGS pp.54–55** ● **BASTING STITCHES p.89** ● **HAND SEWING pp.90–91** ● **APPLYING INTERFACING TO A FACING p.153**

▶ FUSIBLE INTERFACINGS

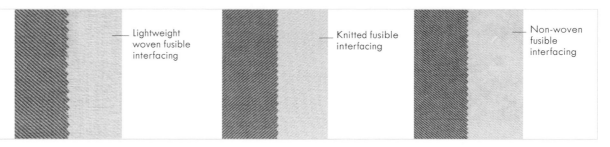

A fusible interfacing is used in the same areas as a sew-in interfacing. To prevent the fusible interfacing from showing on the right side of the work, use pinking shears on the edge of the interfacing.

Lightweight woven fusible interfacing

Knitted fusible interfacing

Non-woven fusible interfacing

▶ INTERFACINGS AND INTERLININGS COMBINED

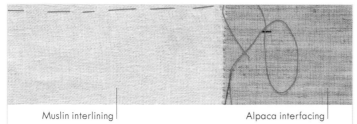

Muslin interlining

Alpaca interfacing

On structured garments there may be both interlining and interfacing. The interlining is applied first and the interfacing is attached on top. Baste around the outside edge and herringbone stitch the inner edges.

▶ FRAME FUSING

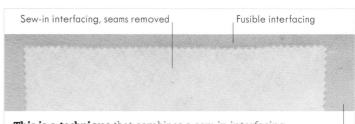

Sew-in interfacing, seams removed

Fusible interfacing

Seam allowance

This is a technique that combines a sew-in interfacing with a fusible. It is used in more structured garments to create tailored collars and cuffs. The fusible interfacing is placed on top to seal the sew-in interfacing in place in the seam allowances.

▶ STRAIGHT FUSIBLE TAPE

Straight grain tape is about ¾in (2cm) wide and has little give in it. Use it to stabilize edges. On some seams it may replace stay stitching. To fuse around curves, snip through the tape at 90 degrees.

▶ BIAS FUSIBLE TAPE

Bias tape has a straight stitch through it. As the tape is cut on the bias, it will bend around curves. When fusing the tape in position, the sewn line in the tape should be on the fabric sewn line.

▶ SLOTTED FUSIBLE TAPE

Slotted fusible is wider than other fusible tapes, and has a slotted edge. The tape is used to shape pocket tops and hems on jackets. Fuse in position so that the slots correspond to the foldline in the fabric.

INTERFACINGS, FACINGS, AND LININGS

Difficulty level ★★☆☆☆

On tailored and more structured garments, the facing will be interfaced and this is then attached to the lining.

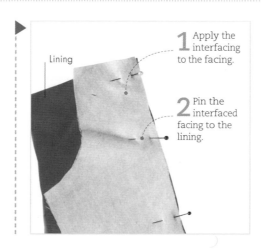

Lining

1 Apply the interfacing to the facing.

2 Pin the interfaced facing to the lining.

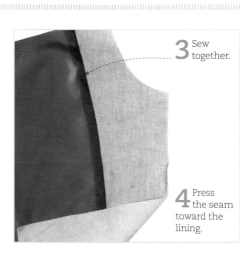

3 Sew together.

4 Press the seam toward the lining.

FLAT COLLAR p.175 ● REINFORCED STRAIGHT BELT pp.202–203 ● CUFFS AND OPENINGS pp.228–235

STORAGE **BASKETS**

Encourage children to have fun cleaning up their toys with this set of fabric baskets.
Heavyweight interfacing creates the boxy shape of each basket, and handles make them portable. Of course,
the baskets are ideal for storing all sorts of other objects, too, including your sewing items.

TECHNIQUES USED Sewing corners and curves **p.102**, Layering a seam **p.108**, Interlinings and interfacings **p.324–325**

YOU WILL NEED

- 28 x 54in (70 x 137cm) medium-weight cotton for large basket outer
- 28 x 43in (70 x 110cm) medium-weight cotton for large basket inner
- 24 x 54in (60 x 137cm) medium-weight cotton for small basket outer
- 24 x 43in (60 x 110cm) medium-weight cotton for small basket inner
- 48 x 36in (120 x 90cm) firm fusible interfacing
- 110 x 12in (280 x 30cm) ultra-heavy fusible interfacing
- Matching thread for each fabric

PIECES TO CUT

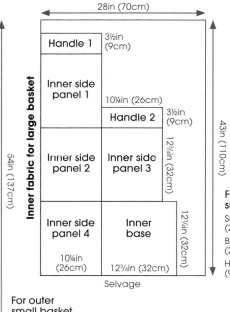

Outer fabric for large basket

28in (70cm)

10¼in (26cm)

Outer side panel 1 — 12¾in (32cm)

Outer side panel 2 — 12¾in (32cm)

Outer side panel 3 — 12¾in (32cm)

12¾in (32cm)

Outer side panel 4 — 10¼in (26cm)

Outer base — 12¾in (32cm)

54in (137cm)

12¾in (32cm)

Selvage

For outer small basket
Side panels: 11 x 9in (28 x 22cm)
Base: 11 x 11in (28 x 28cm)

Inner fabric for large basket

28in (70cm)

Handle 1 — 3½in (9cm)

Inner side panel 1

Handle 2 — 3½in (9cm)

10¼in (26cm)

Inner side panel 2 — Inner side panel 3 — 12¾in (32cm)

Inner side panel 4 — 10¼in (26cm) — Inner base — 12¾in (32cm)

12¾in (32cm)

43in (110cm)

Selvage

For inner small basket
Side panels: 11 x 9in (28 x 22cm)
Base: 11 x 11in (28 x 28cm)
Handles: 3½ x 10¼in (9 x 26cm)

▶ MAKE THE OUTER SIDES

WRONG SIDE OF OUTER SIDE PANEL

1 For each basket, cut a piece of firm fusible interfacing to the same size as the outer base and apply to the wrong side of the base.

2 Cut four pieces of ultra-heavy fusible interfacing to the same size as the four outer side panels.

3 Apply the ultra-heavy interfacing to the wrong side of each panel. As the interfacing is thick, you will need to press the fabric on the right side, too.

4 Sew the side panels together, right side to right side, in pairs along one short edge using a seam allowance of ⅜in (1cm). Finish the seam ⅜in (1cm) above the lower edge. Press the seams open.

Seam stops ⅜in (1cm) above lower edge

PROJECT

PROJECT

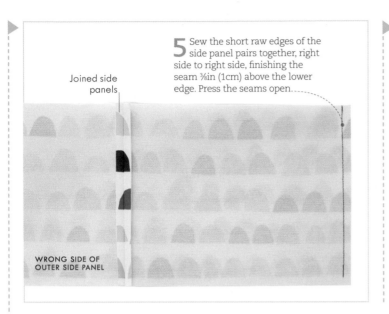

5 Sew the short raw edges of the side panel pairs together, right side to right side, finishing the seam ⅜in (1cm) above the lower edge. Press the seams open.

Joined side panels

WRONG SIDE OF OUTER SIDE PANEL

▶ MAKE THE HANDLES

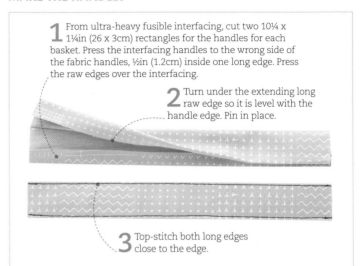

1 From ultra-heavy fusible interfacing, cut two 10¼ x 1¼in (26 x 3cm) rectangles for the handles for each basket. Press the interfacing handles to the wrong side of the fabric handles, ½in (1.2cm) inside one long edge. Press the raw edges over the interfacing.

2 Turn under the extending long raw edge so it is level with the handle edge. Pin in place.

3 Top-stitch both long edges close to the edge.

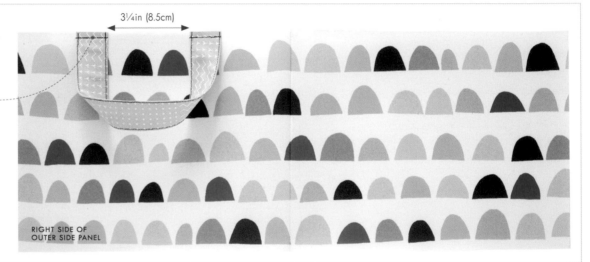

4 Pin the ends of one handle to the upper edge on the right side of one side panel. Make sure the inner edges of the handle are 3¼in (8.5cm) apart. Sew using a ¼in (6mm) seam allowance.

3¼in (8.5cm)

5 Repeat to sew the other handle to the opposite side panel on the other joined pair of side panels.

RIGHT SIDE OF OUTER SIDE PANEL

▶ ATTACH THE OUTER PANELS TO THE BASE

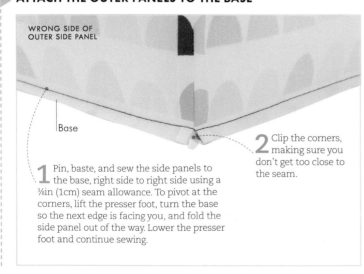

WRONG SIDE OF OUTER SIDE PANEL

Base

1 Pin, baste, and sew the side panels to the base, right side to right side using a ⅜in (1cm) seam allowance. To pivot at the corners, lift the presser foot, turn the base so the next edge is facing you, and fold the side panel out of the way. Lower the presser foot and continue sewing.

2 Clip the corners, making sure you don't get too close to the seam.

3 Turn the basket right side out. The interfacing will crease but it will smooth out flat again when ironed.

4 From ultra-heavy fusible interfacing, cut one 12 x 12in (30 x 30cm) square for the large basket base and one 10¼ x 10¼in (26 x 26cm) square for the small basket base. Position the interfacing base inside the basket on the base, slipping the interfacing under the seam allowance. Press in place, turn the basket over, and press the underside.

HOW TO APPLY A FUSIBLE INTERFACING p.54 ● **HAND SEWING pp.90–91** ● **SEWING CORNERS AND CURVES pp.102–103**

► MAKE THE INNER BASKET

WRONG SIDE OF
INNER SIDE PANEL

Turning gap in
base seam

1 Cut pieces of firm fusible interfacing to the same dimensions as the inner side panels and base, and apply to the wrong side of the pieces.

2 Repeat the steps for joining the side panels and base, without handles, to make the inner basket. Leave a 8–9½in (20–24cm) gap in the base seam, to turn through. Press the seams open.

► JOIN THE INNER AND OUTER BASKETS

1 Insert the outer basket into the inner basket, right side to right side, matching the seams and upper raw edge. Sew the upper edge using a ⅜in (1cm) seam allowance. Layer the seam allowance.

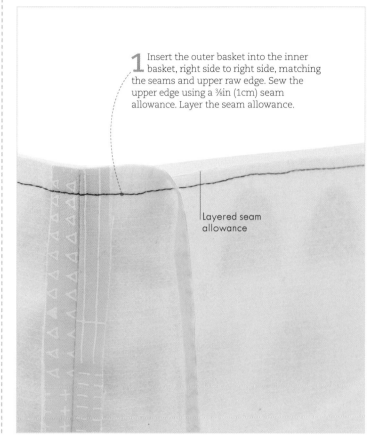

Layered seam
allowance

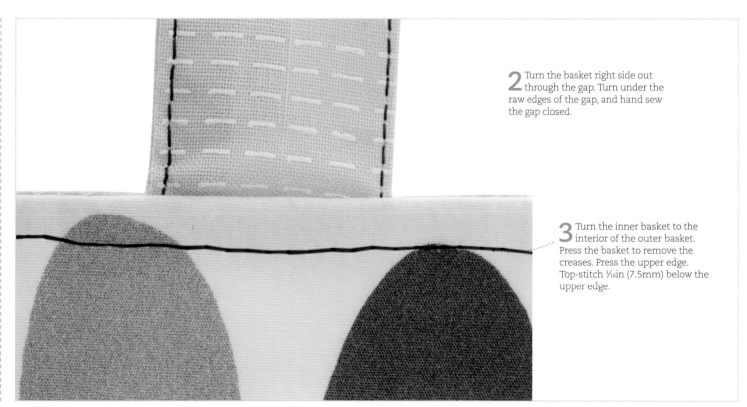

2 Turn the basket right side out through the gap. Turn under the raw edges of the gap, and hand sew the gap closed.

3 Turn the inner basket to the interior of the outer basket. Press the basket to remove the creases. Press the upper edge. Top-stitch ³⁄₁₆in (7.5mm) below the upper edge.

LININGS

A lining is placed inside a garment primarily to make the garment more comfortable to wear—it will prevent the garment from sticking to you. It will also make the garment last longer. Choose a good-quality lining made from rayon or acetate as these fabrics will breathe with your body. Polyester linings can be sticky to wear.

LINING A BODICE

On dresses and fitted tops, a lined bodice is comfortable and it reduces bulk. The insertion of a lining is done prior to the center back seam being joined and the side seams being joined.

Difficulty level ✱✱✱✱✱

1 Place the lining bodice to the fabric bodice, right side to right side. Match the shoulder seams and the neck and armhole edges.

2 Sew together around the neck edge and the armhole edge using a ⅝in (1.5cm) seam allowance.

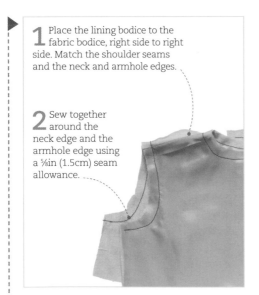

3 Clip the seam allowance around the neck and armhole.

4 To turn through to the right side, pull the back bodice through the shoulder.

5 Repeat for the other shoulder. Press.

6 Join the side seams by sewing through the fabric and lining in one continuous seam.

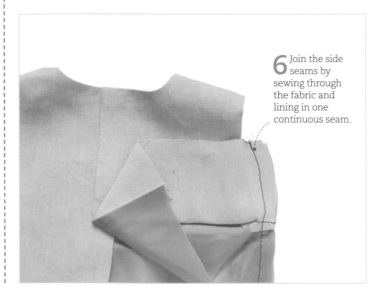

7 Press all the seams.

BASTING STITCHES p.89 ● HAND SEWING pp.90—91 ● STITCHES MADE WITH A MACHINE pp.92—93

LINING A SKIRT

Difficulty level ★★★★★

Cut the lining out the same as the skirt, using the same pattern pieces, and join together, leaving a gap for the zipper. Do not sew in the darts.

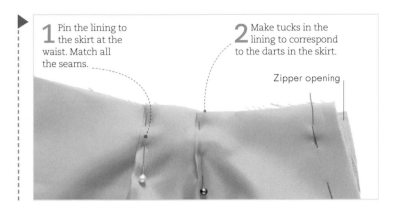

1 Pin the lining to the skirt at the waist. Match all the seams.

2 Make tucks in the lining to correspond to the darts in the skirt.

Zipper opening

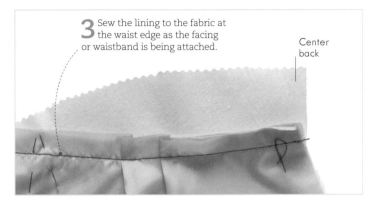

3 Sew the lining to the fabric at the waist edge as the facing or waistband is being attached.

Center back

HEMMING A LINING

Difficulty level ★★★★★

The lining on a skirt or dress should be slightly shorter—about 1½in (4cm)—than the finished garment, so that the lining does not show when you are walking or sitting.

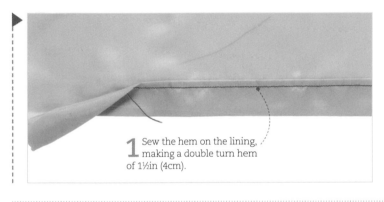

1 Sew the hem on the lining, making a double turn hem of 1½in (4cm).

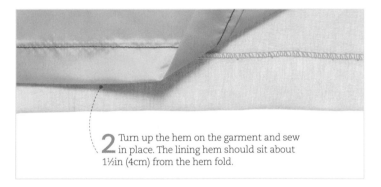

2 Turn up the hem on the garment and sew in place. The lining hem should sit about 1½in (4cm) from the hem fold.

LINING AROUND A SPLIT

Difficulty level ★★★★★

If there is a split in a hemline, the lining will need to be stitched around it securely. First construct the skirt, with its split finished, corners mitered, and hemmed. Finish the lining hem in the same way.

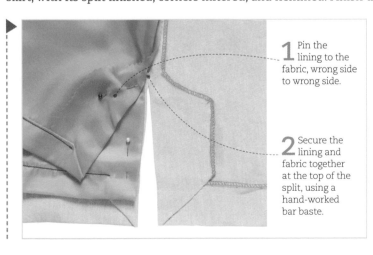

1 Pin the lining to the fabric, wrong side to wrong side.

2 Secure the lining and fabric together at the top of the split, using a hand-worked bar baste.

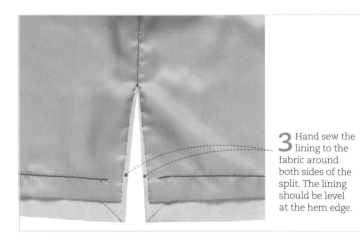

3 Hand sew the lining to the fabric around both sides of the split. The lining should be level at the hem edge.

REDUCING SEAM BULK pp.108–109 • **ATTACHING A STRAIGHT WAISTBAND p.192** • **MACHINE-SEWN HEMS p.266**

LINING AROUND A VENT

Difficulty level ★★★★★

Some skirts and jackets feature a vent at the hemline, where the fabric overlaps to allow for movement. Lining around a vent can be tricky though, as the pattern pieces for the vent can be confusing.

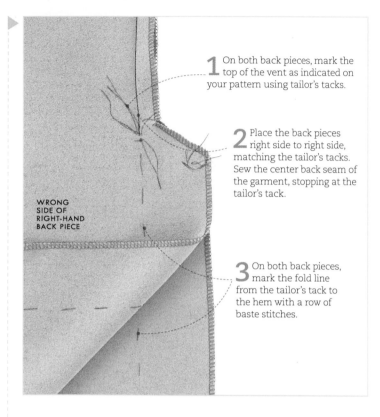

1 On both back pieces, mark the top of the vent as indicated on your pattern using tailor's tacks.

2 Place the back pieces right side to right side, matching the tailor's tacks. Sew the center back seam of the garment, stopping at the tailor's tack.

WRONG SIDE OF RIGHT-HAND BACK PIECE

3 On both back pieces, mark the fold line from the tailor's tack to the hem with a row of baste stitches.

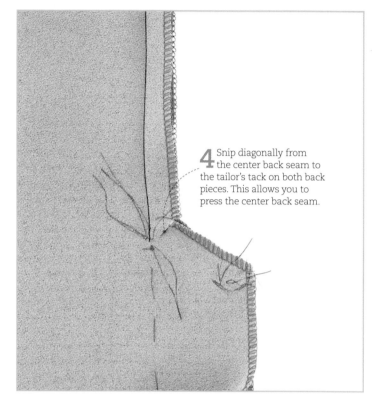

4 Snip diagonally from the center back seam to the tailor's tack on both back pieces. This allows you to press the center back seam.

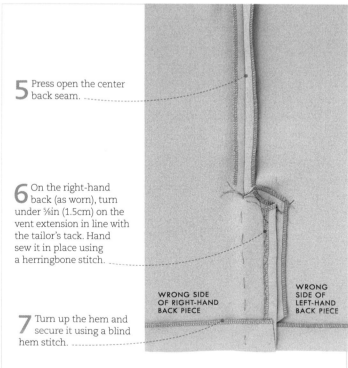

5 Press open the center back seam.

6 On the right-hand back (as worn), turn under ⅝in (1.5cm) on the vent extension in line with the tailor's tack. Hand sew it in place using a herringbone stitch.

7 Turn up the hem and secure it using a blind hem stitch.

WRONG SIDE OF RIGHT-HAND BACK PIECE

WRONG SIDE OF LEFT-HAND BACK PIECE

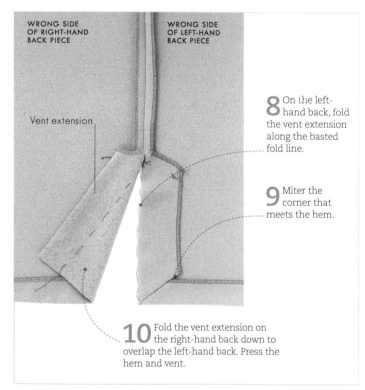

WRONG SIDE OF RIGHT-HAND BACK PIECE

WRONG SIDE OF LEFT-HAND BACK PIECE

Vent extension

8 On the left-hand back, fold the vent extension along the basted fold line.

9 Miter the corner that meets the hem.

10 Fold the vent extension on the right-hand back down to overlap the left-hand back. Press the hem and vent.

11 Cut the lining pieces according to your pattern.

12 On both back pieces, mark the vent as indicated on your pattern using tailor's tacks.

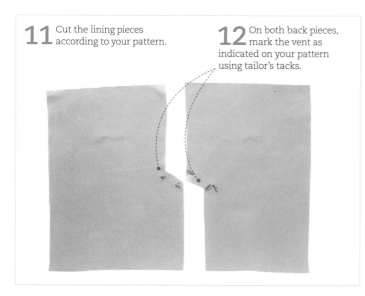

13 Neaten the center back edges using a 3-thread serger stitch or zigzag stitch.

14 Reinforce the inner corners as shown, sewing through the tailor's tacks about ¾in (2cm) from, and parallel to, the edge.

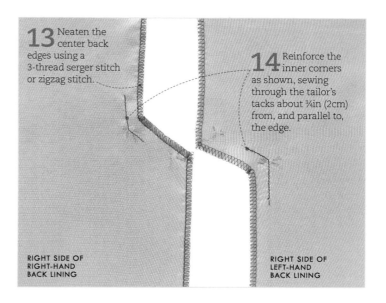

RIGHT SIDE OF RIGHT-HAND BACK LINING

RIGHT SIDE OF LEFT-HAND BACK LINING

15 Place the back lining pieces right side to right side, matching the tailor's tacks. Sew the center back seam of the garment, stopping at the tailor's tack.

16 Press the center back seam open then cut diagonally from the center back edge into the reinforced corners.

17 At the bottom edge, make a double-turn hem and sew it in place.

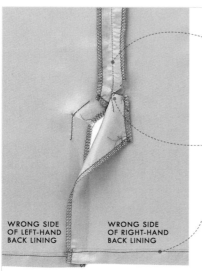

WRONG SIDE OF LEFT-HAND BACK LINING

WRONG SIDE OF RIGHT-HAND BACK LINING

RIGHT SIDE OF LEFT-HAND BACK LINING

RIGHT SIDE OF RIGHT-HAND BACK LINING

18 Place the lining to the skirt wrong side to wrong side, matching them at the center back seam. Pin in place.

19 On the right-hand back lining (as worn), turn under the edge of the opening by ⅝in (1.5cm) and pin to the seam on the skirt vent extension.

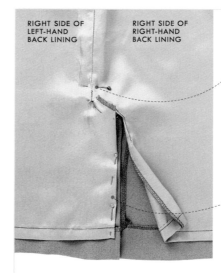

RIGHT SIDE OF LEFT-HAND BACK LINING

RIGHT SIDE OF RIGHT-HAND BACK LINING

20 On the left-hand back lining (as worn), turn under the edge of the opening by ⅝in (1.5cm). This should fit alongside the right-hand side of the vent. Pin in place.

21 At the top of the vent, push the seam allowance of the right-hand back lining under the diagonal part of the left-hand back lining.

22 Fold the diagonal part under and pin.

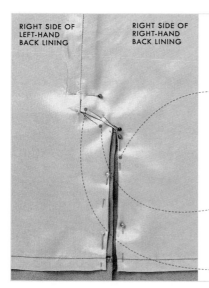

RIGHT SIDE OF RIGHT-HAND BACK LINING

RIGHT SIDE OF LEFT-HAND BACK LINING

23 Sew the lining to the skirt around the vent using a flat fell stitch.

24 Sew diagonally from the center back seam to the top of the vent, sewing through all layers. Pin in place.

25 Press to finish. The lining hem should remain unattached to the skirt hem.

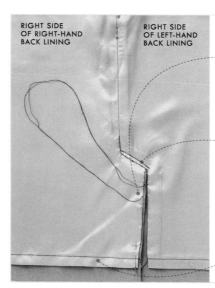

REDUCING SEAM BULK pp.108—09 ● **HAND-SEWN HEMS pp.264—265** ● **MACHINE-SEWN HEMS p.266** ● **MITERED CORNERS p.269**

PROFESSIONAL TECHNIQUES

Once you have mastered the basics of sewing it is time to try some advanced techniques, such as those involved in modern tailoring or boning a bodice for special-occasion wear. These take a little more time and care to execute.

SPEED **TAILORING**

Speed tailoring is the term given to modern tailoring techniques that use fusible interfacings to give shape and structure to a jacket or coat. Choose woven fusible interfacings and cut on the same grain as the jacket fabric pieces. If possible, use two different interfacings—one a medium weight and one a light weight— in conjunction with fusible tapes to stabilize the edges of the jacket. If interfacings of different weights are not available, choose a lightweight product and use two layers if required in the front of the jacket.

COMPONENTS OF A JACKET

Difficulty level ★★★✷✷

These photographs show where to place the fusible interfacing on a jacket or coat. Your pattern may be cut differently to this—the front and back may be one piece, not two as shown here, and you may have a two-piece sleeve—but the same principle will apply, of a heavier interfacing at the front and a lighter one at the back, with reinforcement through the shoulder.

▶ **FRONT**

Medium-weight fusible interfacing with ⅝in (1.5cm) seam allowances removed

Shoulder plate, cut on a bias grain to reinforce the shoulder

A ¾in (2cm) wide stitch-reinforced fusible tape to stop the leading edges of the jacket stretching

▶ **SIDE FRONT**

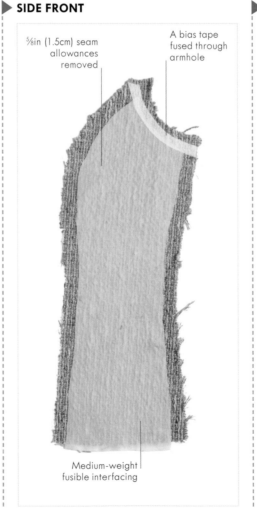

⅝in (1.5cm) seam allowances removed

A bias tape fused through armhole

Medium-weight fusible interfacing

▶ **SIDE BACK**

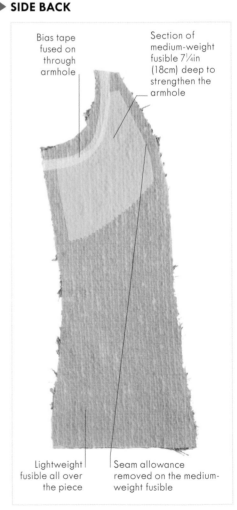

Bias tape fused on through armhole

Section of medium-weight fusible 7¼in (18cm) deep to strengthen the armhole

Lightweight fusible all over the piece

Seam allowance removed on the medium-weight fusible

FUSIBLE INTERFACINGS p.54 ● **FABRIC GRAIN AND NAP p.76**

▶ BACK

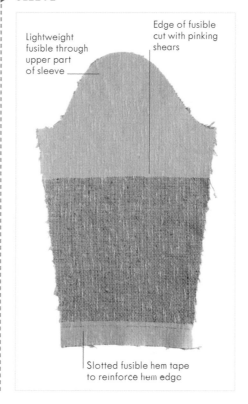

Bias tape fused on at armhole

Bias tape fused on at neck edge

Medium-weight fusible over the shoulders to reinforce, cut 7¼in (18cm) deep at armhole edge and 10in (25cm) deep at center back, seam allowances removed

Lightweight fusible all over

▶ SLEEVE

Lightweight fusible through upper part of sleeve

Edge of fusible cut with pinking shears

Slotted fusible hem tape to reinforce hem edge

▶ FRONT FACING

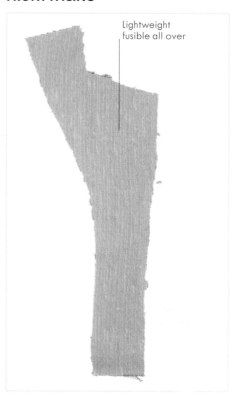

Lightweight fusible all over

▶ UPPER COLLAR

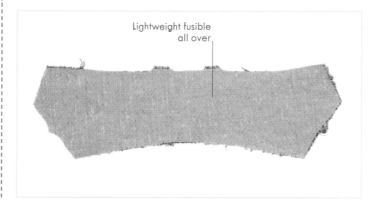

Lightweight fusible all over

▶ FINISHED JACKET

▶ UNDER COLLAR

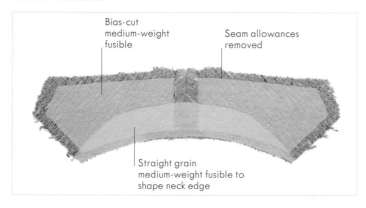

Bias-cut medium-weight fusible

Seam allowances removed

Straight grain medium-weight fusible to shape neck edge

PATTERN LAYOUT **pp.78–79** ● INTERFACINGS **pp.324–325**

JETTED POCKET

Difficulty level ✳✳✳✳✳

This is a professional pocket found on many suit jackets. Great care has to be taken when making this pocket because there is no flap for it to hide behind!

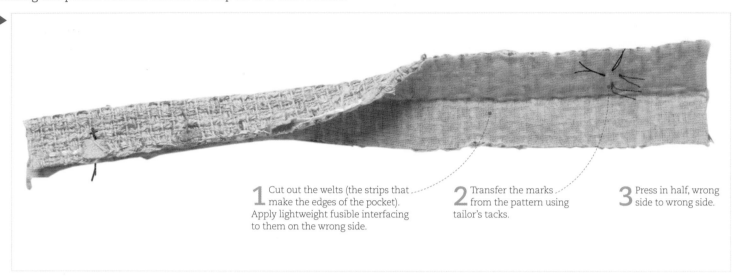

1 Cut out the welts (the strips that make the edges of the pocket). Apply lightweight fusible interfacing to them on the wrong side.

2 Transfer the marks from the pattern using tailor's tacks.

3 Press in half, wrong side to wrong side.

4 Mark the pocket position on the fabric, as indicated on your pattern, using tailor's tacks.

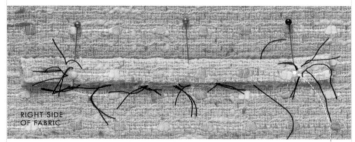

RIGHT SIDE OF FABRIC

5 Start with the upper welt. Place it to the right side of the jacket front. The raw edge of the welt is toward the hem. Match the tailor's tacks. Pin in place.

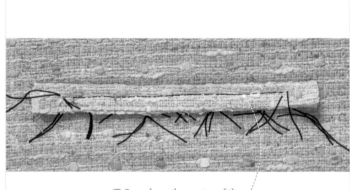

6 Sew along the center of the welt. Sew between the tailor's tacks only.

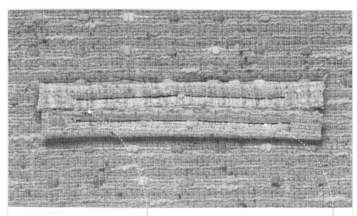

7 Position the lower welt on the jacket, placing the raw edges together.

8 Sew through the center of the lower welt. Ensure both rows of stitches are exactly the same length.

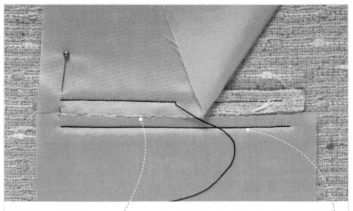

9 Place the lining over the welts, raw edges to the center. Pin to secure.

10 Sew the lining in place over the sewn line of the welts—you can feel the indentation of welt stitches.

FUSIBLE INTERFACINGS **p.54** ● PATTERN MARKING **pp.82–83**

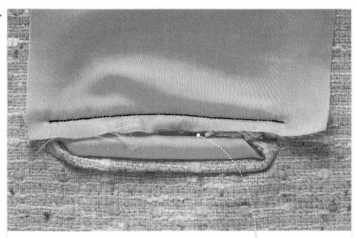

11 Snip through the jacket fabric between the welts (see Jetted pocket with flap, pages, pp.246–247).

12 Push the lining and the ends of the welts through to the back.

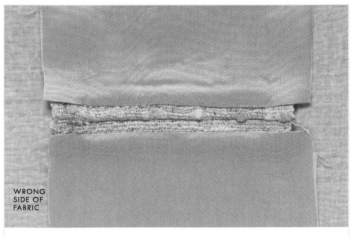

WRONG SIDE OF FABRIC

13 Press the lining and welts on the wrong side as shown.

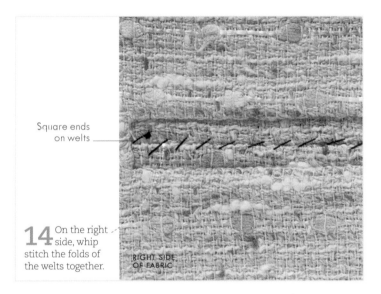

Square ends on welts

RIGHT SIDE OF FABRIC

14 On the right side, whip stitch the folds of the welts together.

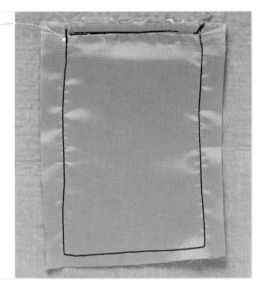

15 On the reverse, sew around the lining to make the pocket bag. The sewing starts and ends on the ends of the welts.

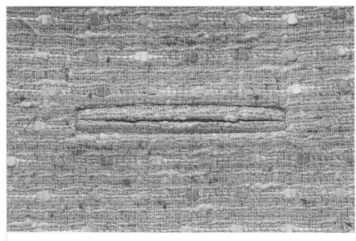

16 Remove the whip stitches from across the pocket opening.

HAND SEWING **pp.90–91** ● STITCHES MADE WITH A MACHINE **pp.92–93** ● JETTED POCKET WITH FLAP **pp.246–247**

TECHNIQUES

COLLAR APPLICATION

Difficulty level ★★★★☆

A notched collar is a sign of a tailored jacket. This type of collar consists of an upper and under collar, and a facing that folds back to form the lapel on either side. Careful sewing and accurate marking are required.

1 Attach the upper collar to the front facing and back neck lining.

Upper collar

2 Stop sewing at the tailor's tack at the front edge.

Back neck lining

Front facing

4 Clip the seam as necessary.

3 Press the seam open over a tailor's ham.

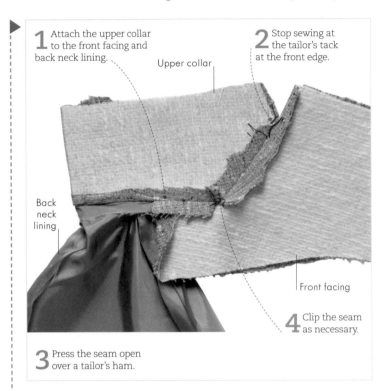

5 Join the under collar to the jacket front and back.

Under collar

JACKET FRONT

6 Stop sewing at the tailor's tack at the front edge.

7 Press the seam open. Clip as necessary.

8 Place the jacket and the lining together. Match the collar sections.

UNDER COLLAR

JACKET FRONT

9 Sew around the collar, stopping and starting the sewing at the tailor's tacks at the front edge.

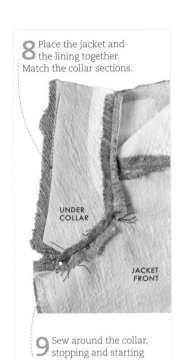

10 Sew the front facing to the jacket front. Start sewing at the tailor's tack at the front edge. The sewing line from the collar and the sewing line from the facing should line up but not cross each other.

11 Layer the seam.

JACKET FRONT

12 On the inside, herringbone stitch the neck seams together.

13 Turn the collar and lapel to the right side.

14 Press using a steam iron and cloth. Roll the seam toward the back of the garment so that it does not show on the right side.

SET-IN SLEEVE

Difficulty level ★★★★★

On a tailored jacket, the sleeve needs to be set in to have a rounded sleeve head, which is created with polyester batting. The sleeve head will ensure that the sleeve hangs perfectly.

1 Cut a piece of polyester batting to fit the sleeve head. The batting should be approx 2in (5cm) deep at the center. Pin in place.

2 Insert two rows of gather (ease) stitches to attach the batting to the sleeve.

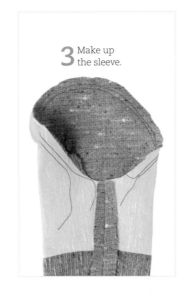

3 Make up the sleeve.

4 Insert the sleeve into the armhole, right side to right side. Pin in place.

5 Pull up the ease stitches to fit. The sleeve head will absorb the fullness.

6 Sew in place. Make a second row of stitches close to the first stitches.

Concave side
Front slope
Back slope

7 The shoulder pad can now be inserted. The back slope of the shoulder pad is longer than the front slope. The concave side will face the jacket lining.

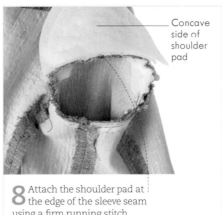

Concave side of shoulder pad

8 Attach the shoulder pad at the edge of the sleeve seam using a firm running stitch.

9 On the right side, the finished sleeve has a rounded sleeve head.

HEM AND LINING

Difficulty level ★★★★★

When making a jacket, the jacket hem is turned up first and then the lining is hemmed. The jacket hem needs to be reinforced first with a slotted fusible hem tape. Make sure that the hem edge is parallel to the ground.

1 Turn up the hem on the jacket by about 1½in (4cm). Pin to secure.

2 Roll back the edge of the hem and herringbone stitch in place.

3 Bring the lining down over the jacket hem. Turn up the hem of the lining so that it is level to the jacket hem, then push up to ¾in (2cm) from the hem edge. At the facing edge, the lining is level with the hem edge. Pin.

4 Use a slip hem stitch to secure the lining in place.

REDUCING SEAM BULK pp.108–109 ● **HOW TO MAKE AND FIT GATHERS p.135** ● **INSERTING A SET-IN SLEEVE p.211** ● **INTERFACINGS pp.324–325**

BONED BODICES

A strapless bodice will require boning inserted to prevent the bodice from falling down. The boning will also give extra structure to the bodice and prevent wrinkles. Boning can be a simple process, or more complex using interfacings for additional structure and shape.

COUTURE BONED BODICE

Difficulty level ✱✱✱✱✱

A couture boned bodice is the more complicated of the two methods of bodice construction, but it is well worth the extra work involved as the finished result is wrinkle-free and self-supporting. This technique can be used for bridal bodices and special-occasion wear.

▶ COMPONENTS OF THE BODICE

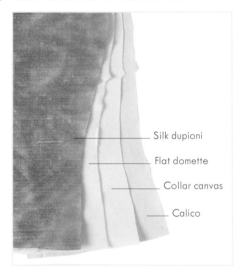

- —— Silk dupioni
- —— Flat domette
- —— Collar canvas
- —— Calico

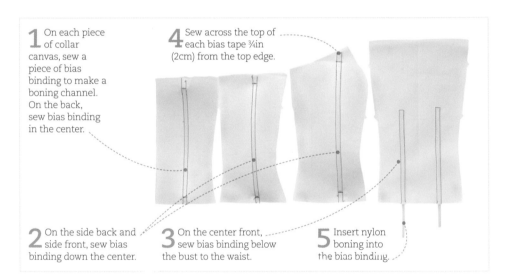

1 On each piece of collar canvas, sew a piece of bias binding to make a boning channel. On the back, sew bias binding in the center.

2 On the side back and side front, sew bias binding down the center.

3 On the center front, sew bias binding below the bust to the waist.

4 Sew across the top of each bias tape ¾in (2cm) from the top edge.

5 Insert nylon boning into the bias binding.

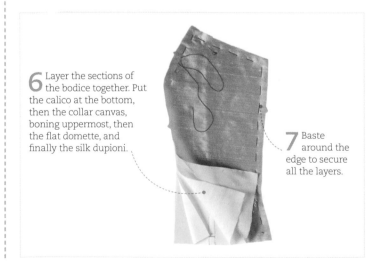

6 Layer the sections of the bodice together. Put the calico at the bottom, then the collar canvas, boning uppermost, then the flat domette, and finally the silk dupioni.

7 Baste around the edge to secure all the layers.

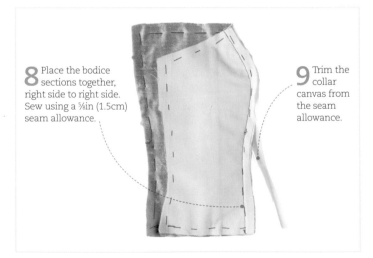

8 Place the bodice sections together, right side to right side. Sew using a ⅝in (1.5cm) seam allowance.

9 Trim the collar canvas from the seam allowance.

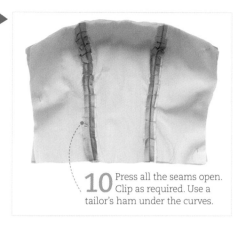

10 Press all the seams open. Clip as required. Use a tailor's ham under the curves.

11 After pressing, the princess seams at the front will be smoothly tapered to the waist.

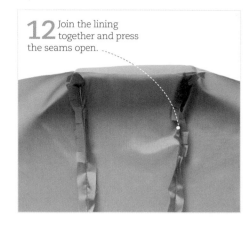

12 Join the lining together and press the seams open.

13 Pin the lining to the bodice around the top edge and down the center back. Match all vertical seam allowances.

14 Clip and layer the seam, then turn to the right side. Press.

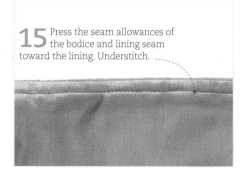

15 Press the seam allowances of the bodice and lining seam toward the lining. Understitch.

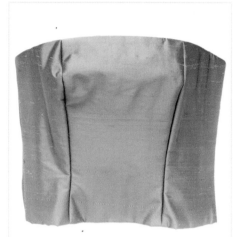

18 The completed bodice will stand on its own!

16 At the hem edge, turn up the silk bodice and herringbone in place.

17 Turn up the lining hem and pin, then hand stitch to the silk.

A BASIC BONING TECHNIQUE

Difficulty level ★★★★☆

For a simpler bodice on a dress or as a bodice on its own, this is a lightweight, quick technique.

1 Join the lining sections together.

2 Press the seam allowances together toward the center.

3 Sew a piece of narrow polyester boning to each set of seam allowances. Use a zigzag stitch to secure.

4 Repeat on all seams to complete the lining.

5 Apply a fusible interfacing to all the bodice sections.

6 Join the bodice sections together. Press the seams open.

7 Join the bodice and lining together at the upper edge.

8 Press the seam toward the lining and understitch.

STITCHES MADE WITH A MACHINE **pp.92–93** • REDUCING SEAM BULK **pp.108–109** • STITCH FINISHES **p.109** • LINING A BODICE **p.330**

TECHNIQUES

APPLIQUÉ AND QUILTING

Simple finishing touches can be used to good effect on many items. The term appliqué applies to one fabric being sewn to another in a decorative manner. The fabric to be appliquéd must be interfaced to support the fabric that is to be attached. Appliqué can be drawn by hand, then cut and sewn down, or it can be created by a computer pattern on the embroidery machine. The embroidery machine can also be used to create quilting, or this can be done by hand or with a sewing machine.

HAND-DRAWN APPLIQUÉ

Difficulty level ★★★☆☆

This technique involves drawing the chosen design on to a piece of double-sided fusible web, after which the design is fused in place on fabric prior to being sewn.

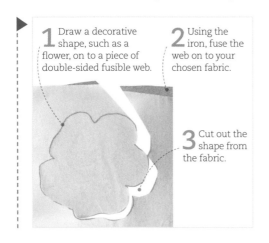

1 Draw a decorative shape, such as a flower, on to a piece of double-sided fusible web.

2 Using the iron, fuse the web on to your chosen fabric.

3 Cut out the shape from the fabric.

4 Place the shape, fusible web side down, where it is to be positioned on fabric and fuse in place.

5 Using a wide, close zigzag stitch, sew around the shape.

6 For a flower, sew on top of the fabric appliqué to make petal shapes.

MACHINE APPLIQUÉ

Difficulty level ★★☆☆☆

There are designs available for appliqué if you have an embroidery machine. You will need to use a special fusible embroidery backer on both the fabric for the appliqué and the base fabric.

1 Place the base fabric and appliqué fabric in the embroidery hoop and stitch out the first part of the design.

2 Trim the appliqué fabric back to the stitched lines.

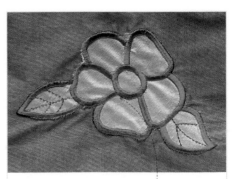

3 Complete the computerized embroidery.

QUILTING

This is a technique that involves sewing through two layers of fabric, one of which is a batting. The sewing sinks into the batting, creating a padded effect. Quilting can be done by hand, with a sewing machine, or using computerized embroidery.

Difficulty level ★★☆☆☆

▶ COMPONENTS OF QUILTING

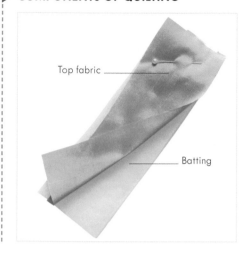

Top fabric

Batting

▶ HORIZONTAL QUILTING

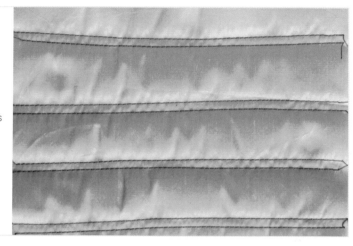

Baste the batting and top fabric together. Sew double lines with spaces between. Use a stitch length of 4.0 on your machine.

▶ DIAMOND QUILTING

1 Diagonally baste the batting and top fabric together.

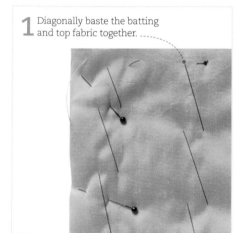

2 Set the machine to a sew length of 4.0, with the needle on one side of the foot. Stitch rows of machining diagonally across. Use the width of the machine foot as a guide to keep the rows parallel.

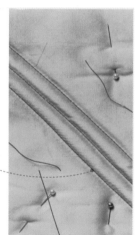

3 Sew parallel rows in the opposite diagonal directions, to create diamond shapes.

▶ FREEFORM QUILTING

Baste the batting and top fabric together. Sew at random.

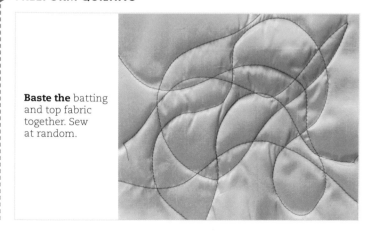

▶ COMPUTERIZED QUILTING

Baste the batting and top fabric together, then sew on a quilted pattern with the embroidery machine.

STITCHES MADE WITH A MACHINE pp.92–93 ● **INTERFACINGS pp.276–277**

OVEN **MITT**

Difficulty level ✱✱✱✱✱

You can customize this attractive kitchen accessory with fabrics that coordinate with your kitchen, but this small-scale project is also great for using up spare fabric. Be sure to choose insulated wadding, which is heat-protective, so that your oven mitt is safe for handling hot items.

TECHNIQUES USED Zigzagged seam neatening **p.95**, How to cut bias strips **p.154**, Quilting **p.345**

YOU WILL NEED

- Pattern template on p.387
- 2 pieces of 15¾ x 10½in (40 x 27cm) medium-weight cotton for outer pieces
- 2 pieces of 15¾ x 10½in (40 x 27cm) medium-weight cotton for lining pieces
- 2 pieces of 15¾ x 10½in (40 x 27cm) insulated wadding
- 16 x 12in (40 x 30cm) medium-weight cotton for the bias binding
- Matching or contrast thread
- Tailor's chalk or air-soluble ink pen

PIECES TO CUT

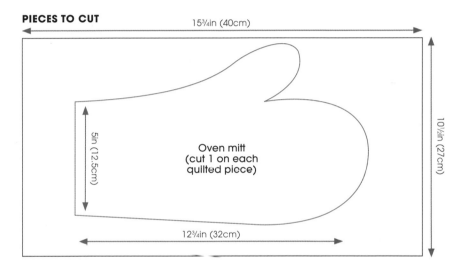

15¾in (40cm)

5in (12.5cm)

Oven mitt
(cut 1 on each
quilted piece)

10½in (27cm)

12¾in (32cm)

▶ MAKE THE BIAS BINDING FOR THE TRIM AND LOOP

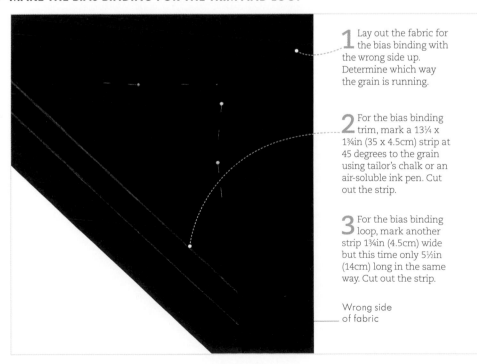

1 Lay out the fabric for the bias binding with the wrong side up. Determine which way the grain is running.

2 For the bias binding trim, mark a 13¼ x 1¾in (35 x 4.5cm) strip at 45 degrees to the grain using tailor's chalk or an air-soluble ink pen. Cut out the strip.

3 For the bias binding loop, mark another strip 1¾in (4.5cm) wide but this time only 5½in (14cm) long in the same way. Cut out the strip.

Wrong side of fabric

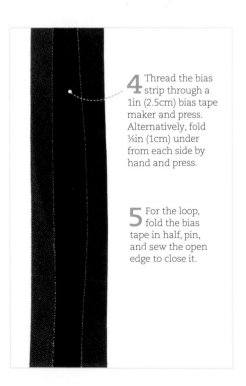

4 Thread the bias strip through a 1in (2.5cm) bias tape maker and press. Alternatively, fold ⅜in (1cm) under from each side by hand and press.

5 For the loop, fold the bias tape in half, pin, and sew the open edge to close it.

▶ **MAKE THE QUILTED PIECES**

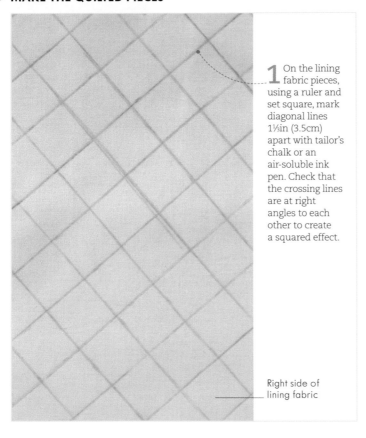

1 On the lining fabric pieces, using a ruler and set square, mark diagonal lines 1⅓in (3.5cm) apart with tailor's chalk or an air-soluble ink pen. Check that the crossing lines are at right angles to each other to create a squared effect.

Right side of lining fabric

2 Create two "sandwiches" of the pieces: place a patterned fabric piece wrong side up on a flat surface, lay a piece of the wadding on top, and finish with a piece of the lining fabric.

3 Pin the three layers together.

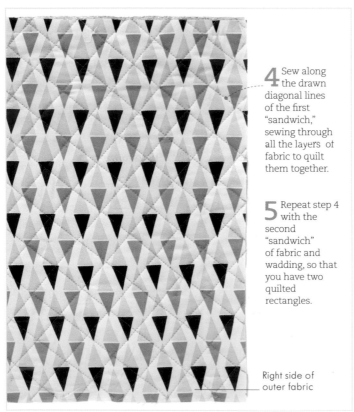

4 Sew along the drawn diagonal lines of the first "sandwich," sewing through all the layers of fabric to quilt them together.

5 Repeat step 4 with the second "sandwich" of fabric and wadding, so that you have two quilted rectangles.

Right side of outer fabric

▶ **ASSEMBLE THE MITT**

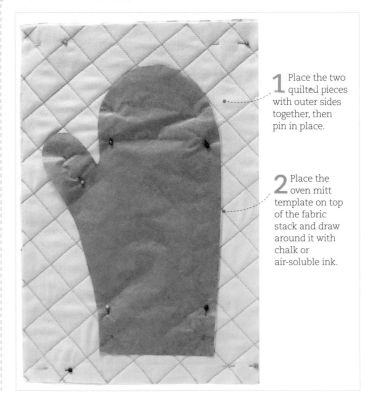

1 Place the two quilted pieces with outer sides together, then pin in place.

2 Place the oven mitt template on top of the fabric stack and draw around it with chalk or air-soluble ink.

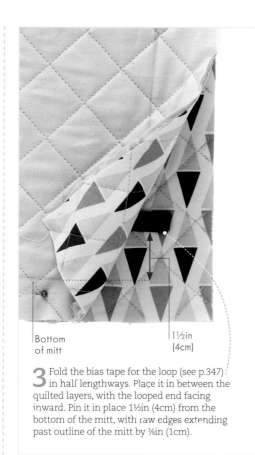

Bottom
of mitt

1½in
(4cm)

3 Fold the bias tape for the loop (see p.347) in half lengthways. Place it in between the quilted layers, with the looped end facing inward. Pin it in place 1½in (4cm) from the bottom of the mitt, with raw edges extending past outline of the mitt by ⅜in (1cm).

4 Sew around the marked shape of the mitt, sewing through all layers. Sew over the loop, but be sure to leave the bottom edge open.

5 Trim around the outside of your seam leaving a ³⁄₁₆in (5mm) seam allowance.

6 Use a zigzag stitch to neaten the edge.

7 Cut into the fabric between the fingers and thumb, but take care not to cut any of the stitches.

BIND THE EDGE

1 Turn the mitt the right side out. Place the bias binding right side to right side on the bottom edge of the mitt, aligning the raw edges.

2 Pin in place, and sew together in the crease of the binding.

3 Turn the mitt inside out and bring the binding to the inside. Hold the folded part of the tape down and sew in place by hand, using a slip stitch.

TECHNIQUES

ROSES AND BOWS

Difficulty level ★★☆☆☆

On special-occasion wear, a rose can add a superb finishing touch. When the raw edges of a rose are exposed, as in version 2 below, it also looks great made in tweed and suiting fabrics, to add a decorative finish to a tailored jacket. A bow that is permanently fixed in place is a beautiful embellishment on bridal wear.

▶ ROSE VERSION 1

1 Cut a bias strip 4in (10cm) wide. Fold in half lengthwise, wrong side to wrong side.

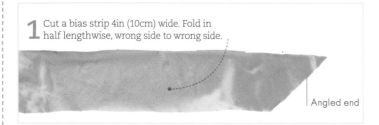

Angled end

2 Pin the raw edges together.

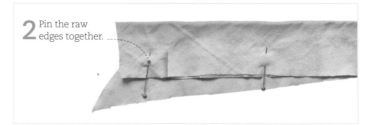

3 Insert two rows of gather stitches at the raw edge—one row at ⅜in (1cm) from the edge and the other row at ½in (1.3cm).

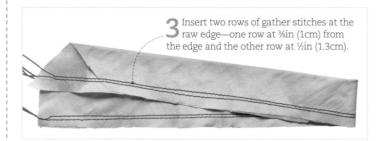

4 Pull up the gathers, grouping them together and leaving spaces between the groups. The groups and spaces will give the impression of petals.

5 Hold the lower edge of one end in your left hand and loosely wrap the strip around.

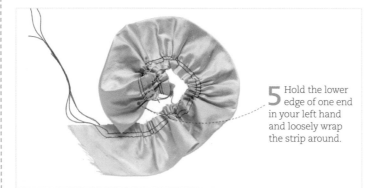

6 When you have a rose shape, tuck any raw edges that show into the base.

7 Secure at the base edge with hand stitches.

▶ ROSE VERSION 2

1 Cut a bias strip 4in (10cm) wide.

2 Insert two rows of gather stitches along the center of the strip. Leave a gap of ⅛in (3mm) between the rows sewn.

3 Pull up the gathers into groups and spaces (see step 4 above).

4 The groups and spaces will pull up to give a diagonal effect. Fold in half along the sewn lines.

5 Hold the end of the gathers in your left hand and wrap the strip around loosely.

6 Secure at the base with hand stitches. Although the edge is raw, fraying is minimal as the strip has been bias-cut.

◀ BASTING STITCHES **p.89** ● HAND SEWING **pp.90–91** ● STITCHES MADE WITH A MACHINE **pp.92–93** ● SEWING CORNERS AND CURVES **pp.102–103**

▶ BOW

1 To make the loops, cut a piece of silk or other fabric that is four times the length of the loop required and twice the width plus seam allowances.

2 Interline with dress net to the wrong side. Baste the net around the raw edge.

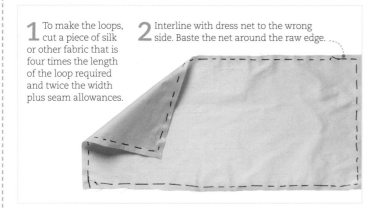

3 Fold in half, right side to right side. Sew along the raw edge leaving a ⅝in (1.5cm) seam allowance.

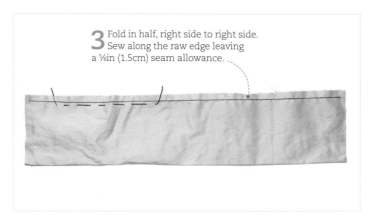

4 Turn through to the right side. Fold so that the seamline is in the center.

5 Bring the short end to the center. Pin in place.

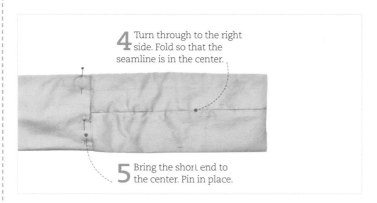

6 Baste through the center, using double thread.

7 Pull along the basting stitches to gather the center.

8 Next make the two ends. Cut two pieces of fabric the required finished length and twice the required width plus seam allowances.

9 Baste dress net to the fabric.

10 Fold each piece of fabric in half, right side to right side, and sew along the long raw edge and at an angle at one end.

11 Remove bulk from the corners.

12 Turn through to the right side. Press. Make sure there are sharp points.

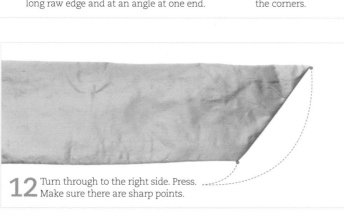

13 To assemble the bow, wrap a piece of fabric around the gathered center of the loops and sew in place by hand.

14 Scrunch the raw ends of the ends together and hand sew behind the loop.

TECHNIQUES

INTERLINING **CURTAINS**

A lined curtain that is also interlined will not only hang beautifully but will also be warm and keep out any drafts. This technique is for hand-sewn curtains and requires a large, flat table to work on. There are different weights of interlining available.

LINED AND INTERLINED CURTAINS

Difficulty level ✳✳✳✳✳

Preparation and accurate measuring of the window and the curtain fabric will ensure that this technique works every time. Choose a thicker quality curtain lining for interlined curtains because it will hang better.

1 Cut out the fabric, lining, and interlining.

Curtain fabric   Interlining   Lining

2 Baste lines to show where the foldlines of the hems will be. There is a double hem at the bottom and a single hem at the sides.

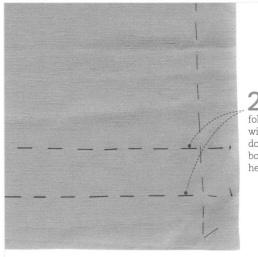

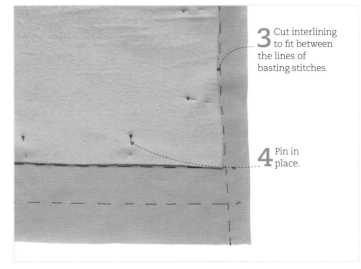

3 Cut interlining to fit between the lines of basting stitches.

4 Pin in place.

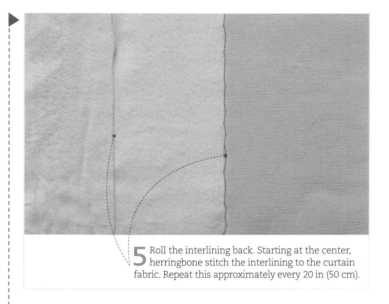

5 Roll the interlining back. Starting at the center, herringbone stitch the interlining to the curtain fabric. Repeat this approximately every 20 in (50 cm).

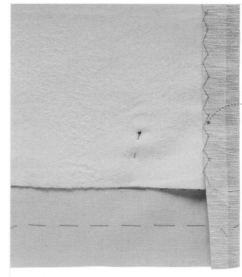

6 Fold the side of the curtain over the interlining and herringbone stitch down.

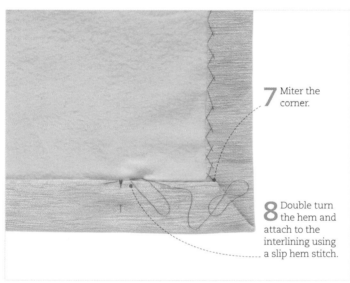

7 Miter the corner.

8 Double turn the hem and attach to the interlining using a slip hem stitch.

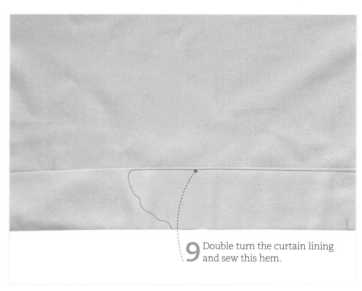

9 Double turn the curtain lining and sew this hem.

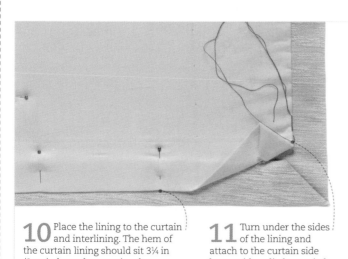

10 Place the lining to the curtain and interlining. The hem of the curtain lining should sit 3¼ in (8 cm) above the curtain edge.

11 Turn under the sides of the lining and attach to the curtain side hems with a slip hem stitch.

12 On the right side the curtain corners will be sharp and there will be no visible stitches.

MITERED CORNERS **p.269** ● INTERLININGS **p.324**

ROMAN **BLIND**

Difficulty level ✱✱✱✱✱

A Roman blind is a simple, elegant way to dress a window and introduce accent color or statement pattern to a room. It requires careful measurement of the window to begin with, but is quick and satisfying to assemble. A professional finish is easily achieved with the inclusion of interlining.

TECHNIQUES USED *Hand-sewn hems* **p.264–265**, *Machine-sewn hems* **p.266**, *Interlining curtains* **p.352–353**

YOU WILL NEED

- Fabric: to calculate the amount you need, measure the window's width (at the widest part where the blind will hang) and also the drop (the finished length of the blind). Add 3¼in (8cm) to the width and 6in (15cm) to the drop for the hems (that's to cover 2in/5cm at the top edge and 4in/10cm at the bottom)
- Lining: add ¾in (2cm) to the width and 10in (25cm) to the drop (for hem and rod pockets)
- Interlining or cotton domette: cut to the desired blind width, with 2in (5cm) extra at the top
- Matching thread
- Sew on Velcro™
- Roman blind fiberglass rods
- 1¼in (3cm) plastic or aluminum weight bar, cut to width of blind minus 1½in (4cm)
- Austrian blind rings ⅜in (1cm) diameter, and safety toggles/orbs
- Blind cord and breakaway cord connector
- Blind cord cleat
- Staple gun
- Screw eyes
- Wooden batten, to attach blind to window, cut to width of blind minus ⅜in (1cm)

Safety note: If babies or small children could come into contact with a blind, it is important to use safety toggles/orbs instead of blind rings on the bottom rod pocket to minimize risk of strangulation. You should also insert a breakaway cord connector, and install a cleat on the wall (see p.359).

PIECES TO CUT

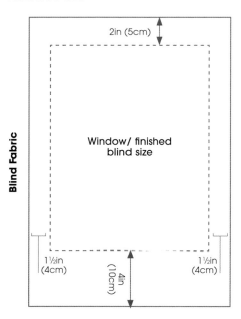

Blind Fabric

2in (5cm)

Window/ finished blind size

1½in (4cm)   1½in (4cm)

4in (10cm)

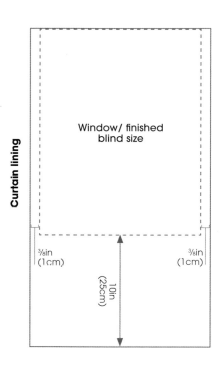

Curtain lining

Window/ finished blind size

⅜in (1cm)   ⅜in (1cm)

10in (25cm)

Interlining = same size as desired finished blind size, plus 2in (5in) at the top.

▶ PREPARE THE HEMS

1 Press under 1½in (4cm) to the wrong side (a single-turn hem) along both side edges of the blind fabric.

2 On the bottom edge, press under 2in (5cm) twice to make a double-turn hem. Pin the side and bottom hems in place. Press.

WRONG SIDE OF FABRIC

▶ **ADD THE INTERLINING**

1 Unfold the side and bottom hems of the blind fabric.

2 Position the interlining fabric on the wrong side of the blind fabric; it should align with the creases of the side and bottom hems.

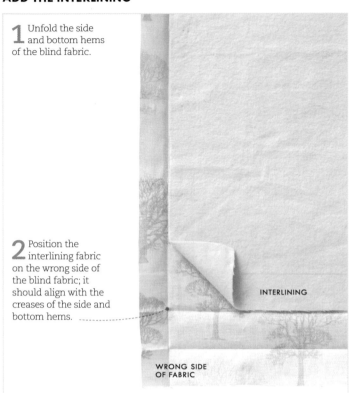

INTERLINING

WRONG SIDE
OF FABRIC

3 Re-fold the side hems and then the bottom hem to enclose the interlining.

4 Baste the side seams with diagonal bastes and pin the bottom hem in place.

▶ **PREPARE THE LINING**

1 Press 1in (2.5cm) to the wrong side, down both side edges of the lining fabric. Pin.

2 Press a 1½in (4cm) hem along the bottom edge. Sew close to the raw edge, at about ³⁄₁₆in (5mm).

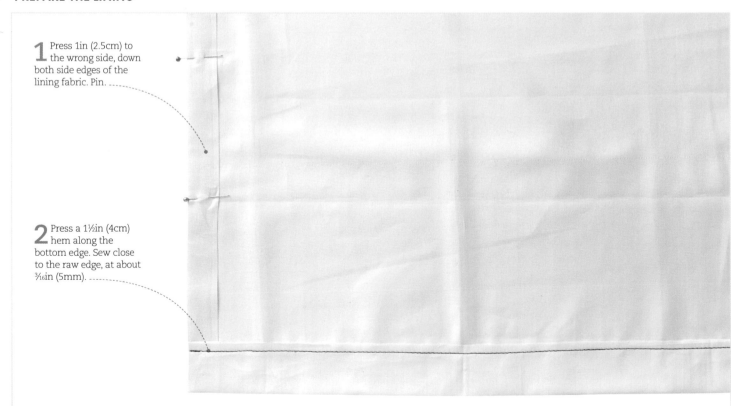

◀ **MARKING AIDS p.19** ● **BASTING STITCHES p.89** ● **HAND SEWING pp.90—91** ● **STITCHES MADE WITH A MACHINE pp.92—93**

▶ **MAKE THE ROD CASINGS AND ATTACH THE LINING**

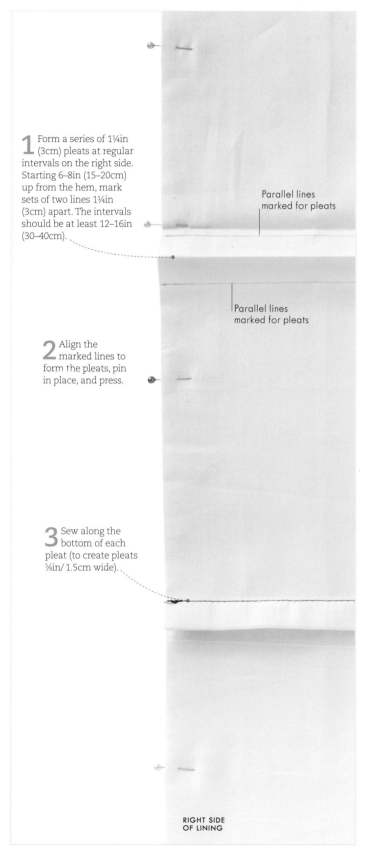

1 Form a series of 1¼in (3cm) pleats at regular intervals on the right side. Starting 6–8in (15–20cm) up from the hem, mark sets of two lines 1¼in (3cm) apart. The intervals should be at least 12–16in (30–40cm).

Parallel lines marked for pleats

Parallel lines marked for pleats

2 Align the marked lines to form the pleats, pin in place, and press.

3 Sew along the bottom of each pleat (to create pleats ⅝in/ 1.5cm wide).

RIGHT SIDE OF LINING

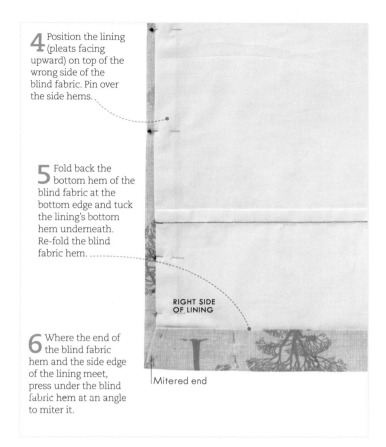

4 Position the lining (pleats facing upward) on top of the wrong side of the blind fabric. Pin over the side hems.

5 Fold back the bottom hem of the blind fabric at the bottom edge and tuck the lining's bottom hem underneath. Re-fold the blind fabric hem.

RIGHT SIDE OF LINING

6 Where the end of the blind fabric hem and the side edge of the lining meet, press under the blind fabric hem at an angle to miter it.

Mitered end

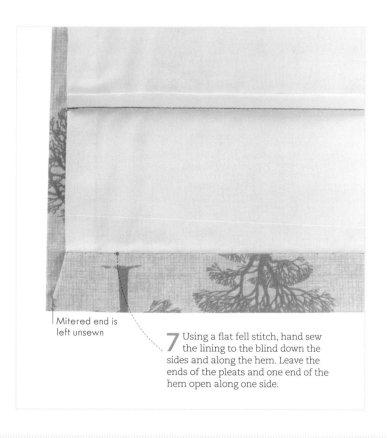

Mitered end is left unsewn

7 Using a flat fell stitch, hand sew the lining to the blind down the sides and along the hem. Leave the ends of the pleats and one end of the hem open along one side.

▶ **ATTACH THE VELCRO™ AND BLIND RINGS**

1 Turn down the top edge so that the blind measures the required finished length. Pin in place.

2 Cut a piece of Velcro™ equal to the width of the blind. Sew the soft loop side of the Velcro™ to the blind along the top hem edge.

3 Using a buttonhole stitch, sew a blind ring on either end of each rod casing, 2in (5cm) in from the blind edge. Sew additional rings at regular intervals in between, no more than 12in (30cm) apart.

4 Sew three small backstitches through both the lining fabric and the blind fabric, above the rod pocket at each ring location. Use a thread that matches your blind fabric color.

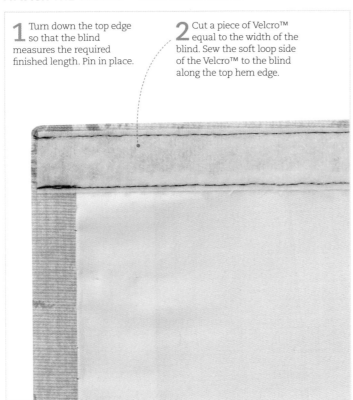

5 Insert a rod into each casing and close the end of the casing using flat fell stitch.

— Roman blind rod

6 Insert the weight bar into the lining fabric pocket in the bottom hem. Press the blind hem corner under to re-fold the mitered end and close it using flat fell stitch.

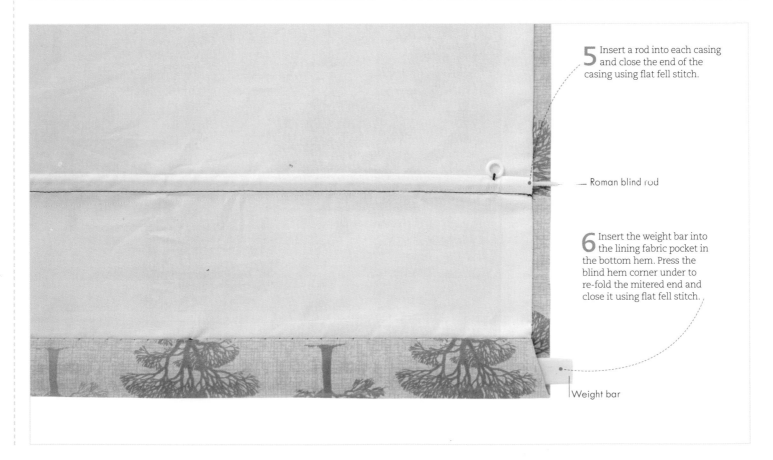

Weight bar

▶ ASSEMBLE THE BLIND

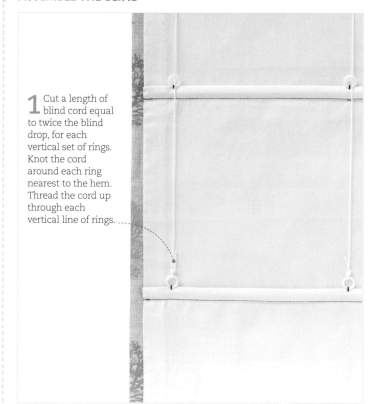

1 Cut a length of blind cord equal to twice the blind drop, for each vertical set of rings. Knot the cord around each ring nearest to the hem. Thread the cord up through each vertical line of rings.

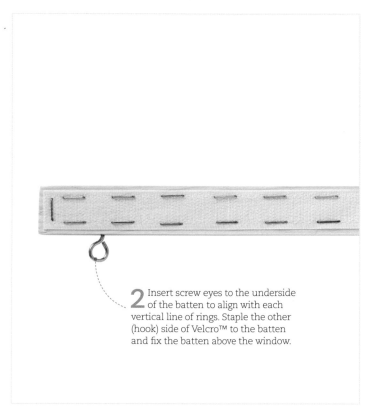

2 Insert screw eyes to the underside of the batten to align with each vertical line of rings. Staple the other (hook) side of Velcro™ to the batten and fix the batten above the window.

3 Attach the blind to the batten and pass the cords through the screw eyes and along to one side (see illustration).

4 To comply with child safety regulations, insert a breakaway cord connector where the cords gather at the end of the batten, no more than 2in (5cm) below the batten when the blind is fully down. Install a cord cleat 60in (1.5m) from the floor and keep the cord wound around it.

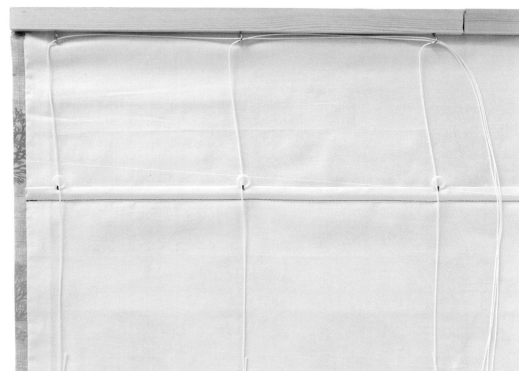

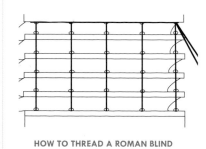

HOW TO THREAD A ROMAN BLIND

MITERED CORNERS **p.269** ● TAPE FASTENERS **p.320**

MENDING

Mending can preserve the life of your favorite clothes or furnishings. Try to fix lost buttons or dropped hems as soon as possible. Here you will find more complex mending techniques for split seams, holes, tears, and broken zippers.

MENDING

Repairing a tear in fabric, patching a worn area, or fixing a zipper or a buttonhole can add extra life to a garment or home good. Repairs like these may seem tedious, but they are very easy to do and well worthwhile. For some of the mending techniques shown here, a contrast color thread has been used so that the stitching can be seen clearly. However, when making a repair, be sure to use a matching thread.

RIPPING STITCHES

Difficulty level

All repairs involve ripping stitches. This must be done carefully to avoid damaging the fabric because the fabric will have to be re-sewn. There are three ways you can rip stitches.

▶ **SMALL SCISSORS**

Pull the fabric apart and, using very small, sharply pointed scissors, snip through the stitches that have been exposed.

▶ **SEAM RIPPER**

Slide a seam ripper carefully under a stitch and cut it. Cut through every fourth or fifth stitch, and the seam will unravel easily.

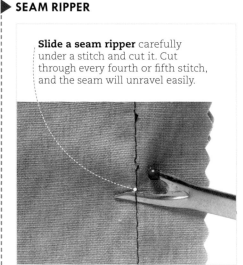

▶ **PIN AND SCISSORS**

On difficult fabrics or on very small, tight stitches, slide a pin under the stitch first to lift it away from the fabric, then snip through with a pair of sharply pointed scissors.

DARNING A HOLE

Difficulty level

If you accidentally catch a piece of jewelry in a sweater or other knitted garment, it may make a small hole. It is worth darning the hole, especially if the sweater was expensive or is a favorite. Holes in the heels of socks can be darned in the same way. Machines often have a darning stitch.

▶

1 Even if the hole is small, the sweater will be unwearable.

2 Work several rows of running stitches vertically around the hole.

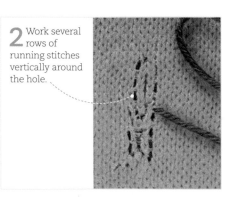

3 Complete the repair by working horizontal rows of running stitches through the vertical stitches.

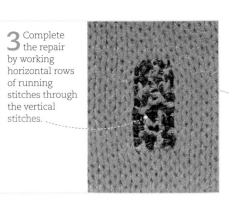

CUTTING TOOLS **pp.16–17** ● HOW TO APPLY A FUSIBLE INTERFACING **p.54** ● HAND SEWING **pp.90–91**

REPAIRING FABRIC UNDER A BUTTON

Difficulty level ★★✩✩✩

A button under strain can sometimes pull off a garment. If this happens, a hole will be made in the fabric, which needs fixing before a new button can be stitched on.

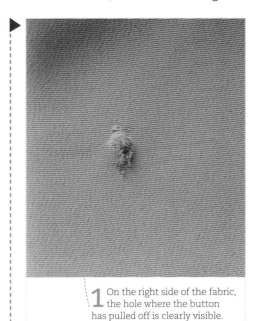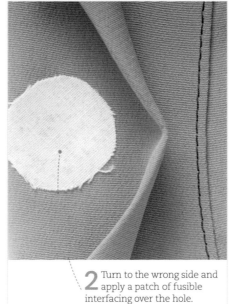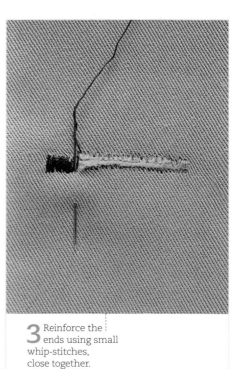

1 On the right side of the fabric, the hole where the button has pulled off is clearly visible.

2 Turn to the wrong side and apply a patch of fusible interfacing over the hole.

3 Work a machine straight stitch over the hole on the right side to strengthen the fabric.

4 Sew the button back in place.

REPAIRING A DAMAGED BUTTONHOLE

Difficulty level ★★✩✩✩

A buttonhole can sometimes rip at the end, or the stitching on the buttonhole can come unraveled. When repairing, use a thread that matches the fabric so the repair will be invisible.

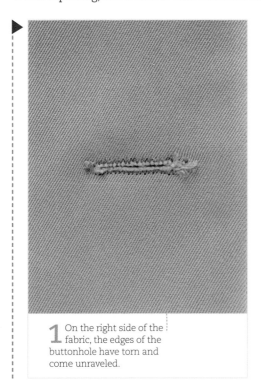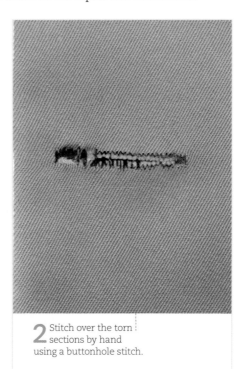

1 On the right side of the fabric, the edges of the buttonhole have torn and come unraveled.

2 Stitch over the torn sections by hand using a buttonhole stitch.

3 Reinforce the ends using small whip-stitches, close together.

SEWING ON BUTTONS **pp.301–303** ● BUTTONHOLES **pp.304–311**

MENDING A SPLIT IN A SEAM

Difficulty level

A split seam can be very quickly remedied with the help of some fusible mending tape and sewing.

1 Where the split has occurred in the seam, rip the seam on either side. Press the fabric back into shape.

2 Apply a strip of fusible mending tape over the split and the seam on either side of the split.

3 Re-sew the seam using a thread color to match the fabric.

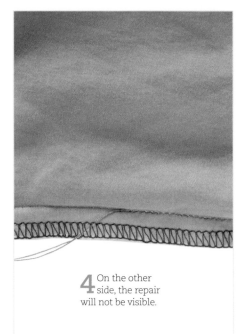

4 On the other side, the repair will not be visible.

MENDING A TEAR WITH A FUSIBLE PATCH

Difficulty level

Tears easily happen to clothing, especially children's wear, and they may occur on home goods, too. There are several methods for mending a tear. Most use a fusible patch of some kind, which may or may not be seen on the front, but you can also use a patch cut from matching fabric (see p.366).

▶ **FUSIBLE APPLIQUÉ PATCH**

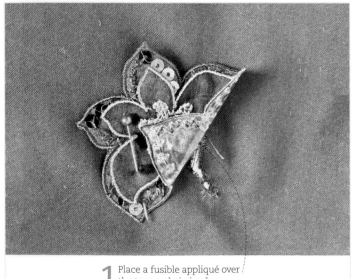

1 Place a fusible appliqué over the tear and pin in place.

2 Apply heat to fuse the decorative patch in place.

HOW TO APPLY A FUSIBLE INTERFACING p.54 ● HAND SEWING **pp.90–91** ● STITCHES MADE WITH A MACHINE **pp.92–93**

▶ VISIBLE FUSED PATCH

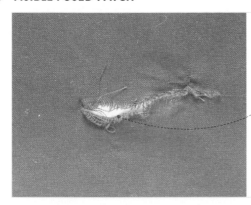

1 Measure the tear in the fabric.

2 Cut a piece of fusible mending fabric that is slightly longer and wider than the tear.

3 Fuse the fabric in place on the right side.

4 Using a zigzag stitch, sew all around the edge of the patch on the right side of the work.

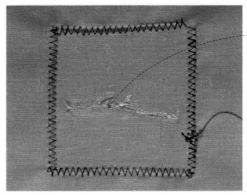

5 On the reverse side of the fabric, the tear will be firmly stuck to the mending patch, which will prevent the tear from getting any bigger.

▶ FUSED PATCH ON THE WRONG SIDE

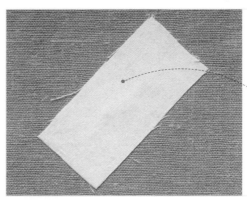

1 Measure the length of the tear. Cut a piece of fusible mending tape to fit.

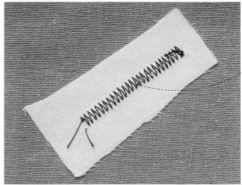

2 On the wrong side of the fabric, fuse the mending tape over the tear.

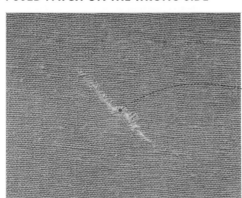

3 Using a zigzag stitch, width 5.0 and length 0.5, sew over the tear, working from the right side.

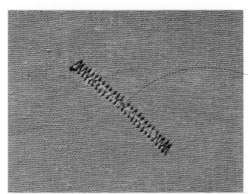

4 On the wrong side, the zigzag stitching will have gone through the fusible tape.

INTERFACINGS **pp.324–325** ● UNPICKING STITCHES **p.362**

MENDING A TEAR WITH A MATCHING PATCH

Difficulty level ★★☆☆☆

On a patterned fabric, such as a checker or a stripe, it is possible to mend a tear almost invisibly by using a patch that matches the pattern.

1 Cut a square hole in the fabric, removing the damaged area.

2 Turn under the raw edges of the hole by ⅜in (5mm) and press.

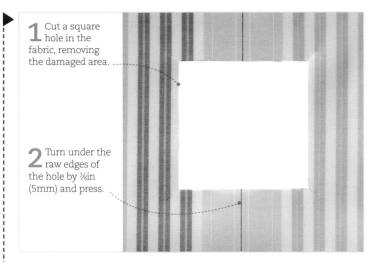

3 Cut a piece of fabric from matching fabric to fill the hole (this fabric could be taken from the hem). Match the stripes or checks. Baste in place.

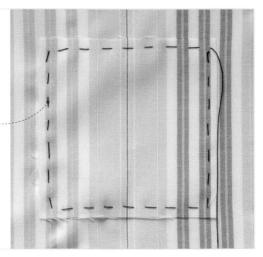

4 Using a small flat fell stitch, sew the patch into the hole, working from the right side of the fabric.

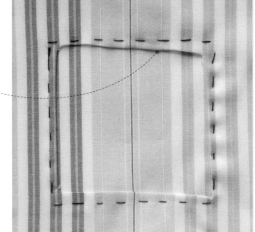

5 This is how it will look on the reverse.

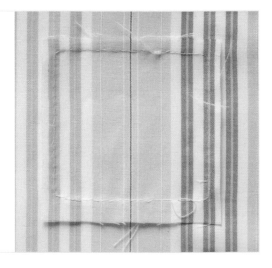

6 Remove the bastes and press.

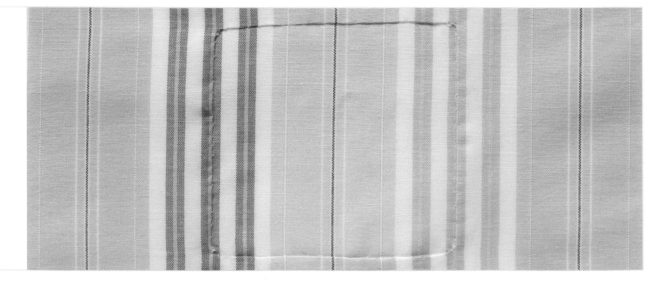

BASTING STITCHES **p.89** ● HAND SEWING **pp.90–91**

REPAIRING OR REPLACING ELASTIC

Difficulty level ✱✱✱✱✱

Elastic can frequently come undone inside the waistband, or it may lose its stretch and require replacing. Here is the simple way to re-insert elastic or insert new elastic.

1 Carefully rip a seam in the elastic casing.

Old elastic

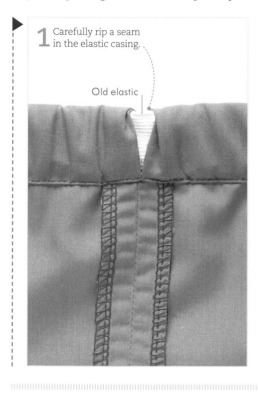

2 Pull the old elastic through the gap in the seam and cut through it.

3 Attach new elastic to the old with a safety pin. Use the old elastic to pull the new elastic through inside the casing.

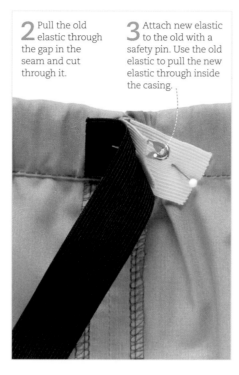

4 Secure the ends on the new elastic.

5 Hand sew the ripped seam back together using a flat fell stitch.

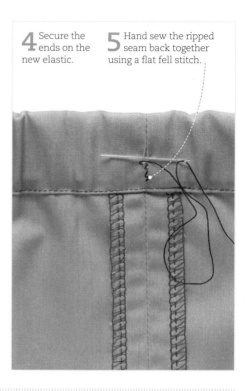

REPAIRING A BROKEN ZIPPER

Difficulty level ✱✱✱✱✱

Zippers can break if they come under too much strain. Sometimes the zipper has to be removed and a new zipper inserted. However, if only a few teeth have been broken far enough down so that the zipper can still be opened sufficiently, you can make this repair.

1 Where there are broken teeth on the zipper, the zipper pull will be attached to one half only. Move the pull up so it is alongside the gap in the teeth on the other side.

Broken teeth

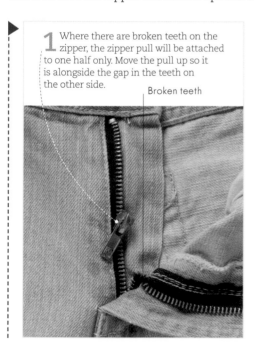

2 Carefully feed the teeth on the broken side into the top of the zipper.

Broken part of zipper

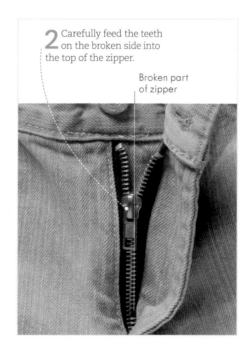

3 Just above the broken part, hand sew over the zipper teeth using double thread. This makes a stop for the puller and the zipper will now have an extended life.

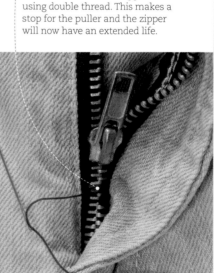

ZIPPERS **pp.284–293** • UNPICKING STITCHES **p.362**

USING THE **PATTERNS SECTION**

To create most of the projects in this book, you will first need to transfer the pattern to paper. You can do this in one of three ways: enlarge it on a photocopier, draw the pattern by hand onto pattern paper, or download it from our website. For garments, you will also need to find the correct size. It is always a good idea to make a garment in muslin first (see pp.74–75) to make sure that the size is right and the garment fits.

CHOOSING A SIZE

Take the relevant body measurements for the garment you are making and find the closest set of measurements in the tables below. If the measurements are between sizes, choose the larger of the two. Sizes may differ from what you would buy in a store.

▶ WOMEN'S SIZING

SIZE	2–4	4–6	6–8	8–10	10–12	12–14	14–16	16–18	18–20
BUST	32¼in (82cm)	33¼in (84.5cm)	34¼in (87cm)	36¼in (92cm)	38in (97cm)	40in (102cm)	42in (107cm)	44in (112cm)	46in (117cm)
WAIST	24½in (62cm)	25¼in (64.5cm)	26¼in (67cm)	28¼in (72cm)	30¼in (77cm)	32¼in (82cm)	34¼in (87cm)	36¼in (92cm)	38in (97cm)
HIP	34¼in (87cm)	35¼in (89.5cm)	36¼in (92cm)	38in (97cm)	40in (102cm)	42in (107cm)	44in (112cm)	46in (117cm)	48in (122cm)

▶ CHILDREN'S SIZING

SIZE	2–3 YRS	4–5 YRS	6–7 YRS
CHEST	21¼–22in (54–56cm)	22½–23⅝in (57–60cm)	24–25¼in (61–64cm)
WAIST	20–20⅞in (51–53cm)	21¼–22⅞in (54–58cm)	22⅞–23⅝in (58–60cm)
HEIGHT	37¾–38⅝in (96–98cm)	41–43¼in (104–110cm)	45⅝–48in (116–122cm)

▶ UNISEX SIZING

SIZE	CHEST
XS	33–34in (84–86.5cm)
S	36–38in (91.5–96.5cm)
M	40–42in (101.5–106.5cm)
L	44–46in (112–117cm)
XL	48–50in (123–127cm)
XXL	52–54in (132–137cm)

▶ PATTERN MARKINGS

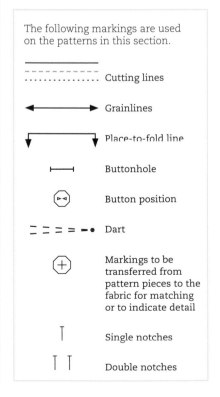

The following markings are used on the patterns in this section.

———————— ·········· Cutting lines

⟷ Grainlines

Place-to-fold line

⊢——⊣ Buttonhole

Button position

= = = – • Dart

⊕ Markings to be transferred from pattern pieces to the fabric for matching or to indicate detail

⊤ Single notches

⊤ ⊤ Double notches

▶ SEAM ALLOWANCE

Seam allowance is the amount of fabric that is taken up by the seam. It is usually given as the distance between the cutting line and the seam line.

The garment patterns in this section include ⅝in (1.5cm) seam allowance. This means that to make a project that is the correct size and shape, you will need to cut along the line on the pattern, and sew ⅝in (1.5cm) inside the cutting line. It can be helpful to mark a seam line onto the pattern pieces before you begin.

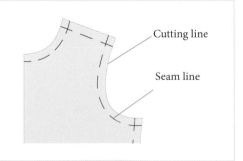

Cutting line

Seam line

COPY OR DOWNLOAD YOUR PATTERN

▶ METHOD 1: PHOTOCOPYING

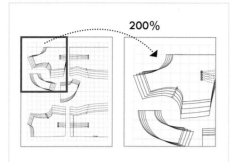

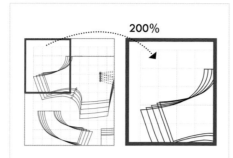

1 To enlarge the pattern on a photocopier, begin by copying it at 100%. Find the line for your chosen size in the pattern, and draw along it in marker or pen. Enlarge the pattern by 200%.

2 Enlarge the pattern pieces again by 200% to reach full size. If you are using a photocopier that has a 400% setting, you can use this setting to enlarge the pieces in one step.

3 Once you have enlarged all parts of the original page, piece them together using the gridlines as a guide, and tape them down. Cut around the line for your chosen size.

▶ METHOD 2: DRAWING THE PATTERN BY HAND

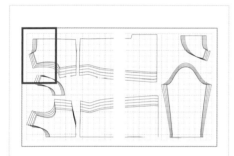

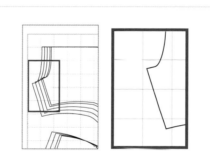

1 Each grid square in the patterns represents a 2in square at full size. To enlarge the patterns by hand, you will need pattern paper with either a ½in or 2in grid.

2 Begin by finding the line for your chosen size in the pattern. Enlarge the pattern onto your paper, mapping each square of the pattern onto a 2in square on the pattern paper.

3 Depending on the size of your pattern paper, you may need to stick together several sheets to fit all the pieces for a single pattern. Once you have copied the pieces, cut them out.

▶ METHOD 3: DOWNLOADING FROM THE INTERNET

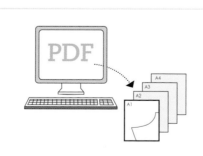

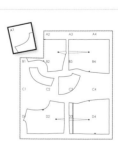

1 Check which pattern is needed to make the project. This is listed on the first page of the instructions. Then go to the website **www.dk.com/thesewingbook**

2 Find the correct PDF for your project. Download the PDF to your computer, and print it out. The pages will be labeled in the order that they fit together.

3 Trim the white margins from the printed pages, and tape the pages together, using the letters and gridlines as a guide. Find the line for your chosen size and cut around it.

A-LINE SHIFT DRESS PATTERN pp.166–171

ENLARGE BY 400% on a photocopier

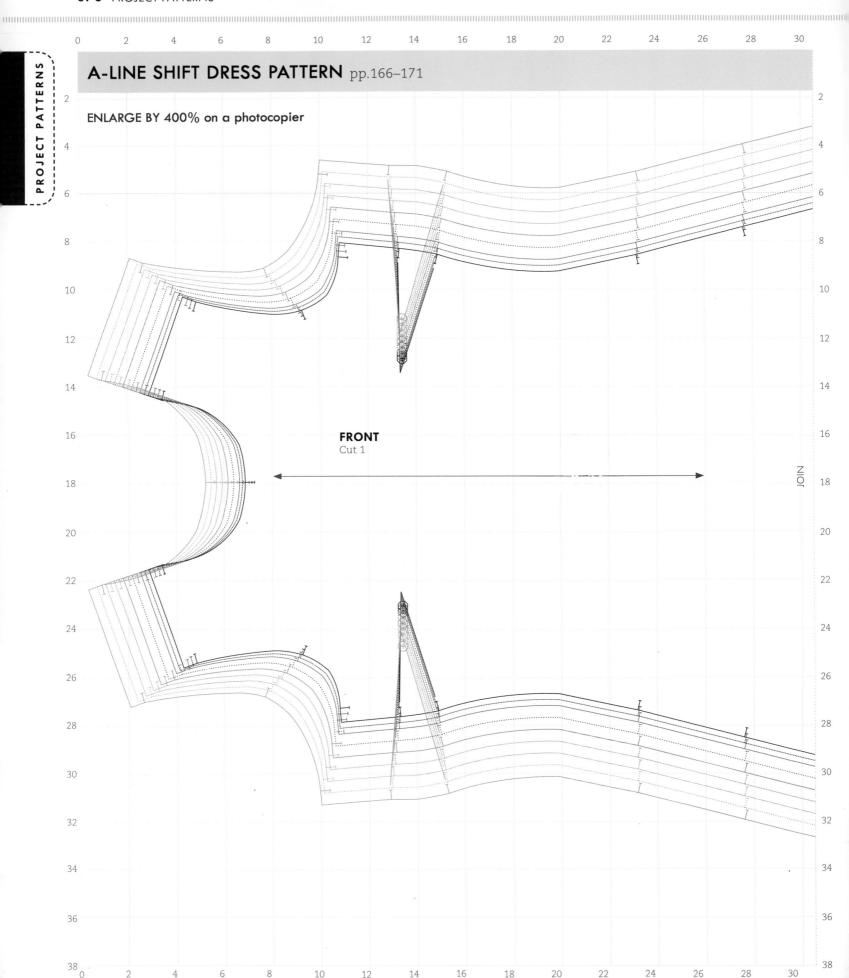

FRONT
Cut 1

JOIN

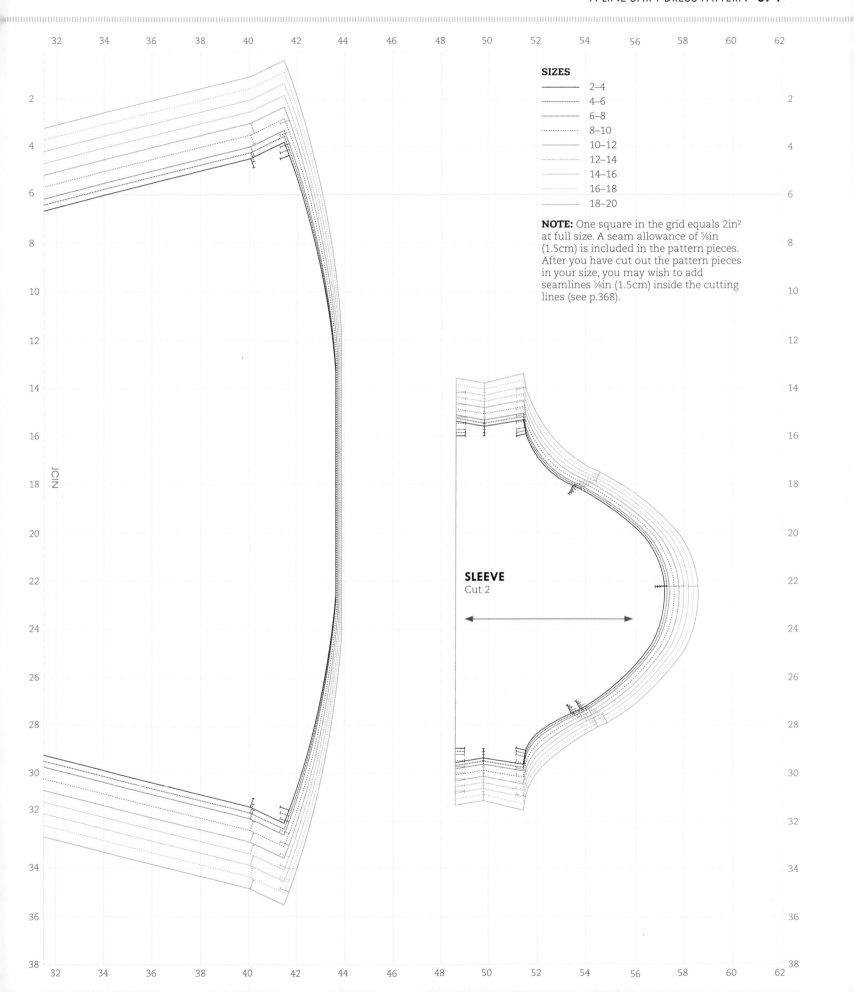

SIZES

———	2–4
········	4–6
————	6–8
········	8–10
———	10–12
———	12–14
———	14–16
········	16–18
———	18–20

NOTE: One square in the grid equals 2in² at full size. A seam allowance of ⅝in (1.5cm) is included in the pattern pieces. After you have cut out the pattern pieces in your size, you may wish to add seamlines ⅝in (1.5cm) inside the cutting lines (see p.368).

SLEEVE
Cut 2

JCIN

A-LINE SHIFT DRESS PATTERN pp.166–171

ENLARGE BY 400% on a photocopier

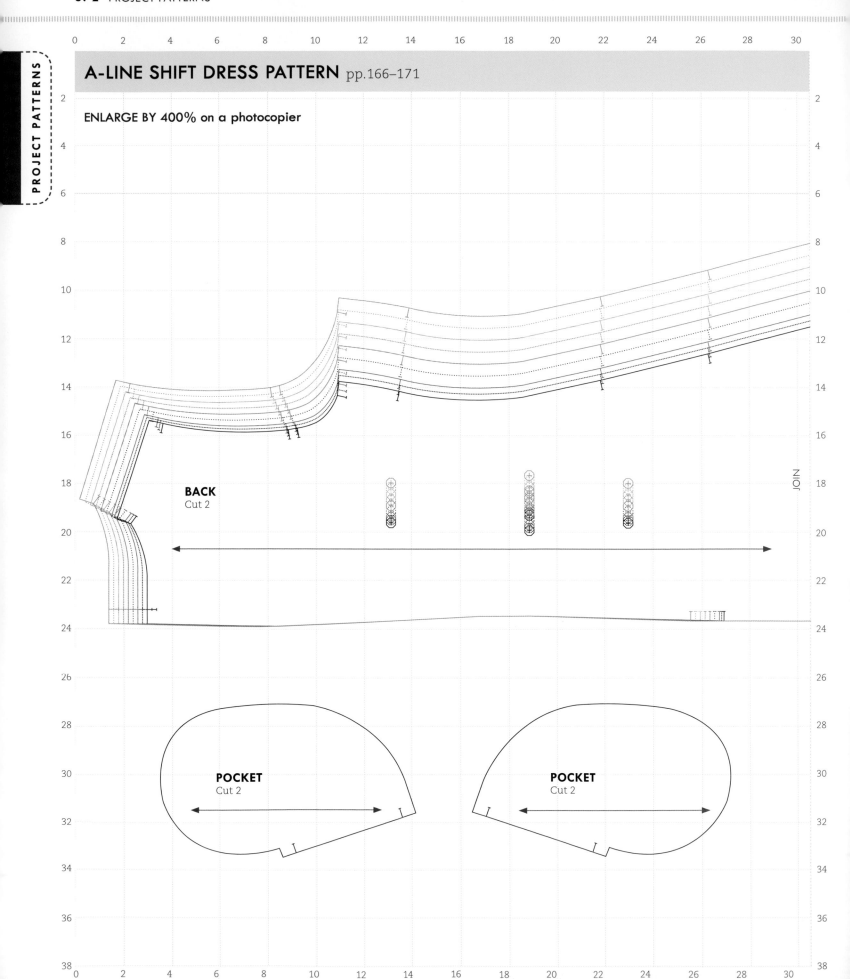

BACK
Cut 2

POCKET
Cut 2

POCKET
Cut 2

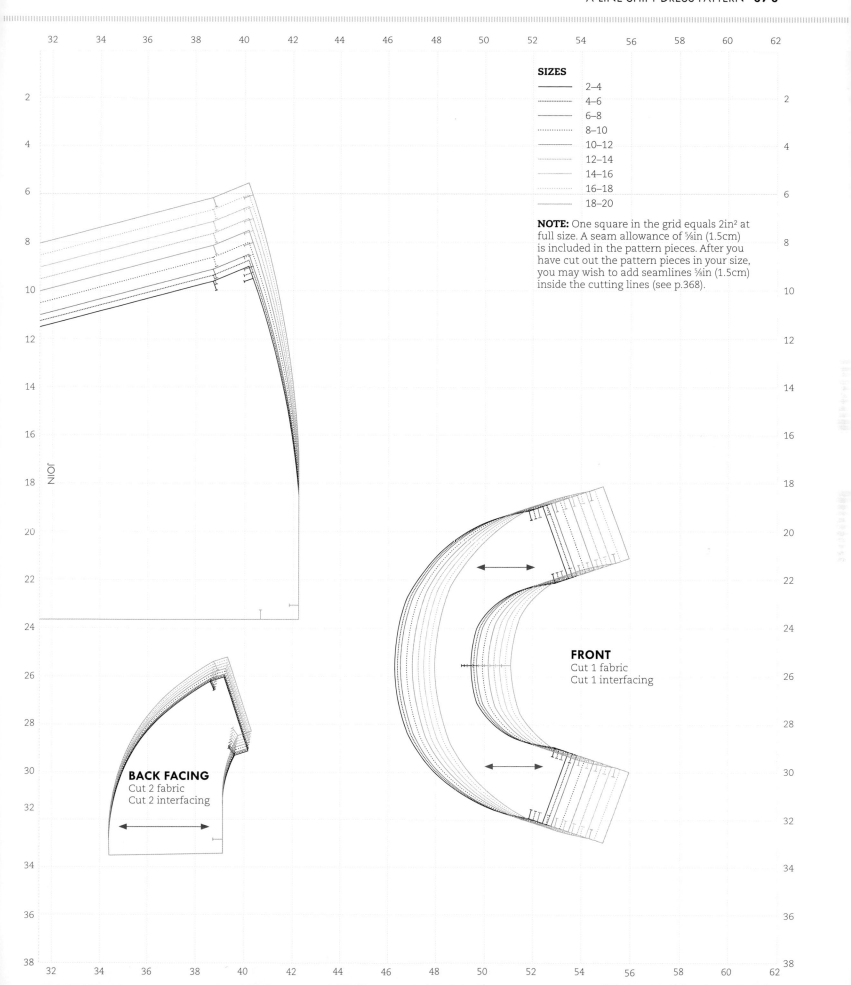

SIZES

——————	2–4
··············	4–6
——————	6–8
··············	8–10
——————	10–12
——————	12–14
··············	14–16
··············	16–18
——————	18–20

NOTE: One square in the grid equals 2in² at full size. A seam allowance of ⅝in (1.5cm) is included in the pattern pieces. After you have cut out the pattern pieces in your size, you may wish to add seamlines ⅝in (1.5cm) inside the cutting lines (see p.368).

JOIN

FRONT
Cut 1 fabric
Cut 1 interfacing

BACK FACING
Cut 2 fabric
Cut 2 interfacing

WRAP SKIRT PATTERN pp.194–199

ENLARGE BY 400% on a photocopier

FABRIC REQUIREMENTS

SIZE	45in (115cm) wide	60in (150cm) wide
2–4	110in (2.75m)	70in (1.75m)
4–6	110in (2.75m)	70in (1.75m)
6–8	110in (2.75m)	70in (1.75m)
8–10	110in (2.75m)	70in (1.75m)
10–12	110in (2.75m)	70in (1.75m)
12–14	110in (2.75m)	70in (1.75m)
14–16	110in (2.75m)	100in (2.50m)
16–18	110in (2.75m)	100in (2.50m)
18–20	110in (2.75m)	100in (2.50m)

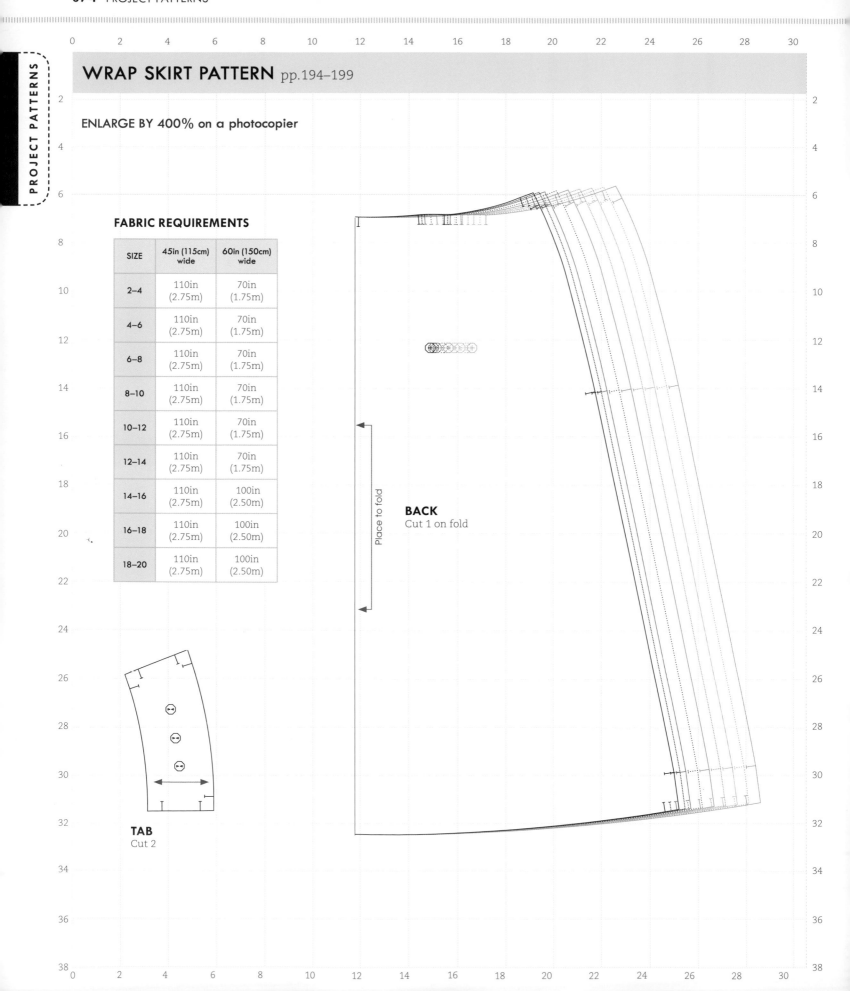

Place to fold

BACK
Cut 1 on fold

TAB
Cut 2

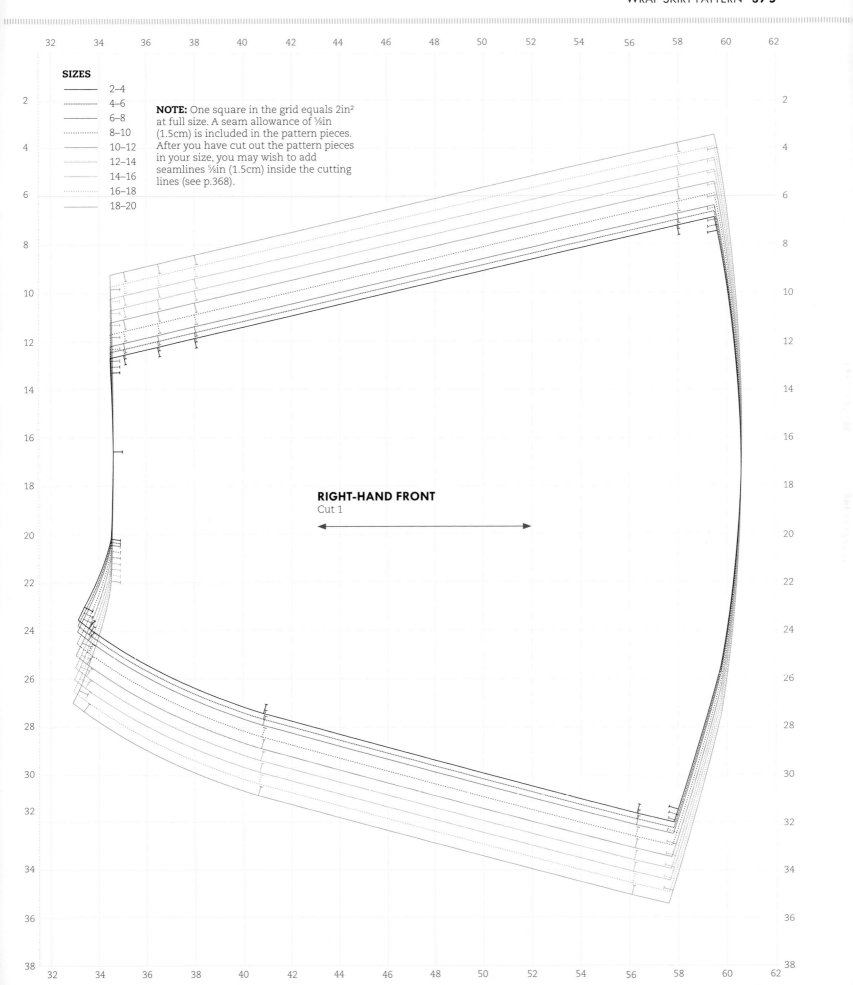

SIZES

——	2–4
····	4–6
····	6–8
····	8–10
——	10–12
——	12–14
——	14–16
····	16–18
——	18–20

NOTE: One square in the grid equals 2in² at full size. A seam allowance of ⅝in (1.5cm) is included in the pattern pieces. After you have cut out the pattern pieces in your size, you may wish to add seamlines ⅝in (1.5cm) inside the cutting lines (see p.368).

RIGHT-HAND FRONT
Cut 1

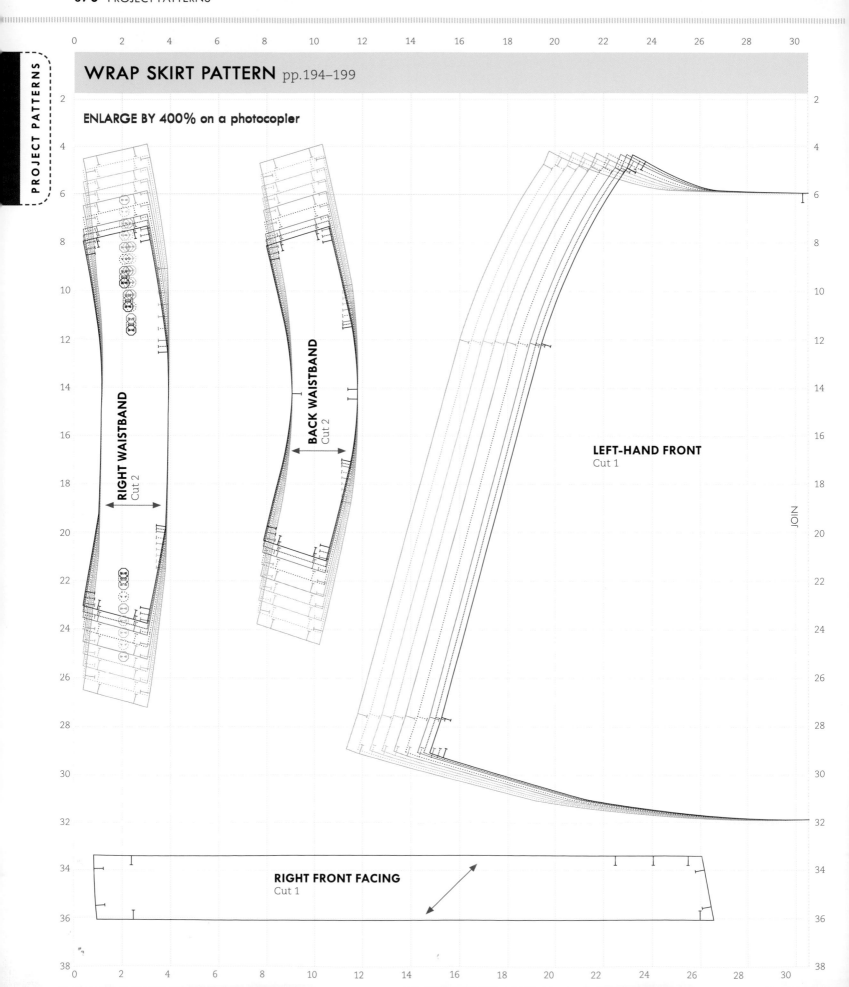

WRAP SKIRT PATTERN pp.194–199

ENLARGE BY 400% on a photocopier

RIGHT WAISTBAND
Cut 2

BACK WAISTBAND
Cut 2

LEFT-HAND FRONT
Cut 1

JOIN

RIGHT FRONT FACING
Cut 1

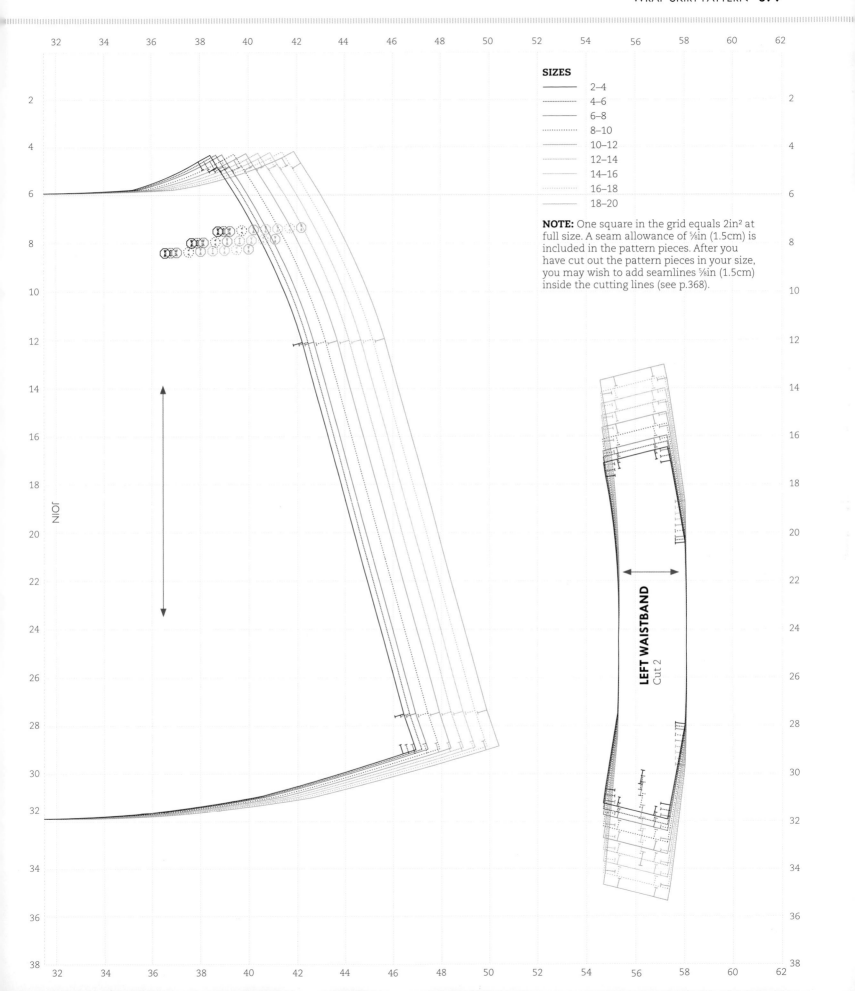

SIZES

——	2–4
········	4–6
–·–·–	6–8
··········	8–10
——	10–12
——	12–14
········	14–16
··········	16–18
——	18–20

NOTE: One square in the grid equals 2in² at full size. A seam allowance of ⅝in (1.5cm) is included in the pattern pieces. After you have cut out the pattern pieces in your size, you may wish to add seamlines ⅝in (1.5cm) inside the cutting lines (see p.368).

JOIN

LEFT WAISTBAND
Cut 2

UNISEX DRESSING GOWN PATTERN pp.216–221

ENLARGE BY 400% on a photocopier

JOIN PIECES 1 AND 2

FABRIC REQUIREMENTS FOR SHORT GOWN

SIZE	45in (115cm) wide	60in (150cm) wide
ALL SIZES MAIN FABRIC	130in (3.30m)	130in (3.30m)
ALL SIZES CONTRAST FABRIC	90in (2.30m)	90in (2.30m)

FABRIC REQUIREMENTS FOR LONG GOWN

SIZE	45in (115cm) wide	60in (150cm) wide
ALL SIZES MAIN FABRIC	130in (3.30m)	130in (3.30m)
ALL SIZES CONTRAST FABRIC	160in (4.00m)	102in (2.60m)

SHORT NECKBAND PATTERN PIECE 1
Cut 2

SHORT NECKBAND PATTERN PIECE 2
Cut 2

POCKET
Cut 2

JOIN PIECES 1 AND 2

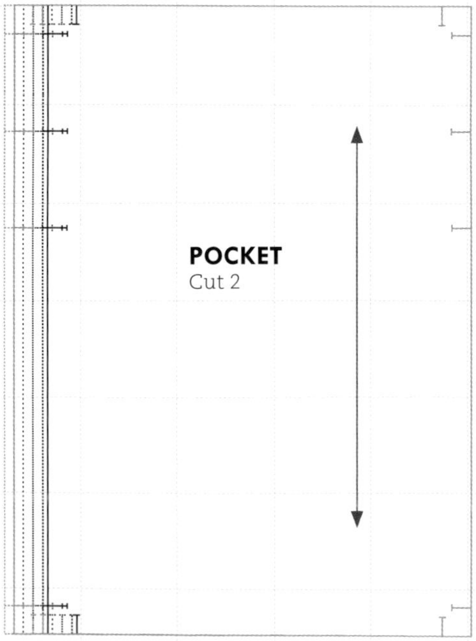

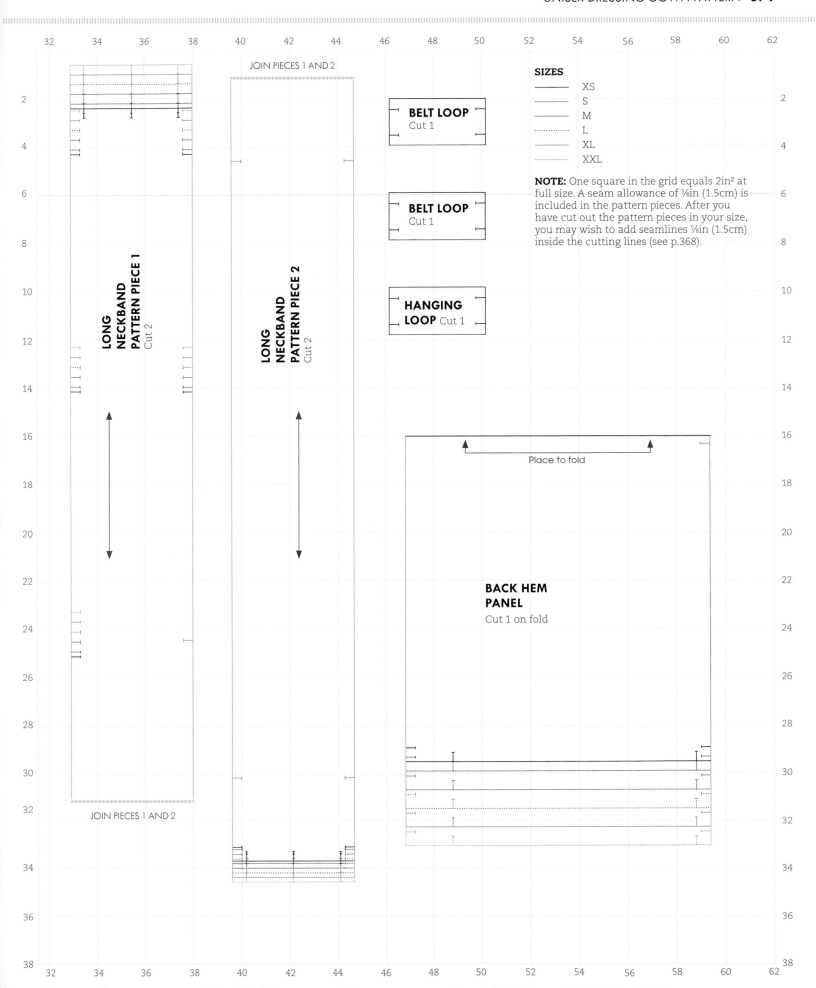

JOIN PIECES 1 AND 2

LONG NECKBAND PATTERN PIECE 1
Cut 2

LONG NECKBAND PATTERN PIECE 2
Cut 2

JOIN PIECES 1 AND 2

BELT LOOP
Cut 1

BELT LOOP
Cut 1

HANGING LOOP Cut 1

SIZES

——	XS
········	S
——	M
········	L
——	XL
········	XXL

NOTE: One square in the grid equals 2in² at full size. A seam allowance of ⅝in (1.5cm) is included in the pattern pieces. After you have cut out the pattern pieces in your size, you may wish to add seamlines ⅝in (1.5cm) inside the cutting lines (see p.368).

Place to fold

BACK HEM PANEL
Cut 1 on fold

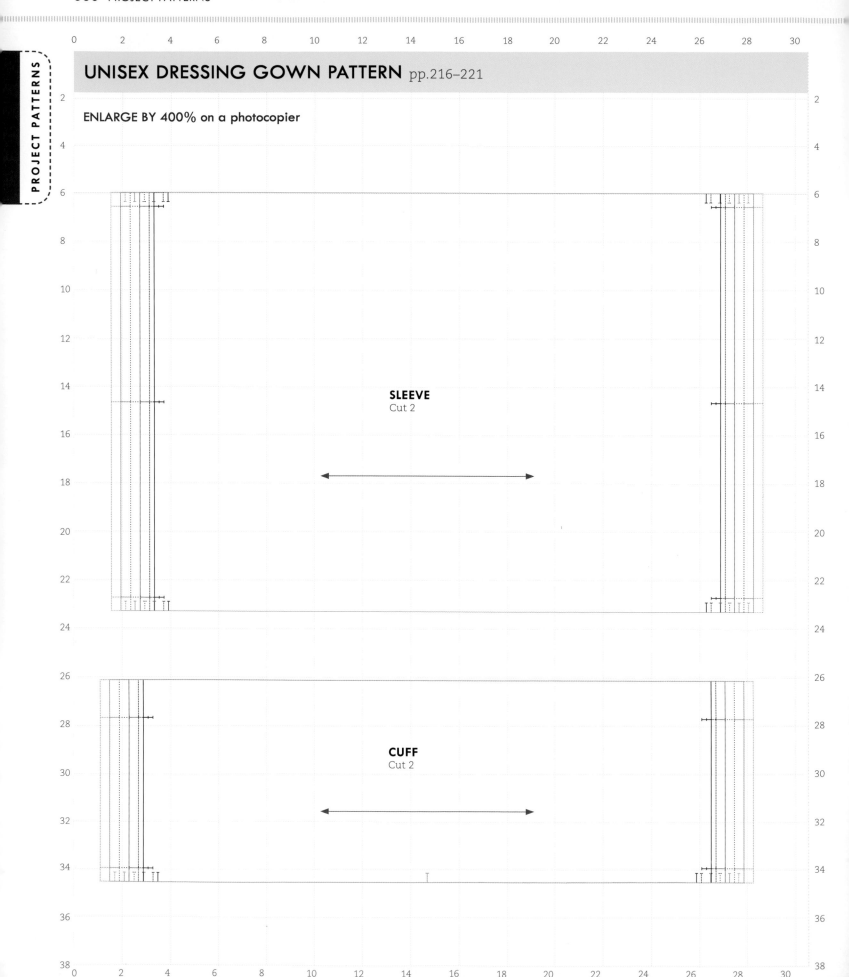

UNISEX DRESSING GOWN PATTERN pp.216–221

ENLARGE BY 400% on a photocopier

SLEEVE
Cut 2

CUFF
Cut 2

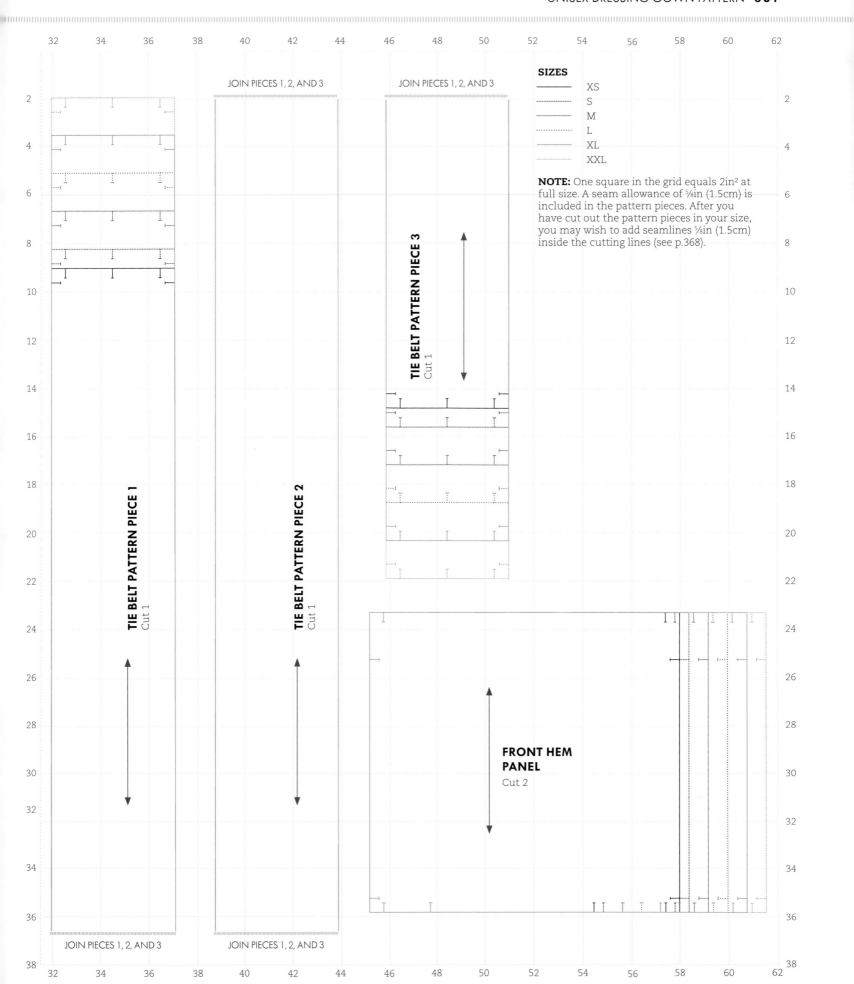

JOIN PIECES 1, 2, AND 3

JOIN PIECES 1, 2, AND 3

SIZES

——	XS
··········	S
------	M
··········	L
——	XL
··········	XXL

NOTE: One square in the grid equals 2in² at full size. A seam allowance of ⅝in (1.5cm) is included in the pattern pieces. After you have cut out the pattern pieces in your size, you may wish to add seamlines ⅝in (1.5cm) inside the cutting lines (see p.368).

TIE BELT PATTERN PIECE 3
Cut 1

TIE BELT PATTERN PIECE 1
Cut 1

TIE BELT PATTERN PIECE 2
Cut 1

FRONT HEM PANEL
Cut 2

JOIN PIECES 1, 2, AND 3

JOIN PIECES 1, 2, AND 3

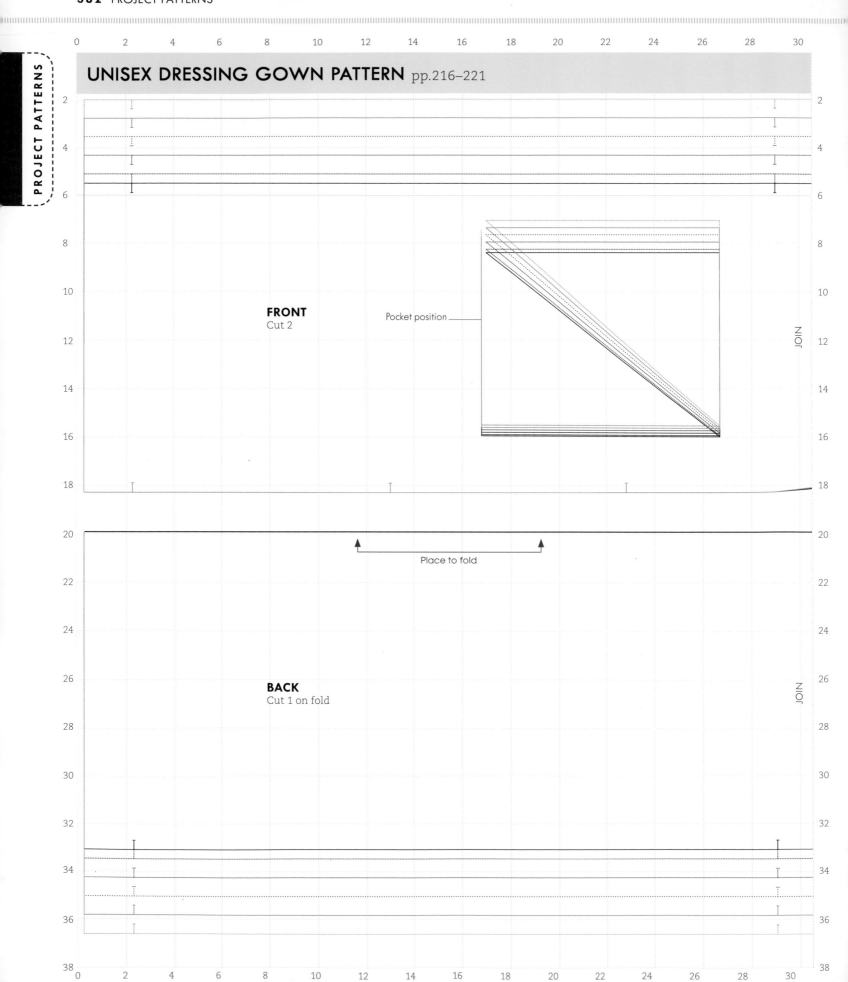

UNISEX DRESSING GOWN PATTERN pp.216–221

FRONT
Cut 2

Pocket position

BACK
Cut 1 on fold

Place to fold

JOIN

JOIN

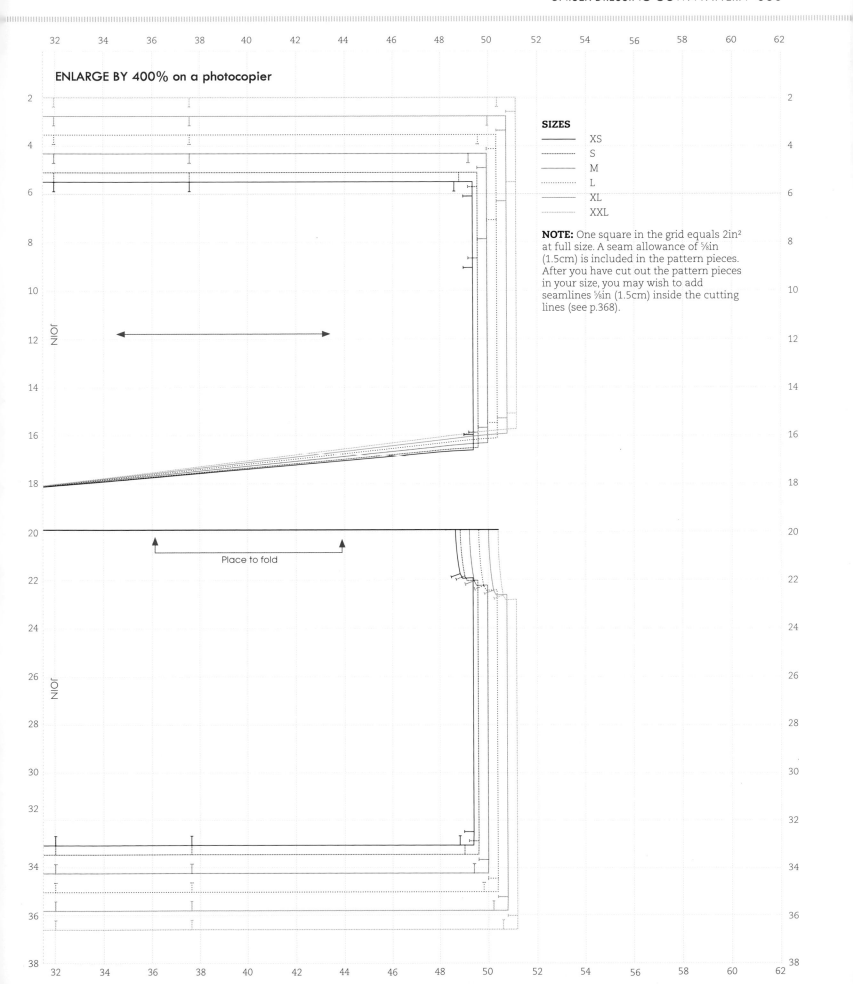

ENLARGE BY 400% on a photocopier

JOIN

JOIN

Place to fold

SIZES

———	XS
·········	S
·········	M
·········	L
———	XL
·········	XXL

NOTE: One square in the grid equals 2in² at full size. A seam allowance of ⅝in (1.5cm) is included in the pattern pieces. After you have cut out the pattern pieces in your size, you may wish to add seamlines ⅝in (1.5cm) inside the cutting lines (see p.368).

CHILD'S REVERSIBLE JACKET PATTERN pp.254–259

ENLARGE BY 400% on a photocopier

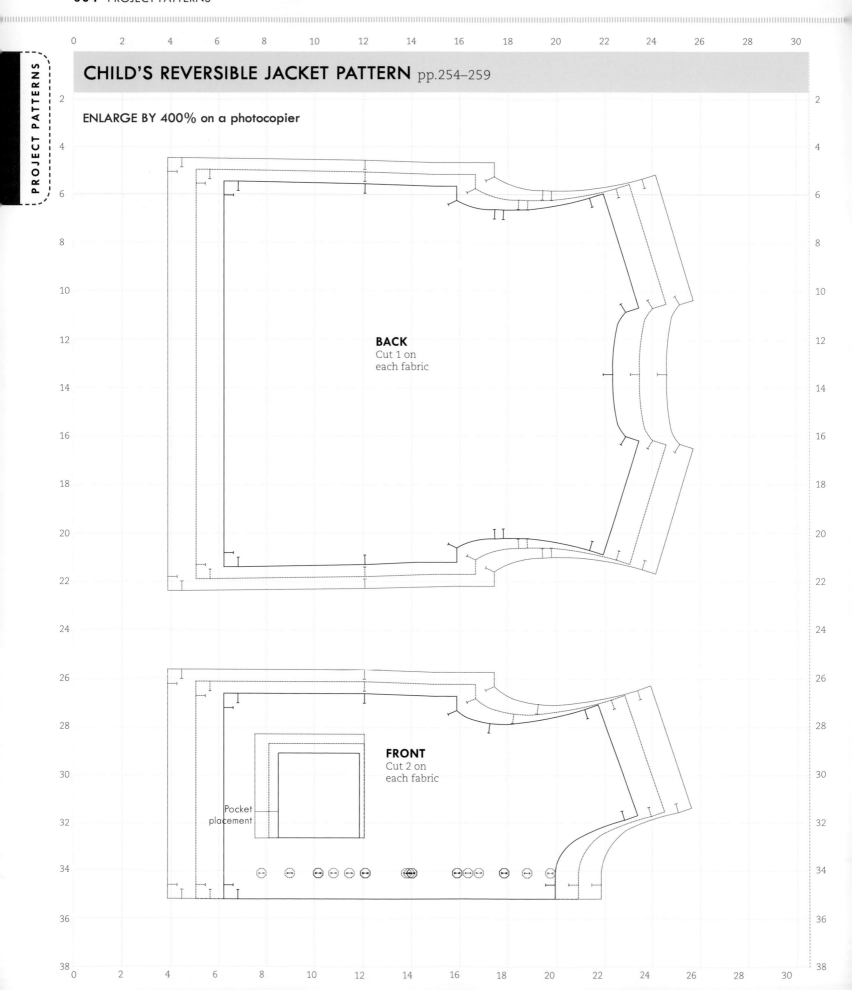

BACK
Cut 1 on
each fabric

FRONT
Cut 2 on
each fabric

Pocket
placement

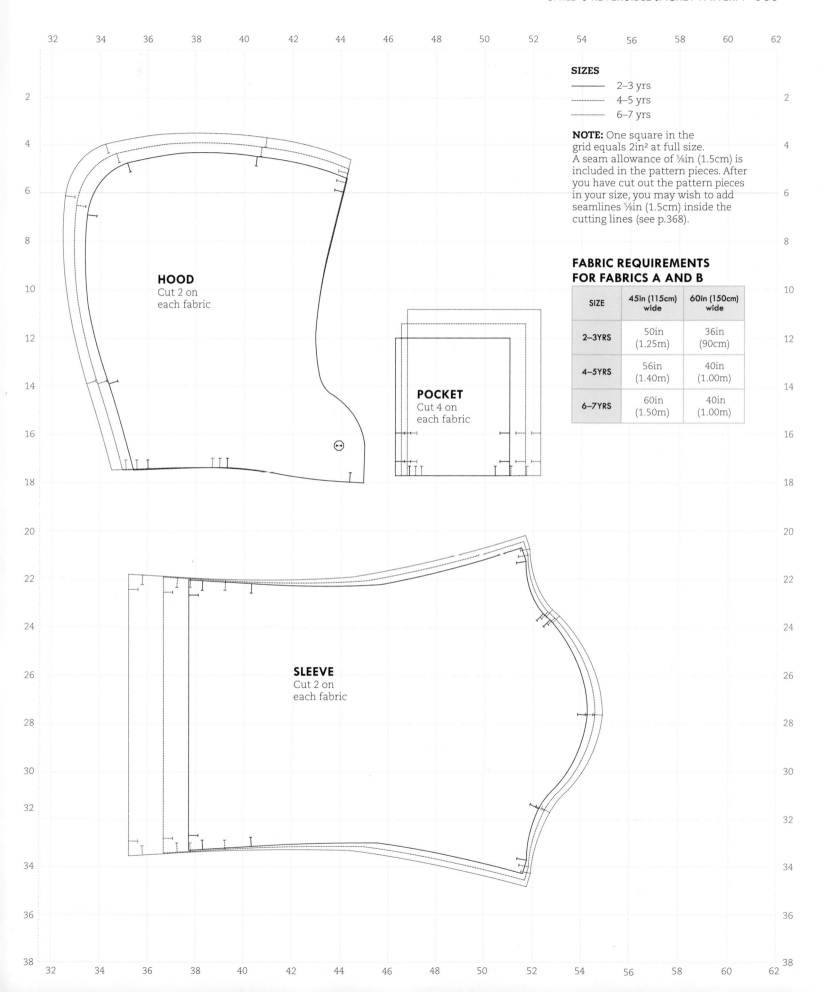

HOOD
Cut 2 on
each fabric

POCKET
Cut 4 on
each fabric

SLEEVE
Cut 2 on
each fabric

SIZES

— 2–3 yrs
····· 4–5 yrs
- - - 6–7 yrs

NOTE: One square in the
grid equals 2in² at full size.
A seam allowance of ⅝in (1.5cm) is
included in the pattern pieces. After
you have cut out the pattern pieces
in your size, you may wish to add
seamlines ⅝in (1.5cm) inside the
cutting lines (see p.368).

FABRIC REQUIREMENTS FOR FABRICS A AND B

SIZE	45in (115cm) wide	60in (150cm) wide
2–3YRS	50in (1.25m)	36in (90cm)
4–5YRS	56in (1.40m)	40in (1.00m)
6–7YRS	60in (1.50m)	40in (1.00m)

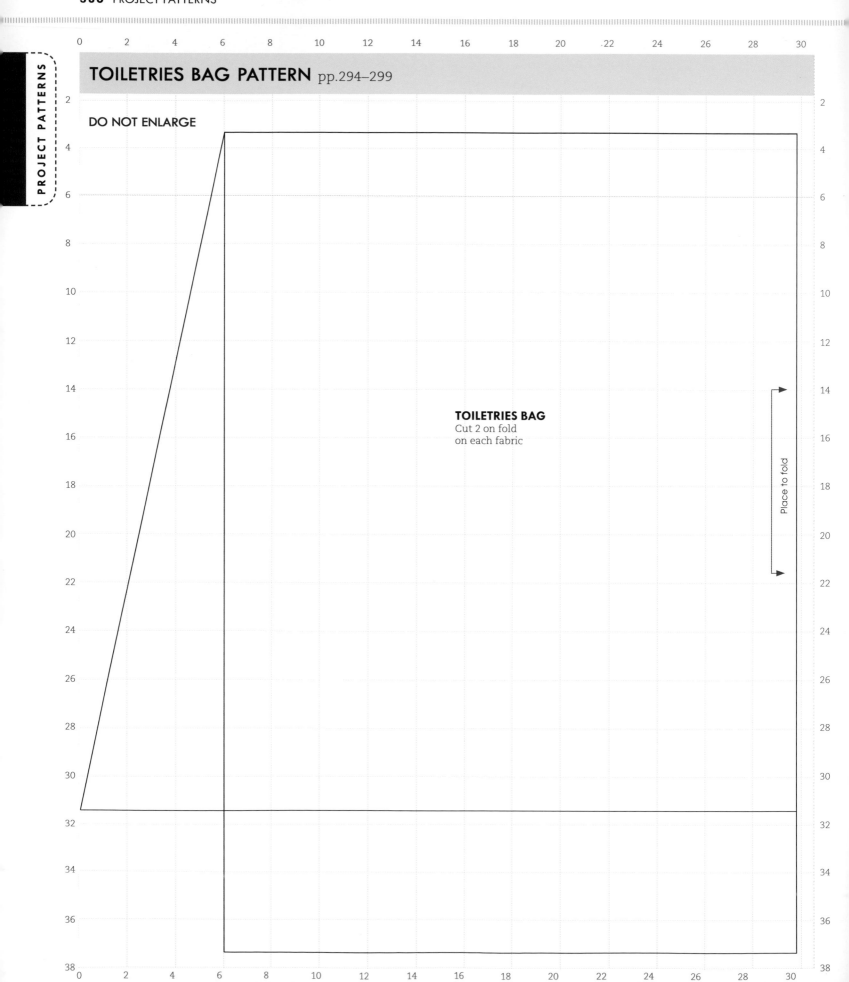

TOILETRIES BAG PATTERN pp.294–299

DO NOT ENLARGE

TOILETRIES BAG
Cut 2 on fold
on each fabric

Place to fold

OVEN MITT PATTERN pp.346–349

ENLARGE BY 200% on a photocopier

NOTE: One square in the grid equals 2in² at full size. A seam allowance of ⅝in (1.5cm) is included in the pattern pieces. After you have cut out the pattern pieces in your size, you may wish to add seamlines ⅝in (1.5cm) inside the cutting lines (see p.368).

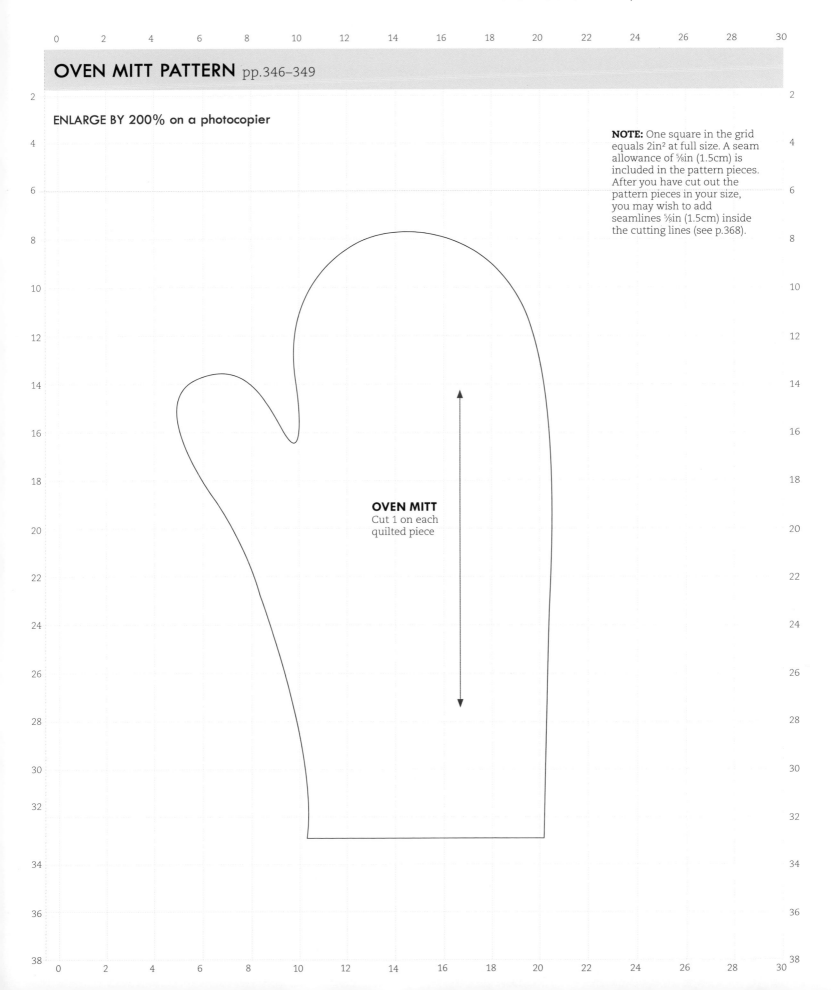

OVEN MITT
Cut 1 on each
quilted piece

GLOSSARY

Acetate Man-made fabric widely used for linings.

Acrylic Man-made fabric resembling wool.

Alpaca Canvas made from wool and alpaca. This fabric can be used as a non-fusible interfacing.

Appliqué One piece of fabric being stitched to another in a decorative manner.

Armhole Opening in a garment for the sleeve and arm.

Arrowhead Small, triangular set of straight stitches worked either by hand or by machine across a seam to add strength at a point of possible strain (for example, at the top of a split).

Back stitch A strong hand stitch with a double stitch on the wrong side, used for outlining and seaming.

Balanced dart A dart with extra fabric added on the wrong side to distribute the fabric evenly on both sides of the dart stitching line.

Banding Method of finishing a raw edge by applying a wide strip of fabric over it. The strip can also be used to add length to a garment.

Bar baste A hand-worked bar of buttonhole stitches used to loosely attach two layers of fabric.

Basting stitch A temporary running stitch used to hold pieces of fabric together or for transferring pattern markings to fabric.

Belt loop Loop made from a strip of fabric, which is used to support a belt at the waist edge of a garment.

Bias 45-degree line on fabric that falls between the lengthwise and the crosswise grain. Fabric cut on the bias drapes well. *See also* **Grain.**

Bias binding Narrow strips of fabric cut on the bias. Used to give a neat finish to hems and seam allowances.

Bias tape maker Tool for evenly folding the edges of a fabric strip, which can then be pressed to make bias binding.

Binding Method of finishing a raw edge by wrapping it in a strip of bias-cut fabric.

Blanket stitch Hand stitch worked along the raw or finished edge of fabric to neaten, and for decorative purposes.

Blind hem stitch Tiny hand stitch used to attach one piece of fabric to another, mainly to secure hems. Also a machine stitch consisting of two or three straight stitches and one wide zigzag stitch.

Blind tuck A tuck that is stitched so that it touches the adjacent tuck without machine stitches showing. *See also* **Tuck.**

Bobbin Round holder beneath the needle plate of a sewing machine on which the thread is wound.

Bodice Upper body section of a garment.

Bodkin Blunt-headed needle used for threading elastic or cord through a casing or heading.

Boning Narrow nylon, plastic, or metal strip, available in various widths, that is used for stiffening and shaping close-fitting garments, such as bodices.

Box pleat Pleat formed on the wrong side of the fabric, and fuller than a knife pleat. *See also* **Pleat.**

Buttonhole Opening through which a button is inserted to form a fastening. Buttonholes are usually machine-sewn but may also be worked by hand or piped for reinforcement or decorative effect.

Buttonhole cutter Very sharp, small chisel that cuts cleanly through a machine-stitched buttonhole.

Buttonhole stitch Hand stitch that wraps over the raw edges of a buttonhole to neaten and strengthen them. Machine-stitched buttonholes are worked with a close zigzag stitch.

Button shank Stem of a button that allows room for the buttonhole to fit under the button when joined.

Calico Inexpensive, cotton floral-print fabric.

Cashmere The most luxurious of all wools.

Casing Tunnel of fabric created by parallel rows of stitches, through which elastic or a drawstring cord is threaded. Often used at a waist edge. Sometimes extra fabric is required to make a casing; this can be applied to the inside or outside of the garment.

Catch stitch *See also* **Slip hem stitch.**

Challis Fine woollen fabric with uneven surface texture.

Chambray A light cotton fabric with a colored warp thread.

Chiffon Strong, fine, transparent silk fabric.

Chintz Floral print or plain cotton fabric with a glazed finish.

Clapper Wooden aid that is used to pound creases into heavy fabric after steaming.

Contour dart Also known as double-pointed dart, this is used to give shape at the waist of a garment. It is like two darts joined together. *See also* **Dart.**

Corded gathers Gathers that are pulled up over a narrow cord or thick thread, used for thicker fabrics. *See also* **Gathers.**

Corded seam A seam with piping in it, often used to join together two different fabrics.

Corded shirring A method of shirring where a piece of piping cord is sewn into a fold in the fabric. *See also* **Shirring.**

Corded tuck *See* **Piped tuck.**

Corduroy A soft pile fabric with distinctive stripes.

Cotton Soft, durable, and inexpensive fabric widely used in dressmaking. Made from the fibrous hairs covering the seed pods of the cotton plant.

Crease Line formed in fabric by pressing a fold.

Crepe Soft fabric made from twisted yarn.

Crepe de chine Medium-weight fabric with uneven surface, often made from silk.

Crinkle cotton Cotton fabric with creases added by a heat process.

Cross stitch A temporary hand stitch used to hold pleats in place and to secure linings. It can also be used for decoration.

Cross tuck Tuck that crosses over another by being sewn in opposite directions. *See also* **Tuck.**

Curtain tape Wide fabric tape containing loops that is stitched to the top of a curtain. Hooks are inserted into the loops and then attached to a rail. The curtain tape is drawn up to make pleats.

Curtain weight Weight inserted into the bottom hem of a curtain to hold the curtain in place and make it hang properly.

Cutting line Solid line on a pattern piece used as a guide for cutting out fabric.

Cutting mat Self-healing mat used in conjunction with a rotary cutter to protect the blade and the cutting surface.

Damask Woven cotton fabric with a floral pattern.

Darning Mending holes or worn areas in a knitted garment by weaving threads in rows along the grain of the fabric.

Dart Tapered sewn fold of fabric used on a garment to give it shape so that it can fit around the contours of the body. There are different types of dart, but all are used mainly on women's clothing.

Darted tuck A tuck that can be used to give fullness of fabric at the bust or hip. *See also* **Tuck.**

Denim Hard-wearing twill weave fabric with colored warp and white weft.

Double-pointed dart *See* **Contour dart.**

Double ruffle Decorative trim made from two plain ruffles where one side is longer than the other. Also a ruffle made from doubled fabric.

Drape The way a fabric falls into graceful folds; drape varies with each fabric.

Dressmaker's carbon paper Used along with a tracing wheel to transfer pattern markings to fabric. Available in a variety of colors.

Drill Hard-wearing twill or plain-weave fabric with the same color warp and weft.

Drop The length of fabric required to make a curtain, the "drop" being the measurement from top to bottom of the window.

Duchess satin Heavy, expensive satin fabric.

Ease Distributing fullness in fabric when joining two seams together of slightly different lengths, for example a sleeve to an armhole.

Ease stitch Long machine stitch, used to ease in fullness where the distance between notches is slightly greater on one seam edge than on the other.

Embroidery machine A machine that is capable of embellishing fabric with embroidery designs.

Enclosed edge Raw fabric edge that is concealed within a seam or binding.

Eyelet fabric A fine plain-weave cotton embroidered to make small decorative holes.

Fabric loop Button loop made from a strip of bias binding. It is used with a round ball-type button.

Facing Layer of fabric placed on the inside of a garment and used to finish off raw edges of an armhole or neck of a garment. Usually a separate piece of fabric, the facing can sometimes be an extension of the garment itself.

Felt A natural wool fabric can "felt" when it is stimulated by friction and lubricated by moisture and the fibers bond together to form a cloth. Felting can also be done in a washing machine on a hot cycle.

Filament fibers Very fine synthetic thread, made using plant materials and minerals.

Flannel Wool or cotton fabric with a lightly brushed surface.

Flat fell seam This seam is made on the right side of a garment and is very strong. It uses two lines of stitches and conceals all the raw edges, reducing fraying.

Flat fell stitch A strong, secure stitch used to hold two layers together permanently. Often used to secure linings and bias bindings.

French dart Curved dart used on the front of a garment. *See also* **Dart**.

French seam A seam traditionally used on sheer and silk fabrics. It is sewn twice, first on the right side of the work and then on the wrong side, enclosing the first seam. *See also* **Mock French seam**.

Frog fastener Decorative fastener made from cord arranged into four overlapping loops sewn at the center. Used with a Chinese ball button.

Fusible tape Straight grain tape used to stabilize edges and also replace stay stitches. The heat of the iron fuses it into position.

Gabardine Hard-wearing fabric with a distinctive weave.

Galloon lace Decorative lace trim shaped on both sides, used to edge a hem.

Gathers Bunches of fabric created by sewing two parallel rows of loose stitches, then pulling the threads up so that the fabric gathers and reduces in size to fit the required space.

Georgette Soft, filmy silk fabric.

Gingham Two-color, plaid cotton fabric.

Goblet pleat Decorative curtain heading in which the fabric is stitched into narrow tubes that are then stuffed with batting. *See also* **Pleat**.

Godet A section that is inserted into a garment to give fullness at the hem edge. It is usually triangular in shape but it can also be a semicircle. *See also* **Pleat**.

Grain Lengthwise and crosswise direction of threads in a fabric. Fabric grain affects how a fabric hangs and drapes.

Grosgrain Synthetic, ribbed fabric often used to make ribbons.

Gusset Small piece of fabric shaped to fit into a slash or seam for added ease of movement.

Habutai Smooth, fine silk fabric originally from Japan.

Hem The edge of a piece of fabric neatened and stitched to prevent unraveling. There are several methods of doing this, both by hand and by machine.

Hem allowance Amount of fabric allowed for turning under to make the hem.

Hemline Crease or foldline along which a hem is marked.

Hemming tape Fusible tape with adhesive on both sides. Iron in place to fuse and secure hems that are difficult to hand sew.

Herringbone stitch Hand stitch used to secure hems and interlinings. Worked from left to right.

Herringbone weave A zigzag weave where the weft yarn goes under and over warp yarns in a staggered pattern.

Hong Kong finish A method of neatening raw edges particularly on wool and linen. Bias-cut strips are wrapped around the raw edge.

Hook and eye fastening Two-part metal fastening used to fasten overlapping edges of fabric where a neat join is required. Available in a wide variety of styles.

Horsehair braid A braid that is woven from strands of nylon thread and sewn into the hemlines of dressy garments to stiffen the lower edge.

Interfacing A fabric placed between garment and facing to give structure and support. Available in different thicknesses, interfacing can be fusible (bonds to the fabric by applying heat) or non-fusible (needs to be sewn to the fabric).

Interlining Layer of fabric attached to the main fabric prior to construction, to cover the inside of an entire garment to provide extra warmth or bulk. The two layers are then treated as one. Often used in jackets and coats.

Jacquard loom Device used in weaving to control individual yarns. This allows looms to produce intricately patterned fabric such as tapestry, brocade, and damask.

Jersey Cotton or wool yarn that has been knitted to give stretch.

Jetted pocket A type of pocket found on tailored jackets and coats. It consists of strips of fabric that form the edges of the pocket (welts) and the lining

Keyhole buttonhole stitch A machine buttonhole stitch characterized by having one square end while the other end is shaped like a loop to accommodate the button's shank without distorting the fabric. Often used on jackets.

Kick pleat Inverted pleat extending upward from the hemline of a narrow skirt to allow freedom when walking. *See also* **Pleat**.

Knife pleat Pleat formed on the right side of the fabric where all the pleats face the same direction. *See also* **Pleat**.

Lapel The turned-back front edge of a jacket or blouse to which the collar is attached.

Lapped seam Used on fabrics that do not fray, such as suede and leather, the seam allowance of one edge is placed over the edge to be joined, then top-stitched close to the overlapping edge. Also called an overlaid seam.

Linen Natural fiber derived from the stem of the flax plant, linen fabric is available in a variety of qualities and weights.

Lining Underlying fabric layer used to give a neat finish to an item, as well as concealing the stitches and seams of a garment.

Locking stitch A machine stitch where the upper and lower threads in the machine "lock" together at the start or end of a row of stitches.

Madras Brightly colored, unevenly checkered plaid cotton fabric from India.

Matka A silk suiting fabric with uneven yarn.

Miter The diagonal line made where two edges of a piece of fabric meet at a corner, produced by folding. *See also* **Mitered corner.**

Mitered corner Diagonal seam formed when fabric is joined at a corner. After sewing, excess fabric is cut away.

Mock casing Where there is an effect of a casing, but in fact elastic is attached to the waist, or is used only at the back in a partial casing.

Mock French seam Similar to a French seam, but best used on cotton or firmer fine fabrics. It is constructed on the wrong side of the work. *See also* **French seam.**

Mohair Fluffy wool yarn cloth used for sweaters, jackets, and soft furnishings.

Multi-size pattern Paper pattern printed with cutting lines for a range of sizes on each pattern piece.

Muslin A test or dry run of a paper pattern using muslin fabric. The muslin helps you analyze the fit of the garment.

Muslin fabric Fine, plain open-weave cotton.

Nap The raised pile on a fabric made during the weaving process, or a print pointing one way. When cutting out pattern pieces, make sure that the nap runs in the same direction.

Needle threader Gadget that pulls thread through the eye of a needle. Useful for needles with small eyes.

Notch V-shaped marking on a pattern piece used for aligning one piece with another. Also V-shaped cut taken to reduce seam bulk.

Notions Term that covers all the bits and pieces needed to complete a pattern, such as fasteners, elastics, ribbons, and trims. Notions needed for a project are normally listed on the pattern envelope.

Nylon Hard-wearing, man-made fabric.

Organza Thin, sheer fabric made from silk or polyester.

Overedge stitch Machine stitch worked over the edge of a seam allowance and used for neatening the edges of fabric.

Overlaid seam *See* **Lapped seam.**

Over-stitch *See* **Buttonhole stitch.**

Pattern markings Symbols printed on a paper pattern to indicate the fabric grain, foldline, and construction details, such as darts, notches, and tucks. These should be transferred to the fabric using tailor's chalk or tailor's tacks.

Pencil pleat The most common curtain heading where the fabric forms a row of parallel vertical pleats. *See also* **Pleat.**

Petersham Stiff, ridged tape that is 1in (2.5cm) wide and curved. It can be used as an alternative finish to facing.

Pile Raised loops on the surface of a fabric, for example velvet.

Pill A small, fuzzy ball formed from tangled fibers which is formed on the surface of a fabric, making it look old and worn; it is often caused by friction. To remove fabric pills, stretch the fabric over a curved surface and carefully cut or shave off the pills.

Pinch pleat Decorative curtain heading in which groups of two or three pleats are sewn together. *See also* **Pleat.**

Pinking A method of neatening raw edges of fray-resistant fabric using pinking shears. This will leave a zigzag edge.

Pinking shears Cutting tool with serrated blades, used to trim raw edges of fray-resistant fabrics to neaten seam edges.

Pin tuck Narrow, regularly spaced fold or gather. *See also* **Tuck.**

Piped tuck Substantial fold of fabric that has a cord running through it. *See also* **Tuck.**

Piping Trim made from bias-cut strips of fabric, usually containing a cord. Used to edge garments or soft furnishings.

Pivoting Technique used to sew a corner. The machine is stopped at the corner with the needle in the fabric, then the foot is raised, the fabric turned following the direction of the corner, and the foot lowered for sewing to continue.

Placket An opening in a garment that provides support for fasteners, such as buttons, snaps, or zippers.

Plain weave The simplest of all the weaves; the weft yarn passes under one warp yarn, then over another one.

Pleat An even fold or series of folds in fabric, often partially sewn down. Commonly found in skirts to shape the waistline, but also in soft furnishings for decoration.

Pocket flap A piece of fabric that folds down to cover the opening of a pocket.

Polyester Man-made fiber that does not crease.

Presser foot The part of a sewing machine that is lowered on to the fabric to hold it in place over the needle plate while sewing. There are different feet available.

Pressing cloth Muslin or organza cloth placed over fabric to prevent marking or scorching when pressing.

Prick stitch Small spaced hand stitch with large spaces between each stitch. Often used to highlight the edge of a completed garment.

Raw edge Cut edge of fabric that requires finishing, for example using zigzag stitch, to prevent fraying.

Rayon Also known as viscose, rayon is often blended with other fibers in fabrics.

Reverse stitch Machine stitch that simply sews back over a row of stitches to secure the threads.

Right side The outer side of a fabric, or the visible part of a garment.

Rotary cutter Tool for cutting fabric neatly and easily, and useful for cutting multiple straight edges. It has different sizes of retractable blade.

Round-end buttonhole stitch Machine stitch characterized by one end of the buttonhole being square and the other being round, to allow for the button shank.

Ruching Several rows of stitches worked to form a gathered area.

Ruffle Decorative gathered trim made from one or two layers of fabric.

Running stitch A simple, evenly spaced straight stitch separated by equal-sized spaces, used for seaming and gathering.

Satin A fabric with a satin weave.

Satin weave A weave with a sheen, where the weft goes under four warp yarns, then over one.

Seam Sewn line where two edges of fabric are joined together.

Seam allowance The amount of fabric allowed for on a pattern where sections are to be joined together by a seam; usually this is ⅝in (1.5cm).

Seam edge The cut edge of a seam allowance.

Seamline Line on paper pattern designated for sewing a seam; usually ⅝in (1.5cm) from the seam edge.

Seam ripper A small, hooked tool used for undoing seams and unpicking stitches.

Seam roll Tubular pressing aid for pressing seams open on fabrics that mark.

Seersucker Woven cotton fabric with a bubbly appearance due to stripes of puckers.

Self-bound seam Similar to the flat fell seam, except that it is sewn on the wrong side of the fabric.

Self-healing mat *See* **Cutting mat.**

Selvage Finished edge on a woven fabric. This runs parallel to the warp (lengthwise) threads.

Serger Machine used for quick sewing, trimming, and edging of fabric in a single action; it gives a professional finish to a garment. There are a variety of accessories that can be attached to a serger, which enable it to perform a greater range of functions.

Serger stitch A machine stitch that neatens edges and prevents fraying. It can be used on all types of fabric.

Sewing gauge Measuring tool with adjustable slider for checking small measurements, such as hem depths and seam allowances.

Shantung Fabric with a distinctive weft yarn with many nubbly bits; made from 100 percent silk.

Sharps General purpose needle used for hand sewing.

Shell tuck Decorative fold of fabric sewn in place with a scalloped edge. *See also* **Tuck.**

Shirring Multiple rows of gathers sewn by machine. Often worked with shirring elastic in the bobbin to allow for stretch.

Shirting Closely woven, fine cotton fabric with colored warp and weft yarns.

Silk Threads spun by the silkworm and used to create cool, luxurious fabrics.

Slip hem stitch Similar to herringbone stitch but is worked from right to left. Used mainly for hems.

Slotted seam A decorative seam where the edges of the seam open to reveal an under layer, which can be in a contrasting fabric.

Smocking Traditional way of gathering fabric using multiple rows of parallel gathers, sewn by hand, to produce fine tubes in the fabric.

Smocking dots Heat-transfer dots that can be transferred to fabric to be used as a guide for hand gathers.

Snaps Also known as press studs, these fasteners are used as a lightweight hidden fastener.

Snips Spring-loaded cutting tool used for cutting off thread ends.

Spandex Lightweight, soft, stretchable fabric.

Staple fibers These include both natural and manufactured fibers such as cotton, wool, flax, and polyester. They are short in length, and relatively narrow in thickness.

Stay stitch Straight machine stitch worked just inside a seam allowance to strengthen it and prevent it from stretching or breaking.

Stay tape Tape sewn to a specific area of an item for reinforcement, for example to help strengthen a seam.

Stem stitch An embroidery stitch frequently used to outline other stitched decoration.

Stitch in the ditch A line of straight stitches sewn on the right side of the work, in the ditch created by a seam. Used to secure waistbands and facings.

Stitch ripper *See* Seam ripper.

Straight stitch Plain stitch, used for most applications. The length of the stitch can be changed to suit the fabric.

Stretch stitch Machine stitch used for stretch knits and to help control difficult fabrics. It is worked with two stitches forward and one backward so that each stitch is worked three times.

Taffeta Smooth plain-weave fabric with a crisp appearance.

Tailor's buttonhole A buttonhole with one square end and one keyhole-shaped end, used on jackets and coats.

Tailor's chalk Square or triangular-shaped piece of chalk used to mark fabric. Available in a variety of colors, tailor's chalk can be removed easily by brushing.

Tailor's ham A ham-shaped pressing cushion that is used to press shaped areas of garments.

Tailor's tacks Loose thread markings used to transfer symbols from a pattern to fabric.

Tape measure Flexible form of ruler made from plastic or fabric.

Tartan Fabric made using a twill weave from worsted yarns. Traditionally used for kilts.

Terry cloth Cotton fabric with loops on the surface.

Thimble Metal or plastic cap that fits over the top of a finger to protect it when hand sewing.

Top-stitch Straight stitches worked on the right side of an item, close to the finished edge, for decorative effect. Sometimes sewn in a contrasting color.

Top-stitched seam A seam finished with a row of top-stitches for decorative effect. This seam is often used on crafts and soft furnishings as well as garments.

Trace basting A method of marking fold and placement lines on fabric. Loose stitches are sewn along the lines on the pattern to the fabric beneath, then the thread loops are cut and the pattern removed.

Tracing wheel Tool used along with dressmaker's carbon paper to transfer pattern markings on to fabric.

Tuck Fold or pleat in fabric that is sewn in place, normally on the straight grain of the fabric. Often used to provide a decorative addition to a garment.

Tweed Traditional tweed is a rough fabric with a distinctive warp and weft. New tweed is a mix of chunky wool yarns, often in bright colors.

Twill weave Diagonal patterned weave fabric.

Underlay Strip of fabric placed under the main fabric to strengthen it, for example under a pleat or buttonhole.

Understitch Straight stitch through facing and seam allowances that is invisible from the right side; this helps the facing to lie flat.

Velcro™ Two-part fabric fastening consisting of two layers, a "hook" side and a "loop" side; when pressed together the two pieces stick together.

Velvet Luxurious pile-weave fabric.

Venetian Luxurious wool with a satin weave.

Waistband Band of fabric attached to the waist edge of a garment to provide a neat finish.

Warp Lengthwise threads or yarns of a woven fabric.

Warp knit Made on a knitting machine, this knit is formed in a vertical and diagonal direction.

Weft Threads or yarns that cross the warp of a woven fabric.

Weft knit Made in the same way as hand knitting, this uses one yarn that runs horizontally.

Welt Strip of fabric used to make the edges of a pocket. *See also* Jetted pocket.

Whip stitch Diagonal hand stitch sewn along a raw edge to prevent fraying.

Wool A natural animal fiber with fabric available in a range of weights, weaves, and textures. It is comfortable to wear, crease-resistant, and ideal for tailoring.

Wool worsted A light, strong cloth made from good-quality fibers.

Wrong side Reverse side of a fabric, the inside of a garment or other item.

Yoke The top section of a dress or skirt from which the rest of the garment hangs.

Zigzag stitch A stitch used to neaten and secure seam edges and for decorative purposes. The width and length of the zigzag can be altered.

Zipper Fastening widely used on garments consisting of two strips of fabric tape, carrying specially shaped metal or plastic teeth that lock together by means of a pull or slider. Zippers are available in different colors and weights.

Zipper foot Narrow machine foot with a single toe that can be positioned on either side of the needle.

INDEX

A

A-line shift dress 166–171
  pattern 372–375
acetate 51, 388
acrylic 51, 388
air-soluble pens 19
all-in-one in-seam pockets 249
alpaca 388
  interfacings 55
altering patterns 62–73
applied casings, waist edges 187
appliqué 344, 388
appliqué scissors 16
armholes 388
  facings 158, 159
arms, measuring 61
arrowheads 388
  hand-stitched 91
  machine-stitched 93
awls 20

B

back stitch 88, 90, 388
back waist, measuring 61
bags
  toiletries bag 294–299, 386
  two-tone tote bag 104–107
balanced darts 116, 388
ball buttons 317
banding 388
  hems with 274–277
  necklines in stretch knits 164
  for a V neck 165
bar bastes 89, 388
baskets, storage 326–329
basting stitches 89, 391
batiste interfacings 55
beading foot 33
beading needles 22
beeswax 20
belts 200–207
  belt carriers 201, 388
  directory of 200
  obi sash 204–205
  reinforced straight 202–203
  tie belts 204
bent-handled shears 17
betweens 22
bias 388
bias binding 388
  bias-bound ruffles 147
  cased waist edges 187
  cuff openings 231

cutting strips 154
  finishing waistband edges 191
  hems 264, 272
  neatening edges with 155
  neck edges 160–161
  sleeve hems 223
bias fusible tape 325
binding 388
blanket stitch 91, 388
blind hem foot 32
blind hem stitch 90, 93, 388
blind hems 266
blind tucks 119, 388
blinds, Roman 354–359
blouse collar with lapel 180
bobbins 388
  sewing machine 32
bodices 388
  altering patterns 62
  boned 342–343
  components of 342–343
  joining fitted skirts to 185
  joining gathered skirt to 185
  lining 330
bodkins 22, 388
body measurements 60–61
boning 27, 388
  bodices 342–343
bound neck edges 160–161
bows 347
box pleats 388
  hemming 128
  self-staying 127
  top-stitching 126
braids 27
  horsehair 389
  horsehair braid hems 273
bridal pins 23
bust
  altering patterns 65–66
  darts 65
  measuring 60
button loops 316–317, 390
  corded loops 316
  frog fastenings 317, 389
  Rouleau loop 316
  spacing 317
buttonhole chisels 15, 16, 388
buttonhole foot 32
buttonhole stitch 91, 93, 388
buttonholes 304–311, 388
  directory of 304
  in-seam 308
  keyhole buttonhole stitch 389
  machine-corded 306

machine-made 305, 306–307
  patch method bound 308–309
  piped 306
  positioning 305
  repairing damaged 363
  stages of 305
  triangular 310
  vertical vs horizontal 305
buttons 26, 300–303
  ball 317
  button placket 311
  button shanks 388
  covered 303
  directory of 300
  repairing fabric under 363
  sewing on 301–302

C

calico 43, 388
carbon paper 19, 388
cashmere 40, 388
casings 388
  applied 187
  mock 188, 390
  partial 189
  sleeve edges 224
  waist edges 186–189
centered zippers 287
chalk
  pencils 19
  tailor's 19
challis 40, 388
chambray 43, 388
checks, cutting out fabrics 80–81
chenille needles 22
chest, measuring 60
chiffon 48, 388
children
  children's sizing 370
  child's reversible jacket 254–259, 384–385
chino pockets 251
chintz 43, 388
chisels, buttonhole 15, 16, 388
circular ruffles 148–149
clappers 29, 388
clean finish
  hems 264
  seam neatening 95
clipping lines 82
cloths, pressing 390
collar point turner 21
collars 174–181
  blouse collar with lapel 180
  directory of 174

ACKNOWLEDGMENTS

FIRST EDITION

AUTHOR'S ACKNOWLEDGMENTS No book could ever be written without a little help. I would like to thank the following people for their help with the techniques and projects: Jackie Boddy, Nicola Corten, Ruth Cox, Helen Culver, Yvette Emmett, Averil Wing, and especially my husband, Nigel, for his continued encouragement and support, as well as my mother, Doreen Robbins, who is responsible for my learning to sew. The following companies have also provided invaluable help, by supplying the sewing machines, notions, and fabrics: Janome UK Ltd, EQS, Linton, Adjustoform, Guttermann threads, The Button Company, YKK zips, Graham Smith Fabrics, Fabulous Fabric, Simplicity patterns, and Freudenberg Nonwovens LP.

DORLING KINDERSLEY WOULD LIKE TO THANK: Heather Haynes and Katie Hardwicke for editorial assistance; Elaine Hewson and Victoria Charles for design assistance; Susan Van Ha for photographic assistance; Hilary Bird for indexing; Elma Aquino; Alice Chadwick-Jones; and Beki Lamb. Special thanks from all at DK to Norma MacMillan for her exceptional professionalism and patience.

PICTURE CREDITS: Additional photography Laura Knox p76 tl, tr, 78 t, 80 t/2 and 4, 81b; Alamy images: D. Hurst, front jacket c. Illustrator Debajyoti Datta. Patterns John Hutchinson, pp 58-9, 62 b row, 63 t and c row, 65, 66, 67 t row, br, 68, 69 t row, bl, 70 tr, bc, br, 71, 72 tl, b row, 73, 81. Additional artworks Karen Cochrane p59 r.

Project Editor Norma MacMillan
Project Designers Viv Brar, Nicola Collings, Mandy Earey, Heather McCarry
Photography Peter Anderson (Tools and Techniques), Kate Whitaker (Projects)

FOR DORLING KINDERSLEY

Project Editor Ariane Durkin **Project Art Editor** Caroline de Souza
Managing Editor Dawn Henderson **Managing Art Editor** Christine Keilty
Senior Jacket Creative Nicola Powling
Senior Production Editor Jenny Woodcock
Senior Production Controller Mandy Inness
Creative Technical Support Sonia Charbonnier

SECOND EDITION

AUTHOR'S ACKNOWLEDGMENTS For this revision of my book I would like to thank the following people for their help with the projects: Bethany Blight, Elisalex de Castro Peake, Georgina Jeffries, Emma May, Cheryl Owen, and Debbie Seton. I would also like to thank Tia Sarkar at DK for her continued patience and keeping me in check! Thanks also to Debbie Shepherd at Janome UK, and my students for their support. Finally, I would like to thank my husband, Nigel, not only for his encouragement but also for the endless cups of coffee.

DORLING KINDERSLEY WOULD LIKE TO THANK: Ruth Jenkinson and her assistants Sarah Merrett and Julie Stewart for the new photography; Keith Hagan and Patrick Mulrey for the illustrations; Steve Crozier for color retouching; MIG Pattern Cutting for creating the garment patterns; Deborah Shepherd at Janome UK for lending us machines to photograph; Arani Sinha, Ishita Sareen, Madhurika Bhardwaj, Nisha Shaw, Priyadarshini Gogoi, Katie Hardwicke, and Bob Bridle for editorial assistance; Jomin Johny, Kanupriya Lal, Roshni Kapur, Shipra Jain, Amy Child, Louise Brigenshaw, Charlotte Johnson, and Alison Gardner for design assistance; Nityanand Kumar for DTP assistance; Angela Baynham for proofreading; and Vanessa Bird for creating the index.

DK UK

Project Editor Shashwati Tia Sarkar
Senior Art Editor Karen Constanti
US Editor Megan Douglass
US Consultant Jennifer Kosek
Editorial Assistant Alice Horne
Senior Jacket Creative Nicola Powling
Jackets Coordinator Laura Bithell
Preproduction Producer Rebecca Fallowfield
Senior Producer Ché Creasey
Managing Editor Dawn Henderson
Managing Art Editor Marianne Markham
Art Director Maxine Pedliham
Publishing Director Mary-Clare Jerram

DK INDIA

Senior Art Editor Chhaya Sajwan
Project Art Editor Vikas Sachdeva
Art Editors Anjali Sachar, Meenal Goel, Sourabh Challariya
Assistant Art Editors Anukriti Arora, Ankita Sharma, Hansa Babra
Project Editors Janashree Singha, Virien Chopra
Assistant Editors Devangana Ojha, Nonita Saha
Managing Editor Soma B. Chowdhury
Managing Art Editor Arunesh Talapatra
Production Manager Pankaj Sharma
Preproduction Manager Sunil Sharma
Senior DTP Designers Pushpak Tyagi, Tarun Sharma
DTP Designers Anurag Trivedi, Manish Chandra Upreti, Rajdeep Singh, Rajesh Singh Adhikari, Satish Gaur, Syed Md Farhan

First American Edition, 2009

This edition published in the United States in 2018 by DK Publishing, 345 Hudson Street, New York, New York 10014

Copyright © 2009, 2018 Dorling Kindersley Limited
DK, a Division of Penguin Random House LLC
18 19 20 21 22   10 9 8 7 6 5 4 3 2 1
001–307519–Mar/2018

Published in Great Britain by Dorling Kindersley Limited.

A catalog record for this book is available from the Library of Congress.
ISBN 978-1-4654-6853-6

DK books are available at special discounts when purchased in bulk for sales promotions, premiums, fund-raising, or educational use. For details, contact: DK Publishing Special Markets, 345 Hudson Street, New York, New York 10014
SpecialSales@dk.com

Printed and bound in China

All images © Dorling Kindersley Limited
For further information see: www.dkimages.com

A WORLD OF IDEAS:
SEE ALL THERE IS TO KNOW
www.dk.com

ABOUT THE AUTHOR

ALISON SMITH MBE A trained fashion and textiles teacher, Alison taught for many years at one of the largest schools in Birmingham, where she was Head of Department. In 1992 she set up the School of Sewing—the first of its kind in the UK—teaching all aspects of sewing, including dressmaking, tailoring, and corsetry. Alison has also taught at the Liberty Sewing School in London and at Janome's sewing school in Stockport. In 2004, she opened a fabric shop in Ashby de la Zouch to complement the School of Sewing. In 2013, Alison was awarded an MBE for her services to sewing and corsetry. She also teaches online for Craftsy.com and writes regularly for sewing magazines, including *Love Sewing*. Alison lives in Leicestershire with her husband and has two adult children.

www.schoolofsewing.co.uk

www.sewwardrobe.co.uk

www.etsy.com/uk/shop/SewWardrobe

- *Alison's projects in the book are the A-line Shift Dress on pages 166–171 and the Child's Reversible Jacket on pages 254–259.*

CONTRIBUTORS

BETHANY BLIGHT Beth studied costume, set design, and animation at Central St. Martins at the University of the Arts London. Since leaving school, she has been an online contributor to several sewing and craft magazines, run sewing workshops in her local community, and worked as a dressmaker. She now divides her time between raising her two boys and designing and making craft projects for blogs, magazines, and books. Beth has also contributed projects to DK's *Quilting*.

- *Beth contributed the* **Oven Mitt** *project on pp.346–349*

ELISALEX DE CASTRO PEAKE Co-founder of indie sewing pattern label By Hand London, Elisalex originally trained as a shoemaker, working in the fashion industry before turning her passion for sewing and self-sufficient style into a successful new career. She heads up the creative side of BHL, designing and sampling new patterns, creating online tutorials and blog content, and teaching sewing and handcrafts all over London. She is a regular contributor to a range of sewing publications.

- *Elisalex contributed the* **Wrap Skirt** *project on pp.194–199 and the* **Unisex Dressing Gown** *on pp.216–221.*

GEORGINA JEFFRIES Georgina graduated from Bath Spa University in 2008 with a degree in Fashion and Textiles. Since then she has worked as a designer and sewing tutor for various schools, social enterprises, and businesses, including Neema Crafts in Tanzania, Sew Over It in London, and Watts Gallery in Surrey. Georgina is currently Artist in Residence at Ochre Print Studio in Guildford, where she launched Fair Imprint—a business specializing in handmade and printed organic homeware that donates a percentage of its profits to charities supporting refugees.

www.fairimprint.com

www.facebook.com/Georgiejaydesign

www.etsy.com/uk/shop/georgiejaydesign

- *Georgina contributed the* **Envelope Cushions** *project on pp.312–315.*

EMMA MAY Emma is a traditionally trained soft furnisher, making bespoke curtains, blinds, and cushions from her studio in Oxfordshire. She is passionate about passing on her skills and empowering other homemakers through inspiring and accessible sewing workshops. Emma is fascinated by color and pattern, and the role they play in people's homes. She is a firm believer that with dedication and a few simple, soft-furnishing techniques you can create a beautiful, individual home with little expense.

www.emmamaystitching.co.uk

- *Emma contributed the* **Roman Blind** *project on pp.354–359.*

CHERYL OWEN An innovative and experienced crafter, Cheryl originally trained and worked in the fashion industry before applying her design and making skills to sewing—as well as other crafts such as paper crafts and jewelry making. She is the author of many craft books and is a regular contributor to magazines. Cheryl has also contributed craft projects to DK's *Craft* and *Quilting* books.

www.chirpymakes.com

- *Cheryl contributed the* **Storage Baskets** *project on pp.326–327.*

DEBBIE SETON Debbie has been a professional designer and maker since 2012, creating a variety of accessories for her small business, The Crimson Rabbit. Working from her home studio in Essex, she sews a variety of pieces—from bags to cat toys—and also knits and crochets luxurious wraps, cowls, and baby accessories. She's passionate about combining print and color, sourcing beautiful fabrics and yarns, and incorporating traditional hand-sewing techniques into her designs.

www.etsy.com/shop/CrimsonRabbitBurrow

- *Debbie contributed the* **Two-Tone Tote Bag** *project on pages 104–107 and the* **Toiletries Bag** *project on pp.294–299.*